Peter, Paul, and Mary Magdalene

Also by Bart D. Ehrman

Misquoting Jesus: The Story Behind Who Changed the Bible and Why

The Text of the New Testament: Its Transmission,
Corruption, and Restoration, Fourth Edition
(with Bruce M. Metzger)

Truth and Fiction in The Da Vinci Code

The New Testament: A Historical Introduction
to the Early Christian Writings,
Third Edition

A Brief Introduction to the New Testament

The Apostolic Fathers: Volumes I and II

Lost Christianities: The Battles for Scripture
and the Faiths We Never Knew

Lost Scriptures: Books That Did Not Make It
into the New Testament

Christianity and Late Antiquity, 330–450 CE:
A Reader
(with Andrew Jacobs)

The New Testament and Other Early Christian Writings:
A Reader, Second Edition

Jesus: Apocalyptic Prophet of the New Millennium

After the New Testament: A Reader in Early Christianity

The Orthodox Corruption of Scripture: The Effect of
Early Christological Controversies on the Text of the New Testament

PETER, PAUL, and MARY MAGDALENE

THE FOLLOWERS OF JESUS IN HISTORY AND LEGEND

Bart D. Ehrman

OXFORD
UNIVERSITY PRESS

2006

OXFORD
UNIVERSITY PRESS

Oxford University Press, Inc., publishes works that
further Oxford University's objective of excellence
in research, scholarship, and education.

Oxford   New York
Auckland   Cape Town   Dar es Salaam   Hong Kong   Karachi
Kuala Lumpur   Madrid   Melbourne   Mexico City   Nairobi
New Delhi   Shanghai   Taipei   Toronto

With offices in
Argentina   Austria   Brazil   Chile   Czech Republic   France   Greece
Guatemala   Hungary   Italy   Japan   Poland   Portugal   Singapore
South Korea   Switzerland   Thailand   Turkey   Ukraine   Vietnam

Copyright © 2006 by Oxford University Press, Inc.

Published by Oxford University Press, Inc., 2006
198 Madison Avenue, New York, NY 10016
www.oup.com

Oxford is a registered trademark of Oxford University Press.

Library of Congress Cataloging-in-Publication Data
Ehrman, Bart D.
Peter, Paul, and Mary Magdalene: the followers of Jesus
in history and legend/by Bart D. Ehrman.
p. cm. Includes bibliographical references and index.
ISBN-13: 978-0-19-530013-0
ISBN-10: 0-19-530013-0
1. Peter, the Apostle, Saint.
2. Paul, the Apostle, Saint.
3. Mary Magdalene, Saint.
I. Title.
BS2515.E37 2006
225.9'22—dc22
2005058996

Credits and permissions for the use of illustrations and
song lyrics appear on page 273.

9 8 7 6 5 4 3 2 1

Printed in the United States of America
on acid-free paper

To the entire Beckwith Clan—

Jack, Barbara, Tommy, Mike, Simon, James, Julia, Peter, Gill, Holly, Emily, and Charlie—

for welcoming me and letting me listen in

Contents

PART THREE: Mary Magdalene

Preface

The hardest part in writing a book about three such prominent figures of the past as Simon Peter, the apostle Paul, and Mary Magdalene is knowing what to leave out. So much could be said—especially where our evidence is so abundant, as in the cases of Peter and Paul, about whom very large books can be, and have been, written. I can't include everything here. For my friends in the field who think I could have done more, let me say that, well, I agree. For everyone else, let me say that I've tried to include the best bits.

I have written this book for the nonspecialist who is interested in these figures from early Christianity but doesn't know much about them. These three could in fact be considered the key players at the foundations of the most important historical, cultural, social, political, and, of course, religious institution of Western civilization—the Christian church. But not only are they historically significant, they are also endlessly fascinating.

Many readers may not know much about Peter, Paul, and Mary as historical figures—that is, what they actually said and did during their lives, both before and after the death of Jesus. But most readers will almost certainly not know the stories widely circulated about them in later times, the legends about Peter's spectacular miracles converting entire cities, Paul preaching that salvation comes only to those who refuse to have sex, or Mary setting sail in a rudderless boat, only to arrive in France, where she became the first missionary.

I would like to acknowledge several scholars who have selflessly read my manuscript and made helpful comments on it, in hopes that I would somehow make it as good as they might wish: Dale Martin, professor at Yale and one of the top scholars in the field, who has the dubious distinction of being my oldest friend in the business; Andrew Jacobs, from the University of California at

Riverside, a former student (though a Dukie) whose keen insights are some-times beyond belief; Stephanie Cobb, from Hofstra University, another former student who has in these latter years developed a deft touch with her mean red pen; the anonymous and extraordinarily smart reader for Oxford University Press who pushed me hard and brought me kicking and screaming into impor-tant revisions; and my wife, Sarah Beckwith, a professor of English at Duke, who is an intellectual nonpareil and a person and partner extraordinaire. In addition, my talented editor and friend at Oxford University Press, Robert Miller, has read the manuscript, supported its progress through several stages, and discussed numerous related issues during long nights over fine wine. All au-thors should be so lucky.

Translations of the early Christian literature, including the New Testament, are my own, unless otherwise indicated; for the Hebrew Bible I have used the New Revised Standard Version.

Introduction

Even though this book is not about the folk-singing trio of the 1960s, Peter, Paul, and Mary, I'd like to begin by making reference to them and one of their best-known songs:

> If I had a hammer, I'd hammer in the morning,
> I'd hammer in the evening all over this land;
> I'd hammer out danger, I'd hammer out a warning,
> I'd hammer out love between my brothers and my sisters,
> All over this land.

Peter, Paul, and Mary burst onto the folk music scene in an apocalyptic moment in American history. In the early 1960s, the Cold War was heating up. Nuclear proliferation was moving apace on both sides of the Soviet-U.S. divide. Schoolchildren throughout the country were being drilled to hide under their desks if a nuclear bomb exploded over their cities. And the American involvement in the war in Vietnam was just starting—soon to become a real "apocalypse now," to use the term later coined for the Francis Ford Coppola film. On the home front, the civil rights movement was at its height, racial violence and desegregation were tearing apart communities, and it was not at all clear how the tensions would come to be resolved. It was a time of danger, a time of warning of worse yet to come, and a time to turn from war, hatred, and oppression to love, all over the land.

At the end of their popular song, after singing of a hammer, a bell, and a song, the trio unpacks their meaning:

> It's the hammer of justice, it's a bell of freedom,
> It's the song about love

Between my brothers and my sisters,
All over this land.[©1]

In the context of the 1960s, when hard social issues of poverty, oppression, racism, sexism—not to mention the international clashes of power and dominance—confronted us all, the folk singers pled for a return to the humane: justice, freedom, and love.

As it turns out, matters were not so different in the first Christian century in Roman Palestine. It too was a time of international political domination and imperialistic expansion, a time of class division, oppression, hatred, violence, and war.

Into that world there appeared the predecessors of our 1960s folk singers. These were prophets, who had a word from above addressing the ills of their world. One of them—far and away the best-known to us today—was Jesus of Nazareth. He also had a message of justice, freedom, and love. Like other Jews of his day, Jesus maintained that the evils of this world were caused by cosmic powers opposed to God and his people, who were wreaking havoc here on earth. These powers brought pain, misery, and suffering; they were responsible for wars, epidemics, droughts, famines, violence, oppression, and hatred. But their days were limited. Jesus believed that God was soon to reassert his power over this world and overthrow the forces of evil, to bring in a new kingdom on earth, a kingdom of God, in which there would be no more injustice, violence, pain, or suffering. God himself would rule supreme, and people would live the lives of paradise.

Jesus had numerous followers who adored him and committed themselves to his message. After his death, they took the message further afield, proclaiming that it was through Christ himself—now raised from the dead and exalted to heaven—that this future kingdom would be brought to earth. Three of these followers were named Peter, Paul, and Mary.

These three may well have been the most important of Jesus' followers: Simon Peter, his right-hand man during his public ministry, the leader of the twelve disciples; the Apostle Paul, the greatest missionary and theologian of the burgeoning Christian church after Jesus' death; and Mary Magdalene, his closest woman follower, the one who first recognized that he had been raised from the dead, and was therefore, arguably, the *first* Christian.

Peter, Paul, and Mary are significant not only because of who they actually were, as historical figures of the first century, but also because of how they were remembered in later centuries as legends sprang up about them, legends that were often assumed to be "gospel truth" by those who heard and told them. During the first three hundred years of Christianity—which will be my focus in this book—Peter was widely known as one who could do spectacular miracles leading to massive conversions to the faith. He was said to have the power to heal the sick, cast out demons, and raise the dead. Some of the stories about him will strike modern readers as more than a bit bizarre—as when he raises a smoked tuna fish from the dead in order to convince his onlookers of the power of God, or when he deprives a maleficent magician of his power of flight over the city of Rome, leading to the magician's crash landing and death. Paul as well had legends told about him as a great miracle worker whose hand-kerchiefs and aprons could be taken to the sick to restore them to health and who baptized a talking lion that later refused to devour him when he was thrown to the wild beasts in the arena. Paul in particular came to be known as a great advocate of asceticism, preaching that eternal life would come to those who abstained from the joys of sex, even if married. Modern readers may find it surprising that this message resonated among many ancients, some of whom abandoned their marriage bed in exchange for a more blessed existence in the hereafter. Mary Magdalene herself came to be known for her sex life—or at least for her previous sex life, as stories began to circulate that she had been a prostitute whom Jesus reformed and who then shared an unusually intimate relationship with him before his death. Later legend sent her to France as one of the first missionaries to western Europe.

None of these stories about Peter, Paul, and Mary is historically accurate. But that does not mean they are unimportant. The people who retold these stories—and those who heard them—believed them to be accurate portrayals of the past. What is more, they told these stories because they expressed so well their own beliefs, concerns, values, priorities, and passions. If we are interested not only in the lives of the original followers of Jesus but also in the lives of those who told stories about them in later times, there is no better place to turn than the stories circulating about Peter, Paul, and Mary.

Some scholars would argue that we ourselves are not so different from the storytellers of the ancient world—that when we recount what happened in the past, we too do so not merely to show what really happened but also because what happened is important to us today for our own lives. That is to say, at the end of the day, no one has a *purely* antiquarian interest, an interest in the past for its own sake. Instead, we are interested in the past because it can help us make sense of the present, of our own lives, our own beliefs, values, priorities, of our own world and our experience of it. If this view is right—and I happen to think it is—then, strictly speaking, there is no such thing as a "disinterested" study of the past: all of us who study it are in fact interested in it for how it can help us think about ourselves and our lives.

This "interested" approach to the past was certainly the one taken by the ancient people who recounted the stories about Jesus' early followers. They told these stories not merely in order to convey objective facts about what had happened, but also because these stories *meant* something to them—whether the stories were, strictly speaking, historically accurate or not. Among other things, this means that modern historians have a two-pronged task. On one hand, we try to determine, to the best of our ability, what actually happened in the past: what did Peter, Paul, and Mary really say, do, and experience? At the same time, we explore how the past came to be remembered by people who later talked about it and told stories about it—even when these stories were not historically accurate.

Somewhat ironically, it is often easier to know how the past was remembered than to decide what actually happened. Indeed, it is sometimes impossible to separate the legend from the history, the fabricated accounts from the historical events, despite our best efforts. The most unfortunate aspect of history is that it is gone forever. Once something happens, it is over and done with, and while there may be traces of past people and events, these traces are always incomplete, partial, slanted, vague, and subject to a range of interpretations. Historians do their best to reconstruct past events based on surviving evidence, but history is not an empirical science that can establish high levels of probability based on assured results obtained by repeated experimentation. History is as much art as science.

To a large extent this is because our sources of information are so problematic. Can we trust the ancient source that says that Peter raised a smoked tuna fish to life? How would we know? Another source indicates that his shadow could heal the sick when he passed by them on a sunny day. Is that true? Yet another source indicates that he raised a Roman senator from the dead by speaking a word in his ear. Did he really do so? Some of the stories of Peter's miracles are found in the writings of the New Testament, while others are found in books outside the New Testament. Does the historian accept what is found in Scripture as being historically accurate and what is found outside of it as inaccurate? On what grounds? We have a number of writings that claim to be Peter's: 1 and 2 Peter in the New Testament, the Gospel of Peter and the Apocalypse of Peter outside of it. Do we know whether he wrote any or all of these books? Or should we take seriously what the New Testament book of Acts says, that Peter was in fact illiterate and couldn't write at all?

These are just a few of the problems we face when trying to know what Peter was really like and what really happened during his life. Analogous problems attach themselves to Paul and Mary. Doing history is not an easy matter.

This is not to say that it is unimportant. On the contrary—speaking as a historian who does this for a living—knowing about the past matters. It matters whether the Khmer Rouge practiced genocide in Cambodia. It matters whether the experiment with communism in Eastern Europe succeeded. It matters whether weapons of mass destruction were discovered in Iraq.

And it matters whether Jesus actually existed and whether his followers did the things that our sources indicate they did. And so we should do our best to know what happened in the past—whether in the recent past with the destruction of New Orleans and the rather feeble efforts on the part of the government to deal with the crisis, in the slightly more distant past with our country's waffling over how to deal with crises in Rwanda or Bosnia, or in the far distant past with the causes of the fall of the Roman Empire or the rise of the Greeks—or the life of the historical Jesus.

At the same time, as I have been suggesting, history is not the only thing that matters, and separating history from legend is not the only interesting and important exercise that scholars perform on our surviving materials. For history is not simply a matter of separating the historical kernel (what *really* matters) from the legendary husk (what can be discarded). In part that's because, as I've indicated, the people who told and retold the stories—of New Orleans, of Rwanda, of Julius Caesar, of Jesus, or of Peter, Paul, and Mary—did not themselves often distinguish between historical fact and legendary imagination. Historical memories, later embellishments, legendary expansions, and pure fabrications were all told and retold because they related truths, beliefs, views, and ideas that Christians wanted to convey and to which they responded.

We should see what these truths, beliefs, views, and ideas were, by examining the stories that survive. And so our study of Peter, Paul, and Mary will consider both historical fact and legendary embellishment, together. We will ask what we can learn about these followers of Jesus as real, historical figures, what we can know about who they were, what they did, what they believed, what they taught, how they lived. At the same time we will ask about them as legendary figures who came to play such an important role in the imaginations of those who embraced the Christian religion, at its very foundations, before it became the religion of the Roman Empire and, eventually, the most important social, cultural, political, economic, and religious institution in the history of Western civilization.

Part One

SIMON PETER

Chapter One

The Quarry: Our Sources for Peter the Rock

Simon Peter is undoubtedly the best-known disciple of Jesus. But how well known is he, really? We know his name, Simon, and his nickname, allegedly given by Jesus himself, Cephas, which in the first century was not a name at all but a noun meaning "rock." The modern equivalent would be "Rocky." This at least was his nickname in Aramaic—the language that both Jesus and Simon spoke. In Greek, the language of the New Testament, the word for rock is *petra,* whence we get his more commonly known name, Peter. The name Simon Peter, then, literally means "Simon the Rock." Given Simon's impetuous and unfailingly fickle character during Jesus' lifetime, one almost wonders if Jesus was being ironic.

But back to our question: how well do we know Peter from our surviving sources? It is much to be regretted that we don't have anything like a full biography of him written by any of his contemporaries, even though a number of ancient accounts narrate what he allegedly said and did, both during Jesus' lifetime and afterward. One of the difficulties confronting historians is knowing which of these accounts, if any of them, can be trusted as historically accurate and which were colored by the legendary impulses prevalent among Christian storytellers of the first several centuries. The problem involves not only the legends found outside the canonical writings of the New Testament but even the stories that eventually came to be regarded by Christians as sacred Scripture.

Fact and Fiction in the Stories about Peter

In one of our early accounts of Peter's missionary activities after the death of Jesus, we find him in the Forum in Rome, trying to persuade the pagan (i.e., polytheistic) crowds to abandon their false gods and to believe in the power of Jesus, the only son of God. A woman appears on the scene completely distressed: her only son, her love and joy, has just died. Out of desperation, she appeals to Peter to raise him from the dead. Peter replies to her: "In the presence of these witnesses go and bring your son, that they may be able to see and believe that he was raised up by the power of God."[1] He sends a group of men to retrieve the corpse. They check to be sure the young man is dead and then bring him to Peter in the middle of the Forum. Peter says a brief prayer over the dead body and then commands, "Young man, arise and walk with your mother as long as you can be of use to her." And we are told that the "dead man rose immediately, and the multitude saw and were amazed, and the people cried, 'You, God the Savior, you, God of Peter, you are the invisible God and Savior.'" Peter's power is thus vindicated, God is glorified, and the masses convert to follow Christ.

But did this event really happen? As it turns out, it is found not in the New Testament but in a collection of writings known as the Acts of Peter, written some 150 years after Peter himself had passed from the scene. Is it actual history or a pious legend? Compare it to an account written somewhat earlier. In the town of Joppa, on the eastern coast of the Mediterranean, a good Christian woman named Tabitha has recently died. The disciples are distressed and send for Peter to come and do something. Without delay he makes his way to town and ascends to the upper room where the body is laid out. Sending everyone out of the room, Peter kneels by the dead Tabitha and prays. He then says to her "Tabitha, rise." She opens her eyes and gives her hand to Peter, to the amazement of all in Joppa, many of whom come to believe in the power of Jesus as a result. Here is a story similar to the other, but this one is found in the New Testament (Acts 9:36–43). How can the historian claim that one of the stories is a fictional narrative and the other is a biographical fact? Is it enough to say that the author of Acts was recording historical events simply because church fathers living many, many years later decided to include his writings in the canon of Scripture?[2]

The resuscitation of dead bodies may not seem all that remarkable to readers of the New Testament. To be sure, we don't see this kind of thing happen every day, but it does seem to happen in the Bible. Other miraculous events, though, while no less impossible in a literal sense, may strike us as a bit more peculiar and subject to doubt. Consider the episode of Peter and the smoked tuna fish. Peter is back in Rome, trying to convince the crowds that his God is all-powerful and deserves to be worshiped. They ask him for a miracle to prove his point, and he notices a smoked tuna hanging in the window of a fishmonger's shop. He takes hold of the fish and asks the crowd, "When you see this swimming in the water like a fish, will you be able to believe in him whom I preach?" They all answer in one voice, "Indeed we shall believe you." And so he says the magic words: "In your name, O Jesus, Christ, in whom they do not yet believe, I say, 'Tuna, in the presence of all these, live and swim like a fish.'"

And the fish immediately comes back to life—not just for an hour or so, but for good, as people see when they stay and feed it bits of bread. This display of divine power has then a spectacular result: "very many who had witnessed this followed Peter and believed in the Lord."

This is a rather strange moment in the life of Peter—and again, one found not in Scripture but in the second-century Acts of Peter. But there are strange events in the New Testament as well. In one passage of the book of Acts, we are told that Peter is so powerful that he no longer even needs to touch the sick or demon-possessed to heal them. If he passes by on a sunny day, his shadow cures them (Acts 5:15–16).

Or consider another pair of stories. In the New Testament, Peter speaks in the name of God to Ananias, a man who has withheld money from the apostolic trust fund. As a result of Peter's intervention, Ananias (and later his equally culpable wife) falls down dead, to the amazement of the crowds. Outside the New Testament, Peter speaks in the name of God to Simon Magus, a magician who tries to prove that he represents the truth of God by flying like a bird over the hills and temples of Rome. As a result of Peter's intervention, Simon is deprived of his ability of flight, crashes to the earth, breaks his leg in three places, and eventually dies. This too, sensibly, amazes the crowd. On what grounds can we say that one of the stories is fact and the other fiction?

We can broaden the question to include the words of Jesus that Peter, his closest disciple, is alleged to have heard. In one account we are told that Jesus was seated on the Mount of Olives teaching his disciples about what would happen at the end of time. When Peter asks him for more details, Jesus launches into a long exposition of what could be expected for nonbelievers on the day of judgment, and appears actually to show Peter the realm of the damned. The graphic and lurid images that appear in the account clearly make their point: those who habitually practice sin will be condemned to severe and painful suffering in the afterlife, and to some extent their punishments will match their crimes. So women who braid their hair to make themselves attractive to their illicit lovers will be hanged by their hair for all eternity, and the men who have had illicit sex with them will be hanged by their genitals over fire. As one might expect, these men lament, "We did not know that we should come to everlasting punishment!" Those who revel in their riches will be clad in rags and filthy garments and cast for all eternity upon a stone topped with a pillar of fire that is "sharper than swords." Those who have lent money out at interest (usury) will spend eternity in a pit with filth up to their knees. And so it goes.

This narrative can be found in a book called the Apocalypse of Peter, which was considered Scripture by many Christian leaders for centuries before the canon was finally agreed upon, but which, obviously, did not finally come to be included in the New Testament. No less striking, however, is the account found within the Christian New Testament, where Jesus is recorded as saying to Peter (and James and John) that "before this generation passes away" (Mark 13:30) the entire universe will fall apart: "the sun will be darkened, and the moon will not give its light, and the stars will be falling from heaven, and the powers in the heavens will be shaken. And then they will see the Son of man coming in clouds with great power and glory" (Mark 13:25–26). If people can see the Son of Man coming, that might be the greatest miracle of all, since there will no longer be any sun, moon, or stars.

More could be said about the amazing stories surrounding Peter both within the canon of Scripture and outside it, but this is enough to make my basic point. Most readers of the noncanonical accounts will have no trouble realizing that they are filled with legendary reports about the things Peter said, heard, did, and experienced. These reports are often based on pious legends, as storytellers among the Christians wanted to celebrate the life of this chief disciple of Jesus. But the legend-making tendencies did not start only after the canon of the New Testament had been completed. Quite the contrary, there are legendary materials within the books that Christians eventually came to call sacred Scripture. It is not the case that the New Testament presents us only with facts and the books outside the New Testament present us only with pious fictions. There are facts and fictions in all our books, both inside the Bible and outside of it. And in many cases it is difficult—one might say well nigh impossible—to separate one from the other.

And maybe that's not the most important task in any event. Both kinds of story, the historically accurate and the highly legendary, were told and retold by Christian storytellers and authors for *reasons,* and often for precisely the same reasons. We need to realize that the people telling the stories about Peter (as well as Paul, Mary, and even Jesus) were not interested simply in providing history lessons, objectively verifiable reports for students needing to learn about history "as it really was." Christian storytellers had an entirely different range of purposes. They wanted to explain, illustrate, explore, and embody important Christian beliefs, perspectives, worldviews, ideas, biases, purposes, practices, and so on.

So, given the nature of the material, possibly the most important task is not the rather dry academic exercise of separating history from legend but rather to understand what the stories were trying to accomplish on their own terms, that is, to see what the storytellers wanted to achieve by telling the stories the ways that they did.

Sources for Peter: The Unusual Case of the Gospel of Mark

Before exploring this matter further, I need to point out that some scholars have argued that despite all the foregoing, there is at least one ancient source that gives a historically accurate account of what happened in Peter's life during the years of Jesus' ministry. This source is allegedly based on a firsthand account (Peter's own) and is none other than the Gospel of Mark.

The Gospel of Mark is our earliest surviving Gospel. Most scholars today think that it was written sometime around 65 or 70 CE, about thirty-five to forty years after Jesus' death.[3] But how did Mark get his information about Jesus? The early church tradition is that Mark was not himself a disciple of Jesus (and was not, therefore, an eyewitness to the events he narrates) but was a personal secretary of sorts for the chief disciple, Simon Peter. This tradition can be traced back to the writings of an otherwise little-known church father of the early second century named Papias, bishop of the city of Hieropolis in Asia Minor (modern Turkey).

The Witness of Papias

Papias was the author of a five-volume work called *An Exposition of the Sayings of the Lord.* To our knowledge, this was the first attempt to interpret the sayings of Jesus in writing. It is difficult to know much about the character of these lengthy interpretations. We do not know, for example, whether Papias was interested only in the teachings of Jesus or if he also discussed the various things that Jesus did and experienced. The reason we don't know is that the work has almost completely disappeared. Christians of the early centuries who read Papias's *Exposition* were not altogether impressed by it and either suppressed it or, at least, did not bother to copy it for posterity. No copy survives today. The only reason we know anything at all about it is that several later church writers quoted it on occasion. That these church writers were more impressed by the fact that Papias had written the book than by what he actually says in it is evident in some of the remarks that they make. Most notably, an important author of the early fourth century, Eusebius, sometimes known as the "father of church history" because he wrote the first account of the history of Christianity's early centuries, read the work (or perhaps only parts) and concluded that "Papias was a man of very small intelligence" (*Church History,* 3, 39, 13).

Still, it is a great pity that Papias's work does not survive in its entirety, for the bits that do survive are of enormous historical interest. In part this is because Papias indicates how he acquired his information about Jesus and his teachings. In one of the quotations that Eusebius gives from the *Expositions,* Papias states that his preferred method of research was not to read what others had written about Jesus (e.g., the Gospels) but to converse with Christian leaders who had been acquainted with one or more of Jesus' own apostles:

> But whenever someone arrived who had been a companion of one of the elders, I would carefully inquire after their words, what Andrew or Peter had said, or what Philip or what Thomas had said, or James or John or Matthew or any of the other disciples of the Lord.[4]

And so, even though Papias was not himself an eyewitness to the ministry of Jesus nor a companion of any of Jesus' disciples, he did come to know people acquainted with the disciples and received valuable information from them. This information served as the basis of his five-volume exposition of Jesus' teachings.

The reason this matters for our purposes here is that one of the few surviving quotations from Papias's work provides a reference to the authorship of and authority behind Mark's Gospel. At one point Papias says:

> And this is what the elder used to say, "When Mark was the interpreter of Peter, he wrote down accurately everything that he recalled of the Lord's words and deeds—but not in order. For he neither heard the Lord nor accompanied him; but later, as I indicated, he accompanied Peter, who used to adapt his teachings for the needs at hand, not arranging, as it were, an orderly composition of the Lord's sayings. And so Mark did nothing wrong by writing some of the matters as he remembered them. For he was intent on just one purpose: to leave out nothing that he heard or to include any falsehood among them." (Fragment 3, 15)

On the basis of this quotation, some scholars have maintained that in the Gospel of Mark, we actually have a highly accurate account of Peter's understanding of Jesus—and, of course, of the things that Peter himself said and did. It is argued that Mark's Gospel is based on the eyewitness report of Peter, as Papias himself faithfully records.[5]

Some of the Problems with Papias's Witness

Historians' lives would be so much easier if this were, in fact, such an open-and-shut case. But unfortunately, there are problems with taking Papias's statement at face value and assuming that in Mark's Gospel we have a historically reliable account of the activities of Peter. To begin with, some elements of Papias's statement simply aren't plausible. When he says that Mark wrote down "everything" that Peter recalled about Jesus' words and deeds, can he really mean it? Our Gospel of Mark is not a large book—just over twenty pages in the English Bible sitting on my desk. It takes probably a couple of hours to read, from start to finish. Are we to imagine that the apostle Peter, who was with Jesus from the very beginning of his ministry to his crucifixion, remembered only enough stories about what Jesus said, did, and experienced to take up a two-hour narrative? Surely if he spent months with Jesus, let alone years, he could talk about him for days on end. The Gospel of Mark can't be a collection of everything Peter would have remembered.

But is Papias even referring to the Gospel of Mark that we now have in our New Testament? It might be natural to assume that he is, but it is important to note several intriguing facts. The first is that our Gospel of Mark was not originally entitled "The Gospel according to Mark." As is true of our other New Testament Gospels, this one was written anonymously. Our author never tells us who he is. The title of the book was added later (we don't know how much later) by scribes who were copying the book and wanted their readers to know what authority the account was based upon.[6] For this reason, there is no guarantee that the book Papias mentions is the book that we call Mark.

Second, consider the one other Gospel that Papias mentions: the Gospel of Matthew (he doesn't discuss Luke or John). This is what he says about it: "Matthew composed the sayings in the Hebrew tongue, and each one interpreted them to the best of his ability." Again, one might uncritically assume that he is referring to the Gospel that we call Matthew. But is he? The two things he says about this book are that it contained (only) sayings of Jesus and that it was written in Hebrew. But our Gospel of Matthew contains much more than sayings, as it also gives an account of Jesus' activities, miracles, death, and resurrection. And it was written not in Hebrew but in Greek.[7] Papias appears to be thinking of some book other than our Gospel of Matthew. When he refers to Mark, then, is he referring to our Mark? Since he never quotes any of the passages of the Gospel, it is hard to say.

There's an even bigger problem with taking Papias at his word when he indicates that Mark's Gospel is based on an eyewitness report of Peter: virtually everything else that Papias says is widely, and rightly, discounted by scholars as pious imagination rather than historical fact. This is one of those interesting instances in which scholars who want certain comments to be factual accept them as fact, even when there are other comments they are willing and eager to admit are fictitious. In other words, it is a case of selective preference—preferring to regard as fact what one wants to be fact, and discounting everything else.

Consider a couple of the other well-attested comments of Papias, which no one credits as factually accurate. In one place in his *Expositions* he mentions a tradition allegedly received from John, the disciple of Jesus, about what Jesus taught about the future millennium on earth:

> The days are coming when vines will come forth, each with ten thousand boughs; and on a single bough will be ten thousand branches. And indeed, on a single branch will be ten thousand shoots and on every shoot ten thousand clusters; and in every cluster will be ten thousand grapes, and every grape, when pressed, will yield twenty-five measures of wine. And when any of the saints grabs hold of a cluster, another will cry out, "I am better, take me, bless the Lord through me." So too a grain of wheat will produce ten thousand heads and every head will have ten thousand grains and every grain will yield ten pounds of pure exceptionally fine flour. So too the remaining fruits and seeds and vegetation will produce in similar proportions. (Fragment 1, 3)

No one thinks this is a teaching that John actually passed along from Jesus; it is a fantastic (and terrific) expectation of a utopian kingdom on earth—intriguing and attractive, but not historically accurate as a description of Jesus' words.

Or consider the rather lurid description of the death of Judas, who, according to Papias, did not "hang himself," as found in Matthew 27:5, but experienced the torment of girth until he literally burst open (more along the lines of Acts 1:18):

> But Judas [after the betrayal] went about in this world as a great model of impiety. He became so bloated in the flesh that he could not pass through a place that was

easily wide enough for a wagon—not even his swollen head could fit. They say that his eyelids swelled to such an extent that he could not see the light at all; and a doctor could not see his eyes even with an optical device, so deeply sunken they were in the surrounding flesh. And his genitals became more disgusting and larger than anyone's; simply by relieving himself, to his wanton shame, he emitted pus and worms that flowed through his entire body. And they say that after he suffered numerous torments and punishments, he died on his own land, and that land has been, until now, desolate and uninhabited because of the stench. Indeed, even to this day no one can pass by the place without holding his nose. This was how great an outpouring he made from his flesh on the ground. (Fragment 4)

Papias was obviously given to flights of fancy. Why do scholars trust him when he says that Peter was the source of Mark's Gospel? It is only because they *want* to trust him in this instance—even though they know full well that when he gives other pieces of "historical" information he is in fact passing on pious fictions.[8]

The Nature of Our Surviving Sources

As I have already intimated, it is important to recognize the nature of our surviving Christian texts, Mark and all the others, when trying to investigate them as sources for what actually happened in history. The narratives that we have— for example, the Gospels and Acts—probably do contain some historical recollections of things that actually happened in the life of Peter (and of Mary, and of Jesus, etc.). But they also contain historically inaccurate statements, many of which are made for the same reasons that the more accurate ones are made: not in order to provide us with history lessons about life in first-century Roman Palestine, but in order to advance important Christian points of view. This is neither a good thing nor a bad one. It is not as if someone could have written a completely "objective" account of things that happened, even if she wanted to do so. Anything that happens has to be observed before it can be described. And the person observing and describing it will always have beliefs, perspectives, worldviews, loves, hates, likes, dislikes, biases, tendencies, and a range of other things that make humans human. All these human traits necessarily affect how we observe what happens in our world, what we choose to describe about it, and how we go about doing so. This is true not just of the writers of early Christian literature but of all of us, all of the time. As a consequence, historians who want to know what really happened in the past always have to take this element of subjectivity into account.

This is especially true of the early Christian Gospels, which were never *intended* to be disinterested descriptions of historical data. They are, after all, called "Gospels," which means something like "the proclamation of good news." Whoever wrote these books meant to show that the life, death, and resurrection of Jesus brought salvation—that is, they had a theological agenda. These books are not "objective" descriptions of what Jesus said and did.

This can be seen by approaching the Gospels in a new way. Most people who are serious about reading the Gospels (and there seem to be fewer and fewer such people) read them in a way that I would call "vertically." That is to say, they start with Matthew and read it from the top of the page to the bottom, from beginning to end. Then they read Mark from beginning to end. Mark sure sounds like Matthew: a lot of the same stories, many of them in the same sequence, often in the same exact words. Then they read Luke, beginning to end, and they have the same sense of things. It's basically the same story, with some new material thrown in. John, to be sure, is different, but when read vertically (top to bottom) it doesn't seem all *that* different.

This, of course, is the way we normally read books. But there is another way to read the Gospels: horizontally. A horizontal reading does not focus on the similarities among them but instead highlights their differences. It involves reading a story in one of the Gospels, and then reading the same story in another one of them, and then the same story in a third. It's like having them laid out on the page in three (or four, if you count John) columns, and you read across the columns instead of top to bottom. When you do that, you start seeing differences among the Gospels. Sometimes these are small differences that are impossible to reconcile (even if the stories are basically the same). Sometimes they are bigger differences that might actually matter to the sense of the story. And sometimes they are enormous differences with real consequences for interpretation.

Let me give some examples that affect our understanding of the life of Peter, just to make the point.

1. In Mark's Gospel one of Jesus' early miracles is to heal Peter's mother-in-law of a fever (which allows her to get up and make dinner for him and his hungry disciples) (Mark 1:30–31). This happens well before Jesus gets a cool reception in his own hometown of Nazareth after the sermon he preaches there, weeks or months later (Mark 6:1–6). In Luke's Gospel Jesus performs the same miracle for Peter's mother-in-law (Luke 4:38–39), but now it is almost immediately *after* his sermon in Nazareth (4:16–30)—before Jesus' activities described in Mark chapters 2–5, instead of after them. Maybe the difference isn't all that important. But if you want to write a biography of Peter, isn't it important to know what happened when?

2. Another chronological problem comes at the end of Jesus' ministry. In Mark's Gospel, Jesus holds a last supper with Peter and the other disciples during the Jewish feast of Passover (14:12). In John's Gospel, however, the supper takes place the day *before* Passover (John 19:14). Which is it? Here the chronology matters: is the Lord's Supper in the Christian tradition supposed to be related to the Jewish Passover seder (perhaps as a "replacement"), or is it unconnected to it?

3. How (and when) is Peter called to be a disciple? Does Jesus call him while he's fishing, telling him to put up the net and follow him, at the very outset of his ministry, as in Mark (1:16–17)? Or does the call come after Jesus has done some miracles (including the healing of Simon's mother-in-law), after Simon and his partners have made a miraculous catch of fish, as in Luke (5:1–11)? Or does Peter find Jesus (instead of the other way around) at his brother Andrew's urging, when there are no fish involved, as in John (1:38–41)?

4. When does Peter recognize that Jesus is the messiah? Is it halfway through the ministry, as in Mark (8:29)? Or is it at the very beginning, as in John (1:41–42)?

Examples of this kind can be multiplied all day long. All you need to do is read the Gospels horizontally, and you'll find plenty of them yourself. And so I have my students do an exercise: I assign a key narrative, such as the accounts of Jesus' resurrection, and ask them to compare all of the Gospel accounts carefully. Who goes to Jesus' tomb the day after the Sabbath? How many women are there? What do they see there? Who meets them there—an angel, a man, or two men? What are they told there? What do they do once they're told? And so on. The same can be done with Peter's role at the resurrection. Is he the first to see Jesus, or is Mary Magdalene? What does he do at the tomb? Whom does he believe? Whom does he disbelieve? Read the accounts for yourself and you'll see the problems. These are not historical narratives of what actually took place. They *can't* be—they disagree far too often to be that.

The same exercise works with the book of Acts, in which Peter also features prominently (at least in chapters 1–12). In this case we do not have a *second* account of the early life of the church to compare and contrast with Acts (i.e., that can be read horizontally with it): Acts is the only book of its kind in the New Testament. But one of the key figures in Acts is the apostle Paul, and it is possible to compare what Paul says about his relationship with Peter with what Acts says about Paul's relationship with Peter. Look carefully at the different accounts and you'll find important differences. When did Peter and the other apostles meet Paul: right after Paul's conversion in Damascus, as in Acts, or years later, as Paul insists (Acts 9:26–29; Gal. 1:16–18)? Did Peter start the mission to the Gentiles, as in Acts, or did he restrict his mission to the Jews while Paul was the missionary to the Gentiles, as in Paul's own letters (Acts 10–11; Gal 1–2)? Did Peter agree with Paul's understanding that Gentiles should not be urged to keep the Jewish law, as in Acts, or did he disagree, as according to Paul (Acts 15:6–11; Gal. 2:11–15)?

Some readers over the years, of course, have tried to reconcile all of these differences. And if you are willing to do enough fancy interpretive footwork, you can interpret just about *anything* in a way that irons out all the problems. When I was in college, for example, I found a book called *The Life of Christ in*

Stereo, which took the four Gospels and smashed them all together into one big Gospel in which all the discrepancies were reconciled. And so what did the author do, for example, when Matthew indicates that Peter denied Jesus three times before the cock crowed but Mark indicates that Peter denied Jesus three times before the cock crowed twice? Very simple: Peter must have denied Jesus *six* times, three times before the cock crowed and three times before it crowed again.[9]

The problem with this kind of interpretation is that, at the end of the day, it is nothing other than an attempt to write an entirely new Gospel, one that is completely unlike any of the four in the New Testament. There may be advantages to doing this—anyone can have the Gospel that he or she wants, produced by his or her own hands. But it's probably not the best way to go if we want to understand the Gospels and Acts in light of their own (as opposed to our) teaching.

Conclusion: History and Legend in the Stories of Peter

As I said in the Introduction, it is important to know what happened in the past. But there are times when we simply can't know what happened. With respect to Peter, there are some things that we can say with relative certainty, as we will see in later chapters: he probably was an Aramaic-speaking fisherman from Galilee, for example. There are other things that are almost certainly legendary accretions created by Christian storytellers who talked about his life and activities: he probably did not, for example, make a smoked tuna come back to life in order to convert the crowds in Rome. And there are yet other events that are possibly historical but harder to establish: Did he preach to a crowd of Jews in Jerusalem two months after Jesus' death, leading to some conversions? Was he the first bishop in Antioch of Syria? Or in Rome? Did he die by crucifixion during the reign of the Emperor Nero?

Whether historically accurate or not, however, there are a large number of stories told about Peter. These stories are worth our attention, not simply to inform us concerning what actually happened in his life but also to help us see what was happening in the lives of the people who told the stories. For these stories functioned in important ways for the Christian storytellers who told and retold them, as the stories helped them express their own beliefs, perspectives, loves, hates, fears, and understandings—not just about Peter but also about themselves and their relationship to both God and the world in which they lived.

Chapter Two

Peter: Solid Rock or Shifting Sand?

We can begin our study of Simon Peter by considering something about his personal character. The stories of the New Testament regularly portray him as fickle and impetuous, the last person you'd expect to be called the Rock. Yet the consistent testimony of the Gospels is that Jesus himself provided the nickname. When did this happen, and how apt a description, really, is it?

Peter's Nickname

As happens so often, the Gospels appear to disagree on when Jesus bestowed the name Peter (Rocky) on Simon. The first Gospel to be written was probably Mark, dated by most scholars to around 65 or 70 CE, that is, about thirty-five or forty years after the events it narrates. Here, in virtually his first public act, Jesus calls Andrew and his brother Simon from their fishing business to be his followers. The brothers live in Capernaum, a small fishing village on the sea of Galilee. Soon after they meet Jesus one of his first miracles involves healing Simon's mother-in-law, in bed with a fever that has kept her from preparing the evening meal (1:29–31). Jesus proceeds to engage in his ministry of healing and casting out of demons, acquiring followers, and disputing aspects of Jewish law with his opponents, the Pharisees, for a couple of chapters. It is not until chapter 3 that he chooses twelve followers to be his closest disciples—an inside circle, as it were. Here we are told that he chooses Simon first and gives him the surname Peter (3:16; this agrees with Luke's version of the story, Luke 6:14). One would assume that the renaming happened at this point, after Jesus had gotten to know Simon a bit.

One of the earliest surviving pictures of Peter, Jesus, and Paul from a catacomb painting in Rome.

The Gospel of Matthew was written some ten or fifteen years after Mark, around 80 or 85 CE. Many of Mark's stories are replicated in Matthew, probably because Matthew simply copied them, changing them as he saw fit (as well as adding a number of stories not found in Mark). As it turns out, Matthew doesn't mention Jesus' naming of the twelve disciples until much later in his ministry. In fact, it does not come until after he has delivered his famous Sermon on the Mount (which is found in Matthew but not in Mark) and performed a number of miracles in Matthew 8–9. Moreover, in his naming of the apostles Matthew has slightly altered the wording of Mark's account. Instead of saying that "he gave to Simon the name Peter," Matthew simply says that the first of the disciples was "Simon who was called Peter" (Matt. 10:2). In other words, in this later account, "Peter" appears simply to be Simon's well-known nickname, not the epithet that Jesus himself gave him.

This makes it all the more interesting that Jesus does appear to give Peter the epithet at a later point in Matthew's Gospel. About halfway through the account, Peter is portrayed as making a significant confession concerning Jesus' true identity. When Jesus asks his disciples who they think he is, Peter responds: "You are the Christ, the Son of the Living God" (Matt. 16:16). It is at that point that Jesus replies to him (this is in Matthew, not in any of the other Gospels) by bestowing upon him his nickname: "Blessed are you Simon son of Jonah! For flesh and blood did not reveal this to you, but my Father who is in heaven. And I say to you that you are Peter [*petros*], and upon this Rock [*petra*] I will build my church" (Matt. 16:17–18). For centuries, interpreters have wrangled over the meaning of these words: is Peter the foundation (rock) of the church, as Roman Catholic theologians have typically argued? Or is his confession that Jesus is the Christ the foundation, as argued by many Protestants? Or do the words mean something else?[1] In any event, what is clear is that for Matthew, Simon is named the Rock on the basis of his correct perception of the identity of Jesus.

When we come to our final New Testament Gospel, John, written probably around 90 or 95 CE, we have a different scenario altogether. Here, Jesus doesn't find Simon fishing and call him to be his follower; Simon instead is the one who finds *him*. Actually, it's his brother Andrew who finds Jesus first. As a disciple of John the Baptist, Andrew overhears his teacher call Jesus the "Lamb of God who takes away the sins of the world," and, naturally, his interest is piqued (John 1:35). Andrew decides to follow after Jesus and speak with him. What he learns is evidently impressive, as he immediately goes to find his brother Simon and says to him, "We have found the Messiah" (John 1:41). Simon comes to see for himself, and the first words out of Jesus' mouth are his new name: "You are Simon son of John; you will be called Cephas" (i.e., Peter). It is hard to know what to make of this declaration, as this is the first time Jesus has laid eyes on the man. Is John trying to show that Jesus had a preternatural insight into his character, as he does with Nathaniel, whom he also appears to know without seeing, later in the same chapter?

In any event, just looking at the Gospels, it is not clear when, or under what conditions, Simon received the nickname Rock. All the Gospels, in any event, agree that it was Jesus himself who gave him the name. It was an auspicious moment in the history of names. Even though *rock* (Peter) was just a noun before this, it became a popular name in the early Christian period, on down, of course, until today.

The Rocky Start:
Peter During Jesus' Ministry

It is hard to know how many people called Peter have actually displayed a rocky disposition. What is clear, however, is that the original Peter did not. On the contrary, rather than a rock, Peter seems much more like shifting sand, at least in the time he spent with Jesus.

Peter's vacillation is a constant refrain throughout the stories of the New Testament Gospels. A number of them show that Peter was impetuous, fickle, constantly open to rebuke, and, in the end, unfaithful. Whether or not all of these stories are historically accurate descriptions of what took place, they occur with enough frequency to make one suspect that Simon was widely known for having a brash and dithering disposition.

Halfway through Jesus' public ministry, according to the early Gospels, he takes Peter, along with James and John, up on top of a mountain, where he is transfigured before their eyes into a radiant being. Two other men then appear—none other than Moses and Elijah—who speak with him. Peter, a bit flummoxed by it all, blurts out that they should make three tents for them, evidently wanting to stay on the mountain and keep the experience going. The narrator of our earliest account, Mark, aptly comments that Peter made the remark "because he did not know what to say" (Mark 9:6). The other disciples had the good sense to say nothing.

On a different occasion in Matthew's Gospel, Peter again is shown to speak at an inopportune moment. Jesus has sent the disciples in a boat across the sea of Galilee while he remains behind to pray. When he finishes it is dark, and a storm has come up, making it difficult for the disciples to make much progress rowing against the wind. Jesus then walks out to them, on the water. When they see him, in the middle of the lake, the disciples are terrified, thinking it is a ghost. Jesus assures them it is he, and then Peter, in a characteristically unreserved moment, calls out, "Lord if it is you, command me to come to you on the water" (Matt. 14:28). Jesus grants his wish, and Peter hops out of the boat and begins walking on the water. But when he realizes what he is doing ("when he saw the wind"), he falters and begins to sink. Only Jesus' helping hand saves him from real calamity. And that is Peter all over: impetuous and vacillating, as seen in Jesus' rebuke to him, "O you of little faith, why did you doubt?"

Peter's inconstancy is seen in his famous confession of Jesus' identity in the early Gospels, especially as portrayed in the Gospel of Mark. For the first half of this Gospel, Peter and the other disciples, much to Jesus' chagrin, appear to have no clue as to who he really is. As Jesus finally says in desperation at one point, after doing miracles for eight chapters and confronting their constant inability to perceive his true character: "Do you not yet understand?" (8:21). He soon asks them who people regard him to be, and they tell him: some think he is John the Baptist or the prophet Elijah, or one of the other prophets, come back from the dead. He then turns the question on them: "And who do you say that I am?" (8:29). Peter, as spokesperson for the group, shows that at last he has some insight: "You are the messiah." But the insight is partial at best. As we will see in a later chapter, most Jews of the first century—Peter included, evidently—thought of the future messiah as a great, powerful figure who would overthrow God's enemies and establish a new kingdom for Israel.[2] That, however, was not who Jesus was, especially according to the Gospel of Mark, which emphasizes that he was a messiah who had to die for the sins of others to put them into a right standing before God (see Mark 10:45). For Mark, Jesus was a suffering messiah, not a glorious, powerful one.

But this isn't Peter's view. Immediately after his confession, Jesus goes on to instruct Peter and his fellows that "the Son of Man [i.e., Jesus] must suffer many things, and be rejected by the elders and the chief priests, and the scribes, and be killed, and after three days rise again" (8:31). And it is Peter, the one who has just said that Jesus is the messiah, who takes him aside to rebuke him. Why the rebuke? Because Jesus evidently can't know what he's talking about.

If he's the messiah, he's certainly not going to suffer and die. But Jesus knows exactly what he's talking about and realizes that Peter has gotten it all wrong. He is so wrong, in fact, that he is standing diametrically opposed to God. And so comes the famous counterrebuke, where Jesus tells his chief disciple: "Get behind me, Satan, for you are thinking the thoughts not of God but of humans" (Mark 8:33). Peter seems always to be the one to open his mouth to say what he thinks, and often the one to be severely rebuked for thinking the wrong thing.

Or consider John's Gospel, where Jesus, at his last supper with his disciples before his arrest, takes a basin of water, girds himself with a towel, and begins to wash the disciples' feet in an act of servitude, showing them how they should act toward one another, not as masters but as slaves (John 13:1–11). When it is his turn, however, Peter says, "You shall never wash my feet." His motives seem good, but it is a rash comment. If Jesus is master, he can do as he wants— and what he wants is to take the role of a servant. Jesus quickly puts him in his place: "If I don't wash you, you have nothing to do with me." Peter then makes an abrupt about-face: "Lord, then wash not only my feet but also my hands and head." With Peter it's nothing or everything.

In all of the Gospels Peter's rash inconstancy is best seen in his most infamous act of denying Jesus. What is striking is that before the event, he is outspoken in his bravado, claiming that even if everyone else falls away at the moment of crisis, he at least will remain faithful to the end (Mark 14:29), and that he is willing to be imprisoned and killed for Jesus' sake (Luke 22:33). Jesus replies that Peter will deny him three times. Peter responds with a solemn disavowal: "Lord, even if I should have to die with you, I will never deny you." Falser words were never spoken. When the moment of truth comes, Peter's valor disappears. After Jesus' arrest, he shamelessly declares, on three occasions, that he doesn't know him, fearing the implications of his association. Even though Jesus predicted it, Peter is responsible for his actions and, understandably, leaves the scene with bitter tears, lamenting his own inability to stand firm, like a rock.

The Rocky Aftermath:
Peter in the Early Church

As we will see later, there are reasons for thinking that Peter's character improved with age. Still, even after Jesus' death and the establishment of the Christian church Peter occasionally reverted to his fickle and unreliable ways.

If we move the clock forward some twenty years, we find Jesus' followers encountering a very different situation. Originally, the twelve disciples—and probably all the others who followed Jesus during his ministry—were Jews who observed Jewish customs, worshiped the Jewish God, and saw Jesus as a Jewish rabbi who gave the proper interpretation of the Jewish law as given by Moses. After Jesus' death, those who converted to believe that he was the Son of God who died for the sins of the world were themselves Jewish, people who saw in Jesus' life and death the fulfillment of the promises made by the Jewish God in the Jewish Scriptures.

Jesus was executed in Jerusalem, and that is where the earliest Christians (i.e., those who acknowledged him as the Christ, whose death brought salvation) started their mission to convert others to believe in him. The community of followers grew, and with growth came the need for leadership. The natural leaders were those who had known Jesus during his lifetime and who could attest to his resurrection. Over time, three main leaders emerged in the church of Jerusalem: Peter, his chief disciple; John, another of the inner circle of the Twelve; and James, Jesus' earthly brother.

It was not long before this movement began to attract non-Jews into its midst. After all, the message of Jesus' followers was that his death brought salvation for *everyone* who was alienated from the one true God. That would include everyone on earth, as all had gone against God's will, whether Jew or Gentile (that is, non-Jewish). Christian missionaries began to proclaim the salvation of Christ to non-Jews, trying to convert them away from their polytheistic religions to the belief that only the God of Israel should be worshiped as God, and that his son, Jesus, died to bring about a reconciliation of humans with him.

The best-known missionary to the Gentiles, of course, was not Peter but the apostle Paul, about whom we will be speaking at greater length in later chapters. Paul and other Jewish missionaries were confronted with a pressing set of questions when taking their message of Christ to pagan (i.e., polytheistic, Gentile) audiences. If Jesus was the son of the Jewish God who taught the correct view of Jewish law to his Jewish followers, in fulfillment of Jewish law, didn't anyone who came to believe in Jesus have to become Jewish? Some missionaries and Christian leaders insisted that the answer was a resounding and obvious yes. God gave his promises to Israel, and now the entire world could enjoy the benefits of those promises as fulfilled in the Jewish messiah, Jesus. But to follow the Jewish messiah, you obviously had to be Jewish. And that meant following Jewish law, as found in the Torah—the Jewish Bible as given by Moses. This included circumcision for all males, keeping kosher food laws, observing the Sabbath day, celebrating Jewish festivals, and the like.

But there were other Christian leaders who took the other side of the debate and argued just as vehemently that to become followers of Jesus, Gentiles did *not* first have to become Jewish. Paul, notably, was the outspoken proponent of this view. Paul argued that since a person could not be made right with God by keeping Jewish law, forcing a non-Jew to keep the law made no sense. Quite the contrary, those who thought that by keeping the law they had improved their standing before God, had completely misunderstood the truth of the gospel of Christ's death and resurrection, for only by Christ's death could a person be reconciled with God. Keeping the law in addition to having faith in Christ could only imply that Christ's death was not sufficient for a right standing before God. That was a blasphemous idea for Paul, the missionary to the Gentiles.

Now, what does all this have to do with Peter in his later life? Paul's letter to the Christians in Galatia (central Turkey) describes an incident involving Peter that suggests his ongoing inconstancy about matters of real moment.[3] According to Paul, there was a sizable Christian community located in the Syrian city of Antioch. This community was made up of both Jewish and Gentile believers in Christ. The Jewish Christians evidently continued to observe their own Jewish customs, but the Gentiles did not keep the requirements of the law (other than the requirements, for example, to worship only the God of Israel and to avoid sexual immorality). It is not clear whether these different sets of believers in Antioch met in the same locations or if they held different, more segregated gatherings (at this period, Christians met in the larger homes of their more wealthy members, not in church buildings). Paul, even though he was a Jew, associated with both groups—and why not? Christ's salvation came equally to both Jew and Gentile.

According to Paul's account in the book of Galatians, Peter came to visit Antioch and followed suit, meeting with both Jews and Gentiles (Gal. 2:11–12). Now, for strict (non-Christian) Jews, this kind of meeting practice could pose serious problems, since eating a meal with Gentiles would entail not keeping kosher. At first, Peter, like Paul, evidently did not see this as a problem. After all, what mattered for salvation was not kosher food but the death of the messiah.

But then other Jewish Christians arrived from Jerusalem. These were close associates of James, the brother of Jesus, who was evidently the ultimate authority in the Jerusalem church at this time. These visitors did not subscribe to Paul's view of Gentiles, maintaining instead that it was important for them to keep the Jewish law if they were to be followers of the Jewish messiah. Peter appears to have been thrown into a bit of a quandary: how was he to act given the new situation? Should he continue associating with Gentiles, or, in deference to the Jerusalem visitors, should he refrain from breaking the Jewish laws he had been raised with? He decided that it was best not to alienate the visitors from Jerusalem. And so he stopped holding fellowship with the Gentile Christians and ate meals only with the Jewish Christians, thereby keeping kosher.

In fairness to Peter, this may have been simply an attempt to avoid offending someone with sensibilities different from his own. But Paul did not see it that way, and once again—Peter may have been used to it by this time—he issued a severe and public rebuke: "And when I saw they were not straightforward about the truth of the gospel, I said to Cephas before them all, 'If you, a Jew, live like a Gentile even though you are Jewish [i.e., if you normally don't keep kosher], how can you compel the Gentiles to live like Jews [i.e., how can you now insist that Gentiles do keep kosher]?" (Gal. 2:14). Paul's logic was that when Peter withdrew from eating with Gentiles, he was showing that deep down he thought that keeping the Jewish law mattered for a right standing before God. But if that's what he thought, then he was previously behaving hypocritically. So he was a hypocrite either earlier or now—either way, it was fickle and it wasn't good.

We don't know how this dispute resolved itself. This is one of those instances when we hear only one side of the argument, and it's never safe to assume that the side that reports the debate is the one that came out on top. Still, there is something remarkably consistent about the incident. Peter, once more acting rashly without thinking out the consequences, changed his mind, repented of his behavior, and was rebuked for it. The Rock appears to be sand.

Peter the Inconstant

What are we to make of this consistent portrayal of Peter in our early surviving sources? I have suggested that it is important not only to know what actually happened in history but also to see why people remembered historical events (and nonhistorical events) in the ways they did. In the present case, all the surviving evidence seems to point in the same direction with regard to Simon Peter's personality: he was fickle, impetuous, and vacillating. But why was it important for early Christians to remember (or create) him in this light?

Preachers over the centuries have had no trouble finding an answer. Jesus' followers have always comprised an enormous range of people, of all types. But one constant among all churches established in Jesus' name is that there have always been people who find it difficult to be faithful to what they consider to be their religious commitments. It is easy to want to be faithful, hard to attain the goal; easy to make promises to God, hard to keep them; easy to display religious bravado when the sailing looks smooth, hard to pay the price when things get rough; easy to think you'll withstand persecution, hard to stand firm when the implements of torture are laid out in front of you.

Peter was like that in many of the oldest stories told about him. More than almost anyone else in the early Christian tradition, he is someone whom followers of Jesus have been able to relate to: good-hearted and eager to please but, when it comes to the moment, vacillating, impetuous, unreliable—one who claims to be willing to die for his master but then in fact denies him not just once but three times. For Peter, the spirit was willing but the flesh was weak. That has been the experience of many thousands of Jesus' followers in the centuries ever since. No wonder it's precisely these characteristics that make the chief apostle so appealing to those who, like him, want to do what is right but seem unable to do so.

And Yet, the Rock

Despite his personal characteristics, there is one respect in which it makes perfect sense to think of Simon as the Rock. For whatever one might say about his personal shortcomings, it is clear that Peter's life and work became absolutely foundational to the establishment of the Christian church as a fervent and coherent group of believers in the death and resurrection of Jesus. This is no doubt what is implied in the tradition, preserved only in one of our later Gospels, Matthew, when Jesus declares that Simon will be called *Petros* (Peter), and upon this *petra* (rock) Jesus will build his church (Matt. 16:18). To a great extent, it was the work of Peter that led to the establishment of the church.

Peter was clearly important to the earliest Christian community. That community was located in Jerusalem soon after Jesus' death, and it was Peter, along with the disciple John and Jesus' brother James, who stood at its head. Since the Jerusalem church became the fountainhead for the church throughout the world, these three—whom Paul calls the "pillars" of the church—were the leaders of all Christianity. It is not at all implausible that Peter, as the chief disciple of Jesus, was himself the head of the three, at least in the earliest phases. James evidently became more important later on, possibly after Peter left Jerusalem to engage in a mission to convert fellow Jews to the new faith in Christ. In Paul's view, in fact, Peter was *the* missionary to the Jewish people, par excellence, just as he himself was the missionary to the Gentiles (Gal. 2:7–8). Since the church, both Jewish and Gentile, was rooted in the earliest mission within Jerusalem and to Jews outside of Jerusalem, and since Peter was the principal leader in converting Jews to Christ in the early phases of the mission, in a very real sense he became the foundation of the entire church, for time immemorial. He was the Rock on which the Kingdom of Christ was built.

Nowhere is this view laid out more clearly than in the book of Acts. This is an account of the spread of the Christian church throughout the Roman Empire. It was written by the same author who produced the Gospel of Luke, possibly at about the same time, around 80–85 CE. Looking back on the foundational events of a half century earlier, Luke indicates that from the beginning—immediately after Jesus' resurrection and ascension—it was Peter who took charge of Jesus' earthly followers. In this narrative, one of the first major events that transpires occurs fifty days after Jesus' death, on the Jewish festival of Pentecost. The followers of Jesus are gathered together in a room in Jerusalem, and suddenly they experience the promised coming of the Holy Spirit. They hear the sound of a mighty wind, they see tongues of flame resting on their heads, and, rushing outside, they begin to speak in foreign languages, preaching the gospel in the native tongues of nonlocal Jews visiting Jerusalem for the holiday (Acts 2:1–13). Many onlookers are perplexed by the commotion, but it is Peter who takes charge by preaching to the gathered crowd. In his impromptu sermon he indicates that what they are observing is a fulfillment of God's promises in his prophets. Peter goes on to inform them about Jesus and the significance of his death and resurrection, urging them to repent. The outcome is as astounding as the event itself: three thousand Jews convert on the spot (Acts 2:14–41).

So according to Acts, Peter stands at the foundation of what was to become the worldwide Christian church. And his work has only just begun. In the next chapter, Acts 3, Peter and John are seen going into the Temple of Jerusalem, where they notice a lame man by the gate, begging for alms. The apostles have nothing to give except what the man needs most. Peter commands him to be healed in the name of Jesus. Immediately he leaps up, praising God. Everyone around sees what has happened, and Peter uses it as an opportunity to deliver another sermon. Again he urges the people to recognize Jesus as the one promised by God, one who was wrongly put to death but was raised by God from the dead. The result? Another five thousand Jews convert. At this rate, there won't be any non-Christians left in town.

That is one of the reasons scholars question the historical accuracy of Luke's narrative. For a Christian wanting to know about the early success of Jesus' apostles, it is almost too good to be true. In fact, maybe it *is* too good to be true, in a historical sense. But Luke's point is nonetheless clear. After Jesus' death, his tiny band of followers quickly multiplied by converting other Jews to believe that in him the promises of the God of Israel had come to fulfillment, and through his death and resurrection they could be reconciled with God. This was the beginning of the church. And who was principally responsible for it? Simon Peter, the Rock upon whom the foundation of the church was built.

Now that we've considered something of Peter's personality traits, we can begin to examine more closely the accounts of his life—both within the New Testament and outside it—from his rocky beginning to the end, when he was martyred for his faith in Christ some thirty-five years later.

Chapter Three

The Rocky Beginning

Christianity is the largest religion in the world today. And among the Christian denominations, the largest is the Roman Catholic Church, with around one billion members. The official Catholic view is that Peter was the first pope, the bishop of Rome, the leader on whom all else was built. Apart from whether that's a historically tenable position or not, I think everyone would agree that the Christian church allegedly founded on Peter—embracing not just Catholics but also Protestants and Orthodox—has been the most important religious, cultural, political, economic, and social institution in the history of Western civilization. Given the almost unimaginable reach of the church in both the public and private spheres over the centuries, one might expect that its beginning was equally spectacular. Is that the case? Who was the chief disciple of Jesus, the one who in some sense stands at the very beginning of it all, the foundation for the superstructure that stands as a mighty bulwark in the history of the West and large parts of the East?

The Unlikely Foundation Stone

As it turns out, the few historical facts that can be known about Peter are anything but impressive. One could hardly pick a less likely candidate as the foundation stone upon which to build a church. From what we can tell, the historical Simon was an illiterate peasant from the remote rural backwaters of the Roman Empire. When we break through the legends surrounding his later life, we find a completely ordinary man.

Our earliest sources are unified in presenting him as a fisherman from rural Galilee, the sparsely inhabited region in the north of what is now Israel. He may have owned his own boat, or he may have rented one from a wealthier merchant. He appears to have labored with his brother Andrew, so he may have been involved in some kind of small family business. But we shouldn't romanticize the hard labor involved. For most people of his class, life involved a very simple hand-to-mouth existence, with long, backbreaking hours and very low wages.

The earliest tradition indicates that Simon lived in the small village of Capernaum on the western shore of the Sea of Galilee (calling it a "sea" is a bit of an overstatement; it's actually a fairly small lake). There is a passage in the Gospel of John (1:44) that indicates he came from Bethsaida, which was a somewhat larger place. But this may not represent a historical datum. The name Bethsaida means "house of fish," and locating Peter there may simply reflect an early tradition about his occupation. The earliest sources speak only of Capernaum (see Mark 1:21, 29).

Capernaum was not a major center of cultural activity. Archaeologists have dug there and shown that it was small, poor, and uncultured.[1] Probably during Simon's lifetime it had a population of something like a thousand. No public buildings of any kind have been uncovered from the period, not even any paved roads. The village was a bunch of houses. The houses used local basalt rock for their foundations and were constructed out of simple materials—probably wood structures insulated with field straw and animal manure, dirt floors, and thatched roofs. It is true that the excavated remains of Capernaum include a synagogue: the ruins can still be seen today by the steady flow of tourists into and out of the village. But the structure that now stands dates from the fifth century (four hundred years after Simon's time). There's no archaeological evidence to suggest any synagogue structure at all in Simon's day: at that time, a synagogue was simply a gathering (the literal meaning of the word) of Jews for the reading of Scripture and prayer, which could have happened anywhere.

Most Jews of the period, in fact most people of the period, could not read. And so it is not surprising to find an early tradition indicating that Peter himself was not schooled, that he was "illiterate"—the literal translation of the Greek term used of him and his fisherman companion John in Acts 4:13: "When they [the Jewish leaders in Jerusalem] saw the boldness of Peter and John and realized that they were unlettered [illiterate] and common, they were amazed." It should be born in mind that fishermen were typically uneducated peasants who had been put to work on the water in their early years and worked the nets until old age. They usually would not have had any schooling. Even a basic primary education meant being able to afford the leisure time and lost wages associated with going to school. And so far as we know, there was no school in the small village of Capernaum.

I emphasize Peter's probable lack of education not because it makes him stand out as an anomaly in his day but because it makes him altogether typical. Modern scholars have engaged in detailed studies of the extent and function of literacy in the ancient world and have come up with conclusions that strike many people as surprising. It appears that before the Industrial Revolution, most societies were highly illiterate, since they could not afford to devote the necessary time and resources to the mass education of their young, and saw no need to do so. Only with the need for a literate workforce, as in the modern world, was there a reason to remove so many able-bodied people from employment to teach them to read and write.[2]

The most reliable estimates indicate that at the best of times in the ancient world, only 10–15 percent of the population could read and write. And by "write" I mean "being able to sign your name." The percentage was much lower, of course, in rural areas, where people as a rule just scraped by. In a place such as rural Galilee, the vast majority of people, 90 or more likely 95 percent, could not read a simple text. Those who could do so were in demand, as the only way most people could read a book was by hearing it read by someone else. And the only way someone could engage in writing—for example, in drawing up a simple contract or divorce certificate or land lease—was by hiring the services of someone who had taken the time and effort to be trained. It is no wonder that the scribes were such authorities in first-century Palestine: they were the literary elite among the Jews. Peter was not among them.

He was, instead, an illiterate fisherman. His native language, living in that part of Galilee, would have been Aramaic, the language of Jesus himself. There is little evidence or reason to think that Peter could speak any other language— not Greek, and certainly not Latin—although he may have been able to understand Hebrew if it was read to him, as that was the language in which the Jewish Scriptures were written. The idea that everyone in the Roman Empire could speak Greek is certainly wrong. The educated elite could do so, but not the average person, who had enough to do simply to keep the family fed.[3]

Some people have argued that since Peter had a house, he must have been somewhat wealthier than average. It is true that archaeologists have identified a structure in Capernaum that in the second century had some graffiti written on the walls, suggesting that it was important to Christian pilgrims. Moreover, this structure appears to have been built over a small house of the first century.[4] But that is skimpy evidence to go on to show where the historical Peter actually laid his head at night. It is just as conceivable that a hundred years after he was long gone someone wanted to venerate his name and chose a likely spot for his house. In any event, Peter's house is mentioned in the New Testament Gospels, so there's nothing unreasonable in assuming he had one. But there really wasn't much choice for someone living in a poor village such as Capernaum. There weren't any condominiums for rent.

Other bits of information that we can glean from the Gospels about Simon's background are that his (and presumably Andrew's) father's name was John (or Jonah) (John 1:42; Matthew 16:17), that he was married, and that his mother-in-law was still living after he started following Jesus (Mark 1:30). He was not, therefore, single and celibate, like most of his papal successors down through the ages. But there is an additional piece of evidence concerning his marriage from outside the Gospels. The Apostle Paul indicates that Cephas was in the habit of taking his wife along with him on his missionary endeavors (1 Cor. 9:5). And so Peter's wife was still living some decades after the death of Jesus and also had converted to faith in him. We never learn her name or anything else about her, other than that she had a living mother who once had a fever. It's not at all implausible that the entire family lived together in the same house in Capernaum: Peter, Andrew, wives, mothers-in-law, and so on.

We might assume that the men of the family (Peter and Andrew) made enough money from their fishing business to support the rest. Once they began following Jesus, of course, they lived off the beneficence of others: that is, either by begging or by being given their food without begging. How their families continued to survive without the bread- (or fish-) winners is a question never dealt with in any of our sources.

Two of our early sources indicate that after Jesus' death, Peter planned to return to work (John 21; Gospel of Peter 60). But Peter soon became a believer in the resurrection of Jesus and ended up with more serious matters on his hands than fishing for a living. As Jesus is recorded to have told Simon and his brother Andrew at the outset of his ministry, "Follow me and I will make you fish for people" (or as the older Bible translations would have it, "I will make you fishers of men") (Mark 1:17). For our earliest Gospel, Mark, this marks the beginning of Peter's association with Jesus.

One might wonder why the early Christians chose to remember Peter as coming from poor peasant stock, an illiterate day laborer who was to become the head of the church. Why not sugarcoat his reputation, or choose someone else to remember as the head of the apostolic band that led the church into the world? The answer may well be that many Christians in the first two centuries— the vast majority of them, in fact—were themselves from the lower classes. From all reports, they stood amazed at the grace of God that had reached down to the likes of them with salvation. Moreover, remembering that God could work so powerfully through one as lowly as a peasant fisherman from a virtually unknown village in the rural backwater of Galilee may have comforted Christians and convinced them that the power that was at work in the gospel was not human-inspired or human-produced. The only way to explain the amazing success of the religion, whether judged by its personal effects or its rapid growth, was that God had chosen to work through weakness, not through strength. He had, after all, taken someone as unpromising as Simon and made him the Rock on whose labors the church could be built.

Peter in the Ministry of Jesus

We have already seen that the New Testament Gospels give differing accounts of when Simon acquired his nickname, the Rock, and how Simon became acquainted with Jesus in the first place (contrast Mark 1:16–18, John 1:35–42, and Luke 5:1–11). But they agree that soon after their initial meeting, Jesus acquired a larger number of followers. From them he chose twelve to be his closest disciples, with Simon Peter chief among them.

The Place of the Twelve

It is obvious in the Gospels that the twelve disciples have a special place among Jesus' followers. They accompany Jesus on his travels, they are privy not only to his public teaching but also to private instruction given to them alone (including, sometimes, explanations of the mysterious parables he delivers to the crowds), and they are given special authority and power to work wonders in his name. What is not so obvious is why Jesus chose specifically twelve men to be his disciples. Why not nine, or fourteen?

To make sense of the apostolic band of the Twelve, and Peter's place among them, we need to digress briefly into a related question of how to understand Jesus' own ministry and mission. This is a matter of ongoing debate among scholars who devote their lives to the question. The debate, in fact, has been carried on since the end of the eighteenth century, and it shows no signs of abating anytime soon. In recent decades, the one thing that virtually all scholars have come to agree on is that whatever else one might say about Jesus, he must be understood within the context of his own day, and not ripped out of that context as if he were a twentieth-century European or a twenty-first-century American. Jesus was a first-century Palestinian Jew. Any attempt to understand his words and deeds must take that historical fact seriously.

I won't recount the various options for understanding Jesus advanced by serious scholars (and by quacks) in modern times. Anyone interested in such matters can turn to books that deal with just this issue, starting with the great classic in the field, Albert Schweitzer's 1906 *Quest of the Historical Jesus*.[5] But I will indicate the view of Jesus that has been dominant among scholars since Schweitzer's groundbreaking work. This is the view that Jesus is best understood as a Jewish apocalyptic prophet.[6]

We know from a range of ancient sources about the first-century Jewish worldview that scholars have labeled "apocalypticism." There are references to apocalyptically minded Jews in historical works written during the period. Yet, more important, there are writings by Jewish apocalypticists themselves, including a number of the Jewish apocrypha from outside the Bible and such works as the Dead Sea Scrolls.

The term *apocalypse* means "unveiling" or "revealing." Jewish apocalypticists are so named by modern scholars because they believed that God had revealed to them the heavenly secrets that could make sense of earthly realities. This involved knowing why there was such evil and suffering in the world and knowing what God was going to do about it. Apocalypticists believed that the world is controlled by evil forces such as the Devil and his demons. That's why pain and misery are so rampant among us. God himself obviously isn't responsible for this cesspool of suffering. His personal opponent, the Devil, is, along with his nefarious allied forces.

But according to apocalypticists, God will eventually make right all that has gone so badly wrong. He will once again manifest his sovereignty by saving the world from the evil that now runs so rampant. Many apocalypticists were especially concerned about God's chosen people—the nation of Israel— and were intent to show that despite Israel's suffering, God has not abandoned them. He will send a deliverer who will overthrow the enemies of his people and set up a kingdom here on earth, to be ruled by his special emissary, the messiah. Other apocalypticists had a more cosmic view, thinking that not just Israel but the entire world is in the throes of the forces of evil, and that God will send not just an earthly king (the messiah) but a cosmic judge of the whole earth. This one will destroy the Devil and all his minions, and bring in a paradisal world, the Kingdom of God, in which there will be no more pain and suffering of any kind. God himself will rule supreme.

And when will this happen? Jewish apocalypticists maintained that the end is right around the corner. Those who are suffering need to hold on for just a little while longer. They should not cave in to the forces of evil and abandon their faith in the God who is ultimately in charge of this creation, for soon he will intervene in a mighty act of judgment on all those who oppose him and set up his new Kingdom. How soon? "Truly I tell you, some of those standing here will not taste death before they see that the Kingdom of God has come in power." These are the words of Jesus (Mark 9:1). Jesus himself appears to have subscribed to an apocalyptic view of the world and thought that God's act of vindication was absolutely imminent. "Truly I tell you, this generation will not pass away before all these things take place," says Jesus in our earliest surviving account of his teachings (Mark 13:30).

Jesus' mission and message are about the coming Kingdom of God, in which all evil will be destroyed, all suffering will be overcome, and only the good will rule.[7] In fact, Jesus maintains that the Kingdom is already beginning to appear. In the coming Kingdom there will be no demons, and so Jesus engages in a ministry of casting out demons. In the Kingdom there will be no disease, and so Jesus heals the sick. In the Kingdom there will be no hunger, and so Jesus feeds the multitudes. In the Kingdom there will be no natural disasters, and so Jesus calms the storms. In the Kingdom there will be no death, and so Jesus raises the dead.

Jesus' proclamation in our earliest surviving sources is about this coming Kingdom and the need for people to prepare for it. It will be an actual kingdom, here on earth, where people will lead joyous lives under the governance of God. It will be a kingdom brought from heaven by a cosmic judge, whom Jesus mysteriously calls "the Son of Man." This evidently refers to the figure called "one like a son of man" in a passage in the Jewish Scriptures describing the future judgment (Daniel 7:13–14). This Son of Man will come in judgment on the earth, bringing destruction upon those who have opposed God and salvation for those who have obeyed him. Indeed, anyone who adheres to the teachings of Jesus himself will be saved when this Son of Man arrives (Mark 8:38; 13:26–27). Those who are saved will enter then into God's eternal kingdom. And how will God govern this kingdom? Through his messiah, and those whom he chooses to administer his will.

And so we return to the question of why Jesus specifically chose *twelve* disciples, Peter among them. According to ancient Jewish tradition, the people of God were originally organized into twelve tribes, with a tribal leader over each (the patriarchs of Israel in the Hebrew Bible). When the people of God—Israel and all those who truly worship the God of Israel—enter into the Kingdom, how will *they* be organized? As they were in the beginning. There will be twelve tribes in the new Israel of the Kingdom, and twelve leaders. Who will these twelve be? In one of his best-attested sayings, Jesus clearly gives his answer. Speaking privately to Peter and the others, Jesus tells them: "Truly I say to you that in the new world [i.e., the Kingdom of God], when the Son of Man sits on the throne of his glory [as ruler of all], you who follow me [the disciples] will also sit on twelve thrones judging the twelve tribes of Israel" (Matt. 19:28; cf. Luke 22:28–30). It is the twelve disciples who will rule in the Kingdom.

Choosing specifically twelve disciples, in other words, is an apocalyptic statement that the kingdom is soon to arrive and that these twelve men, the closest followers of Jesus, will be its rulers.

Who will enter into this kingdom, to be ruled by the twelve, once the Son of Man arrives? One of the most striking features of Jesus' teaching is that it will not be the rich and powerful, the highly religious and honored. It will be the lowly, the downtrodden, the oppressed, the poor, the sinful. "For the first shall be last and the last first," and "whoever humbles himself will be exalted and whoever exalts himself will be humbled." It is the rich and powerful who side with the forces of evil in this world (how do you imagine they get their wealth and power?); it is the poor and oppressed who side with God. And they will be rewarded when the Son of Man arrives with God's Kingdom. It is no accident that the rulers of this Kingdom will be those who are lowly and of no consequence now. Chief among them will be an illiterate fisherman from the rural backwaters of Galilee.

Peter and the others, then, are the insiders around Jesus who will be his co-rulers when the Kingdom arrives and Jesus himself, also a lower-class peasant from the hinterland, becomes the messiah of God. No wonder the disciples are portrayed as incredulous of their good fortune as they anticipate the inbreaking of God's Kingdom. They want to know if Jesus is himself the messiah. They want to know if it is now that he will be restoring the Kingdom to Israel (Acts 1:6). They want to know if they can have special positions of authority once it arrives, for example, by sitting at his right hand and his left when he is on his throne (Mark 10:35–37). The Twelve, then, are a special group, not just because they are receiving special attention and instruction from the one who will rule the earth, but because they will rule with him in the Kingdom that is to come.

Special Privileges of the Three

Our earliest accounts of Jesus and his disciples—the Gospels of Matthew, Mark, and Luke—indicate that among the Twelve there was an inner group of three who were especially close to Jesus: Peter and the two sons of Zebedee, James and John. We see these three given special privileges in several scenes of the Gospels.

In the Gospel of Mark, a Jewish leader named Jairus appeals to Jesus to come cure his daughter, who is on the verge of death. By the time Jesus arrives at the house, the girl has already died. But Jesus is undeterred: he sends out all the mourners and takes with him just the girl's parents and Peter, James, and John. In their presence alone, he raises the girl from the dead (Mark 5:21–24, 35–43).

Halfway through his ministry Jesus goes up to the Mount of Transfiguration, taking with him only Peter, James, and John. There he is transformed before them and begins to speak with his two predecessors from the Jewish Scriptures, Moses and Elijah, to the amazement and fear of the three onlookers (Mark 9:2–8).

Prior to his arrest Jesus is speaking to his disciples about the future destruction that will take place when the Kingdom of God arrives. Then Peter, James, and John, along with Peter's brother Andrew on this occasion, ask him for more information privately. Jesus complies with their request, delivering the longest speech of his ministry (in Mark's Gospel) to tell them about the disasters that will strike the earth before the Son of Man arrives in judgment on the earth (Mark 13:1–36).

After he holds his Last Supper with his disciples, he goes out to the garden of Gethsemane to pray, and he leaves the other disciples, taking with him only Peter, James, and John, before whom he becomes greatly agonized, knowing that his end is soon (Mark 14:32–34). He asks them to keep watch for him while he prays. But three times he returns to them, only to find them asleep. Of the three, it is Peter alone he rebukes: "Simon, are you asleep? Could you not watch one hour? Watch and pray that you not enter into temptation" (Mark 8:37).

So while the Twelve were accorded a special place among Jesus' followers, as those who received private instruction and special authority, there was yet an inner group who accompanied Jesus in his even more private moments and with whom, presumably, he was particularly close: three fishermen from Galilee.

The Special Connections of the One

Among these three, there was one who, in particular, was widely understood to be Jesus' right-hand man, Simon the Rock. He was the one who openly acknowledged that Jesus was the Messiah; he was the one who spoke out to Jesus on the Mount of Transfiguration; he was the one who called out to Jesus while he was walking on the water. He was also the one who was subjected to Jesus' occasional rebuke: "Get behind me, Satan, for you are thinking the thoughts not of God but of humans"; "Simon, are you asleep? Could you not watch one hour?" Just on the level of historical fact, it appears that Jesus' closest disciple was Peter.

And so it is interesting to notice the various conversations between Jesus and Peter in some of our surviving traditions, and to consider why these conversations may have been remembered by Christians who told and retold their stories about Jesus. If nothing else, these conversations can show us how early storytellers understood what it meant to be a follower of Jesus.

It is probably safe to say that following Jesus during his earthly life meant, above all else, accepting his message that the Kingdom of God was soon to appear, and that people needed to prepare for its imminent arrival. The moment was urgent; the word needed to be proclaimed, to warn people of the coming disaster and the possibility of salvation. This can help explain the puzzling situation I mentioned earlier, that Simon and Andrew, along with others, apparently left their families in the lurch in order to go off with Jesus. How would those left behind survive in the months and years to come without the family income? Maybe Peter and the others were so convinced that the end of this age was imminent that survival for the long haul was not really an issue. For them, there was not going to *be* a long haul! The Son of Man would soon arrive from heaven and so the Kingdom was right around the corner. And in that Kingdom, there would be no need for backbreaking labor, for God would provide all that is needed to his children. And so, as Jesus told them, God's people should "seek first the Kingdom . . . and all these other things [food and clothing] will be provided" them (Matt. 6:33).

The disciples themselves appear to have been all too aware of what they sacrificed for the sake of following Jesus, in anticipation of this coming Kingdom. When Jesus indicated that it is not the wealthy but the poor who will enter the Kingdom of God, Peter is said to have replied: "Look, we have left all things and followed you" (Mark 10:28). Jesus' response embodies his apocalyptic message in a nutshell: "Truly I tell you, there is no one who has left house or brothers or sisters or mother or father or children or fields for my sake, and for the sake of the good news, who will not receive a hundredfold houses and brothers and sisters and mothers and children and fields in the present age, along with persecutions, and in the age that is coming eternal life. For many who are first will be last, and the last first" (Mark 10:29–32).

Peter and the others appear to have accepted Jesus' message that this coming new age would be imminent, and that Jesus himself would be the messiah, the ruler of that kingdom, with themselves as his co-rulers. What a shock, then, when it didn't turn out as planned.

Peter and Jesus as the Coming Messiah

Here I need to stress a point that I have only intimated until now. Today when Christians talk about Jesus as the messiah, they seem to mean a range of things. Some appear to think that being the messiah would make Jesus divine. Others think that being the messiah required him to die for the sins of the world. Others think Jesus is the messiah because he is the spiritual ruler of God's kingdom in our hearts. Others think that being the messiah means all these things. But historians have long known that none of these understandings of the messiah can be found in any Jewish writings—and, therefore, that none of them was likely held by any Jews—prior to Christianity itself. That is to say, these may be Christian understandings of the messiah, but they were not Jewish understandings of the messiah. And Jesus, Peter, and the other disciples were not Christians, but Jews. What, then, did Jews expect of a messiah?[8]

It may be that in Jesus' day most Jews were not expecting any kind of messiah at all, just as most Jews today aren't. But those who *were* expecting a messiah had a range of ideas about what that one might be like. The word *messiah* itself comes from the Hebrew word meaning "anointed one" (the Greek equivalent is *christos,* whence we get the term "Christ"). Since the kings of Israel were anointed as part of their inauguration ceremony, it came to be thought, once Israel had been overrun by other nations and made subservient to them, that there would be a future king to sit on Israel's throne, a future anointed one like David, the great king of old. And so some Jews anticipated a future warrior-king who would overthrow their enemies and reestablish Israel as a sovereign state in the land. Other Jews who embraced a particular kind of apocalyptic mind-set thought that the future anointed (or chosen) one would be a cosmic judge of the earth, for example, the "one like a son of man" described in the book of Daniel, who would destroy the forces of evil to bring in God's rule here on earth. Yet other Jews who were more focused on the ritual laws God had prescribed in Scripture thought that the future anointed one would be a great and powerful interpreter of God's law who would lead his people in righteousness.

There were, in short, a variety of expectations of what the future messiah might be like. But all of these expectations had one thing in common: the messiah was presumed to be a figure of grandeur and power who would overcome God's enemies in the age to come. The idea that he would be weak and easily crushed, that he would be tortured and executed by the enemy, was as far removed from the Jewish notions of messiahship as you can imagine. Why, then, do Christians talk about the messiah as if he was *supposed* to suffer and die? Because Christians, from the very beginning, have confessed that Jesus himself is the messiah, and Christians know full well that he suffered and died. It's a matter of logic: if Jesus is the messiah and Jesus suffered and died, then the messiah had to suffer and die.

To support their view, Christians have always appealed to certain passages of Scripture that speak of God's righteous one being subject to the abuse and torture of others, passages such as Psalm 22 and Isaiah 53. Non-Christian Jews have pointed out, however, that these texts never speak about the messiah (you can look for yourself: the term *messiah* never occurs in them). That's why for most ancient Jews the claim that Jesus was the messiah was ludicrous. From their standpoint, Jesus was everything that the messiah was *not* supposed to be: a lowly, powerless, crucified criminal.

What has all this to do with the traditions about Peter in our early Gospels? We have already seen that when asked, Peter confesses Jesus to be the messiah (e.g., Mark 8:29). If that was the actual expectation of the historical Peter, then his hopes were severely dashed by the brutal facts of history. For rather than establishing God's kingdom, either in Israel or over all the earth, Jesus was arrested for conspiracy against the state and summarily tortured and executed in a humiliating and public way.

No Jew would come away from the crucifixion thinking that this one was the messiah. The crucifixion radically disconfirmed Peter's deepest hopes. As we will see in a later chapter, however, that was not the end of the story. For Peter came to believe that three days after the crucifixion, God raised Jesus from the dead. He evidently claimed to have seen Jesus alive afterward. Whatever he actually saw, this resurrection experience turned everything on its head once again. For if Jesus was raised from the dead, he *must* be God's chosen one. That would mean that he is the messiah in some way unlike any previously imagined. But could Jesus himself not have imagined what kind of messiah he was? This is where the Christian tradition takes over, for early on Christian storytellers portrayed Jesus as knowing all along what was to happen to him. As a result, he had an understanding of what it meant to be the messiah that was completely different from what was commonly understood.

That is why, in the later stories of our Gospels—developed after Christians had devised innovative ways of understanding the messiah—when Peter confesses Jesus to be the messiah, Jesus warns him not to tell anyone (Mark 8:30). He doesn't want the misunderstanding (i.e., that he was the Jewish messiah of normal expectation) to spread. And that's why Jesus allegedly tells Peter that he must suffer and die in Jerusalem (the storytellers imagine Jesus saying some such thing because, after all, that's exactly what did happen). Peter, of course, is portrayed as not understanding what Jesus means. Thus Jesus rebukes him: "Get behind me, Satan."

In this later Christianized understanding of Jesus as the messiah, he is the one who must suffer and die for others. But that's not all. Jesus is also the messiah in the more traditional Jewish sense, in that he will *still* inherit the Kingdom of God when it comes. In fact, he himself will bring it. For he is the very one he predicted, the Son of Man to come from heaven in judgment on the earth. Jesus will come again in glory to judge the living and the dead.

Peter and the others no doubt expected this to happen right away: after all, Jesus is recorded as saying that it will happen within their generation, before the disciples have "experienced death" (Mark 9:1). But as time passed and they proclaimed the message of salvation through the death of the messiah, problems set in and it became clear to Jesus' followers that there would be an interim between the beginning of the end (the death and resurrection of Jesus) and the culmination of the end (his second coming in power).

Peter, Jesus, and the Time of the Church

Some of the conversations recorded between Peter and Jesus deal with just this interim. Some early Christian storytellers, for example, recognized that before the Kingdom comes into power, the church must be spread throughout the world. And so in Matthew's Gospel, written ten or fifteen years after Mark's, Peter's confession of Jesus as the messiah comes to be worded differently. As in Mark, Peter, when asked, indicates, "You are the messiah" (though in Matthew 16:16 he adds, "the Son of the living God"). Jesus' immediate response is not to urge them to tell no one, as in Mark. First he affirms the identification and indicates something of its implications:

> Blessed are you Simon Son of John, for flesh and blood did not reveal this to you, but my Father in heaven. And I say to you that you are Peter [*Petros*], and upon this rock [*petra*] I will build my church, and the gates of Hades will not prevail against it. I will give you the keys of the kingdom of heaven, and whatever you bind on earth will be bound in heaven, and whatever you loose upon earth will be loosed in heaven. (Matt. 16:17–19)

For the later storytellers who shaped the account in this way, the end is not to come right away after Jesus' death (as indeed, Matthew, writing half a century later, knew full well). First the church needs to be built. And at the foundation of it would be Peter.

Some interpreters, principally Protestant theologians, have argued that Jesus in this passage cannot mean that the "rock" on which he is to build the church is Peter himself, because the word for rock is *petra* and the nickname of Peter is the slightly different *Petros*. This actually is a debatable point, since Peter's nickname could not be *petra*—in Greek *petra* is a feminine noun, whereas Peter, obviously, is masculine (and so the invented name *Petros*, the masculine form of *petra*). Moreover, if any such saying did go back to Jesus or to a storyteller who was telling the story in Aramaic, both *petra* and *Petros* would have been the same word, *cephas*.

But whether Jesus is saying that Peter himself is the rock on which the church will be built (the view of most Catholic interpreters) or that the solid confession that Peter has just made of Jesus' messiahship is the rock (the view of many Protestants), it is clear that (for Matthew) there will be an interim before the Kingdom of God arrives. During this period the church will provide a kind of alternative existence here on earth, in which God's kingdom (i.e., his rule among people) will be manifest. The decisions that Peter makes as head of the church will reflect the will of God in heaven ("what you bind will be bound . . . what you loose will be loosed"). And the church will be victorious, even in the face of the forces of evil ("the gates of Hades will not prevail against it").

Peter and the Problems in the Meantime

As time went on, some Christians became less assured that belonging to the church provided protection from the forces of evil (the "gates of Hades"). This is evident in a conversation that was later ascribed to Peter and Jesus. For over three hundred years our only knowledge of this conversation came from a second-century writing known as the book of 2 Clement, which was discovered in the early seventeenth century and first published in 1633. But in recent times archaeologists have turned up virtually the same conversation in some Greek fragments of a Gospel that apparently claimed to have been written by Peter himself (we will talk more about this Gospel in a later chapter). This Gospel of Peter was written in the early second century, some thirty or forty years after Matthew. The conversation recorded between Peter and Jesus is fully indicative of the new situation that Christians had found themselves in during the intervening period. For here there is a clear understanding that evil still continued to exercise its power unabated in that age, and that its wrath was especially directed against those who sided with Christ.

The conversation, which I give here in the more complete form found in 2 Clement, begins with words that will sound familiar to those who know their New Testament: "For the Lord said, 'You will be like sheep in the midst of wolves.'" A surprising question then comes from Peter, and an even more surprising response from Jesus. Peter asks, "What if the wolves rip apart the sheep?" And Jesus responds:

> After they are dead, the sheep should fear the wolves no longer. So too you: do not fear those who kill you and then can do nothing more to you; but fear the one who, after you die, has the power to cast your body and soul into the hell of fire. (2 Clement 5:2–4)[9]

What is particularly striking about this back-and-forth is that it assumes that God will vindicate his chosen people not in the future Kingdom that is coming to earth but in the afterlife. This is what we might call a "de-apocalypticized" message—one in which the original apocalyptic expectation of an actual kingdom in this world has been transformed into an expectation that when a person dies, his or her soul will face an individual judgment, either heaven or hell. Peter is told that what happens to the physical body in the here and now (e.g., being ripped apart by one's enemies) should be of little concern. What matters is what happens after one dies. This is a message, of course, that Christians continue to affirm, despite the fact that it was not the apocalyptic view taught by the historical Jesus himself.

Peter and the Afterlife

A final conversation between Peter and Jesus appears in an intriguing work of the second century known as the Apocalypse of Peter. This was an important book in the early Christian church. Several church fathers thought that it should be included as part of the New Testament, either together with the Apocalypse of John (i.e., the book of Revelation) or on its own without John. Unfortunately, we have only a fragment of the work in the original Greek language in which it was written. There is, however, a much fuller translation of the text into Ethiopic. There are important differences between the surviving Greek and Ethiopic accounts that have puzzled scholars for nearly a century. But both versions narrate a revelation given by Jesus to Peter concerning what will happen to the souls of the saved and the damned in the afterlife. In fact, in the Greek version it appears that Jesus actually takes Peter on a guided tour of heaven and hell, the first such tour narrated by any Christian author on record and a distant relation to Dante's *Divine Comedy*.

In the fuller Ethiopic version, the account begins with Jesus talking to his disciples on the Mount of Olives, an obvious allusion to the episode related in Mark 13. Here too the disciples want to know what the future holds in store. Jesus tells them in graphic, and at times lurid, detail. He assures them that the end is indeed coming soon. Those who have remained faithful to God will be rewarded with eternal bliss, whereas those who have lived lives of habitual sin will face unspeakable torments. As it turns out, the punishments often match the crimes:

> And some there were hanging by their tongues; and these were the ones who blasphemed the way of righteousness, and under them was laid fire flaming and tormenting them. . . .
>
> And I saw the murderers and those who were accomplices cast into a gorge full of evil, creeping things, and smitten by those beasts, writhing about in that torment. And upon them were set worms like clouds of darkness. And the souls of those who were murdered stood and looked upon the torment of those murderers and said, "O God, righteous is your judgment."
>
> And other men and women were being burned up to their middle and were cast down in a dark place and were scourged by evil spirits, having their entrails devoured by worms that never rested. And these were the ones who had persecuted the righteous and delivered them up.

And near to them were women and men gnawing their lips and in torment having heated iron in their eyes. And these were the ones who did blaspheme and speak evil of the way of righteousness.

And over against these were yet others, men and women, gnawing their tongues and having flaming fire in their mouths. And these were the false witnesses. (Apocalypse of Peter, 21–29)

Here, then, in the Apocalypse of Peter we have a fuller description than any found in the earlier Gospels about what lies in store both for those who support God (eternal bliss) and for those who oppose him (eternal torment). It is clear that we are dealing here with a kind of ancient theodicy, that is, an attempt to explain how God can be righteous if there is so much suffering in the world. For according to this text, the powers of evil and those who side with them will not have the last word. God will have the last word. This world may appear to be a cesspool of misery and suffering, but all will be made right in the world that is to come. God will vindicate his name and his people, rewarding them for their faithfulness and punishing their enemies for the evil they have done.

This is a clear case—as are most of the conversations between Peter and Jesus—in which Christians who tell the stories are expressing their own hopes, fears, longings, desires, loves, and hates. In other words, Christians appear to be using stories of Peter to "think with," that is, to work out their own sense of who God truly is, what it means to obey him, and what awaits those who choose not to do so.

Chapter Four

Peter at the Passion

The New Testament Gospels have sometimes been called "Passion narratives with long introductions." The scholar who came up with this phrase meant that these books are largely about the suffering, death, and resurrection of Jesus. Everything else in Jesus' life—his entire public ministry—is a preliminary to these key events. This can be seen to some extent simply in the amount of space the Gospel writers devote to the events of Jesus' last days. Our earliest Gospel, Mark, for example, devotes six of its sixteen chapters to the last week of Jesus' life. Our latest canonical Gospel, John, covers three years of Jesus' ministry in the first eleven chapters, and the final week in the other ten.

And so we know more about Jesus' final days and hours than about any other period in his life. Correspondingly, there are more significant references to Peter in the accounts of the Passion than in any other portion of the Gospels.

Peter in the Last Supper Traditions

Peter plays a prominent role in the traditions of Jesus' Last Supper with his disciples. In the Synoptic Gospels of Matthew, Mark, and Luke, this is a Passover meal that Jesus celebrates.[1] Passover was an annual Jewish festival that commemorated the Exodus many centuries earlier, when Moses led the children of Israel out from their slavery in Egypt. Jews understood this event to be the handiwork of God, and every year they held a festival in memory of it. This festival included a special meal with foods that symbolized different aspects of the event: bitter herbs reminded them of the bitter slavery of their ancestors in Egypt, unleavened bread reminded them that the children of Israel needed to flee quickly in order to escape, and so on. At this meal in the Synoptic Gospels,

Jesus takes some of the symbolic foods of the Passover and invests them with new symbolism that reflects the new act of God's salvation. The bread represents Jesus' own body, which would be broken, and the cup of wine represents his own blood, which would be shed.

John's Gospel, on the other hand, does not portray Jesus' Last Supper as a Passover meal. Instead, it is a meal that took place the evening *before* Passover.[2] As a consequence, there is no reference in John to Jesus instilling new symbolic significance in the already symbolic foods of the supper. Instead, in John, Jesus performs a different symbolic act. He, the master of the Twelve, girds himself with a cloth, pours water into a basin, and begins to wash the disciples' feet, a job normally reserved for a slave (John 13:1–11). Peter, as John tells the tale, puts his foot in his mouth instead of the basin. He asks Jesus if he is really planning to wash his feet; Jesus replies that Peter will understand later what he's doing. Peter retorts that he will never let Jesus wash his feet. Jesus then makes a stark reply: "If I don't wash you, you have nothing to do with me." That's more than enough for the rash Peter, who now pulls a complete about-face and asks for even more than Jesus has been graciously willing to give: "Lord, then wash not only my feet but also my hands and head." But Jesus stays firm in his resolve and informs Peter that "the one who is washed is clean all over, and needs to wash only his feet."

This account is found in none of the Gospels other than John, and it is difficult to establish as a conversation that really took place. Its interpretation is open to a number of possibilities. Many interpreters think that storytellers narrating the account were thinking of the importance of baptism for the remission of sins. The one who is washed (that is, baptized) is clean all over, and only on occasion needs to have the feet recleansed (for example, through coming to Jesus for forgiveness of sins). If so, then Peter's impetuous response to Jesus represents the reaction of some early Christians who may have wondered if, after they had broken faith with Jesus, they needed to be baptized again. This conversation makes it clear that there is no need for rebaptism, only a return to Jesus for forgiveness.

The scene at the Last Supper that most fully exemplifies Peter's character is one found in all four of the Gospels, one of the best-known incidents from Peter's life. Given its deep roots in all the traditions, it may refer to something that actually happened. Jesus in the Gospels is portrayed as knowing that he is about to be betrayed, and he predicts that his disciples will abandon him. It is hard to know if Jesus' prediction is historical or if it is a story told later to explain that Jesus was not caught off guard by the events that took his life. But the tradition of Peter's bravado in the face of trouble may well be authentic. For in all the accounts, when Jesus predicts that he will be deserted by all, Peter declares that he, at least, will never abandon him. As he says in our earliest account: "Even if everyone falls away, I will not" (Mark 14:29). Or as he says yet more boldly in Luke's version, "Lord, I am ready to go with you to prison and to death" (Luke 22:33). Thirty years later, he did just that, but at the time of Jesus' arrest, things turned out differently. How quickly is a rock crushed.

Peter at Jesus' Arrest

We have already noticed how the character of Peter gets played out at the crucial juncture of the story of Jesus' arrest. Even though he is one of the trusted "inner circle" of three that Jesus takes with him when he goes off to pray in solitude, Peter turns out not to be trustworthy at all. Jesus makes a simple request that Peter, James, and John remain awake and watch while he prays, but three times (according to Mark's account) he comes back to find them napping (Mark 14:32–42).

When Judas Iscariot arrives with the armed guard to arrest Jesus, we learn that one of the disciples pulls a sword and strikes off the ear of a servant of the high priest. In the last of our canonical Gospels (but not the others) we're told that this disciple was none other than Peter the impetuous, who, as one might have come to expect by this point, earns yet another rebuke from Jesus: "Put the sword in its scabbard; will I not drink the cup the Father has given me?" (John 18:11). What Peter is doing with a sword we're never told (weren't Jesus and his followers pacifists?).

But soon the bravado melts away. We're told in the Gospels that Peter did not flee the scene directly but followed the crowds who took Jesus off to stand trial before the Jewish court on charges of blasphemy. The flight of the other disciples makes sense: if their leader was a criminal, what does that make them? Peter, however, is said to have "followed at a distance" (Mark 14:54), evidently to see how things would turn out.

They did not turn out well, either for Jesus, who was condemned for his teachings, or for Peter, who out of fear denied knowing his master three times in rapid sequence: either before the cock crowed twice, as in Mark, or before it crowed at all, as in the other Gospels. This threefold denial of Jesus embodies a moment that Peter himself no doubt would have wanted very much to forget. But it's a story that Christians have long been eager to remember. Here Jesus' closest follower, his right-hand man, the one on whom he said he would build his church, turns his back on his master in order to save his own hide, concealing his knowledge of the one to whom he had sworn allegiance and for whom he had professed a willingness to suffer and die. The appeal of the story to Christian storytellers should be obvious, for how many of us have not let fear get the better of us, turned coward at the moment, sought to protect our own well-being even if it meant going back on our promises or turning our backs on those we otherwise love and cherish? Peter's denials didn't hurt Jesus; he was on the road to the cross as it was. But they hurt Peter, showing him to be faithless when the moment of truth arrived.

If Peter's story had ended there, this instance of pathos probably would not have had the allure it has had over the centuries to Christian storytellers and listeners. But the faithlessness of Peter is set, in the fuller story of the Gospels, against the faithfulness of Jesus, who, as we will see, remained true to his companion despite his act of denial.

Peter at the Crucifixion

According to our earliest account, when Jesus was crucified the only followers who looked on (from a distance) were some of the women who had accompanied him on his trip from Galilee to Jerusalem for the annual Passover celebration: Mary Magdalene, another woman named Mary, and one named Salome (Mark 15:40). Matthew cites a group of women as well, with some names different from the ones in Mark. John indicates that along with Mary Magdalene was Jesus' own mother, Mary, and an unnamed disciple whom Jesus loved (not Peter). Only Luke suggests that Peter may have been present at the crucifixion: in his account, we're told that "all of Jesus' acquaintances" watched from afar (Luke 23:49). This must be an exaggeration, since Jesus would have had hundreds of acquaintances and surely not all of them were there looking on.

There are noncanonical accounts, however, that indicate that Peter had special knowledge of the events that transpired during the crucifixion. Several of these accounts have intrigued modern scholars because they have been discovered only in modern times and claim to be written by none other than Peter himself.

The Gospel of Peter

Scholars had long known of the existence of a Gospel allegedly from Peter's own hand, because the so-called father of church history, Eusebius, narrates a story in his ten-volume *Church History* that mentions the book and says something about its character. This Gospel was used by some late-second-century Christians in Syria as sacred Scripture. It came to be proscribed, however, when the local bishop, a man named Serapion, read it for himself and found that it contained passages that could easily be interpreted to present a heretical understanding of Christ. The heresy (false teaching) involved a teaching known as docetism. This word comes from the Greek term *dokeo,* which means "to seem" or "to appear." Docetism taught that Jesus Christ was not actually a human being made of flesh and blood but only appeared to be human. The basic idea behind docetic views of Jesus was that if Christ was completely God, he obviously could not be subject to the limitations, pain, suffering, and death of humans. Then how is it that he *seemed* to be a human? Because it was, in fact, all an appearance.

We know of docetic Christians, some of them by name, from about the time of Bishop Serapion. In rough terms, there were two kinds of docetists. Some thought that Christ only appeared to be human because his body wasn't a real flesh, blood, and bone composition but a phantasm that simply took on the appearance of flesh, blood, and bone. And so when Jesus died on the cross, he didn't really feel pain, didn't really shed blood, didn't really die. He only seemed to do so.

The other kind of docetism was a bit more complicated. According to this view, there were two separate beings in Jesus Christ: Jesus, who was an actual flesh-and-blood man, and Christ, who was a divine being who temporarily came down into Jesus to dwell in him, empowering him to do miracles and deliver supernatural teachings, and then leaving him prior to his death to die alone. Docetists of this kind sometimes appealed to the Gospel of Mark, where we are told that at Jesus' baptism, the heavens opened up and the Spirit of God descended "into" (the literal rendering of the Greek) Jesus (Mark 1:10). This is when the divine being came to inhabit Jesus' body. But then, at the end of the Gospel, when Jesus is hanging on the cross, he cries out, "My God, my God, why have you forsaken me?" (literally, "why have you left me behind?") (Mark 15:34). This is because at this point the divine spirit, the Christ, had left Jesus, to suffer his fate and die on the cross.

According to Bishop Serapion, as recounted for us by Eusebius, the Gospel allegedly written by Peter lent itself to a docetic interpretation of Christ. Unfortunately, Serapion doesn't tell us which passages of the Gospel he has in mind, or which kind of docetism he was concerned about. Yet more unfortunately, the book itself came to be lost, unavailable to inquiring minds for many centuries.

Then, in one of the flukes of archaeological history, a portion of the Gospel of Peter turned up in an excavation in Akhmim, Egypt, in 1868. A French archaeological team, digging in an ancient Christian cemetery, unearthed the tomb of an eighth-century monk. He had been buried with a book. Among other things, the book contained a fragmentary Gospel that is written in the first person. The author claims to be Peter.[3]

This is not a complete Gospel but only a fragment of a much larger narrative: the surviving fragment begins in the middle of a sentence and ends in the middle of a sentence. How much else was lost we may never know. But what now survives is spectacularly interesting for historians of early Christianity, even though the book was actually written sometime in the early second century, fifty years or so after Peter himself had died. For here is a book that gives a narrative of Jesus' trial, death, and resurrection, forged in the name of Peter as if he himself were the one authorizing the validity of the account.

It is true that the pseudonymous author does not insert himself into the narrative very frequently. Most of the story is told in the third person. But there are some striking features of the text that make it distinctive among our surviving accounts of Jesus' death. For one thing, in this narrative, the Roman authorities, headed by Pontius Pilate, have very little—almost nothing—to do with Jesus' execution. Our fragment begins right after Pilate has washed his hands of the affair, and we're told that "none of the Jews" would wash his own hands. Already in the first verse, then, the tone is set. It is the Jews and their leaders who are responsible for Jesus' death, not the Romans. This became a set theme in the second and later centuries, when Jews came to be seen as culpable for the death of their own messiah, and eventually labeled with the odious term "Christ-killers."

The narrative contains an account of Joseph of Arimathea requesting Jesus' body, the mockery, and the crucifixion of Jesus. The crucifixion scene itself is presented somewhat differently than in the Gospels of the New Testament. We are told, for example, that when he was crucified, "the Lord . . . was silent, as if he had no pain" (v. 10). Could this be one of those passages that Serapion thought was open to a docetic interpretation? Jesus acted as if he had no pain because, in fact, he did have no pain?

There is also a curious incident not recorded in our other Gospels. As in the other texts, two criminals are crucified along with Jesus. But here, rather than both evildoers mocking Jesus (as in Mark) or one mocking him and the other speaking peaceably to him (as in Luke), one evildoer maligns the Romans for executing Jesus when they had no cause. Angry at this fellow's impudence, the Roman soldiers decide not to break his legs. That is, they choose not to end his misery quickly, but to force him to last longer in the throes of his torment.[4]

When Jesus dies in this Gospel, one other significant verse appears, for here his final cry of dereliction is somewhat different from what we find in Mark and Matthew. Now Jesus calls out, "My Power, O Power, you have left me behind" (v. 19). Is this another verse that could be interpreted docetically, to indicate that the divine element within Jesus had left him to die alone?

After Jesus is deposed from the cross and buried, the author moves from a third-person narrative to a first-person one:

> But I and my companions were grieving and went into hiding, wounded in heart. For we were being sought out by them as if we were evildoers who wanted to burn the Temple. Because of these things we fasted and sat mourning and weeping, night and day, until the Sabbath. (vv. 26–27)

Later in the text, when the author goes on to describe the miraculous events of the resurrection (which we will consider later), we learn that the person speaking is supposed to be none other than Peter himself.

The Christian who forged this account in the name of Peter has an interesting view of the crucifixion. He tells the story, as do all those telling their stories, to convey his own ideas, in this case that the Jews are the ones responsible for the death of the Lord and, possibly, that Jesus was not actually a human like the rest of us, but only seemed to be.

The Coptic Apocalypse of Peter

A more explicitly docetic understanding of Jesus' crucifixion can be found in another second-century document that claims to have been written by Peter himself, a book known as the Coptic Apocalypse of Peter. It is called the Coptic Apocalypse to differentiate it from the document that we examined earlier, the account preserved in Greek and Ethiopic in which Peter is given a guided tour of heaven and hell. The Coptic Apocalypse of Peter is an entirely different work, unrelated to the other. In this instance we did not know of the existence of the book until its fortuitous discovery in relatively modern times, when it turned up in a cache of writings found not by archaeologists digging for buried treasure but by Egyptian peasants digging for fertilizer.

The details of the discovery are still murky, some sixty years after it was made.[5] But it was evidently sometime late in 1945 when a group of seven Egyptian farmhands, headed by a fellow named, remarkably enough, Mohammed Ali, accidentally unearthed a jar in the wilderness near the Egyptian town of Nag Hammadi, close to the Nile, not far from the city of Luxor. They had been digging for fertilizer for their garden plots back home. When they uncovered the jar, they were not sure what to do with it, as it was sealed shut and they were afraid there might be an evil genie inside. On further reflection, they realized it might also contain gold, and so they smashed into it with their mattocks. But there was neither genie nor gold, only a set of thirteen leather-bound books, of little immediate use to a group of illiterate farmhands in the wilderness of Egypt.

Eventually the books came into the hands of museum officials in Cairo, who made the discovery known to scholars of antiquity. To the scholars' amazement, the books were found to contain a veritable library of largely unknown works from the early centuries of Christianity. The books were themselves shown to have been produced in the mid- to late fourth century, but they contained anthologies of earlier texts (fifty-two tractates altogether), most of which appear to have been originally written much earlier, some of them as early as the beginning of the second Christian century.[6]

Many of these texts were immediately recognized as significant because they contain the teachings of early Christian Gnostics, whom I'll discuss momentarily. As a result, sometimes the collection is referred to, somewhat inaccurately, as the Gnostic Gospels. More commonly, it is known by the place of its discovery, as the Nag Hammadi Library. The books in the collection are all written in the ancient Egyptian language Coptic, even though most, or all, of the books were originally written in Greek (so we are dealing with Coptic translations of Greek originals). This includes the Coptic Apocalypse of Peter, one of the most intriguing of the documents discovered in the collection, as it reportedly gives a firsthand report by Peter of what really happened at the crucifixion of Jesus.

To make sense of this report, I first need to say something very briefly about Gnostics and the religious views they had, a matter that we will return to repeatedly throughout this study. The term *Gnostic* comes from the Greek word for knowledge, *gnosis*. It is used in some ancient sources to refer to people who have special, often esoteric, religious knowledge that can bring salvation.

Modern scholars sometimes speak about "Gnostic religion" as if it were one solitary thing in the ancient world, whereas in fact there was an enormous

range of religions that stressed the importance of secret knowledge for salvation. These religions did not always share the same beliefs, practices, and scriptures. But there were groups of religions that can be understood as having the
same basic understanding of the world, in which gnosis played an important
role for salvation. These Gnostic religions by and large maintained that the
world we live in is not the good creation of the one true God. Instead, it came
into existence as the result of some kind of cosmic disaster. Moreover, the
material existence we are forced to live alienates us from our true lives as
spiritual beings. The goal of the Gnostic religions is to allow us to transcend
this evil material world and return to our heavenly home whence we came.
This can happen as soon as we learn the truth about ourselves, the world around
us, how we came to be here, and how we can escape. In other words, we need
special self-knowledge for salvation.

According to many Gnostic religions, it was Christ himself who provided
the special gnosis needed for salvation. But how could Christ reveal this truth
to us without himself becoming a material being, that is, without himself being
trapped in the evil world of matter? Gnostics tended to be docetic in their
understanding of Christ, some of them thinking he was a pure phantasm, others that there was a difference between the man Jesus and the divine Christ.
For those who took the latter view, when Jesus was crucified, it was simply the
material part (the man Jesus) that died. The spiritual being, the Christ, is beyond suffering.

This is where the Coptic Apocalypse of Peter comes into the picture, for
this book provides an account, written in the name of Peter, in which the author claims to observe Jesus' crucifixion. But as it turns out, even though the
Savior appears to be nailed to a cross, it is only an appearance.

The book begins by the Savior warning Peter against other Christian leaders who are "blind and deaf" to the real truth of the gospel, because "they are
without perception" (i.e., they lack true gnosis; Apoc. Pet. 74). These others
blaspheme the truth and proclaim an evil teaching. We later learn that these are
the people known in the churches as the "bishop" and the "deacons." In other
words, in this text, we find a Gnostic Christian, claiming to be Peter, attacking
the non-Gnostic Christians, who appear to be the actual leaders of the Christian churches.

But then comes the really interesting part. Peter claims that "I saw him
apparently being seized by them to be crucified" (Apoc. Pet. 81). But Peter is
confused, because above the cross he sees another person who is "glad and
laughing." Understandably, he wants to know what he is seeing. And the Savior tells him:

> He whom you see above the cross, glad and laughing, is the living Jesus. But he
> into whose hands and feet they are driving the nails is his physical part, which is
> the substitute. They are putting to shame that which is in his likeness.[7]

And so, according to the Peter of this document, there appear to be *three* Christs: the one talking to him, the one whose physical part is getting nailed to the cross (which is only a substitute for the real Christ), and the "living" Jesus who is above the cross laughing.

But what is he laughing at? We're next told that the living Jesus approaches Peter and speaks with him to let him know that the part of him that was being crucified is "the home of demons and the clay vessel in which they dwell, belonging to Elohim." *Elohim* is the Hebrew word for God in the Jewish Bible. Since Gnostics thought that this world was a cosmic mistake, not the creation of the one true God, they insisted that the God of the Jews who created this world was a lesser, ignorant deity. It is to that one that the body, the clay vessel containing the spirit, belongs. The living Jesus is laughing because those who are crucifying him don't have the true knowledge (they "lack perception"). They think that they can kill him. But he can't be killed. He is the true spirit that has been released.

After speaking a bit further with Peter about his true nature, Jesus comforts him: "I will be with you so that none of your enemies will prevail over you. Peace be to you! Be strong!" And then we are told that "when he [Jesus] had said these things, he [Peter] came to his senses."

Here, then, is a vision of the crucifixion that reveals to Peter what it really meant for Christ to be nailed to the cross. It meant the death of his material body, but death was unable to touch the spirit. So too with those who have the true knowledge that can bring salvation: they cannot really be harmed. Only their bodies can be tortured and killed. But their bodies are not who they really are. The body is merely the demonic and evil trapping of the soul within, which will escape and return to its heavenly home.

The Peculiar View of Basilides

Some readers have been put off by this idea of Christ laughing at his own crucifixion. After all, it doesn't seem like much of a joke. But there were yet other traditions of the crucifixion, connected with Peter, that took the bad joke a step farther. One of the infamous Gnostic Christians of the mid-second century was a teacher from Alexandria, Egypt, named Basilides. We don't know much about Basilides's teaching since, unfortunately, none of his own writings has survived. We thus need to rely on the accounts written by his enemies who attacked his views, especially the late-second-century heresiologist (i.e., heresy hunter) Irenaeus of Gaul, who wrote a five-volume attack on Gnostics and their teachings. Irenaeus gives a brief but detailed exposition of Basilides's views about God, the world, and Christ. In places it is hard to know whether he is giving a dispassionate summary of what Basilides actually taught or if he's skewing the picture a bit (or a lot) in order to make it easier to discredit and mock his views.

In any event, according to Irenaeus, Basilides also taught a doctrine of the laughing Jesus at the crucifixion. But in this case it worked quite differently. If you'll recall, in the early Gospels we're told that when Jesus was en route to Golgotha to be crucified, the Roman soldiers compelled a passerby, Simon of Cyrene, to carry the cross for him (Mark 15:21). According to Basilides, it was at that point that Jesus—who, after all, was divine and could do pretty much anything he wanted—pulled an identity switch. He miraculously transformed Simon of Cyrene to make him look like himself, and changed his own appearance to look like Simon of Cyrene. As a result, the Romans crucified the wrong person. Jesus, incredibly, stood by the cross laughing at his little stunt.

The motivation for thinking there may have been some such identity switch is the one we have discussed already under the broad rubric of docetism. Christ, in this view, could not really suffer, because he was not really human. How, then, is it that he appeared to suffer? It was a false appearance: someone else suffered in his stead.

And what has this to do with Peter? In an ancient tradition that goes back to the late-second-century author Clement of Alexandria, we learn that Basilides claimed to be the disciple of a man named Glaukia, who had been a disciple of Peter. In other words, here again a docetic interpretation of the crucifixion is (indirectly) tied to the views allegedly held by the chief of the apostles.

Peter's Letter to Philip

A final example of docetic views put on the lips of Peter can be found in another of the documents discovered at Nag Hammadi, a book that allegedly contains a letter written by Peter himself to the apostle Philip. It is therefore called the Letter of Peter to Philip. Much of this book contains a conversation between the resurrected Jesus and his disciples, who have been gathered together by Peter. Here Jesus reveals to them the nature of this worldly reality and instructs them how they can attain the salvation of their souls. This instruction embodies a Gnostic understanding of the world and the path of enlightenment. After Jesus delivers it he returns to heaven and Peter begins to speak to the other apostles about their need to suffer in this life. In the course of his talk he speaks as well of Jesus' own suffering and crucifixion, indicating that in fact, despite appearances, the suffering could not really touch Jesus himself:

> [Peter] spoke thus: "Our illuminator, Jesus, [came] down and was crucified. And he bore a crown of thorns. And he put on a purple garment. And he was [crucified] on a tree and he was buried in a tomb. And he rose from the dead. My brothers, Jesus is a stranger to this suffering." (Peter to Philip, 139)[8]

One might wonder why Christians would tell the stories this way, in which Peter insists that Christ only appeared to suffer. It is important to recall that in the early centuries of the church there were Christians who understood that this world is not the ultimate reality, the good creation of the one true God, but that it came into existence as the result of a cosmic disaster and is not the soul's real home. Our real home is in heaven, and we need to escape this material world in order to find our salvation. Christ himself, then, as Peter expresses it in these texts, could not belong to this evil world, could not be subject to its limitations and passions and sufferings. How is it, then, that he appeared to suffer? Because it was in fact all part of an appearance. Christ is a completely divine being, and the divine is beyond all suffering. Our own suffering, in this view, is temporary and rooted in the fact that we are entrapped in this alien, deficient world. But we too can follow Christ's example and escape the trappings of this world, returning to our heavenly home, where there will be no material evil, only peace and repose.

Peter and the Resurrection

It is safe to say that if no one had come to believe that Jesus was raised from the dead, the religious movement he started would have died with him. There never would have been a Christianity. To be sure, traditional Christianity has taught that it was the death of Jesus that brought about salvation. But it was the resurrection that showed the death to be what it was. Once a person came to believe that God had vindicated Jesus by raising him from the dead, it became clear that the crucifixion was no simple miscarriage of justice: it was the plan of God to bring about the salvation of the world. The resurrection is thus the linchpin in the founding of the Christian religion. Without it, Jesus would have been yet one more Jewish prophet who experienced a tragic and undeserved end.

As might be expected, Peter, as the chief of the apostles, plays a central role in the early traditions about Jesus' resurrection from the dead.

An Account of the Resurrection

It may be somewhat surprising to learn that the Gospels of the New Testament do not narrate the events of the resurrection. They do indicate that Jesus was buried in a tomb by Joseph of Arimathea, and they tell stories about the tomb being discovered empty three days later. But they do not give any description of what happened as Jesus emerged from the tomb.

There is such a description from outside the New Testament, however, and it happens to be in the Gospel of Peter. The author does not narrate this account in the first person, as something he himself saw. But he does describe it as a factual event, which is authorized, then, by the alleged author, Peter himself.

And an amazing account it is. After Jesus' burial the Jewish leaders are afraid the disciples will steal Jesus' body from the tomb, and so they convince the governor, Pilate, to provide them a guard to keep watch for three days. Pilate appoints a centurion named Petronius along with a group of soldiers. They roll a huge stone in front of the door of the tomb and seal it with seven seals (presumably to ensure that no one can break in), and take turns keeping watch.

But on the morning of the third day, a booming sound comes from the sky, the heavens open, and two men descend to the tomb. The stone rolls aside under its own power, and the two men enter. The soldiers on guard go to wake Petronius, and as they are telling him what has happened they see three men come out of the tomb. Two of them are as tall as mountains, with their heads reaching up to the sky. They are supporting the third, who is taller still, with his head up above the sky. And behind them, out of the tomb, there emerges the cross. A voice comes from heaven: "Have you preached to those who are asleep?" And the cross replies, "Yes."

This wonderfully legendary account is clearly trying to emphasize several points. Most obvious is that the tomb was empty on the third day, not because someone had stolen the body but because God had effected a miracle in bringing Jesus out alive. The miraculous nature of the event is stressed by the fact that a stone so huge and sealed with seven seals rolled away of its own accord as the angelic figures descend from heaven. The account also stresses the divine nature of Jesus as he emerges from the tomb, with his head reaching above the sky. (Is he being supported by the others because he is still weak from the physical ordeal of crucifixion? One would think that with a glorified body, that wouldn't be a problem.) And it emphasizes that salvation has extended even to the realms of the dead by the sacrifice of Christ. Hence the conversation with the cross, a metaphor for the instrument of Jesus' death: the good news of salvation has been proclaimed to those who had previously died, presumably the righteous saints awaiting their redemption in the holding place of Sheol.

This, then, is "Peter's" sole surviving account of what the resurrection of Jesus means: that he is divine and that through his death, as vindicated by the powerful act of God, salvation has come to the world.

The Discovery of the Empty Tomb

Even though the other surviving Gospel accounts do not narrate the events of the resurrection itself, they do indicate the two pieces of evidence that Jesus was raised from the dead: his tomb was discovered empty on the third day, and he appeared to his followers afterward. What has long struck careful readers, however, are the wide-ranging differences among the canonical accounts in their descriptions of these events. Just with respect to the empty tomb, the Gospels differ on who went to the tomb, what they found there, whom they encountered, what they were told, and what they did in response. We will deal more with these stories in a later chapter, as Mary Magdalene is a key figure in them. For now we are interested in Peter's role.

In none of the stories is Peter said to be the first to find the empty tomb. It is always the women (or Mary Magdalene alone) who make the discovery. And in most of the accounts, they are the only witnesses to the empty tomb—

so it is narrated in Matthew, Mark, the Gospel of Peter, and the original version of the Gospel of Luke. But there is another tradition about the empty tomb in some manuscripts of Luke, and this involves Peter.

To make sense of this alternative tradition, I need to say a brief word about the texts of our surviving accounts. Unfortunately, we do not have the original copies of any of the Gospels: these were lost or destroyed after they were produced and copied by scribes who wanted to circulate the books in their communities. We also don't have the first copies made of these books or copies of the copies. What we have are handwritten copies (manuscripts) that come from many decades—in most instances, many centuries—after the originals had been produced, copied, and lost.[9]

There are thousands of copies altogether, mainly from the Middle Ages. One of the problems confronting scholars is that all of these copies differ in their wording (this is true for all our early Christian texts, not just the Gospels). This is because the scribes who copied their texts sometimes altered them, either making accidental mistakes in the process of transcription or intentionally changing what they were writing in an effort to "improve" the stories a bit.

We have one such attempt at improvement in Luke's story of the empty tomb, and it involves Simon Peter. According to Luke, the women who went to the tomb found that Jesus' body was not there. But two men, evidently angels, appeared on the scene, telling them that Jesus had been raised from the dead. The women went off to tell the disciples, but "their [the women's] words seemed to them [the disciples] to be a foolish tale, and they did not believe them" (Luke 24:11).

It wouldn't be until Jesus actually appeared to the disciples that they would believe for themselves. But in a verse that was probably not originally in Luke's account, which instead came to be added by later scribes, we have a reference to one of the disciples going to the tomb and seeing for himself:

> But Peter got up and ran to the tomb, and stooping down he looked in to see the linen cloths by themselves, and he went away, astounded at what had happened. (Luke 24:12)[10]

This is a significant addition, because now the report of the empty tomb is not simply an idle tale told by unreliable women: it is verified by the chief of the apostles. Moreover, what Peter is said to see is significant. Technically speaking, the tomb is not empty. Jesus' body is not there, but his burial cloths are. In other words, Jesus has emerged from the tomb in a glorified body, no longer needing to be clothed with earthly raiment. This is apt testimony to the powerful, physical resurrection of Jesus.

It is interesting that we find a similar tradition about Peter and the empty tomb in the Gospel of John, the final canonical Gospel to be written. As John tells the tale, Mary Magdalene goes on the third day and finds the tomb empty.

Rather than reporting to all the disciples, she runs to tell Simon Peter and one other unnamed and mysterious disciple, whom John identifies simply as "the one whom Jesus loved." This is a figure who turns up several times in the final chapters of John's Gospel, who is often simply called by students of the Fourth Gospel "the beloved disciple." The ancient tradition is that this "beloved disciple" is none other than John, the son of Zebedee and the alleged author of the Fourth Gospel.[11]

In any event, once Mary tells them, "They have taken the Lord out of the tomb, and we do not know where they have laid him" (in John 20:2 she obviously doesn't realize yet that Jesus has been raised from the dead), the two disciples make a rush to the tomb. The beloved disciple outstrips Peter and arrives first to look inside, but it is Peter who actually enters the tomb first "and saw the linen cloths lying there, along with the napkin which had been placed on [Jesus'] head, not lying with the linen clothes but separate, folded up in its own place" (20:6–7). Apparently Jesus had neatly folded his grave clothes before making his exit from the tomb.

The text does not say that Peter came to believe in the resurrection on the basis of his discovery. Strikingly, the *other* disciple, who enters after Peter and sees the bizarre sight, recognizes it for what it is: "and he saw and believed." But Peter too will believe soon enough, as Jesus is about to appear to him and the others.

The Post-Resurrection Appearances of Jesus

The accounts of who was the first to see Jesus alive after his resurrection vary from one author to another in the earliest surviving sources. According to the Apostle Paul, Christ "first appeared to Cephas and then to the Twelve" (1 Cor. 15:5). This account coincides with at least one of the Gospel narratives. In Luke's story, after the women tell the disciples about the empty tomb, two of Jesus' other followers (not members of the Twelve, but others who had been accompanying them) are walking along the road to the village of Emmaus when Jesus himself appears to them. They don't recognize him, however, and begin talking to him as to a stranger. They have been discussing the tragic events of the past few days, and one of them, Cleopas, expresses his surprise that the stranger hasn't heard about what happened to Jesus, who had been rejected by the Jewish leaders and turned over to the Roman authorities and crucified. But his tomb, he indicates, has now been discovered empty.

Jesus, still "in disguise," rebukes the two disciples for not understanding that all these things had to take place in accordance with the Scriptures. He accompanies them to the village, and they persuade him to stay with them. When they sit at table he breaks bread and gives it to them, and we're told that "their eyes were opened and they recognized him" (Luke 24:30). But immediately he vanishes from their sight.

They rush out to tell the eleven remaining disciples what has happened, and when they arrive they learn from them that "the Lord has risen indeed, and has appeared to Simon" (Luke 24:34). This *may* then coincide with Paul's account of the events, that Jesus' first appearance was to Peter, although it's not clear from Luke's version whether the appearance of Jesus to Simon was before or after he appeared to Cleopas and his unnamed companion on the road to Emmaus.

In Luke's story, Jesus next appears to all the eleven remaining disciples, Peter among them, who are obviously frightened, thinking that they are seeing a spirit. Jesus, though, shows them his hands and feet and tells them to handle him; when they still have their doubts, he asks for some food. They give him a piece of broiled fish, and he eats it before their eyes (Luke 24:36–43).

One of the points of this account is obviously to stress that Jesus was *physically* raised from the dead. After the resurrection, he still had a bodily existence. He could be seen and handled, and he could still eat food. This was not some kind of phantasm. It was Jesus himself, his body come back to life.

The other canonical Gospels have other narratives about Jesus' appearances after the resurrection. The most striking account is probably Mark's, for in its original version, there was evidently no appearance to Peter or to anyone else at all. According to Mark, when the women go to the tomb, they find a young man dressed in a white robe—but no Jesus. The young man informs them that Jesus has been raised from the dead. He then gives them an explicit instruction: "But go, tell his disciples and Peter that he will precede you to Galilee, and you will see him there, just as he told you" (Mark 16:7). It is striking that Peter is explicitly mentioned in addition to the other disciples. This surely is not because he was not considered to be one of the disciples, but because he in particular is being told to go meet Jesus. And why him in particular? No doubt because he was the one who had denied his Lord not three days earlier. This, then, is a way of affirming that Jesus has and will extend his forgiveness to the fickle Peter despite his act of faithlessness.

But what is really odd is how the story ends in the Gospel of Mark. In the next verse—the last verse of the entire book—we're told that the women in fact don't tell Peter and the others anything: "And they [the women] went out and fled from the tomb, for fear and astonishment seized them, and they said nothing to anyone, for they were afraid" (Mark 16:8). And that's where the book ends.[12]

I earlier mentioned that there are places where scribes modified the texts they were copying in order to try to "improve" them (at least from their own perspective). Here is another place where that happened. Most readers of Mark over the years, scribes included, have been taken aback by this abrupt and unexpected conclusion. The women told no one? Didn't Peter and the others hear the good news? If they didn't hear, how is it that Mark knows that Jesus was raised from the dead?

For some scribes, the ending was too abrupt, and so they made up one of their own, in which Peter and the others do learn about the resurrection and come to see Jesus himself afterward. In fact, different scribes added different endings, so that in our surviving manuscripts, there is a variety of ways that Mark's Gospel comes to be concluded. In one ending, we're told that the women reported to "Peter and to those with him" what they had been told, and that then Jesus met with them and sent them forth to preach the gospel. In a longer ending, which found its way into English Bibles by way of the King James translation, Jesus does not meet with Peter alone but appears to Mary Magdalene (whose report the disciples do not believe), two unnamed disciples (who also are not believed), and then finally to the eleven—Peter included, obviously— as a group.

In contrast to Mark's Gospel, in Matthew the women do tell the disciples to meet Jesus in Galilee. They go there as a group and meet him there. Nothing specific is said about an appearance to Peter individually.

In John's Gospel there is a series of appearances of Jesus after his resurrection: first to Mary Magdalene alone, then to ten of the disciples—Thomas wasn't there—and then to all eleven (John 20:11–29). Then comes one of the most interesting accounts of Jesus' resurrection appearances, one that is particularly significant for Simon Peter and his relationship with Jesus. We're told in John that Simon and six other disciples return to Galilee, and Simon announces that he is going fishing. The others decide to join him, and they fish all night with no luck. Then at dawn Jesus appears on the beach, but again he is in disguise. The disciples don't recognize him. He asks if they've caught anything. When he learns they haven't, he instructs them to cast their net on the right side of the boat. They do so, and make an enormous haul. It is then that the unnamed disciple "whom Jesus loved" tells Peter that "it is the Lord." Impetuous Peter throws on his clothes (he had stripped for work) and dives into the sea to swim to shore (one might have expected him to leave his clothes off if he was going for a swim, but that is how it is in John 21:1–8).

The others come ashore with a net filled with fish, and they have a breakfast of fish and bread with Jesus. Again, as in Luke, this may be emphasizing that it was precisely a bodily Jesus who was raised from the dead, not just some phantasm. Then after breakfast comes a significant conversation, in which three times Jesus asks Peter, "Do you love me?" And each time Peter affirms, "Yes Lord, you know I love you."[13] After each of Peter's affirmations, Jesus tells him to take care of his sheep ("Feed my lambs"; "Tend my sheep"; "Feed my lambs").

Here again, as was the case in Mark's Gospel, we appear to have an account in which Jesus is restoring Peter to fellowship with himself after the abrupt breach in their relationship caused by Peter's denials. Three times Peter claimed not to know Jesus. And now three times he has the opportunity to affirm not only that he knows him but also that he loves him. Jesus responds kindly and urges him to take up the task that is to be set before him: watching over those placed under his authority, like a good shepherd over his sheep.

Jesus then predicts Peter's own death:

> Truly, truly I say to you, that when you were young, you girded yourself and walked wherever you wanted; but when you are old, you will reach out your hands and someone else will gird you and lead you where you do not want to go. (21:18)

The Gospel writer comments that Jesus said this in order to "signify by what kind of death he would glorify God" (21:19). It may be that the Gospel of John was written after Peter's death and the author knew that he had been martyred as a witness to Jesus, a subject we will be dealing with more fully in the next chapter.

It appears that the Gospel of Peter had an ending similar to John's in which Jesus appeared to the disciples after their fishing expedition in Galilee. Unfortunately, as I indicated earlier, we don't have this Gospel in its entirety, and the portion we have breaks off in midsentence. But it is reasonably clear that there will be an appearance of Jesus to his disciples by the Sea of Galilee. We're told that after the women discover the empty tomb and learn that Jesus has been raised, the twelve disciples were grief-stricken.[14] And then comes the tantalizing end of the story:

> But I, Simon Peter, and Andrew, my brother, took our nets and went to the sea; and with us was Levi, the son of Alphaeus, whom the Lord

And that's where our fragment of the Gospel of Peter ends.

Peter and the Resurrected Jesus

There are several important themes that recur throughout these stories about Peter's encounter with the resurrected Jesus, themes that the early Christian storytellers who narrated the accounts would have wanted to emphasize. One constant refrain is that the resurrection of Jesus was not simply an idle story made up by foolish women—a theme we will want to revisit when we discuss Mary Magdalene and the significant role she plays in the stories of Jesus. That early Christian storytellers had this concern in the first place probably does not speak highly of their views of women, although it should be noted that several of the surviving stories also indicate that *men* were sometimes not believed when reporting that Jesus had been raised from the dead (Mark 16:13; John 21:24–25). But the point of several of the stories, in any event, is that the reports of the women were verified by the disciples themselves, and by the chief of the disciples, Simon Peter, in particular.

Moreover, several of these resurrection accounts emphasize the physical character of Jesus' existence once he has been raised from the dead. Peter and the others can see, hear, and handle him. They can give him fish and bread to

Portrayal of one of Jesus's apostles, possibly Peter, preaching the Gospel with scroll in hand, from a fifth-century ivory panel now in the Louvre (Paris).

eat. They can observe that he is not a phantasm but a real bodily presence. This was to become an important doctrine for some early Christians who wanted to deny a docetic Christology, on one hand, and also wanted to insist that eternal life for believers was to be a bodily existence, not a disembodied life of the spirit, on the other (cf. Paul in 1 Cor. 15).

Others of the stories stress that after his resurrection Jesus restored the frayed relationship he had with Peter. During his lifetime, Jesus had chosen Peter to be his chief disciple, his right-hand man. But at the end, when it really mattered, Peter turned tail and denied Jesus three times. This denial did not lead, however, to a permanent estrangement. In Mark, the earliest surviving account, the messenger in the tomb instructs the women to tell Peter in particular to meet the risen Lord in Galilee. And in the final canonical account, John, Jesus has a private conversation with Peter, three times asking if he loves him. Receiving the expected reply, he then commissions Peter to take care of those under his charge and to prepare for a martyr's death.

There is one other account of Peter's encounter with Jesus after his resurrection, however, that stands at considerable odds with the ones we have considered to this point. In the previously mentioned Letter of Peter to Philip we are told that Peter assembled the disciples after the resurrection and they prayed to Christ, and that he then appeared to them. But he did not come to them in the body. In fact, that text speaks about him having been "in the body" in the past tense, as if he were now no longer so (Peter to Philip, 133, 16). Instead, he appears to them as a great light on top of a mountain. A disembodied voice comes from the light, telling them, "I am Jesus Christ who am with you forever."

The disciples then ask Christ several questions about how the world has come to be the (awful) place it is and how they might escape it—questions of real concern to Gnostic Christians, who found this material world to be an evil realm of entrapment. They, like Jesus himself, seek to escape the wicked rulers of this world, and they need guidance from him about how that is possible. Jesus gives them the answers they seek, telling them that he did come in the appearance of a mortal body but that in fact this was only the "mortal mold" that held his spirit while on earth and that he fooled those who looked upon him, who thought that he was "a mortal man" (136, 20). They too are to "strip off" from themselves that part that "is corrupted" (i.e., the material, physical body) in order for them to be enlightened and so receive their salvation. It is after this that Peter goes on to explain, as indicated earlier, that when Jesus himself appeared to suffer, he was in fact "a stranger to this suffering."

In this account, in contrast to the canonical ones, Peter is shown supporting a docetic understanding of Jesus and a belief, evidently, in his disembodied existence after the resurrection. In other words, since the body is a material entity, and since matter forms no part of the truly divine, Jesus, along with all those who join him in his resurrection, lives a spiritual, nonfleshly existence in the afterlife.

It should be clear from this alternative vision of Jesus after his resurrection that the stories about Peter are being used by a variety of Christians in a variety of ways. Different Christian storytellers are inventing stories that can buttress their own beliefs. Even when these stories are about the same events—Peter's encounter with his risen Lord—they are shaped according to the ideas and theological agendas of those who tell them, rather than, say, by a concern to preserve a historical record of what really transpired on the third day after Jesus' death. What matters to these storytellers is Peter as he is to be remembered, whether the accounts reflect events that transpired in history or represent fabrications of later times, or a combination of both.

Chapter Five

On This Rock I Will Build My Church

Peter is historically significant, and not only because he was Jesus' chief disciple and was among the first to realize that Jesus had been raised from the dead. To be sure, even on their own terms, these two facts would have made Peter one of the most important people in the history of the Christian religion. But his story was to continue long after the days of Jesus. For Peter played an important role, indeed several important roles, in the burgeoning Christian community that sprang up once the followers of Jesus became convinced of the resurrection. Peter is recorded as having been the first Christian evangelist and missionary; he is portrayed as the first Christian preacher; he is reputed to have been one of the first Christian authors; he is thought by some to have been one of the first Christian "bishops," the bishop, in fact, of Rome and therefore the first pope; and he is widely regarded as being one of the earliest Christian martyrs. For an illiterate fisherman from Galilee, it's a pretty impressive resumé.

Peter as Missionary

The New Testament book of Acts portrays Peter as the first Christian evangelist. On the day of Pentecost, he preaches to a crowd of Jews who are amazed at the signs of the Spirit that have come upon Jesus' disciples: they are speaking in foreign tongues, proclaiming the gospel to Jews who have come to Jerusalem from around the world, each in his own language. Peter's sermon converts three thousand to faith in Jesus on the spot. Soon thereafter he heals a lame man beside the Temple and proclaims to the gathered crowd that he has done so in the name of Jesus. Another five thousand convert. Peter's burgeoning career as a missionary here in the opening chapters of Acts comes as no surprise to the readers of the Gospels, who will recall that Jesus initially called him from his nets to make him "fish for people," that is, to capture the hearts of others for the gospel.

That this was Peter's career after Jesus' resurrection is also attested to by the apostle Paul, the missionary to the Gentiles, who indicates that his own ministry to non-Jews is paralleled by Peter's as the missionary to Jews (Gal. 2:7–8). In another place Paul indicates that Peter took his wife along with him on his missionary journeys, suggesting that she too was involved in the Jewish mission (1 Cor. 9:5).

The Beginning of the Gentile Mission

Paul's strong statement that Peter's work was restricted to the "circumcised" may stand at some tension with an important narrative found in the book of Acts, a story that Paul never mentions and seems not to know. This is the conversion of the first Gentile to the Christian faith, a Roman centurion named Cornelius, whose acceptance of Peter's proclamation is of such importance to the author of Acts that he takes nearly two entire chapters to narrate it (Acts 10–11). The reason it was important has long been recognized by students of the New Testament. The book of Acts deals with the spread of Christianity from its inauspicious beginnings among a small group of Jesus' followers in Jerusalem to its prevalence throughout the entire Mediterranean world, until the gospel finally reached, at the very end of the book, the capital of the empire, Rome itself. But Acts is concerned not only with the numerical and geographical spread of the new religion but also with what we might call its ethnic spread. For even though it started out as a movement within Judaism, Christianity soon became a religion for all people, Jew and Gentile alike. As we have seen, one of the major debates in the early church was over whether the followers of Jesus needed to become Jewish or not. After all, he was accepted as the Jewish messiah sent from the Jewish God to the Jewish people in fulfillment of Jewish law. And so, naturally, there were those who insisted that to be a follower of Jesus, one had to be Jewish.

Not so for Paul, and Paul's later biographer, Luke, the author of Acts. For them, this movement is for all people, Jew and Gentile, and Gentiles who accept this faith do not need first to become Jewish in order to do so. Acts wants to show that this understanding of Christianity as a religion for all people is not simply a whimsical idea of the relative latecomer to the Christian scene, the apostle Paul, but a view propagated by the earliest disciples of Jesus themselves. In order to make this point, it tells the lengthy story of how the very first Gentile accepts the gospel when it is proclaimed by Jesus' chief apostle, Simon Peter.

In the account, Cornelius is said to be a non-Jew in the city of Caesarea, on the coast of the Mediterranean, who devoutly worships the God of Israel and who receives a vision from God to send for Simon Peter, staying in the town of Joppa. In the meantime, Peter in Joppa has a midday vision in which he sees a sheet containing animals of every description lowered from the sky. He hears a voice from heaven telling him to "kill and eat." Peter is naturally taken aback, because eating some of these animals would mean breaking the Jewish rules about kosher foods. But then he hears a voice that tells him, "What God has cleansed, you must not call common [unclean]" (that is, you do not need to refrain from eating nonkosher foods; 10:15). The same sequence of events happens three times. And while Peter is trying to figure out what it all means, the messengers arrive, asking him to come to Caesarea to meet with Cornelius and his household.

Based on his vision, Peter decides that this is a divinely appointed mission, and so he goes to meet with Cornelius, even though, as a Jew, he is to have no contact—so Acts indicates—with non-Jews. This is not actually true, historically, since Jews regularly had contact with Gentiles in all sorts of situations. But it is true that eating with Gentiles could pose problems, since this would make it difficult, or maybe even impossible, to keep the kosher food laws. In any event, Peter goes to meet Cornelius. When he arrives, he learns that God had instructed Cornelius to send for him, and he begins to proclaim the good news of the salvation that Jesus has brought through his death and resurrection.

While he is telling the assembled crowd these things, suddenly the Holy Spirit comes upon them all, and they begin speaking in tongues just as the apostles did on the Day of Pentecost. This is surefire proof to Peter that non-Jews, Gentiles, can have a standing before God equal to that of the Jews, simply on the basis of faith in Jesus. It is not important for them first to convert to Judaism and follow the Jewish laws set forth in Scripture. After all, they have received the Spirit while remaining Gentiles. This, then, was the meaning of his vision of the sheet. Peter proceeds to baptize the new believers (showing their acceptance into the church) and returns to report to the apostles and others that the good news of salvation has now reached Gentiles as well as Jews.

This story, as I've indicated, serves as a kind of linchpin in the narrative of Acts. Much of the rest of the book will be about the success of the Christian mission not among Jews but among Gentiles scattered throughout the Roman Empire, especially through the missionary activity of the apostle Paul, the greatest advocate of the view that salvation in Christ does not hinge on the observance of the prescriptions of the Jewish law. For Luke, this wasn't Paul's novel idea. It was the plan of God, as shown to Jesus' hand-chosen chief disciple, Peter himself.

Peter's Miraculous Mission

What accounts for Peter's success as a missionary? In the book of Acts, there is no ambiguity about the matter: God works miracles through him, and this convinces the crowds that he represents the truth they need to accept. The first conversions come when the apostles miraculously receive the Spirit and begin speaking in tongues on the day of Pentecost. Peter preaches a sermon and thousands convert. He heals a lame man at the temple, a crowd gathers, he preaches a sermon, and thousands convert. Eventually we're told that all the apostles begin doing "many signs and wonders" with the result that "many more were added to those who believed in the Lord, both men and women" (5:14). It gets to the point where Peter is so powerful that throughout Jerusalem people can simply lay their sick out on the street on a sunny day, and if his shadow passes over them, they become well (5:15–16). Everyone who is diseased or demon-possessed is healed. It must have been great while it lasted. And it is surprising that anyone bothered to persecute this movement. You would think they'd set up enormous apostolic hospitals around the Mediterranean to solve the world's problems.

The view that miracles are what drew the masses to convert continues in the legendary accounts of Peter in later works, such as the Acts of Peter. There was a logic to this view. People throughout the ancient world knew all too well that there were powerful forces of nature that could not be controlled by human effort. You can't control when and where it will rain, and so you can't protect against drought; you can't defend the body against disease or demons, or the crops against blight; you can't control if a woman dies in childbirth or if a child is stillborn; you can't determine who is born blind or deaf or lame; you can't control the hour of your death. Humans are limited in what they can provide for themselves when it comes to what really counts—not just happiness, but health and life itself.

The gods, however, were known to be superhuman beings who could control such things. Any god who manifested his or her power deserved human devotion: in fact, devotion to such a god would obviously increase the chances of divine intervention in the case of drought, famine, disease, or death.

Throughout the Roman Empire, there were hundreds—probably thousands—of religions, all of which promoted the worship of gods who could provide their devotees with what they needed. One of the things that made Christianity different from all the other religions, with the exception of Judaism, is that it insisted that there was only one God who was to be worshiped. None of the others was a true god. That meant that if you converted to the worship of this one God, you had to abandon your worship of the others. This was unlike the other religions of the empire. For them, if you accepted a new god you could keep your old ones as well. All these "pagan" religions were polytheistic, none of them insisting on exclusive devotion. In fact, for these other religions it was perfectly acceptable to worship a wide range of deities who could perform a wide range of functions. Why, then, would someone decide to give up all their other gods in order to worship the one God of the Christians? The only reason would be if this one God was shown to be superior to all other gods, the one who could in fact provide all that was needed for healthy and happy lives. And how could this be shown? Through the miracles he did.

According to our earliest records of Christian missionary activity, then, it is no surprise that it is precisely the logic of miracles that drives people to convert. We find this logic in a wide range of tales told about the early Christian missionaries in the legendary accounts known as the Apocryphal Acts. These are stories about such apostles as John, Thomas, and Andrew that record their missionary activities and show how the powerful miracles they did led to massive conversions to the faith. Among the Apocryphal Acts are accounts of the missionary exploits of Paul (which we will be examining in a later chapter) and of Peter.

The Acts of Peter is especially interesting because it is largely about a contest of miracles between Peter and a magician (that is, a false miracle worker) named Simon, otherwise known as Simon Magus (Simon the Magician). This contest is over who is the true representative of God, and the outcome will be decided on the grounds of power. Whoever does the most spectacular miracles represents the truth. The miracles narrated in these stories may seem incredible to modern readers. But as I have suggested, if the miracles in the book of Acts weren't found in the Christian Bible (such as the healing power of Peter's shadow or his ability to raise the dead by speaking a word), these might seem just as incredible. One impossible occurrence is no more possible than any other impossible occurrence. And what, after all, is a miracle but an impossible event that occurs?

Simon Magus is a figure who first turns up not in the Acts of Peter but in the Acts of the Apostles in the New Testament. The later legends about him are all based on the account of his initial encounter with the apostles in Acts 8. According to the story, the apostle Philip travels to a city in Samaria and does a series of miracles there. He casts out demons and heals the paralyzed and the lame. This leads, naturally enough, to a large number of conversions to worship his God. But there is a person named Simon who had previously amazed the Samaritan people by his power, so that everyone there said about him, "This is the power of God that is called Great." That is, they took Simon to be the representative of the greatest of the gods until Philip came along and outshone him, leading everyone to convert to Philip's God and belief in Jesus. Simon himself is impressed and converts and is baptized (Acts 8:4–13).

When the apostles in Jerusalem hear that many have been converted and baptized in Samaria, they send two of their leaders, Peter and John, to continue the work there. As it turns out, even though the Samaritans have become followers of Jesus, they have not yet received the gift of the Holy Spirit, which empowered the apostles themselves, starting with the Day of Pentecost. Peter and John arrive and lay hands on the baptized believers, and the Spirit comes upon them (presumably through some miraculous and public sign, such as speaking in tongues). When Simon of Samaria sees the power of Peter and John, he is moved by jealousy and offers the apostles money, saying, "Give me this power too, so that I can lay hands on someone for them to receive the Holy Spirit." Peter rebukes him for thinking that God's power can be bought, and warns him to repent, "for I see that you are filled with bitter poison and unrighteous fetters."

Simon asks the apostles to pray for him that he might escape the wrath of God for his wicked thoughts (Acts 8:14–24). And there the story ends.

But later legends picked up where Acts left off. According to these legends, Simon Magus never did learn his lesson, but continued trying to compete with the apostles by convincing people that his own miracles were equal to or better than theirs, and that he was the true representative of God.

Eventually Christian authors came to portray Simon Magus as the first arch-heretic. In the works of later writers, such as the late-second-century Irenaeus—one of the great heresy hunters of the orthodox Christian tradition—Simon was the first Gnostic, the one from whom all Gnostics could trace their origin. In the Acts of Peter he is portrayed not as a Gnostic but simply as an opponent to the apostles and their message of salvation in Christ. Simon sets himself up as a great power of God and, in competition for converts, tries to better the apostle Peter in a contest of miracles. This miracle-working contest forms the heart of the Acts of Peter.

The story is designed to show how Peter's powerful presence drove Simon from one place to another (Judea to Rome). It is also designed to show how Peter, the apostle of Jerusalem, ended up in the capital city of the empire, Rome. There, according to tradition, he became the leader of the church and, in fact, its first pope. He went to Rome, in this account, to counter the nefarious doings of the archenemy of God, the maleficent Simon, whose miracles were leading many astray.

It is not altogether clear how far this account is to be taken as a straightforward historical narrative of what happened when Peter arrived in Rome and how much is simply an entertaining set of stories. The narrative begins not with Peter but with the apostle Paul in Rome. Paul has been converting the masses through his miracles but is preparing to leave to take his Christian mission to Spain. His departure, however, creates a vacuum in the religious sphere, which is filled by Simon (Magus), who calls himself "the great power of God" (an allusion to Acts 8). Simon's own followers exalt him, saying to him, "You are the God in Italy, you are the savior of the Romans." He announces to the Romans that he will make a grand, miraculous entrance among them, flying into town over the gate of the city. And so he does, arriving in Rome and wreaking great havoc by doing miracles that turn people away from their faith in Christ to believe in Simon himself as the true representative of God. But in fact he is empowered by the enemy of God, Satan. Peter is therefore summoned by God to counter his work.

Peter sails to Rome with the intention of besting Simon and proving to the Romans that it is faith in Christ that matters before God. When he arrives, he finds that Simon is being housed by a lapsed Christian aristocrat, Marcellus. When the doorman does not allow Peter into the house to confront Simon, Peter performs his first miracle. Seeing a large dog leashed to a chain, he commissions him to fetch Simon. The dog, being loosed, enters Marcellus's house and speaks with a loud human voice: "Simon, Peter, who stands at the door, bids you to come outside in public; for he says, 'On your account have I come to Rome, you wicked man and destroyer of souls.'" Hearing a speaking dog is enough evidence for Marcellus, the host: he immediately repents of his devotion to Simon and rushes out to Peter, begging for forgiveness for his apostasy to the side of evil.

While they are talking, Peter sees a man in the crowd who is inappropriately laughing. Detecting that the man is possessed, Peter orders the demon to depart and show itself. The demoniac rushes forward, throws down a marble statue of Caesar, and kicks it to smithereens. Marcellus is upset, because if the emperor learns that his statue has been abused, he will mete out a severe punishment. Peter, always in control in this account, tells Marcellus to take some running water and sprinkle it on the shattered pieces of the statue. He does so, and it miraculously reassembles itself whole.

In the meantime, the dog returns from Simon and speaks with Peter, telling him that Simon refuses to meet with him. The dog then lies down and dies. Many of the crowd fall down at Peter's feet, ready to convert on the spot. Others want to see yet more miracles, and this is when Peter pulls the stunt with the smoked tuna fish that I described in an earlier chapter, making it come to life and swim in the pond in the name of Christ to convince the crowds that Jesus is Lord of all.

The miracles continue until there is a face-to-face showdown between Peter and Simon Magus in the Roman Forum, a contest to prove once and for all who is the greater miracle worker and who, therefore, is the true representative of God. The entire population of Rome comes to the Forum, including all the Roman senators and other officials. The ruling prefect sets the terms of the contest: he sends forth a slave, who happens to be one of the emperor's favorites, and he orders Simon to kill the young man and Peter to raise him from the dead. Both do their appointed tasks. Simon whispers a word in the lad's ear, causing him to fall down stone dead. Peter, not to be outdone, proclaims, "My God and Lord Jesus Christ . . . is doing many signs and miracles through me to turn you from your sins. In your power, revive now through my voice, O Lord, into the presence of all, him whom Simon killed by his touch." He calls the slave's master over and directs him to take hold of the slave's hand; when he does so, the young man is restored to life. The crowd is impressed, and they all cry out: "There is only one God, the God of Peter."

While he is at it, two parents whose children have recently died beseech Peter to raise them as well. The most telling case involves a deceased senator whose mother begs for Peter's help. He directs the people to bring the son into the Forum, and proposes a new contest. Whichever of them, he or Simon, can raise the man from the dead will be recognized as representing the true God; the other will be seen as an impostor. As he says:

> Romans, let a righteous judgment now take place between me and Simon, and judge which of us believes in the living God, he or I. Let him revive the body which is before us, and believe in him as an angel of God. If he is not able, I will

call upon my God. I will restore the son alive to his mother and then you shall believe that he is a sorcerer and deceiver, this man who enjoys your hospitality. (Acts of Peter, 28)

One may wonder why further demonstration is needed, since the entire city of Rome has already acknowledged that Peter is the representative of the one true God. But the story provides a fitting conclusion to the clash of the titans. The young senator is brought in on his funeral bier, and Simon has the first go at him. Standing next to the bier, he bows over the body three times and shows the crowds that the man lifted his head, opened his eyes, and made a brief nod. The people believe the miracle has been performed and rush out to collect wood for a pyre on which to burn Peter, as the impostor. But Peter stops them, pointing out that the dead man is still lying down and has scarcely moved.

Let the dead man speak, let him rise; if he is alive, let him untie the band from his chin, let him call his mother . . . let him beckon to you with his hand.

The prefect comes over to the bier and sees that in fact the man is still lying motionless. Simon's magic was enough to work a partial reanimation but not a full resuscitation. And then Peter takes over. After speaking to the mother, he goes to the dead man, says a prayer over him, and orders him to rise. The young man arises, unties the cloth around his chin, asks for his clothes, comes down off the bier, and speaks to Peter. This, then, is a real resurrection. Peter turns to the crowd, urging them to repent from their sins and to turn to Christ for eternal life. From then on, Peter is "worshiped like a god" by the Romans, who bring him those who are sick to be cured.

You might think that this would be the end of Simon Magus, but something a bit more dramatic is in store: his ultimate demise in a final contest. Simon decides to have one more shot at proving his superiority over Peter, and announces his decision to ascend directly to God by taking flight over the city of Rome, much as he had first arrived there. Great magician that he is, he succeeds in taking off and sailing above the temples and hills of Rome. But Peter, the representative of the true God, is not one to be bested. He utters a prayer that the truth of God be manifest, causing Simon to be deprived of his powers in midflight. He crashes to the ground and breaks his leg in three places. The crowd responds by attacking him with stones, and he ends up dying as the result of a botched operation. Peter, then, hero of the story, is shown victorious in every way, the true representative of God whose power can overcome the magical shams of the Devil at every turn.

Peter as Preacher

We have seen that the traditions about Peter consistently portray him as a miracle-working evangelist whose spectacular ability to work wonders convinces the masses to convert to belief in Jesus as the son of the one true God.

But what more can we say about what Peter actually preached in his effort to convert others?

Here again we are up against the restraints imposed upon us by our sources. It is much to be regretted that we don't have any direct information about what the historical Peter himself might have actually preached and taught during his missionary activities "among the circumcised." As we will see later, we have a number of writings that allegedly come from Peter's own hand. Some of these we have already considered, such as the Gospel of Peter, the Apocalypse of Peter, the Coptic Apocalypse of Peter, and the Letter of Peter to Philip. There are several others yet to be considered, such as the books of 1 and 2 Peter in the New Testament and the Acts of Peter and the Twelve, discovered at Nag Hammadi. But there are good reasons to suspect that none of these works was actually penned by Peter himself—especially given the circumstance that our earlier traditions indicate that he was an illiterate Aramaic-speaking peasant who had not been trained to read, let alone engage in Greek composition.

For the most part, then, we are restricted to seeing what other authors say about sermons and speeches he delivered. That in itself poses problems for anyone who is more interested in the words of the historical Peter than in the ways he was later remembered. Ancient historians themselves admit that when it comes to the speeches that they record in their writings, they made up the speeches, putting words on the lips of their protagonists as suited the occasion.[1] This appears certainly to be true of the earliest surviving account we have of the apostolic proclamations, the New Testament book of Acts, nearly one-quarter of which is taken up with speeches delivered by its main characters, especially Peter and Paul. As scholars have long recognized, the speeches of Peter and Paul sound very much alike in the book of Acts—so much so that if you didn't know who the speaker was, you often wouldn't be able to tell based on the contents of the speech. Peter sounds like Paul, and Paul sounds like Peter. This may seem a bit odd, given the fact that Peter was an illiterate peasant who spoke Aramaic, whereas Paul was a well-educated, highly astute author raised in a Greek-speaking environment. But it's not odd when the true nature of the situation is recognized. In the book of Acts, these two sound exactly alike not because they would have sounded alike in real life but because their words have been placed on their lips by the same person, the author of Acts himself.

And so here again, when we examine what Peter is alleged to have preached, we are in effect seeing what different authors imagined him to have said—which may come down to the same thing as seeing what different authors would have wanted him to say.

Peter's Sermons in the Book of Acts

In the book of Acts Peter typically makes a public address after a miracle has occurred. The first sermon he delivers is on the Day of Pentecost, fifty days after Jesus' death. The crowds are amazed that the apostles are all speaking the gospel in foreign languages. Peter assures them that this is not drunken behavior (it is only nine o'clock in the morning) but rather is a fulfillment of the prophecies of the Hebrew Bible, that at the end of the age God's Spirit would be poured out on humankind, leading to miraculous signs and wonders. These, in other words, are the last days, and people need to repent. Peter continues by speaking of Jesus, who was himself a great miracle worker but was crucified by those who were lawless. God, however, has reversed this act of injustice, raising Jesus from the dead—again as was predicted in the Jewish Scriptures.

When the Jewish crowds—those who two months earlier had cried for Jesus' death—realize their own culpability before God, they cry out, "What shall we do?" Peter tells them that they are to repent of their sins and be baptized in the name of Jesus, and so receive the gift of the Spirit. Three thousand heed his call and are baptized (Acts 2:22–42).

In the next chapter, after he has healed a lame man at the gate into the Temple, Peter preaches another sermon with many of the same themes: the Jewish people were culpable in the death of God's righteous one, Jesus, but this was also in fulfillment of what was predicted by the prophets. Everyone now needs to repent, that their sins can be blotted out (3:12–26).

In the chapter that follows, he preaches yet again, this time to the Jewish leaders, accusing them of crucifying Jesus but attesting that God had raised him from the dead, and insisting that in his name alone there is salvation (4:8–12).

Even when Peter preaches to a non-Jewish audience, in the home of the centurion Cornelius, his message is similar. Jesus had been empowered by God to do miraculous deeds, but the Jewish people nonetheless rejected him and had him killed. But God raised him from the dead, in fulfillment of the prophecies of Scripture. Everyone, both Jew and Gentile, needs to repent and receive the forgiveness that comes in his name (Acts 10:29–43).

The themes that recur in these sermons come to be repeated in the sermons Paul preaches to win converts. Jesus was unjustly killed by humans, but he was vindicated by God, who raised him from the dead. People now need to repent and turn to God, being baptized in the name of Jesus and receiving salvation. Peter, in other words, is the first spokesperson in this narrative for the message that the book of Acts itself wants to convey, a message that is rooted in the theological views of Luke, the author of the account.[2]

Peter's Preaching in the Acts of Peter

There are some interesting differences in Peter's sermons when we turn to the second-century Acts of Peter. In some respects there is a different audience, as here Peter preaches not to the non-Christian Jews of Jerusalem (or the Gentiles sympathetic to Judaism in the home of Cornelius) but to pagans and former pagans who had earlier converted. The major themes of Peter's speeches in the Acts of Peter can be seen in his first address to the Christian community upon his arrival at Rome. Here he is speaking to people who had been misled to think that Simon Magus was the true representative of God. Peter's speech is meant to disabuse them of this idea, for in his view, Simon is instead the representative of God's archenemy, Satan.

Peter proposes to tell the crowds "why God sent his Son into the world," which was to "dispense some mercy or means of salvation." In particular, God intended to "annul every offence and every ignorance and every activity of the devil." Peter points out that he himself had been inspired by the devil when he denied his Lord three times, and he tells them that "Satan the deceiver sends his arrows upon you too, to make you leave the way." But he exhorts them to hold fast to the true faith, for everyone whom the Devil draws away from the faith "is a child of perdition for all eternity." His hearers are therefore urged to repent, to renounce their attachment to the worker of evil (Simon Magus) and return to the true faith of Jesus Christ (Acts of Peter, 7).

In part this sermon is interesting because it has so little content in it. The entire point appears to be that Satan is intent on disrupting the faith, he uses Simon to do so, and people should turn from Satan (and Simon) to God. But there is very little substance in what it might actually mean to stop following Simon. That is to say, there is no indication of what theological or practical differences there are between Peter's understanding of the faith and Simon's.

This can also be seen in our now well-known case of the tuna fish. The crowd wants to know who is the true servant of God, Simon (Magus) or Peter, and so they say, "Show us another miracle that we may believe in you as a servant of the living God, for Simon too did many wonders in our presence, and on that account we followed him" (Acts of Peter 12). Peter responds, "When you see this [tuna] swimming in the water like a fish, will you be able to believe in him whom I preach?" They reply that they will indeed believe. He performs the miracle, they decide to follow him, and they "believed in the Lord." What it was, exactly, they believed is never spelled out.

And that is true for virtually the entire account. One might have expected that since Simon Magus was widely believed to be the father of the Gnostic religion, Peter would malign the Gnostic system and show how his own theological set of beliefs was superior to it. But there is nothing of that sort in the text. Instead, the emphasis is that Simon is on the wrong side of the divide between Satan and God, Peter is on the right side, and people need to align with Peter or they will pay an eternal consequence. The miracles that Peter performs, then—which are always superior to the rather paltry attempts of Simon Magus—show that in fact he is right, and people need to repent.

Peter's Ascetical Preaching

There is one aspect of Peter's preaching in the Acts of Peter, however, that does contain some real content. It is not the kind of content one finds in his proclamation in the New Testament Acts of the Apostles. It is, on the other hand, consistent with the proclamation of other evangelists portrayed in the Apocryphal Acts of the Apostles. This is the gospel of asceticism, the declaration that to be a true follower of Christ, one must abstain from all bodily pleasures, especially the pleasures of sex.

As we will see later, this becomes a prominent theme in second-century presentations of the Apostle Paul as well, where in fact it is even more pronounced than in the case of Peter. It is yet more pronounced in the works associated with other apostles, such as Thomas and Titus.

In the Acts of Peter, it is this particular aspect of his proclamation that leads to Peter's martyrdom. The prefect of Rome, a man named Agrippa, is said to have four concubines: Agrippina, Nicaria, Euphemia, and Doris. They hear Peter's preaching about the need to maintain chastity before God, and as a result "they agreed among themselves to abstain from cohabitation with Agrippa." As you might imagine, Agrippa is not amused: "That Christian [Peter] has taught you not to consort with me. I tell you that I will destroy you and burn him alive" (Acts of Peter, 33).

Matters get worse. The Roman emperor has a friend named Albinus, whose wife, Xanthippe, hears Peter preach and decides to abstain from having sex with her husband. At that point "many other women delighted in the preaching concerning chastity and separated from their husbands, and men too ceased to sleep with their wives, because they wished to serve God in chastity and purity." With uncharacteristic understatement, the author describes the result: "And there was a great commotion in Rome."

The idea that Peter would preach a life of abstinence may seem novel to readers of the New Testament, where there is nothing quite like that to be found. But in fact it was a common theme throughout the writings about Peter in the second and third centuries. In one of the more intriguing incidents allegedly from Peter's life, discovered in a Coptic manuscript in 1896, we have a fragmentary account of Peter's interaction with his own daughter, whom he means to keep celibate for life. According to the account, known simply as the Act of Peter, a great multitude gathers before Peter, bringing their sick with them for him to cure. But someone in the crowd points out that it seems inconsistent for Peter to heal the multitudes when his own virgin daughter is completely paralyzed on one side, lying helpless in the corner of the room. Why, he wants to know, has Peter neglected his own flesh and blood?

Peter replies that of course he has the power from God to heal the girl if he desires to do so. To prove the point, he orders her to arise and walk toward him. She does so, and the crowd rejoices. But then Peter orders her back to her place, to become helpless once again, and she obeys. The crowd is befuddled and upset, but Peter explains to them that when the girl was born, he received a vision from God warning that his daughter would "harm many souls if her body remains well." And as she grew, the warning came true. The text is fragmentary at this point, but evidently, when the girl was just ten, she had already grown to be a real beauty, and was stolen away by a rich man named Ptolemy, who had seen her bathing (perhaps publicly) with her mother. We are not sure what then happened, as two pages of the manuscript of the Act of Peter are missing at just this point. But when the story resumes, Ptolemy has just returned the girl to the doorstep of Peter's house, paralyzed from head to foot. Evidently God struck the girl to prevent her from being the cause of sexual stumbling to Ptolemy (and maybe others), who eventually repented of his desires, became a follower of Christ, and died to an eternal reward.

The girl, in other words, was too seductive to be allowed to remain well, and so God willed her to be permanently paralyzed. This may not be a generous commentary on the author's view of women, but it is comparable to what can be found in other texts associated with Peter. For example, in a work allegedly by the apostle Titus (Paul's companion in the writings of the New Testament), a work that was forged sometime possibly in the fourth century, we read of another instance of Peter "healing" a young virgin. In this case, it is not his own child but the child of a peasant, who brings his healthy daughter to Peter asking that he say a prayer for her well-being. Peter asks God to do what is best for her soul, and the girl falls down dead. The author of the text thinks this is a great thing: "O reward worthy and ever pleasing to God, to escape the shamelessness of the flesh and to destroy the pride of the blood!" he says. The girl's father, understandably, is somewhat less pleased. To the consternation of the narrator, and of Peter in the story, the man pleads with Peter to raise the girl from the dead. He complies, and several days later a man seduces the girl and runs off with her, never to be seen again. The author ends the story there. The moral is evidently meant to be obvious: death itself is better than a life of sin in the flesh.

A doctrine of renunciation can be found in a final account connected with Peter that we will examine here, a work that is among the Nag Hammadi Library but which, unlike most of the others in the collection, has no obvious ties to any Gnostic group. The Acts of Peter and the Twelve begins with the disciples heading out on their mission to spread the gospel after Jesus' resurrection. They take a boat and end up at a city "in the midst of the sea." Peter disembarks and goes to find lodging. He meets a man on the road who is selling pearls. None of the rich people in the city comes out to buy his pearls, because the man doesn't appear actually to have any. The poor people, on the other hand, want to be shown a pearl, since for them it is such a rare treat. He tells them that if they journey to his city, not only will he show them a pearl, he will give it to them for free.

Peter himself wants to know the way to the city and the hardships that must be endured to get there, since he and his companions are eager to go into every place to spread the gospel. The man tells him that his name is Lithargoel (which means something like "light, gazelle-like stone"), and he tells them that it is not easy to get to his city: "No one is able to go on that road, except one who has forsaken everything that he has and has fasted from stage to stage" (Acts

of Peter and the Twelve, 5). It requires, in others words, a complete abandon-
ment of all that one cherishes, and an ascetic style of life.

Peter and his companions decide to make the trip, and when they arrive at
the city, after many hardships, a physician—who is Lithargoel in disguise—
comes out to meet them. After a brief conversation, he reveals his true identity
to them: he is in fact Christ himself, and they have arrived at his city only
through the hardships that are necessary for those who are to enter the kingdom of heaven. Christ sends them back to the city whence they came, instructing them to provide the poor with what they need to live. The disciples are
perplexed, however, because in order to arrive at Lithargoel's city they have
sacrificed everything they have, and so have nothing to give to the poor. Christ
responds that his name alone is more valuable than gold, silver, and precious
stones, and he gives them medicine that will allow them to heal not the body
but the soul—which is to be valued much more highly than the body. He instructs them, though, not to spend time with the rich, who might badly influence them, but to spend their time with the needy, giving them the spiritual
health that can provide them eternal life. Peter and the other disciples worship
Christ, and he leaves them in peace.

Here is a tale that stresses the need for the ascetic life and associates this
teaching, yet again, with Peter. We will see in subsequent chapters how a similar message of asceticism comes to be associated with Paul and Mary as well,
and we will explore in greater depth why this became a message of such importance for Christians of the second and third centuries. For now it is enough
to say that there developed a strand of Christianity that became very other-
worldly early on in the Christian movement. This view understood the values
and priorities of this world to be antithetical to the values and priorities of
God. For people to attain to God, they have to renounce this world and all it
has to offer. We have already seen that there were Gnostic Christians who held
this perspective. But it was shared by a much wider range of Christians as
well. Many of these Christians believed that ties to this world, and to the human body as a product of this world, could only keep one from God. God
belongs to a different world, the world above, and so one has to choose whether
to be bound to the things of this world and to the passions of the body, or
instead to renounce this world and the body so as to belong to God.

According to this perspective, faith in Christ does not simply entail an ac-
knowledgment that he died for people's sins and was raised from the dead. It
means committing oneself to the kingdom that he represents, the kingdom of
God. This commitment has to be total and involves renouncing life here. Since
bodily pleasure above all else is what ties us to this world, making us long for
more and more of what we can acquire in this material existence, it is precisely
bodily pleasure that must be rejected. So the life of chastity—for those who were
married as well as for those who were not—comes to be seen as the life of total
commitment to God. The rich are to renounce their wealth, the influential their

power, and the sensual their bodies. It is this that will allow one to enjoy the pleasures of the world above.

The historical Peter may not have preached such a message. In fact, in all likelihood he did not. But as it came to be an emphasis of later Christian thinkers, it is no surprise to find the gospel of asceticism placed on his lips in the traditions that were circulated in his name many decades and centuries after his death.

Chapter Six

Peter: Christian Author and Martyr

Anyone who was anyone in the ancient world could write. There were exceptions, possibly exceptions that prove the rule, such as Jesus. But for the most part, the people who were remembered were the literary elite.

People who could not write, if they were thought to be sufficiently important, were often imagined as being able to do so. This is true, for example of Jesus, for whom we have legends that he sent off letters in response to requests for an audience.[1] And it is true of Peter, who was reputed not only to have been an evangelist and preacher in the early church but also to have been a rather prolific author.

Peter as Author

Some Christians, as we have seen, argued that Peter produced a Gospel in his own name, the so-called Gospel of Peter. Other Christian church leaders argued otherwise, on theological grounds: the book contained a potentially docetic Christology, and Peter could never have written such a thing. So too with other writings in Peter's name: the Coptic Apocalypse of Peter and the Letter of Peter to Philip, both of them discovered near Nag Hammadi. These were thought by some Gnostic Christians to be from the hand of the apostle, but other (anti-Gnostic) Christians could not agree. Even the other Apocalypse of Peter, in which the apostle is given a guided tour of heaven and hell, was accepted by some Christians as authentically by Peter, but rejected by others as too bizarre to have come from him.

Modern scholars are unanimous in thinking that none of these writings could have actually been written by Peter himself. For one thing, all of them contain teachings that appear to have arisen long after Peter's death, in the second century. This is true, for example, of the heightened anti-Judaism of the Gospel of Peter or the Gnostic understanding of the Coptic Apocalypse of Peter. For another thing, there is the serious, and debated, issue of whether Peter himself would have been able to write. This is an important question for historians of ancient Christianity, in no small part because two of the books of the New Testament, 1 and 2 Peter, also claim to be written by Peter.

First Peter

The book of 1 Peter claims to come from "Peter, an apostle of Jesus Christ" (1:1), and is addressed to Christians living "in exile" in certain regions of Asia Minor (modern Turkey): Pontus, Galatia, Cappadocia, Asia, and Bythinia. It is not clear from the letter itself whether the recipients actually were exiled from their homelands or whether the author intends for the term *exile* to be taken metaphorically: since the Christian's real citizenship is heaven, life on earth is a temporary resting place away from home.

The latter interpretation would make particularly good sense in light of the situation facing the readers of the letter, for it is clear that the Christians to whom it is addressed are undergoing considerable suffering for their Christian faith and that the author thinks yet more suffering is in store for them. It is interesting to note that the term *suffering* occurs more often in this short five-chapter book than in any other work of the New Testament, including the books of Luke and Acts combined, which take up one-fourth of the entire New Testament. What is this suffering that the readers are experiencing?

Some have argued that 1 Peter is referring to the persecution of Christians by the emperor Nero. As we know from Roman historians, Nero wanted to implement some architectural designs for the city of Rome but was hampered by the fact that Rome already was built (Tacitus, *Annals of Rome,* 15). And so he arranged for arsonists to burn down parts of the city in the great fire of 64 CE, leaving many thousands homeless. When the populace came to suspect Nero for the fire, the emperor decided to blame someone else and lit upon the Christians as easy scapegoats, since they were already hated so widely. He had Christians rounded up and publicly tortured and killed on charges of arson. This is the first recorded instance of a Roman emperor persecuting the Christians.

There are reasons to think, however, that 1 Peter is not referring to the suffering of Christians under Nero. For one thing, this persecution extended only to the Christians living in Rome. It was not an empire-wide affair. The recipients of the letter of 1 Peter, however, live not in Rome but in the provinces of Asia Minor. Moreover, the Christians persecuted by Nero were not actually condemned for being Christians; they were condemned for the crime of arson (even though the charges were false). The recipients of 1 Peter, on the other hand, are said to suffer reproach for the sake of Christ (4:14). In addition, their suffering is not caused by imperial authorities but is occurring on the grassroots level, as former

friends (and family members?) have become upset that they no longer participate in the religious and civic life of their communities, but have started their
own closed social group instead (4:3–5). Finally, this author does not condemn
the state officials for any harsh treatment of the Christians. On the contrary, he
appears to think that the government is set up to reward those who behave well
and to punish only those who disobey the laws (2:13–14).

The situation of the readers, therefore, is not one of official persecution by
the state. These people are suffering because they are under attack from former
friends and colleagues who cannot understand why they have changed their
views and taken to participating in a new and possibly secretive society of
Christians. The author urges his readers to face their suffering strongly, since
they are to suffer as their master, Christ himself, did (4:13). Relatedly, he insists that they should suffer not for doing anything wrong, but only for doing
what is right. That is to say, they should not break the law or do anything else
that would justify punishment. Then, if they suffer simply for being Christian,
they can hold their heads high as those who suffer unjustly. That is probably
why the author urges them to live moral, upright lives (3:14–17; 4:14–15):
they are to show the world that despite the suspicions against them, they are
upstanding citizens who benefit, not harm, society by their presence. The author appears to hope that honorable, moral behavior by the Christians will win
others over to the faith (2:11; 3:1). The followers of Christ are not to be antisocial, but must be willing to explain their behavior, and their faith, to anyone
who asks (2:13–15; 3:15–17).

The author goes out of his way to emphasize that even though his readers
are going through suffering and can expect more to come, they are highly
privileged. When they abandoned their former social worlds, they joined a
new family of faith by being born anew (1:3, 23), so God himself is now their
Father (1:14, 17). As a result, they can
pride themselves in being the chosen
people (2:9), special in the world because they alone have been made holy
by the Spirit and have been the benefi-
ciaries of Christ's death (1:2, 19).

The book of 1 Peter was seen as so
timely in the early church, so full of
solid advice about how to face suffering, that it was widely and enthusiasti-
cally accepted by Christians as having
come straight from the hand of Peter

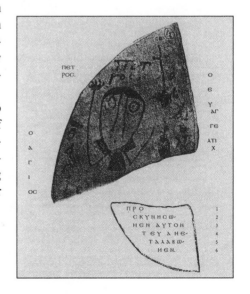

Ostrakon (pottery sherd) from the sixth or
seventh century, depicting the "evangelist
Peter" and (on the reverse) urging its
readers to revere his Gospel.

himself. But modern scholars have found reason to doubt the author's claim and to suspect that here—as was the case with the Gospel of Peter, the two apocalypses of Peter, the Letter of Peter to Philip, and yet other so-called Petrine writings—we are dealing with a pseudonymous work, that is, a work written falsely in the name of someone other than the actual author.

It should be noted that we know of nothing that ties the historical Peter to the Christians in Asia Minor, where the letter is addressed. We know of his life in Jerusalem, Antioch, and Rome—the three areas where he appears to have spent his missionary efforts. But Asia Minor? That was Paul's territory. Of course, Peter may have gone there as well, but Paul explicitly and emphatically tells us that he and Peter had divided up the mission field: Peter's work was among Jews, and his was among Gentiles (Gal. 2:7). And who are the recipients of this letter? Gentiles, not Jews (4:1–5).

Yet more significant is the basic question of whether a book like this *could* have been written by Peter. As we have repeatedly seen, Peter himself was an Aramaic-speaking, lower-class fisherman from rural Galilee. There is nothing to suggest that someone in that socioeconomic situation would have gone to school to learn to read and write. This letter, on the other hand, is written in high-quality Greek by someone who is fluent in the language and who, as it turns out, is thoroughly imbued with the Jewish Scriptures in their Greek translation. Of course, it is technically possible that after Jesus' resurrection, Peter went back to school, took some Greek classes, did some advanced work in Greek composition, mastered the Jewish Bible in Greek, and then penned a letter such as this to a group of people that otherwise he was not known to be ministering to. But it seems unlikely.[2]

Why, though, would someone *claim* to be Peter when writing a letter such as this? The first thing to note is that it was not at all uncommon for people to assume false identities when writing books in antiquity: it happened a lot, even though the practice was widely condemned in pagan, Jewish, and Christian circles—sometimes even by people who were engaging in it.[3] This can be seen in the Petrine pseudepigrapha we have already considered: a handful of books all claiming to be written by Peter, all written by other people.

There were several reasons an author in antiquity might claim to be someone other than he was. With the early Christian writings, most commonly it was to get a hearing for one's views. If you think you have something important to say and you want people to listen to you, what better way than to claim to be someone famous—Jesus' chief disciple, for example?

In the case of 1 Peter, the real author's motives may have been as pure as the driven snow. He may have recognized that Christians in the communities of Asia Minor and elsewhere were experiencing hardship as a result of their faith, and wanted to comfort them, support them in their suffering, and encourage them to keep strong in the face of it. Who better to assure them of their need to suffer and to insist they suffer for what is right rather than what is wrong than the disciple Peter?

There may have been a secondary motive at work as well. One of the features of 1 Peter that has struck scholars over the years is how the author's portrayal of Christ's suffering and death so closely resembles the teaching of the apostle Paul. There are some statements that on the surface sound absolutely Pauline: "He himself bore our sins in his body upon the tree, that we might die to sin and live to righteousness, for by his wounds we were healed" (2:24); "For Christ also died for sins once for all, the righteous for the unrighteous, that he might lead us to God, having been put to death in the flesh but made alive in the Spirit" (4:18); and so on. We know from other sources—for example, Paul himself (cf. Gal. 2:11–14)—that Peter and Paul were sometimes at odds. Could part of the objective of this letter have been to show that the two great apostles saw completely eye to eye on matters of real importance? It is not at all unthinkable: other authors also tried to portray the two apostles as being in complete harmony, including the author of the book of Acts (cf. Acts 15).

Second Peter

One other writer who tried to show that Peter and Paul were on the same wavelength was the author of the so-called Second Letter of Peter in the New Testament. In this particular case there is less disagreement among critical scholars: whoever wrote 2 Peter, it was not Simon Peter the disciple of Jesus.

Unlike 1 Peter, the letter of 2 Peter was not widely accepted, or even known, in the early church. The first time any author makes a definitive reference to the book is around 220 CE, that is, nearly 150 years after it was allegedly written. It was finally admitted into the canon somewhat grudgingly, as church leaders of the later third and fourth centuries came to believe that it was written by Peter himself. But it almost certainly was not.

The letter is principally concerned about false teachers and their harmful effect on the "true" believers in Christ. The opponents of the author are viciously attacked, even though we are never told what it is, exactly, they teach. But the author issues dire warnings against them as those who "bring in destructive heresies," who "deny the Master who bought them," and who will "bring upon themselves quick destruction." These false teachers "follow after their own licentious ways," and because of them "the way of the truth is blasphemed" (2 Peter 2). The author goes on to say lots of negative things about these people. As scholars have long recognized, much of the invective is borrowed, virtually wholesale, from another book that found its way into the New Testament, the epistle of Jude. This is one of the reasons for dating the letter itself somewhat later, possible around 120 CE or so: it is dependent on another letter that appears to have been written near the end of the first century.[4]

One of the faults of these wicked teachers, in the author's opinion, involves their serious misinterpretations of the writings of Paul: "there are some things in them [Paul's letters] that are difficult, which the foolish and unstable twist about, as they do with the rest of the Scriptures, to their own destruction" (3:16). This author is writing, in other words, when there was already a collection of Paul's letters considered to be Scripture. This is yet another reason for thinking that the book comes from the early second century. It is significant that the author makes such a big deal out of Paul being a scriptural authority, for here again we see a reconciliation between the two chief apostles.

This author is particularly concerned about people who scoff at the Christian idea that the end of the age is coming soon, as predicted "through the commandment of the Lord and Savior by the holy prophets and your apostles" (3:2). (Would Peter himself talk about "your apostles"? Wasn't he one of them?) But since the end hasn't come, some unbelievers have begun to mock. For this author, however, it is no laughing matter, for just as the world was once destroyed by water in the days of Noah, so it will be destroyed by fire in days to come (3:1–7). And one should avoid thinking that the end is not coming soon, just because it hasn't happened yet. For God's timetable is not our own, and when God says it will be soon, he means soon by his standards. We must never forget, says the author, that "with the Lord a day is as a thousand years and a thousand years as a day" (3:8). For this author, even if the end is still five thousand years off, it is still coming right away.

Here, then, is a letter written in Peter's name by an early-second-century Christian who wants to attack the false teachers of his community, to urge his readers to hold fast to their faith and to wait in expectation of the glorious judgment of God that is sure to come—if not soon by our standards, then soon, at least, by his.

The Letter of Peter to James

We have observed throughout these discussions that various Christians of the second and third centuries wanted to latch on to Peter as an authority for their views, whether they were docetic or anti-docetic, Gnostic or anti-Gnostic. And so it comes as no surprise to learn that just as the pseudonymous authors of 1 and 2 Peter (who were clearly different writers, judging from their literary styles) both wanted to argue for a close tie between the views of Peter and his apostolic companion Paul, there were other authors who maintained that there was a sharp division between their views. We find such a position staked out in a group of writings that were allegedly produced by one of the early leaders of the church of Rome, a man named Clement. These books are therefore known as the Pseudo-Clementine writings. There are two sets of writings that survive under Clement's name: one is a set of twenty homilies (sermons) that he is said to have delivered *(The Clementine Homilies),* and the other is a ten-volume account of journeys that he undertook to locate long-lost members of his family *(The Clementine Recognitions).* There are extensive similarities between these two sets of writings—so much so that scholars have long been convinced that they both go back to a single, older writing that no longer survives, edited by two different authors in two different ways to give us the two sets of books that we now have.

The reason these writings are important for us here is that they both indicate that in his travels Clement met Peter and then journeyed around the Mediterranean with him. Peter, in fact, gives lengthy addresses in these books. It is significant that in these addresses Peter occasionally appears to malign the apostle Paul as a false teacher. What is directly germane to our purposes here is that the first set of writings, the *Homilies,* is prefaced by a letter allegedly written by Peter to James, the brother of Jesus and head of the church in Jerusalem. This letter also attacks the so-called apostle to the Gentiles.

The letter does not mention Paul by name. But it is not too difficult to see who the author's "enemy" is: it is someone who works among the Gentiles and teaches them that it is not necessary for them to keep the law. As we will see more fully in a later chapter, that is precisely what Paul himself taught (see Gal. 2:15; 5:2–5). And so the words of Peter to James strike a harsh chord:

> For some from among the Gentiles have rejected my lawful preaching and have preferred a lawless and absurd doctrine of the man who is my enemy. And indeed some have attempted, while I am still alive, to distort my word by interpretations of many sorts, as if I taught the dissolution of the law. . . . But that may God forbid! For to do such a thing means to act contrary to the law of God which was made to Moses and was confirmed by our Lord in its everlasting continuance. For he said, "The heaven and the earth will pass away, but not one jot or one tittle shall pass away from the law." (Letter of Peter to James, 2.3–5)

Paul is Peter's enemy; his teaching is "lawless and absurd"; he distorts the teachings of Peter; he contradicts the teaching of Jesus himself. Not high praise for the apostle to the Gentiles!

Most of Peter's letter to James expresses his concern that his teachings not be distorted. And so he insists that his writings be passed on only to those who are reliable and who have proven themselves worthy to receive them, after a long period of initiation.

As might be expected, this polemic against Paul comes to expression also in the Clementine writings themselves. This is especially true of the *Homilies.* Both here and elsewhere we find accounts similar to those in the Acts of Peter where Peter becomes involved with a controversy with Simon (Magus). But in this writing it becomes clear that Simon Magus in fact is a cipher for none other than Paul himself. This is evident, for example, when Peter attacks a thinly disguised Paul for thinking that his very brief encounter with Christ in his vision while on his way to persecute Christians in Damascus (a reference to Acts 9) could authorize him to teach a gospel that stands at odds with that proclaimed by Peter, who spent an entire year with Christ while he was still living and is, according to Christ's own words, the Rock on which the church is built. As Peter says:

And if our Jesus appeared to you and became known in a vision and met you as angry and an enemy, yet he has spoken only through visions and dreams or through external revelations. But can anyone be made competent to teach through a vision? And if your opinion is that that is possible, why then did our teacher spend a whole year with us who were awake? How can we believe you even if he has appeared to you? . . . But if you were visited by him for the space of an hour and were instructed by him and thereby have become an apostle, then proclaim his words, expound what he has taught, be a friend to his apostles, and do not contend with me, who am his confidant; for you have in hostility withstood me, who am a firm rock, the foundation stone of the Church. (*Homilies* 17.19)

To buttress his claim of superiority, in one section of the work Peter sets forth the view that in the working out of God's plan for humans, the lesser always precedes the greater. And so Adam's son Cain, the murderer, preceded his other son Abel, the righteous; Abraham's outcast son, Ishmael, preceded his chosen son, Isaac; Isaac's godless son, Esau, preceded his godly son, Jacob; and on down to more recent times, where there were two who appeared on the Gentile mission field spreading the gospel of Christ, Simon (i.e., Paul), and Peter, who was, as the latter, the greater of the two, "who appeared later than he did and came in upon him as light upon darkness, as knowledge upon ignorance, as healing upon sickness" (*Homilies* 2.17).

In sum, as we have seen in other parts of our study, Peter was a figure who could be used for a wide range of purposes by Christians in the early Church, a kind of lightning rod that drew other Christian thinkers to himself. He could be used by Gnostics to attack orthodox positions and by orthodox Christians to attack the Gnostics; he could be used to promote a docetic Christology or to deny it; he could be used to advance a Pauline teaching of a law-free gospel based in the death of Christ or to oppose it.

He was not only a controversial figure but an all-round useful one: his life and teachings could be invoked to encourage those who found that the "flesh is willing but the spirit is weak," or to show that God worked spectacular miracles in demonstrating the truth of the gospel, or to urge an ascetic lifestyle among those who converted to faith in Christ. Peter may have been the Rock on which the church was founded, but since the church was so many different things to so many different people, in some ways Peter was a rock collection.

Peter as Bishop

In some circles, Peter is best known as the first bishop of Rome, the first pope. In the period I'm interested in for this book, however, there is little evidence to support this view. On the contrary, several authors indicate that Peter was not the first leader of the church there and certainly not its first bishop. There are some traditions, however, that connect him with the Roman church long *after* it had been established.

Before examining these traditions, I should reiterate that there were other churches outside Rome that claimed a special connection with Peter. His importance to such churches is no mystery: if Peter was Jesus' chief disciple and the first to affirm his resurrection, then any church that could claim him as their own would obviously improve its status in the eyes of the Christian world at large. The church in Jerusalem itself could certainly make some such claim, as it is clear that in the beginning months of the church, soon after Jesus' death, it was Peter who took charge and began the mission to convert others to faith in Jesus. Some twenty years later the apostle Paul could still speak of Peter as one of the "pillars" of the Jerusalem church, along with John, the son of Zebedee, and James, the brother of Jesus (Gal. 2:9). As becomes clear from a range of sources, including Paul himself (e.g., Gal. 2:12), James was eventually to take over the leadership of the church in Jerusalem, possibly as Peter pursued his mission to convert Jews in other places. The second-century author Clement of Alexandria indicates that it was James who was the first bishop of Jerusalem (Eusebius, *Church History,* 2, 1).

We have also seen that Peter was present for a time in the large city of Antioch of Syria, where he had a confrontation with Paul over whether it was appropriate to abstain from eating meals with Gentile believers in view of the scruples of Jewish Christians who believed in the need to continue keeping kosher (Gal. 2:11–14). A later tradition indicates that Peter was actually the first bishop there (Eusebius, *Church History* 3, 36).

Peter was also significant for the church of Corinth. When Paul writes his first letter to the Corinthians, he is concerned that there are groups of Christians claiming allegiance to one Christian leader or another: some to him as founder of the church, some to Apollos as an apostle who came in Paul's wake to build up the church, and others to Peter (1 Cor. 1:12). There is nothing to indicate that this allegiance to Peter was because he too had come to visit the church: a fourth group, for example, claims allegiance to Jesus himself, and it is certain that *he* was never there. But it is clear that Peter's reputation as the chief apostle made an appeal to him carry considerable weight.

These cities—Jerusalem, Antioch, and Corinth—contained three of the largest churches in the first two centuries. All three claimed some kind of connection with Peter. In a distant way, so did a fourth, the church of Alexandria, Egypt. According to Eusebius, it was the apostle Mark who first went to Egypt and established the (very large) church there (*Church History* 2, 15). This is the same Mark whom we met earlier as an alleged follower and secretary for Peter, and who, according to the second-century Papias, wrote his Gospel as a set of recollections that he heard from Peter's sermons about the life of Jesus. In other words, through his right-hand man, Mark, Peter is also closely connected with the Alexandrian church.

And so, of course, is the fifth of the largest churches in early Christendom, the church in Rome. We have seen a number of traditions already that presuppose that the church in the city of Rome was well established by the time Peter

arrived there. The second-century Acts of Peter, for example, begins by discussing Paul's work of strengthening the church in Rome (is the assumption
that he too came after it had started?) and his decision to leave to take his
mission to Spain. It is only because the vacuum created by his absence is filled
by the agent of Satan, Simon Magus, that Peter is called by God to journey to
Rome to confront his sworn enemy. Peter then, according to this tradition,
comes into a situation in which there has already been a large number of converts, many of whom have fallen away.

If Peter did not start the church in Rome, who did? As it turns out, our
earliest evidence for the existence of a church in Rome at all is one of Paul's
letters, the letter to the Romans (written in the 50s CE). This letter presupposes
a congregation made up predominantly, or exclusively, of Gentiles (Rom. 1:13).
It does not appear, then, to have been a church established by Peter, missionary
to the Jews. Moreover, at the end of the letter, Paul greets a large number of the
members of the congregation by name. It is striking that he never mentions
Peter, here or anywhere else in the letter. Interpreters are virtually unified, on
these grounds, in thinking that when Paul wrote this letter in the mid-50s,
Peter had not yet arrived in Rome.

A later tradition found in the writings of the late-second-century church
father Irenaeus, however, indicates that the church in Rome was "founded and
organized by the two most glorious apostles, Peter and Paul" (*Against Heresies* 3, 3, 2). As I have just argued, this cannot have been the case—since in
Paul's own letter to the Roman church, he indicates that he has not yet been
there (Rom. 1:13). Irenaeus had a particular polemical point to make by his
claim, for in his view, already here at the end of the second century, the church
in Rome was the predominant church in the Christian world and its views of
the faith were to be normative over all others. And so naturally this most important of churches must have been "founded and organized" by the two most
important apostles, Peter and Paul (who were seen, therefore, in contrast to
other writings we have observed, as being in complete harmony with one another). The reality is that we do not know who started the church in Rome. It
may well have been started simply by anonymous people: since so many people
traveled to and from Rome, it is not at all implausible that early converts to the
faith (say, a decade or more before Paul wrote his letter to the Roman Christians in the 50s) returned to the capital and made other converts, and that the
movement grew from there.

But who was the first bishop of Rome? According to the second-century
Irenaeus, it was a man named Linus, who was appointed to the office by Peter
and Paul (*Against Heresies* 3, 3, 3). In one place the father of church history,
Eusebius, appears to agree with this to some extent when he says that "the first
to be called bishop after the martyrdoms of Peter and Paul was Linus" (*Church
History,* 3, 2), but here Linus is appointed not by Peter but by someone else,
after Peter's death. And to confuse things even further, just a few paragraphs
later Eusebius phrases the matter differently, saying that "Linus . . . was the

first after Peter to be appointed Bishop of Rome. Clement again, who became the third Bishop of Rome." This makes it appear that Peter was the first bishop, Linus the second, and Clement the third. And the tradition becomes yet more confused when we consider the writings of Tertullian, from the early third century, who seems to indicate that Clement was not the third bishop of Rome but the first—appointed by Peter himself (*Prescription of the Heretics* 32).

How is one to resolve this confusion? It is worth pointing out that when Paul wrote his letter to the Romans, he gives no indication that there is *any* single leader of the church there, just as there were not single bishops over any of the churches that Paul addressed in his letters in the 50s. More telling still, some sixty years after Paul we have another letter written to the church in Rome, this time by the soon-to-be-martyred Ignatius, the bishop of Antioch, who has been sent under armed guard to face the wild beasts in the Roman Forum. Even though Ignatius presupposes that there are single bishops in each of the other six letters that he writes (for example, to the Ephesians and the Smyrneans), when he writes to Rome he does not presume this at all, but instead speaks to the entire congregation, never mentioning any one person in charge of the church.

Somewhat before Ignatius's time, and soon thereafter, we have two writings from Christians who actually resided in Rome. Both attest to a situation in which the Roman church was not under the leadership of a single individual, the bishop. The book of 1 Clement was written sometime in the mid-90s CE. This is some thirty years after Peter's death, which the author knows about and mentions (1 Clement 5:4). The letter was allegedly written by that very Clement whom later tradition was to call the Roman bishop. Yet it seems to assume that the churches at that time were run not by individual leaders but by a board of presbyters. The letter, in fact, is addressed to a situation in Corinth in which the presbyters have been ousted from office in some kind of church coup. The Roman Christians (not a bishop) write to try to redress the situation by having the older presbyters reinstated in office.

Another writing, from after Ignatius's day, also was produced in the city of Rome; this is the apocalypse known as the Shepherd of Hermas. Hermas was a Roman Christian living probably near the middle of the second century.[5] In his writing, he mentions Clement—but not as a bishop. Rather, Clement is named as a kind of foreign correspondent for the church (Shepherd 8, 3). More telling still, Hermas speaks of the "presbyters" and the "bishops" of the church, but never of a solitary bishop over the entire congregation.

It was only with the passage of time that the Christian churches developed the hierarchical structures that came to characterize their organization by the end of the second century, where there was one bishop over each church, under whom served a board of elders (or presbyters) and deacons. It appears that the Roman church itself was organized more loosely in its early years, probably because the church consisted of a large number of congregations of Christians who met separately in the homes of some of their wealthier members, scattered throughout the city. Each of these so-called house churches probably had somebody in charge, likely the person who owned the house and provided the space. Eventually these churches would band together to make common cause. And when they did so, they appointed leaders who would be in charge of all the communities found throughout the city. But this was a development that did not transpire until the middle of the second century. Peter, in short, could not have been the first bishop of the church of Rome, because the Roman church did not have *anyone* as its bishop until about a hundred years after Peter's death.

Peter as Martyr

The death of Peter by execution is already alluded to in the Gospel of John—which evidently, then, had been written after the event occurred. As noted earlier, Jesus tells Peter after the resurrection:

> When you were young, you girded yourself and walked wherever you wanted; but when you grow old, you will reach out your hands and someone else will gird you, and lead you where you do not want to go. (21:18)

The author concludes this quotation by noting, "He said this to signify the kind of death he would experience to glorify God."

It is clear that Peter is being told that he will be executed (he won't die of natural causes) and that this will be the death of a martyr (by it he will "glorify God"). Some interpreters have thought that the reference is more specific than that: the author is indicating that Peter will be crucified. The argument is that the text speaks of the immobilization of the hands, which may refer to being nailed or tied to a cross. Such an interpretation is possible, but it should be pointed out that the binding of the hands appears to occur before Peter is to be led off to be executed. And so the passage may simply refer to a martyrdom (by any means) yet to come.

In any event, by the end of the first century and into the second it was widely known among Christians that Peter had suffered a martyr's death. The tradition is alluded to in the book of 1 Clement: "Because of unjust jealousy Peter bore up under hardships not just once or twice, but many times; and having thus borne his witness [or "having been martyred"] he went to the place of glory that he deserved" (5:4). And a hundred years later Tertullian speaks of Peter enduring "a passion like the Lord's"—possibly referring to the tradition that Peter was crucified.

This became the firm tradition of later times, that Peter, along with his companion apostle Paul, had been martyred during the persecution by the emperor Nero. According to this tradition Peter's death came by crucifixion, and in a rather bizarre manner: he had been crucified upside down, with his head to the ground. This tradition is later reported in Eusebius, who says that "Peter came to Rome where he was crucified, head downward at his own request" (*Church History*, 3, 1). But its earliest occurrence appears in the second-century Acts of Peter, which tells the famous "Quo vadis" story of Peter returning to Rome in order to be crucified.

Peter's Death in the Acts of Peter

Peter's death is one of the most interesting tales in the Acts of Peter. As I described earlier, according to the book, Peter had incensed two of the most powerful men in Rome by his preaching of sexual continence. The concubines of the ruling prefect Agrippa and the wife of the emperor's friend Albinus refused any longer to have any sexual relationships with them. In their pique, the men decide to go after Peter.

Albinus's wife, Xanthippe, learns of the plot, however, and warns Peter to flee the city. He is reluctant to do so, but his fellow Christians finally persuade him. As he is walking through the city gate, however, he sees Jesus coming in. Perplexed, he asks him, "Lord, where are you going" (in Latin, "Quo vadis?"). Jesus replies that he is going to Rome to be crucified. Peter is confused: "Lord, are you being crucified again?" And Jesus replies, "Yes, Peter, again I shall be crucified." Peter then wakes up as if from a dream, sees Jesus ascend to heaven, and realizes that he must return to the city to be captured and crucified in Jesus' stead (Acts of Peter, 35).

It should not be thought that Peter reluctantly turns back, recognizing with dread that he too must be crucified. The text indicates quite the opposite: Peter returns to Rome "rejoicing and praising the Lord" that he is to be crucified. This, for Peter, was his ultimate chance to imitate Christ and die a glorious martyr's death.

Peter meets up with his Christian companions, tells them his plan, and urges them not to be angry with Agrippa, since this is the Lord's will. And when the moment comes, he asks to be crucified upside down. This is not because, as some later interpreters would have it, he felt unworthy to be killed in the same way as his Lord. He himself indicates what is meant by the upside-down crucifixion: it is a symbolic statement about the nature of earthly existence and our human need to look past the appearances of life to the realities that they reveal. This idea is conveyed in an address that Peter gives from the cross. He speaks to the onlookers about the "mystery of the whole creation," which itself is all topsy-turvy. When the first man (Adam) came into the world, he came headfirst (as do newborns). That means that Adam's perspective, as the one who brought sin into the world, was entirely reversed and upside down. That is why people seem to think that what is true is false and what is false true, what is right is wrong and what is wrong right, what is real is fake and what is fake real. All of this is because humans have reverse vision, due to the actions of Adam, the first man (Acts of Peter, 38). By hanging upside down, however,

Peter sees things correctly: what is to us right is to him left, what is to us up is to him down, and so forth.

People need to acquire this new vision of reality in our world. Those who are in Christ recognize that the values and priorities and loves and passions of this world are all wrong. But there is an alternative set of values, priorities, loves, and passions: those that come from God. Christians are to adhere to these, even though they seem opposite to what the rest of the world embraces.

Peter, having said his piece, dies. In an interesting aftermath, his friend Marcellus provides for him an expensive and elaborate burial. Peter has to return from the dead to upbraid his friend for not understanding his message: since all things are reversed—as he has just gone to great length to explain while dying—it is not wealth that is to be valued (for example, in expensive funeral arrangements) but poverty, and not death that is to be shunned but life.

Conclusion

Throughout our discussion we have constantly asked why Christian storytellers would tell the accounts of Peter's life the way they did. In the account of his death, there seem to be numerous lessons conveyed by the narrative. On the most basic level, Peter is finally able to redeem himself for the act of unfaithfulness at Jesus' arrest and trial: now, true to his word, he does go to death with Jesus. Moreover, he goes not kicking and screaming but rejoicing and praising God. This is an important lesson, no doubt, for Christians in the second and third centuries, who were themselves sometimes captured by the authorities and confronted with painful tortures and death. And then there is the key point made by Peter himself, hanging upside down on his cross: this world and its values are not to be embraced, for God's ways are not our ways and his views are not ours. We must realign our views to realize that what most people seek and long for in this world is to be shunned. We must avoid the passions of this world and forsake its longings. Only then will we understand our true human nature and be prepared to enter the world that God has prepared for his people.

Part Two

THE APOSTLE PAUL

Chapter Seven

The Apostle Paul:
Polling Our Sources

Has there ever been a Christian figure as controversial as the apostle Paul? It was a new understanding of Paul's letters that led Martin Luther to split from the Catholic Church, leading to the Protestant Reformation and a division within Christendom that continues down to our own day. Churches of all description continue to wrangle over Paul's teachings: some insist that his writings oppose women in the ordained ministry, while others argue just the opposite; some claim that his letters denounce same-sex relations, and others assert the contrary; some argue that his letters support Western forms of capitalism, while others say it is just the opposite.

Debates over Paul—and over who can claim him—are not, however, a product of the modern age: they go all the way back to New Testament times. The letter of 2 Peter speaks of those (Gnostics?) who "twist" the meaning of Paul's letters "to their own destruction" (2 Peter 3:16). This must mean that both the author of 2 Peter and the Christians he was opposing appealed to Paul's authority for their views. On the other hand, there were some Christian groups that wanted nothing to do with Paul—as seen, for example, in the Letter of Peter to James connected with the Pseudo-Clementine writings, where the famous apostle to the Gentiles is referred to by "Peter" (that is, the anonymous author claiming to be Peter) as "the man who is my enemy."

We don't need to wait until the second century for this opposition to arise. Paul had plenty of enemies in his own lifetime. And often these were in the very Christian congregations that he himself founded, among his own converts. In the churches of Galatia there were Christians who insisted that Paul had misunderstood the gospel of Christ when he maintained that Gentile men did not have to become circumcised to belong to the people of God. Paul, they argued, was a relative latecomer to the faith who had perverted the original gospel message. Elsewhere, in the churches of Corinth, Paul was thought by some to have only a rudimentary understanding of the faith, which could now be proclaimed by others who had far greater spiritual power and rhetorical eloquence. In the opinion of these "super-apostles" (as Paul calls them), Paul's "bodily presence is weak, and his speech is contemptible" (2 Cor. 10:10). Paul's ideas were often seen as dangerous: the epistle of James in the New Testament appears to be directed against the teachings of Paul (or at least the interpretation of these teachings by others) that insisted that a person is made right with God "by faith alone, apart from works."

If nothing else, Paul engendered controversy. Since different groups sometimes claimed his support for their opposing views, historians have naturally asked what Paul himself actually believed and taught.

As we saw in the case of Peter, even though this is an important question to ask, it is not the only question. It is also worth asking how different groups *presented* Paul's life and teachings, for this too involves a set of historical questions: not necessarily about the historical Paul as he really was, but about Paul as he was remembered.

In the chapters that follow we will be asking both sets of questions. As I did with Peter, I will begin by observing that there are problems with our sources when it comes to any attempt to separate out the real, historical Paul from the Paul of legend. Then I will explore the many portrayals of Paul, historical and legendary, from the early centuries of the church.

Separating History from Legend

How do we know the difference between what really happened in the life of Paul and what has come down to us as pious legend? An early account indicates that on one of his missionary journeys Paul arrived on the island of Cyprus, where he met a certain magician who was a "Jewish false prophet named Barjesus" (literally "son of Jesus"; he also went by the name Elymas) who had the ear of the local Roman official, Sergius Paulus. Barjesus is said to be afraid that Sergius Paulus would convert to become a follower of Jesus and that he would thereby lose a patron, so he tries to prevent him from accepting the message that Paul proclaims. When Paul realizes what is happening he confronts Barjesus, telling him, "Now see, the hand of the Lord is against you and you will become blind and not see the sun for a while." Immediately the false prophet is struck blind.

Compare this with a second story. Paul has been in Rome, strengthening the faith of the believers there. Before departing to make his way to evangelize Spain, he has a farewell eucharistic service with the faithful. One of the women who comes forward to take communion is an unrepentant sinner named Rufina. Paul stops her with a word: "Rufina, you do not approach the altar of God as a believer, since you rise from the side not of a husband but of an adulterer, and yet you endeavor to receive God's eucharist." He threatens her with eternal punishment, with a very palpable result: "At once Rufina collapsed, being paralyzed on the left side from head to foot. Nor could she speak anymore, for her tongue was tied."

Both stories indicate that Paul is an apostle not to be messed with. Did both, or either, actually happen? It might surprise readers to learn that the first account is found in the New Testament book of Acts (13:6), but the other occurs in the first section of the Acts of Peter (chapters 1–2).

Or consider two comparable resuscitations. In one account Paul is preaching to a group of believers in the city of Troas, in the upper room of a house. His sermon drags on for a very long time. Sitting in the window of the house is a Christian named Eutychus; around midnight, he dozes off and falls three stories from the window to his death. Paul, however, goes down to the corpse, embraces it, and announces that it is alive. Lo and behold, Eutychus rises from the dead. Paul, completely unfazed, returns to the upper room, where he continues to talk until daybreak (Acts 13:7–11). This may sound legendary, but it is, after all, in the New Testament book of Acts.

Yet how different is it from the account of the raising of Patroclus, a servant of the emperor Nero, who also is said to have been listening to Paul late at night, this time in a barn? He too drifts asleep, falls from the window, and dies. Word is sent off to Nero, who very much liked the boy, but Paul once again saves the day, telling the gathered believers to mourn for the boy to the Lord so that he might be revived. And it all goes according to plan: Patroclus is resuscitated and returns to his master, Nero. As I noted in an earlier chapter, though the story of Patroclus is comparable in many ways to the resuscitation of Eutychus, it is found not in a canonical book but in the legendary Acts of Paul from the second century.

A final example is drawn from the tales of Paul's persecution at the hands of his enemies. In one account, Paul is preaching the gospel in the city of Lystra when his enemies from among the Jews rouse the mob against him. Paul is stoned, dragged out of the city, and left for dead. But his followers gather around him, and he gets up to head into the next city to proclaim the gospel yet again, as if nothing had happened. Here is a man you can't keep down.

Is this more or less spectacular than the account of Paul thrown to face the wild beasts in the city of Ephesus? This particular account is admittedly a bit strange—but aren't all impossible stories strange, whether in the Bible or outside it? In this one, a fierce lion is set upon Paul; Paul and the lion, however, recognize each other. This lion is one that Paul had previously met in the wilderness, where it had asked the apostle (in a human voice) to be baptized. And now, when they become reacquainted in the Forum, of course the lion won't touch his master. God sends a hailstorm that kills all the other wild beasts (and a number of people), and both Paul and the lion escape, Paul to preach the gospel in other lands, the lion to return to his natural home.

Of course it's legendary. But perhaps we shouldn't be too quick to say that it is simply a later fabrication, while the accounts found in the New Testament are all factually accurate. Don't we have features of both history and legend in all the stories surrounding the apostle Paul? Aren't we faced with the same situation that we found ourselves in with respect to Peter, that there are some historical records, some legendary accounts, and some stories that probably represent a combination of the two?

Accounts from Paul's Own Hand

We are indeed very much in the same situation as with Peter with regard to the intertwining of history and legend, but with one very important difference: in the case of Paul, we have a number of letters that survive from his own hand, which provide us with bedrock historical information about the apostle to the Gentiles—something that we regrettably lack with respect to Peter. There are thirteen letters within the New Testament that claim to be written by Paul, along with a handful of letters from outside the New Testament, including a third letter to the Corinthians (the New Testament contains 1 and 2 Corinthians), several letters written to the Roman philosopher Seneca (and several from him to Paul), and a letter to the Christians of the town of Laodicea. Surely, then, we are in a better situation historically than with Peter—or even Jesus. Neither Peter nor Jesus left us any writings, but Paul evidently did.

Even so, several caveats are necessary for using these writings to learn about the historical Paul. Most important, as happened in the case of Peter, a number of the writings that claim to be written by Paul were not actually written by him but are pseudepigraphical (which is the highfalutin way of calling them forgeries). This is certainly true of all the writings found outside of the New Testament. None of these Pauline letters (3 Corinthians and the letters to Seneca, for example) was actually written by Paul, as scholars have known for centuries: these other letters presuppose situations that are quite different from those that Paul faced while writing some twenty to thirty years after Jesus' death, mainly in the 50s CE.

But what about the thirteen letters that claim to be written by Paul in the New Testament? These letters pose three problems for anyone trying to reconstruct what the historical Paul himself taught.

Pseudepigraphy

The first problem involves knowing which letters came from Paul's hand. To some extent this is a different kind of problem from what we had with Peter, since in Peter's case, we weren't certain that he could write at all. Paul, at least, was well educated and highly trained, so he could and did write. But there were numerous writings circulating in his name in the early church: how do we decide which ones he wrote? I should stress that this is not a question of whether an early Christian might have forged letters in Paul's name. We *know* that Christians were forging letters in Paul's name—for example, the letter of 3 Corinthians, which attacks the kind of docetic Christologies that came into existence in the early- to mid-second century, some decades after Paul's death, or the letters he allegedly exchanged with the philosopher Seneca, which date from about three centuries after both had died.

We have solid evidence to suggest that already during the New Testament period there were Christians forging letters in Paul's name. The evidence comes in a letter that itself claims to be written by Paul—2 Thessalonians—in which the author warns his readers against a letter circulating in his name that he himself did not actually write (2 Thess. 2:2). The irony is that a number of scholars, for pretty good reasons, suspect that Paul did not write 2 Thessalonians itself. This makes for a rock-solid argument that there were Pauline forgeries in the first century. Either 2 Thessalonians is from Paul's own hand and he knows of a forgery that is floating around in his name, or 2 Thessalonians is not from Paul's hand and is itself a forgery. Either way, there are forgeries circulating in Paul's name.

One important question is whether any of these forgeries made it into the New Testament. We have always to remember that the New Testament did not come into being as a set canon of Scripture until centuries after the books of the New Testament themselves were written.[1] The people who made the decisions concerning what to include in the New Testament were not academic scholars or literary sleuths. Living centuries after the books were written, they often had no means of gauging accurately whether a book's alleged author was its real author. It may seem strange to say, but modern scholars have far more resources at their disposal for uncovering ancient forgeries than ancient people themselves did, since today we have sophisticated methods of literary analysis, indexes of vocabulary and grammatical stylistic preferences, data retrieval systems, and so on.

I won't go into all the details here, but will simply refer you to other books that deal specifically with this issue of which writings allegedly by Paul were actually written by him.[2] For our purposes it is enough to know that almost all scholars are convinced that of the thirteen letters attributed to Paul in the New Testament, seven are indisputably his: Romans, 1 and 2 Corinthians, Galatians, Philippians, 1 Thessalonians, and Philemon.

The other six letters differ from these undisputed seven, sometimes in very significant ways, sometimes in minor but telling ways. The differences involve (1) the vocabulary and writing style used (or not used) in the letters: everyone has a distinctive writing style, and it's possible to determine stylistic characteristics to see if a book actually employs a writer's style; (2) the theological points of view represented: some of the disputed letters appear to contradict the theology of the undisputed letters; (3) the historical situation that lies behind the writing: some of the letters presuppose a situation that arose long after Paul's death; and so on.

These other letters—Ephesians, Colossians, 2 Thessalonians, 1 and 2 Timothy, and Titus—appear to have been written by later Christians who were taking Paul's name in order to propagate their own views, much as happened with Peter in such works as the Gospel of Peter, the Letter of Peter to Philip, and the Apocalypse of Peter. These disputed Pauline letters, then, will be quite useful for us in knowing how Paul was remembered in the years after his death, but they will be of less use in helping us to understand what Paul himself taught.

Interpolations

Even the undisputed Pauline letters occasionally pose problems for us, however, in that there are some places where it appears that later scribes who copied the letters inserted material into them that was not originally there. Remember, this is the age before electronic publishing, photocopy machines, and even printing with movable type. This interpolated material again cannot be used to establish what Paul himself said or thought, but it does show us what later Christians wanted Paul to think.

Just to give one example: an important passage in 1 Corinthians, a letter that Paul indisputably wrote, insists that women should be "silent in the churches," since they "are not permitted to speak" (1 Cor. 14: 24–36). This has been a key passage for arguments in the modern world over women's roles in the churches: can women, for example, be ordained to ministry? Well, not if they can't speak. But as it turns out, there are very convincing reasons for thinking that these verses in 1 Corinthians 14 were not originally penned by Paul but were added later by a scribe who wanted the apostle to be on the side of those who believed women should not participate in the worship services as active members of the congregation.

Among the reasons that scholars have found this view convincing is the circumstance that just three chapters earlier Paul indicates that when women pray and prophesy in church, they should do so with covered heads. Now, it's a little hard to see how Paul can say in chapter 11 that it is acceptable for women to speak if he is going to deny it in chapter 14. Moreover, if you remove the verses from Chapter 14 (i.e., if you assume they were not originally there), the passage flows much better: right before this Paul is speaking about prophets in the church and right afterward he is still speaking about prophets. What is especially telling is that there are some manuscripts of 1 Corinthians in which these very verses are found in a different place in the text—as if they were originally a marginal note made by a scribe that was placed in different spots by different scribes who later copied his manuscript. For these and other reasons it appears that Paul did not write the verses about women having to be silent in church—obviously a significant point for those who want to know Paul's views of women.[3]

The Occasional Nature of the Letters

The final problem posed by Paul's letters for seeing what he taught and believed is that even if you restrict yourself to the undisputed letters in their uninterpolated form, you still need to realize that all of these letters were occasional writings. What I mean by this is that they were letters written for certain occasions. And understanding the occasion for each writing affects how it is to be interpreted.

All of Paul's surviving writings were actual letters—that is, pieces of correspondence that Paul sent through the ancient equivalent of the U.S. Postal Service (in antiquity, this usually involved having someone hand-deliver the letter). These were not meant to be systematic treatises in which Paul spelled out everything he thought was important. Just as you write a letter or an e-mail for a reason—you just want to say hi, you're missing someone, you have important news to share, it's someone's birthday, there's a problem at the office you need to address, you're going to be late on your taxes, and so on—so too Paul wrote his letters for occasions. In Paul's case, nearly all of his letters, with one important exception, were written to Christian communities that he himself had established in urban areas around the Mediterranean by converting former pagans to believe in the one God of Israel and in the death and resurrection of his son. When he would hear about how one of his churches was doing (often the news wasn't good), Paul would write a letter back to them to reestablish their relationship and to deal with the various problems they were facing, whether these problems had to do with ethical issues, false teachings, personality conflicts, or something else.

What this means, though, is that since all of Paul's letters were occasional, they for the most part deal only with the situations at hand. These letters are not systematic treatises dealing with all-important issues of Christian doctrine and ethics. It's a pity we don't have *all* of the letters Paul ever wrote. Then we would have a goldmine of information about him and the Christian churches he established. As it is, we're restricted to seven undisputed letters that are all tied to very specific situations.

Let me illustrate how this may create problems for us. In only one passage in all of Paul's letters does he discuss the importance of the Christian eucharistic meal, the Lord's Supper, and how it ought to be observed. He deals with the matter in 1 Corinthians because problems about the meal had arisen in Corinth. Some of the church members were eating all the food and getting drunk at the meal, and others who had to come late—because they had to work, presumably—found there was nothing left for them to eat. It's quite clear from his discussion that Paul considers the meal and its proper celebration to be of the utmost importance: some Christians have become sick or even died as a punishment for not observing it properly. But if 1 Corinthians had been lost— as most of Paul's other letters were lost—then we wouldn't even know that Paul thought anything about the meal. How many other issues that were highly significant for Paul do we not know about, simply because they never arose in the churches he addressed in the surviving letters?

So when dealing with Paul, we have to be very careful not to assume that we can have a complete picture of what he believed and taught. We know some things, but our picture will, regrettably, be incomplete.

The Special Case of Acts

We have one other relatively early source of information for the life and teachings of Paul: the New Testament book of Acts. In the case of Peter we had reason to suspect that some of the stories told in Acts were not historically accurate but were later reflections on his life by the author of the book, who also wrote the Gospel of Luke. I have already suggested at the beginning of this chapter that the same applies to Paul, that some of the accounts of Acts are as much the stuff of legend as historically verifiable reports.

In the case of Paul, however, we have even firmer grounds for making this judgment. There are places where the book of Acts reports on the same events of Paul's life that Paul himself refers to in his own letters, and we can compare what Acts says about Paul with what Paul says about himself. What is striking is that in almost every instance where this kind of comparison is possible, disparities—sometimes very large disparities—appear between the two accounts.

If Acts was written around 80 or 85 CE, as most scholars think (soon after the Gospel of Luke), then it would have been written at least a generation after Paul himself, no doubt by someone in one of Paul's own communities who would have heard stories about the apostle as they had been in circulation in the decades after his death. But as we all know, stories get changed in the retelling, and thirty years is a long time. Most scholars contend that Paul is a better source for knowing about Paul than Luke is—that where there are discrepancies, it is Paul who is to be trusted.

Inconsistencies in Acts

In part this is because the author of Acts does not seem all that concerned to present an internally consistent portrayal of Paul's life, despite his claims that he wants to give an "accurate" account (Luke 1:1–4). The way I usually try to show this to my students is by giving them a little exercise of comparison. There are three passages in the book of Acts that describe Paul's conversion to Christ. All three accounts agree with the basic point—made by Paul himself in his own letters—that prior to his conversion, Paul was an avid persecutor of the Christians, and that it was on the basis of a vision of Jesus after his resurrection that Paul became convinced God had raised Jesus from the dead. But what was this vision, and what happened when Paul experienced it? It depends on which account you read, the one in Acts 9, 22, or 26. According to the story in chapter 9, when Jesus appeared to Paul on the road to Damascus, Paul's traveling companions "heard the voice but saw no one" (9:7), but when Paul himself recounts what happened in chapter 22, he indicates that his companions "saw the light but did not hear the voice" (22:9). Well, which was it? In chapter 9, Paul's companions are said to be left standing while he himself is knocked to the ground by the vision (v. 7), but according to chapter 26, they all fall to the ground (v. 12). In chapter 9 Paul is instructed by Jesus to go into Damascus to receive instruction by a man named Ananias about what to do, but in chapter 26 he is not sent to Ananias but is instructed by Jesus himself.

These may seem like minor details, but why are the accounts at odds with one another at all? Some interpreters have suggested that the differences are there because Luke made minor changes in the story, depending on the context in which it was being told: in chapter 9 he narrates the event itself, whereas in chapter 22 Paul recounts the story to a hostile crowd and in chapter 26 he tells it during his court trial. This seems like a reasonable view, but it still creates a problem for anyone who wants to know what actually happened. For if Luke was willing to modify his story depending on the context within which he told it, why shouldn't we assume that he modified *all* of his stories whenever he saw fit? And if he did that, how do we know when we're reading the story as it happened?

Inconsistencies with Paul's Letters

The evidence that Luke sometimes modified the information he received—or that his sources of information had already modified it—is even clearer when you compare his account of Paul with Paul's account of himself. Sometimes the differences are minor matters that simply suggest Luke got a piece of information wrong. Other differences are quite important, because they affect the way we understand Paul's gospel message and his mission as a Christian evangelist.

There are discrepancies between the book of Acts and Paul's own letters, for instance, with reference to Paul's traveling itinerary. In the book of Acts, for example, we're told that when Paul makes a trip to Athens after converting a number of people in the city of Thessalonica, he is completely alone: his companions Timothy and Silas do not accompany him (Acts 17:15; see 18:5). But that's not what Paul himself says. In 1 Thessalonians Paul indicates that Timothy had been with him in Athens, and that because Paul is eager to get news of how the new Thessalonian converts are doing, he sent Timothy back to them to find out (3:1–2). Maybe it doesn't much matter, but it does show that Luke doesn't have the details right.

A second, comparable difference really does matter. According to Paul himself, once he was converted by his vision of Christ, he did not go to Jerusalem in order to meet with the apostles (Gal. 1:17). Paul is quite insistent on the point. He stresses the fact and says, "Before God, I do not lie!" (1:20). The reason is quite clear: he wants his readers to realize that the gospel message he preaches was not handed on to him by Jesus' earthly disciples. He got it directly from Christ himself in a vision that led to his conversion. No one, then, can accuse him of perverting the gospel as he inherited it from those who were apostles before him. This makes it all the more interesting to see how the events play out according to the book of Acts. There, after his conversion, Paul leaves Damascus and goes directly to Jerusalem, precisely in order to meet with the apostles (Acts 9:23–30). Luke has his own reasons for wanting Paul to make immediate acquaintance with the apostles. For him, all of the apostles—Peter, James, Paul, and everyone else—were in complete agreement about all the important matters facing the church. The need to show apostolic agreement led him to tell the story of an early apostolic meeting, even though Paul explicitly denies it.

Sometimes the differences between Paul's self-portrait and the portrait in Acts involve the content of Paul's message. According to Acts, for example, when Paul is speaking to a group of pagan philosophers in Athens, he tells them that they and all pagans worship many gods because they simply don't know any better. But God is forgiving of this oversight and wants them to realize that he alone is to be worshiped. Now, having learned the truth, they can repent and believe in Jesus (Acts 17). It is interesting to contrast this with what Paul himself says about the pagan religions in his own writings. In his letter to the Romans Paul is quite blunt: pagans worship many gods not because they are ignorant. In fact, it is just the opposite: pagans know perfectly well there is only one God, and they've rejected that knowledge of God in order to worship other gods. Because they've known all along what they are doing, God is not at all forgiving of them, but is incensed and sends his wrath down upon them (Rom. 1:18–32).

Some interpreters have tried to reconcile these two passages by saying that Paul may have preached one thing when talking to polytheists, so as not to cause offense, even if he thought something else (as in Acts 17). Of course that's theoretically possible—that Paul refused to say what he really thought because he didn't want to offend somebody. But that hardly sounds like Paul, who made a career out of getting in trouble for his outspoken views. And it seems unlikely that Paul would say the opposite of what he really thought (as a kind of white lie) if he felt as strongly about it as he appears to have done in his own writings. Would he preach the opposite of what he believed? Would he propagate a misconception?

Other discrepancies between Paul and Acts have to do with the very heart of his mission. Paul saw himself as the apostle to the non-Jews, the Gentiles, who he insisted did not have to start following the laws of Judaism in order to become believers in Jesus. Paul insists that God called him specifically to this task of taking the gospel to the Gentiles. It is interesting to see that Luke, who wants harmony at every point, claims that it was *Peter* who started the Gentile mission, before Paul (Acts 10–11). Moreover, as we have seen, Peter and Paul are in complete harmony in the book of Acts when it comes to this Gentile mission (Acts 15). But not according to Paul. In his account, he and Peter have a rather nasty confrontation over just this issue in the city of Antioch (Gal. 2:11–14).

What is really telling is how little Paul himself is willing to accommodate the sensitivities of those Jewish Christians who continue to think that it is important for all people to keep the law God gave the Jews (as seen in the Antioch incident). At one point, Paul indicates that he absolutely refused to allow his Gentile companion Titus to be circumcised in order to placate those who believed circumcision was important for a right standing before God (Gal. 2:3). Titus was presumably grateful. But how *could* Paul have had Titus circumcised? Wouldn't that violate precisely his teaching that a person is made right with God by faith in Christ alone, not by following the laws God had given the Jews through Moses? Luke's "Paul" has a different view, however. According to Luke, Paul had another companion, Timothy, circumcised for just this reason, to placate the Jewish Christians they knew (Acts 16). Paul himself, of course, says nothing about having Timothy circumcised. How could he have done so when he sees this as standing diametrically opposed to his understanding of the gospel?

In even larger terms, the book of Acts paints a picture of Paul that would seem strange to anyone who knows Paul only through his own writings. In Acts, Paul is portrayed as a good Jew who never does anything that would compromise his commitment to keeping the entire body of Jewish law. Not so Paul, who claims that when with Gentiles, he lives "as one outside the law" (1 Cor. 9:21). Moreover, if all you had available was the book of Acts, you would not know some of the most important teachings of Paul. Even though he is portrayed as preaching his message in chapter after chapter of the account, you wouldn't know that Paul was an apocalypticist who was expecting the imminent end of the age, you wouldn't know that Paul thought that it was the cross of Jesus that brought about salvation, you wouldn't know that Paul taught his doctrine of justification by faith, you wouldn't know just how active women were in the churches that Paul established, and on and on.

Conclusion

I do not want this to seem like a harsh harangue on the book of Acts. In fact, I think Acts is a terrifically interesting and important book. The problem is that it has been misused over the years by interpreters who have thought that when they were reading the stories in Acts, they were reading history as it actually happened. To be sure, there is historically accurate information in Acts—about Peter, about Paul, about the early Christian movement. But the book is not principally a repository of historically factual data. It is a collection of stories about the early Christian movement and its chief apostles, especially Peter and

Paul. Some of these stories are rooted in historical fact, whereas others represent ways these apostles were remembered by one author (Luke) and the community that passed along the stories over the years before he heard them and wrote some of them down. If we want to know about the historical Paul, we will treat Acts for what it is and not pretend that it records events that you would have been able to capture on your camcorder if you had been there.

This is true of other accounts we have of Paul as well, as a number of legends sprang up about the apostle based to some extent on the things that actually happened in his life. At one point in his own writings, for example, Paul tells us that he had some kind of visionary experience, when he was "taken up to the third heaven" (2 Cor. 12:2). He doesn't tell us what he saw up there in the heavenly places, but later authors were far less discreet and tell us in detail all about Paul's ecstatic visions. And so we have two apocalypses claiming to portray Paul's visions, just as we have apocalypses allegedly by Peter.

Moreover, throughout his letters Paul indicates that he suffered persecution. And so we have accounts that describe in graphic detail what these persecutions entailed—such as the story of him being stoned and then getting up to go on his mission, and the story of his meeting up with his friend the baptized lion. There are also hints in Paul's letters that he expects soon to be executed. And so we have an account of what happened at his execution, which was quite an extraordinary and supernatural affair: when the executioner beheaded him, milk, instead of blood, squirted from his neck.

In the chapters that follow, then, we will be looking at the historical Paul himself, basing our examination principally on the letters that he wrote. At the same time we will look at the legends that sprang up about him—some of those from the New Testament and some from outside of it. Both of these matters—the historical and the legendary—will be important for understanding this great figure at the beginning of the Christian church, since stories about the actual, historical Paul and about the legendary Paul were remembered in later times.

Chapter Eight

Paul the Convert

Paul was undoubtedly the most important convert in the history of the Christian religion. But it is important to understand that, at least from his perspective, he was not converting from one religion (Judaism) to another (Christianity). For one thing, the terms *Christianity* and *Christian religion* are anachronistic: in Paul's day, such terms did not yet exist to denote a particular religion with its own beliefs, practices, scriptures, and so on. I will continue to use the terms here simply for the sake of convenience, as a kind of shorthand for "the religion adopted by the followers of Jesus."

But even more important, Paul did not understand that he was leaving one religion in order to adopt another. In his view, faith in Jesus as the messiah was the fulfillment and correct understanding of the religion that he had always embraced, the religion of his Jewish ancestors: it was, in a sense, "true" Judaism. To say he converted, therefore, is simply to say that he changed his view about one important aspect of his understanding of Judaism, an aspect that had enormous implications for everything else. He changed his views about Jesus, coming to think that he was God's messiah, who had died for the sins of others and then been raised from the dead.

To understand what this conversion toward faith in Jesus might have meant for Paul, we need to learn more about what his life and religion were like before he came to this new faith. What do we know about Paul *before* he became a Christian?

This is one of those areas of historical research—there are billions of them, actually—where we wish we had more extensive source material to work with. We can learn a few things from Paul's own letters, which can be supplemented by a cautious use of the stories found in the book of Acts, along with several inferences that can be drawn from the sheer facts of his writing—for example, the fact that he wrote in Greek, which among other things can tell us that he was educated enough to write and that he was thoroughly trained in Greek.

Paul's Life as a Jew in the Diaspora

There are two passages in Paul's letters that are especially useful in coming to an understanding of his earlier life. Writing to the Christians he had converted in the city of Philippi, Paul insists that if anyone had advantages before God for being a good, law-observant Jew, it was he:

> If anyone else thinks that he can be confident in his flesh, I have greater reason: I was circumcised on the eighth day, of the nation of Israel, and the tribe of Benjamin; a Hebrew born of Hebrews; with respect to the law, a Pharisee, with respect to zeal, a persecutor of the church, with respect to the righteousness that comes through the law, blameless. (Phil. 3:4–6)

And in a passage written to the Christians of Galatia, Paul stresses his serious commitment to the Jewish religion of his ancestors before believing in Christ:

> For you have heard of my former way of life in Judaism, that I persecuted the church of God to an extreme and was trying to destroy it; and I was advanced in Judaism beyond many of my own age in the nation, being more extremely zealous for our ancestral traditions. (Gal. 1:13–14)

At the very least, these passages tell us that prior to becoming a believer in Jesus, Paul was an inordinately religious Jew of the Pharisaic persuasion, who avidly persecuted the followers of Jesus. From the fact that he writes such a high-quality Greek, and from other hints in his letters and from statements in Acts, it is clear that his Jewish upbringing took place outside of Palestine, in what is known as the Jewish Diaspora.

The term *diaspora* literally means "dispersion." In this context it is used to refer to the fact that most Jews in Paul's day (and for centuries before and after) did not live in the Jewish homeland, which the Romans called Palestine, but throughout the world, with major communities located in such far-flung places as Alexandria Egypt, Babylon, and Rome.[1] Being a Jew outside of Palestine had some rather important implications. For one thing, it meant not speaking the same language as the Jews of Palestine, most of whom, like Peter and Jesus, would have spoken Aramaic. As with many highly educated people, Jew and non-Jew alike, Paul's native tongue was Greek. There is some question among scholars whether Paul could have spoken or read any other languages—an ongoing debate, for example, over whether he could have read the Jewish Scriptures in their original Hebrew or if, instead, he knew them in their Greek translation, usually called the Septuagint.[2]

Living in a Pagan World

Even more important than his native tongue is the fact that as a Jew in the Diaspora, Paul would have been surrounded by people embracing religions other than Judaism. Paul, unlike Jesus or Peter, was born and raised in a non-Jewish, "pagan" environment.

Demographic figures are difficult to come by for the ancient world, but most scholars put the population of the Roman Empire at this time at around sixty million people, with something like 7 percent of them Jews. Judaism, in other words, was a small minority religion in the empire as a whole. It is not that all other people were the *same* religion. Quite the contrary—there were hundreds and hundreds of religions around, all of them "minorities" when placed over against the rest of the populace. But most of the other religions held certain beliefs and practices in common, and to that extent it is possible to label them as "pagan."

It is impossible to do justice to the wide range of ancient pagan religions in just a few paragraphs, but a couple of broad generalizations can serve my purposes here. For one thing, all these religions were polytheistic, that is, they all believed in and worshiped many gods. For pagans, there were all sorts of gods and goddesses for all sorts of places and all sorts of functions. There were, of course, the great state gods, including those of Greek and Roman mythology, such as Zeus, Apollo, and Athena. These were understood to be superior, say, to local deities. But there were many other gods as well: gods of the fields, streams, and forests, gods of the cities and towns, gods of the home and hearth, gods of war and peace. There were gods who looked over the various aspects of human life that humans themselves were unable to control: weather, growth of crops, fertility of livestock, health, childbirth. All of these gods deserved worship. No one—apart from the Jews—thought that only one god was worthy of worship. For ancient peoples any such view was literally nonsense. Saying you were to worship only one god was like saying you were to have only one acquaintance or eat only one food or engage in only one activity.

There were two principal ways these various gods were worshiped throughout the empire: by prayer and by acts of sacrifice. Sacrifices were usually of foodstuffs, both vegetable and animal. Some kinds of sacrifices could be made almost anywhere, for example, pouring out a little wine as a sacrifice to the gods before eating, wherever you happened to be. Others, such as annual animal sacrifices on certain holy days, were to be made by specially appointed priests in sacred places, temples.

It was through proper worship that the gods were kept at peace, and so were inclined to do what was good for humans. If they were not placated sufficiently, disasters could happen: drought, famine, epidemic, earthquake, military defeat, and on and on.

There is almost nothing to suggest that any of the pagan religions was exclusive in nature, that is, that any of the gods insisted that if you worshiped him or her, you could not also worship other gods. In fact, the widespread assumption was that all the gods—as superhuman beings—deserved their due; worshiping one had no bearing on whether you also wanted to or were allowed to worship another.

The worship of these gods was typically undertaken according to long-standing, sometimes very ancient custom, in which ritualistic acts of prayer and sacrifice were followed according to set patterns, handed down from one generation to the next. In almost none of these religions were there sacred books containing revelations from the deity concerning how worship was to be conducted. And there was almost no sense of a divine revelation from the deity that was to govern what one was to believe or how one was to behave in daily life. In fact, both doctrine and ethics were of little concern to the pagan religions. This is not to say that pagans were unethical; on the contrary, so far as we can tell, most ancient pagans were about as ethical as most people are today. But ethics was not something taught within the religions, which instead focused on proper modes of prayer and sacrifice to the gods.

On Being a Jew

What would have made a good, upright, highly religious Jew such as Paul stand out in the pagan world? For one thing, Jews were unique for insisting that only one God was to be worshiped and glorified. Many Jews continued to think that other gods did exist. And most Jews had no problem with pagans worshiping whatever gods they wanted. That is to say, most Jews were not missionary, trying to convert others to their religion. But Jews did insist that for themselves, there was only one God, the God of the Jewish ancestors.

Jews also maintained that they were this God's chosen people. The traditions about the ancestors had largely to do with their calling to be a "special people": they were to be God's people, and in exchange, he would be their God. Jews understood, in fact, that God had made a covenant, a kind of political peace treaty, with them. So long as they followed his prescriptions for how they were to worship him and live in community together, he would protect and defend them. Jews, then, were a covenantal community. They were related to one another by blood (except when a non-Jew would go through the rituals of conversion). And they were related to God through a special covenant involving set acts of worship, devotion, and communal life.

The actual acts of Jewish worship, in themselves, were not all that different from the acts of worship in pagan religions: they involved prayers and sacrifices made to God, the latter in a sacred place. Most Jews insisted that the only place for animal sacrifices was in the Temple of God that had been built in the holy city Jerusalem, in Judea—unlike the pagan religions, where temples, say, to Zeus could be found throughout the empire. The procedures for these sacrifices were spelled out in the Jewish writings, which I have earlier referred to as the Torah (the word is sometimes translated as "law").

de it distinct in the religious
n authorities as sacred books.
es and traditions contained in
nd of act of worship. A highly
in the Jewish Scriptures inside
Torah and other sacred books,
remiah, and Ezekiel and some

ctioned for a range of occasions
en instituted by God to allow his
Only priests could perform these
f those others—nonpriests—who
of course, would have a difficult
usalem. For someone such as Paul,
as an occasional pilgrimage to the
pelled out in the Torah.
f Jewish parents, circumcised on the
eighth day, and raised m...   ancestral traditions than most of his
peers, he is saying that he took his commitment to the God of the Jews and to
the Jewish Scriptures with utmost seriousness. Paul was nothing if not serious.
He must have been enormously learned in the texts of Scripture from an early
age. He claims that with respect to the righteousness that could be found in the
law—that is, with respect to doing the things that the law demands of those
who stood in a covenantal relationship with God—he was "blameless." It is
worth emphasizing this point because many readers (Christians especially)
have thought that Paul had a real guilt complex when it came to the law, that he
saw Jewish law as a terrible taskmaster that made unreasonable demands on
people and then punished them for not keeping them. This does not seem to
have been Paul's view, at least as a righteous Jew before coming to faith in
Christ. He appears, on the contrary, to have been like most other righteous
Jews of his day, who saw the law as the greatest gift God had given his people,
and a joy to keep. Rather than claiming to have an enormous burden of guilt
imposed by the law, Paul claims that as far as doing what the righteous demands of the law were concerned, he was "blameless."

Paul also tells us that he was a Pharisee before he came to believe that Jesus
was the messiah. Most of my students—perhaps most Christians—have the
wrong idea about Pharisees in the time of Paul. We are unfortunately hampered yet again by our historical sources in knowing what the Pharisees actually stood for. We have only one author of surviving writings who is known by
name from among the Pharisees before the time the Jerusalem Temple was
destroyed (70 CE). As it turns out, it's the apostle Paul. His surviving writings,
of course, are only those that he produced after converting to faith in Christ. (It
would be absolutely stunning if some of Paul's pre-Christian writings were
discovered. One can only imagine what they must have looked like.) In any

event, we can piece together some information about Pharisees in Paul's day from later references to them—for example, from later writings of the Jewish rabbis and the writings of the Christians who opposed them, and from Paul.

One thing that can be said about Pharisees is that the most common stereotype about them is almost certainly wrong. In the dictionary, today, if you look up the word *Pharisee* you'll find as one of the later definitions "hypocrite." This has always struck me as bizarre—somewhat like defining *Episcopalian* as "drunkard" or *Baptist* as "adulterer." To be sure, there are no doubt Episcopalian alcoholics and Baptist philanderers, just as there must have been Pharisaic hypocrites. But as I tell my students, agreeing to commit hypocrisy was not an entrance requirement for the Pharisaic party. There was no hypocritic oath.

One thing we do know about the Pharisees is that they strove to follow God's law as rigorously as they could.[4] This doesn't make them hypocrites; it makes them religious. Their view is understandable: if God gave a law, shouldn't we try our best to keep it? Pharisees in Paul's day developed a set of oral traditions, sometimes called the "traditions of the elders," which were intended to enable people to keep the written laws of Moses. That is, Pharisees were strict interpreters. One of the ways they were strict—with respect to themselves, at least—is that they appear to have believed that the laws of purity that governed how the priests were to conduct themselves in the Temple in Jerusalem were to be followed in their own daily lives. Doesn't Scripture itself teach that the people of God (Israel) are a "kingdom of priests" (see Exod. 19:6)?

So, for example, if in the Torah priests are told they must wash their hands before performing a sacrifice, then Pharisees taught that they themselves should wash their hands before eating a meal. The life of the priest was to be the life of the ordinary person, seeking to lead a purified existence before God. Paul evidently accepted these Pharisaic teachings. He was, in short, a highly religious Jew, fully conversant with the Jewish traditions found in the Scriptures, and particularly keen to implement the religious teachings of Scripture in his daily life.

Other Traditions about the Early Paul

In addition to the evidence of Paul's devotion to Judaism, there are other traditions about Paul's early life found, for example, in the book of Acts—not in his own writings—that are more difficult to accept as historically authentic. Instead, they appear to represent what the author of Acts, Luke, would have wanted to say about Paul, as he remembered the life of the great apostle. Even though some of these have been widely accepted by modern readers, scholars among them, I think they may be more the stuff of legend than history. With some of them it is difficult to say.

For example, Luke indicates that Paul sometimes went by a Hebrew name, Saul. I should stress that Luke does not indicate that Paul's "Jewish" name was

Saul and that when he converted to follow Jesus his name was changed to "Paul"—as one often hears. On the contrary, even in the book of Acts, he is sometimes called Saul after his conversion (Acts 12:25). This is simply his Hebrew, as opposed to Greek, name. Whether that was really the name he took in Aramaic-speaking circles is anyone's guess. As I noted earlier, Paul actually came from a Greek-speaking, rather than Aramaic-speaking, environment. It may be that Luke wanted to stress his extreme Jewishness by giving him a name that had clear Jewish resonances: the first king of ancient Israel in the Jewish Scriptures was also named Saul.

Luke also claims that Paul was originally from the city of Tarsus in Cilicia (Acts 22:3). Again, this is something that Paul himself never says a word about. It is clear that Paul must have come from some relatively large urban setting in the Jewish Diaspora, and this may have been Tarsus. But we really cannot say for sure. Here again, Luke may have had reasons of his own to locate Paul originally in Tarsus: in antiquity, Tarsus was known as one of the great philosophical centers of the empire, one of the two or three best places for a person to develop his philosophical and rhetorical abilities—at least according to Strabo, the great Roman geographer and describer of exotic places (*Geography*, 13). Luke may have wanted to assist Paul in his intellectual pedigree by making him a resident of a great city of philosophical discourse.

Luke also claims that Paul, as a young man, came to study Judaism in Jerusalem with the great rabbi of his day, Gamaliel (Acts 22:3). This tradition is even more unlikely than the others. Paul himself would have had good reasons to emphasize his educational pedigree when highlighting his pre-Christian credentials in the passages I quoted above, but he is silent about the specifics of his training. In fact, Paul gives no clear indication at all that he was familiar with distinctively Aramaic/Hebrew modes of interpretation: he is thoroughly at home with the Greek Septuagint, on the other hand. Luke, however, would have had plenty of reasons to claim that Paul was trained "at the feet of Gamaliel": this provides the hero of his Acts with the very best Jewish education one could have, with the most famous rabbi of his day, in Jerusalem itself. If these were the circles Paul himself actually ran in, however, it is virtually impossible to explain some of the things that he says in his letters, for example, that the Jewish people who converted to worship Jesus in Judea didn't know him in person—even what he looked like. It appears Paul had never spent much, if any, time in Jerusalem, the capital of Judea, before he became a follower of Jesus.

The book of Acts also indicates that Paul was trained as a professional "tent maker" (Acts 18:3). This is certainly possible, as Paul does refer in some of his letters to supporting himself by working with his hands. He never states what it is that he did. But leatherworking may certainly have been one of the options, whether that involved making tents, belts, or saddles—the word that Luke uses could be interpreted in a variety of ways.

One claim in Acts that recurs in later legends about Paul is that he was a Roman citizen (Acts 22:25). This has struck some historians as highly unlikely. Paul himself never says anything of the sort, and in fact very few Jews were actually citizens of the empire. For one thing, being a citizen meant performing occasional sacrifices to the gods for the well-being of the state. Jews who didn't adhere to some kind of strict Judaism would probably have had few qualms about the matter. But a highly religious Jew such as Paul? It seems unlikely. Moreover, citizenship in this period was, for the most part, restricted to the elite. Paul, on the other hand, even though he was well educated, appears to have been strictly working-class. Here again it may be that Luke is trying to stress just how prominent Paul was—a citizen of Rome, even—before his conversion.

One other description of Paul survives from our ancient sources, this time not from the book of Acts in the New Testament but from an extracanonical book called the Acts of Paul and Thecla. This is a fictional account of the exploits of Paul and his female disciple Thecla, written sometime in the second half of the second century. In it we are told what Paul looked like, and the description is not highly complimentary. We are told that a Christian named Onesiphorus was looking for Paul among the people on the road coming into town, and all he had to go on was a description given him by Titus. Paul was said to be short, bald, bowlegged, in good shape, but with eyebrows that met and a fairly large nose. Some scholars have argued that an ancient reader would have taken this as a positive description, but most don't think so. It appears, in fact, to be the description of someone who is weak, sensual, a bit lazy, not overly intelligent, and a shade cunning.[5]

Why would the Acts of Paul and Thecla portray him this way? There are several possible explanations: one is that the entire point of the narrative is that Paul's superiority was not rooted in his physical presence and demeanor— much like Socrates, one of the greatest philosophers of all time, who was also reported to have been unusually ugly. Another is that the author of this account wants to show that the virgin Thecla's attachment to Paul cannot be explained as a kind of physical attraction, such as happens frequently in fiction from the period, where an astoundingly beautiful girl sees an astoundingly beautiful boy and they both fall madly in love at first sight and forever. Thecla does become obsessed with Paul, but it's not because of his preternaturally good looks!

This account is probably not a historical reflection of what Paul actually looked like. About that, we are completely ignorant. It is a description of what this author imagined him to have looked like. If God could work his power through anyone this ugly, he could work his power through anyone.

Paul as a Persecutor of the Christians

The book of Acts and Paul's own biographical references agree that prior to becoming a follower of Christ, Paul was an avid and violent persecutor of the

Christian church. According to Acts, Paul received authorization from the high priest in Jerusalem to drag Christians off to prison. This too is historically implausible: the high priest in Jerusalem had no jurisdiction over Jews living in other parts of the empire, and Paul himself says nothing about it. He does, however, say that he was a zealous persecutor of the Christians. And why was that? What led Paul not only to reject the Christian message about Jesus but even to oppose, to the point of violence (whatever that entailed), those who proclaimed Jesus to be the messiah?

Once again we are handcuffed by our sparse source material. Some scholars have argued that Paul was frightened by the early Christian movement, that he was afraid of what might happen to the broader Jewish population if the Romans got wind of this upstart new religion. The logic would be that if the Roman authorities learned that a Jewish sect had begun to worship a criminal crucified by the state as a future "king," they might not take kindly to the development and react against it. This explanation strikes me as a bit too speculative. Why would Roman leaders punish non-Christian Jews for what a breakaway Jewish sect was saying? Moreover, Paul never shows fear of Roman reprisals after becoming a follower of Jesus and never hints that this was his problem with Christians before he himself converted.

One of the earliest surviving portrayals of Jesus's crucifixion, from a miniature ivory panel of the fourth century. For Paul, Jesus's crucifixion was the key to salvation.

Some scholars have suggested that Paul persecuted Christians because they were teaching Gentile converts not to keep the Jewish law. Again, this makes some superficial sense, for surely such an avid keeper of the law as Paul would be offended by converts to a form of Judaism who saw no need to follow the commandments of God. But there's very little to suggest that *Jewish* believers in Christ had stopped keeping the law before Paul showed up on the scene. On the contrary, the earliest believers in Jesus were Jewish and continued on in their Jewish ways. Moreover, from what we can tell, they urged their Gentile converts to become Jews so that they could follow the Jewish messiah. It is not at all clear that there were large numbers of Gentiles converting to become Jesus' followers prior to the conversion of Paul, just a few years after Jesus' crucifixion. It was Paul himself, after his conversion, who believed he had been called by God to convert the Gentiles. He explicitly states that he had to convince those who were Christian leaders before him that Gentiles should not be required to keep the law.

There may be a better explanation for what Paul found to be so offensive in the Christian claims about Jesus before he himself converted, an explanation hinted at in Paul's own writings later in life. Paul may have been incensed precisely at the claim that Jesus was the messiah.

What would have been offensive about this claim? On one level, it is what we have already seen: Jews who were expecting the messiah (and not all of them were) anticipated that the messiah would be someone great and glorious, a powerful warrior-king, for example, or a cosmic figure sent from heaven to overthrow God's enemies. And who was Jesus? A crucified criminal.

We can be even a bit more specific than this. In a previous chapter I talked about Jewish apocalypticists. From what little we know about Pharisees, it appears that they adhered to apocalyptic views. This means that Paul would have been an apocalyptic Jew even before coming to believe in Jesus. He would have believed, for example, that the current age was evil but was soon to come to an end, when God intervened in the course of history and brought in his good kingdom on earth, through his powerful messiah. What would it be like for someone with this kind of belief to hear that Jesus, in particular, was the messiah? It would have seemed absolutely ridiculous, and a slur against God himself. For Jesus was not a great and powerful figure come from God, but an itinerant prophet from backwoods Galilee who got on the wrong side of the law and suffered a weak, humiliating, painful death at the hands of the Romans. This was not someone who had conquered God's enemies; he was a gnat that the enemy had swatted. Saying that he was God's chosen one was tantamount to saying that God himself was weak and powerless in this world dominated by Rome—blasphemous!

But there was something even more offensive about the claim that Jesus, in particular, was the Jewish messiah, something that made the claim yet more troubling than the fact that Jesus had none of the characteristics that the messiah was supposed to have and did none of the things that the messiah was supposed to do. This was the fact that he was crucified. It was the specific mode of his execution that may have particularly angered Paul once anyone claimed that Jesus was the messiah. Paul tells us in one of his later writings what the problem was with crucifixion in particular: Scripture indicates that anyone who is "hanged on a tree" (as happens during crucifixion) is cursed by God himself. The Torah teaches, "Cursed is anyone who hangs on a tree" (Deut. 21:23; quoted in Gal. 3:13).

For Paul, someone who was crucified, as opposed to being stoned or beheaded, for example, stood under God's curse. To claim that a crucified man was God's messiah was therefore not simply ridiculous but completely scandalous, for it contradicted what God himself had said. Someone hanged on a tree was the furthest thing from being under God's special favor; he was under God's curse. Jesus was cursed by God; he wasn't his Christ.

It appears that Paul was so incensed by the claim that this Jewish teacher was the messiah of God that he went on the attack, trying to stamp out this outrageous form of Judaism. But then, in one of the greatest turnarounds in the history of religion, the outspoken opponent of Christ became his greatest apostle; the persecutor became the proclaimer. The conversion of Paul was a cataclysmic moment, not just for his own life but also for the life of the fledgling Christian church, which was soon empowered to move outside its Jewish matrix to become a religious influence on the early empire, a religion that would eventually convert the empire, leading to the unprecedented upheavals of religious and social life in the centuries that were to follow in Paul's wake.

Paul and the Resurrection of Jesus

There is little doubt, historically, about what converted Paul. He had a vision of Jesus raised from the dead. This is what he himself says, and it is recorded as one of the key incidents in the book of Acts.

Acts, as we have seen, narrates the tale on three occasions: the narrator himself describes the event in chapter 9, Paul recounts it to a hostile crowd in chapter 22, and he speaks of it again at his trial in chapter 26. There are differences among these three accounts, making it difficult to know what, exactly, the author of Acts wants us to think happened. But the basic story line is similar. According to the fullest description, in Acts 9, Paul has been given authorization by the Jerusalem high priest to track down followers of Jesus in the Jewish synagogues of Damascus, Syria, so that he might capture them and bring them back as prisoners to face charges in Jerusalem.

Before Paul can arrive in Damascus, though, he has a life-transforming revelation. While on the road, a light flashes around him, he is knocked to the ground, and he hears a voice: "Saul, Saul, why are you persecuting me?" He replies, "Who are you Lord?" And the voice responds, "I am Jesus, whom you are persecuting; but rise up and enter the city and you will be told what to do" (9:1–6). Paul is temporarily blinded by the light. Led by the hand, he is taken into Damascus, where a Christian named Ananias is instructed by Jesus in a dream to lay his hands on Paul, heal him, and give him instructions. In particular, he is told that Paul "is a chosen vessel for me to bear my name before the Gentiles and kings and the children of Israel" (Acts 9:15). Ananias does as he is instructed; Paul regains his sight and is baptized, presumably by Ananias. And so we have the conversion of Paul.

This is a turning point in the narrative of the book of Acts, for immediately after Paul's conversion we have the story of Cornelius, the first Gentile to believe in Jesus (Acts 10–11). This leads up to the stories of Paul's missionary journeys among the Gentiles, as he converts pagans in the cities of Asia Minor, Macedonia, and Achaia (modern Turkey and Greece), laying the foundation for the church as a worldwide religion comprising not only Jews but also, significantly, Gentiles.

Paul himself, in his own writings, also claims that his conversion was a call from God to take the gospel to the Gentiles. He is much more reticent than the book of Acts to describe what happened at the time. In his brief autobiographical comments in his letter to the Galatians he simply says:

> When God, the one who set me apart for something special from my mother's womb and called me through his grace, was well pleased to reveal his Son to me, so that I might proclaim his good news among the Gentiles, I did not immediately consult with flesh and blood nor go to Jerusalem to those who were apostles before me, but I departed for Arabia and again I went away to Damascus. (Gal. 1:15–17)

Here Paul portrays his conversion as a special calling from God, just as prophets in the Hebrew Bible were called by God to fulfill his will among the people of Israel (see, for example, Isaiah 49:5; Jeremiah 1:5). In Paul's case, however, God's call involves taking the message of salvation not to Jews but to Gentiles. That is to say, God fulfilled the promises of the prophets that the entire world will come to worship him alone and join the covenant community of Israel. This is made possible by the death and resurrection of Jesus, and Paul himself is to be the one who proclaims this good news to former pagans.

But what does Paul mean that God was pleased "to reveal his Son to me"? Does he mean that he finally realized that Jesus was not the cursed of God but the Christ of God? It appears that he does mean at least that. But what caused the change? Was it simply a moment of inspiration? We get further information on what motivated Paul's conversion in a brief comment that he makes about Jesus' death and resurrection in a famous passage in his first letter to the Corinthians:

> For I delivered to you among the most important matters what I also received, that Christ died for our sins in accordance with the Scriptures, and that he was buried; and that he was raised on the third day in accordance with the Scriptures, and that he appeared to Cephas, then to the twelve; then he appeared to more

than five hundred brothers at one time . . . then he appeared to James, then to all the apostles; and last of all, as to a miscarriage, he appeared also to me. For I am the least of the apostles, and am not worthy to be an apostle since I persecuted the church of God. But I am what I am by the grace of God, and his grace that is in me has not been bestowed in vain. (1 Cor. 15:3–10)

And so, as is also recorded in the book of Acts, Paul indicates that he had a vision of Jesus after he had been raised from the dead. This must have been two or three years after Jesus' death. The vision showed Paul beyond any reasonable doubt that Jesus—who had been crucified, dead, and buried—had come back to life. There was only one possible explanation for Jesus coming back to life: God must have raised him from the dead. And if God raised him from the dead—well, that changed everything.

Paul's New View of Jesus

To understand how Paul's thinking was radically disrupted by his belief that he had seen Jesus alive after his crucifixion, it is important to realize that all of his subsequent reflections on everything of importance to him—including the nature of God, the question of how people are put into a right relationship with God, the relationship of Jews and non-Jews before God, the matter of when the world as we know it would come to an end—were changed by this vision of Jesus. The way to imagine this radical change of understanding is to recognize, as New Testament scholar E. P. Sanders has put it, that Paul started "thinking backwards."[6] That is to say, starting from what he knew to be true, that he saw Jesus alive after his death, he reasoned backward to understand anew the implications for everything else that mattered to him.

First of all, of course, was his view of Jesus. For if Jesus was alive, then God had raised him from the dead. And if God had raised him from the dead, then that must mean that he was the one whom God especially favored. Paul, like other Christians before him, began searching through the Scriptures, or through his vast recollection of what was in the Scriptures, and started thinking about all those passages in the Hebrew Bible that speak of God's vindication of his Righteous One, who had been violently and wrongly mistreated by those who were unrighteous—passages, no doubt, such as Psalm 22:

Dogs are all around me; a company of evildoers encircles me. My hands and feet have shriveled; I can count all my bones. They stare and gloat over me; they divide my cloths among themselves, and for my clothing they cast lots. But you, O Lord, do not be far away! O my help, come quickly to my aid! Deliver my soul from the sword, my life from the power of the dog! . . . All the ends of the earth shall remember and turn to the Lord; and all the families of the nations shall worship before him. For dominion belongs to the Lord, and he rules over the nations. (Psalm 22:16–20, 27–28)

Or possibly Isaiah 53:

> Surely he has borne our infirmities and carried our diseases; yet we accounted
> him stricken, struck down by God, and afflicted. But he was wounded for our
> transgressions, crushed for our iniquities; upon him was the punishment that
> made us whole, and by his bruises we are healed. All we like sheep have gone
> astray; we have all turned to our own way, and the Lord has laid on him the
> iniquity of us all. . . . Yet it was the will of the Lord to crush him with pain.
> When you make his life an offering for sin, he shall see his offspring, and you
> shall prolong his days. (Isaiah 53: 4–6, 10).

If God vindicated Jesus, which he obviously must have done, since Jesus
was alive again, then that must mean, Paul reasoned, that he was the Righteous
One who suffered unjustly at the hands of others.

But how could Jesus be God's Righteous One if he was in fact crucified?
For doesn't Scripture indicate that the one who hangs on a tree is cursed by
God (Deut. 21:23)? Paul began very quickly to think that yes, Jesus was cursed.
But he must not have been cursed for his *own* unrighteous acts, since he was
God's Righteous One. He must have been cursed for the unrighteous acts of
others. That is to say, Jesus did only what was right, and suffered for the sake
of others who had violated God's will and stood under his wrath. Jesus took
the wrath of God (his "curse") upon himself for others. His suffering and death,
in other words, were vicarious: he died for the sake of others, so that they
themselves would not have to pay the price for their own sins. Christ's death
ransomed others from the just payment of death.

Since God raised Jesus from the dead, the death of Jesus must itself have
been according to the plan of God. It wasn't simply an act of Roman oppression or a miscarriage of justice. God wanted Jesus to die for the sake of others.
But if it is Jesus' death that puts people into a right standing before God, what
about the covenant God made with Israel, that he would be their God and they
would be his people, as seen by the fact that they keep the law he gave them?

Paul's New View of Salvation

Paul, thinking backward still, came to believe that it was only through the
death of Jesus that a person could be made right with God. That must mean
that the law God had given the Jews was *not* instrumental in how a person was
put right with God. The only thing that mattered for salvation was the death of
God's chosen one. By implication, then, all people could participate in the
salvation brought by Jesus' death, both the Jews who had the law and the Gentiles who did not. Paul immediately saw the key implication of this new revelation of God's plan: the message needed to be taken to the Gentiles so that
they too could be saved. They would not be saved by becoming Jews and

keeping the law. All that mattered for salvation was the death and resurrection of God's chosen one.

In sum, right off the bat Paul realized that he had been given a revelation of Jesus because he was to be the one to take this good news (the gospel) to pagans, to convert them to believe in the one God of the Jews and Jesus his Son, whose death brought salvation, apart from the law.

As Paul reflected more on the implications of this understanding of salvation, he came to a new understanding of Jewish law, in which he was so thoroughly trained and which he had so vigorously attempted to keep. Even though he saw himself as "blameless" before the law, Paul came to think that this was not what was required for a right standing before God. As he points out in Philippians:

> For [Christ's] sake I have suffered the loss of all things and consider them excrement, so that I might gain Christ, and be found in him, not having my own righteousness that comes through law, but the righteousness that comes through having faith in Christ, the righteousness that comes from God and is received by faith. (Phil. 3:8–9)

Paul came to realize that there was a problem posed by the law of God given to the Jews.[7] According to the law, the faithful Jew, one who keeps the law, will be given "life," that is, an eternal right standing before God. In itself that was not a problem. Nor was there a problem with the law per se. Even after converting to believe in Jesus, Paul continued to think that the law was "holy, and the commandment [of God] is holy, righteous, and good" (Rom. 7:12). The problem was that the law promises life to those who keep it, but people are hindered from keeping it because they are enslaved to the power of sin that is in the world.

Today most people think of sin—if they think of it at all—as something that a person does that is wrong, a violation of what God wants. But for Paul, sin was not simply an act of wrongdoing. As an apocalypticist, he believed that there were cosmic, demonic forces in the world that were aligned against God and that compelled people to behave in ways contrary to God. Sin was one of these demonic forces. Ever since Adam and Eve allowed sin to come into the world, it had dominated the human race (Rom. 5:12–21). As a result, the law of God told people what they needed to do, and its demands were righteous. But ultimately people couldn't do what the law demanded, because they were under the power of sin (Rom. 7:7–25).

Now, it is true that the law itself makes provision for what to do when one sins. That's why it prescribes sacrifices to be made when a person violates what God otherwise demanded. But the fact that Israel needed a sacrificial system in the first place showed that the law itself acknowledges that everyone is under the power of sin, that is, that no one can really do everything that God wants. And so even if Paul once thought of himself as "blameless" before the law (perhaps in that he periodically had a sacrifice performed for his transgressions), he still could not be perfect in God's eyes—until, that is, Jesus died on the cross and bore the sins of others, making it possible for people to be pure in the sight of God.

For Paul, the death of Jesus was, on one hand, a radically new thing that God had done in order to bring salvation to his people. No longer did anyone have to rely on the sacrifices in the Temple for a right standing before God. The perfect sacrifice had now been made. On the other hand, this was not a completely new thing, because it had been part of God's plan all along. This is part of Paul's new realization that came on the heels of his experience of Jesus' resurrection.

The prophets of the Hebrew Bible had predicted that there would come a time when the law of God would no longer be something external to people—demands placed on them that had to be kept. It would be internal—"written on their hearts," as the prophet Jeremiah said (Jeremiah 31). Paul thought this day had now come. Those who believe in the death of Jesus are removed from their old ways of sin and set free to do what God really wants them to do. This happens because when people are baptized as Christians, the Spirit of God comes into them and gives them new life and real power. This is true of all people, Jews and Gentiles. Those who believe in Jesus and are baptized in his name are therefore not only given a right standing before God but also given the power to do the things that his righteous law demands of them (Gal. 5:16–25).

This, then, is a "new" covenant that God has made with his people, which is actually a fulfillment of the old covenant, in that it was anticipated by the ancient prophets. Christ is therefore the fulfillment of what God had planned all along, or as Paul puts it in one place, Christ is the "goal" (or the "end point") of the law (Rom. 10:4).

Paul's New View of the Law

Many Christians today seem to have a rather skewed view of what Jewish law is all about. Some of my students think that Judaism is built on a system of "do's and don'ts"—there are lots of things you have to do (observe the Sabbath) and lots more things that you can't do (eat ham sandwiches), and it's all a huge burden that no one could possibly bear. That's why, in their view, Jews need Christ, because the law leads only to their condemnation, whereas Christ brings salvation. I say this view is skewed because it is not the view of Jews themselves, either now or in the ancient world. Virtually all the Jewish writings from antiquity talk about the law as the greatest thing ever, God's gift to his people to show them how to live and how to worship him. How could there be anything wrong with the law? It tells you God's will and gives helpful guidance about life itself.

This was originally Paul's view as well. Jews were God's chosen people, and observing the law was an act of gratitude and a mark of prestige. But

Paul's view changed once he came to think that Jesus' death is what puts a person in a right covenantal relationship with God.

In looking back on his former life in Judaism, Paul appears to have come to think that the point of the law was not to assure Jews that they were in a secure covenantal relationship with God. God gave the law as a great gift to his people, to be sure. But the gift was a way of showing them his own righteous demands. As Paul puts it in one place, the "law was given on account of transgressions" (Gal. 3:19). That is, it was a pointer to the way God wanted his people to live, and a kind of "custodian" (one who watches over children to make sure they go the right way; Gal. 3:24) to help God's people keep to God's paths.

But Paul evidently came to think that Jews (many Jews? all Jews? himself as a non-Christian Jew?) had misused the law, in that they thought by keeping it they had secured their salvation before God (Rom. 10:3). This, Paul came to believe, was a mistake. Anyone who tried to be justified—that is, put in a right standing before God—by keeping the law instead fell under a curse (Gal. 2:15–16). It is only when people receive God's Spirit, which happens when they are baptized into Christ, that they can do what the law commands (Gal. 5:14; 16–18).

And here is where one of the most difficult aspects of Paul's thought comes into play. If having the Spirit enables one to do what the law commands, which is obviously a good thing, then you would think that Paul would go on to insist that people do just that: keep all of the laws of Scripture. These laws include things such as being circumcised if you are a male, keeping kosher food laws, observing the Sabbath, celebrating certain special holidays, offering sacrifices for sins, and so on. Yet Paul is absolutely clear that he thinks that non-Jews are not to do these things once they believe in Christ. In fact, in his most vitriolic letter, the one to the Galatians, he lays a curse on anyone who thinks that Gentiles who have come to believe in Jesus should engage in such practices (1:8–9; 2:15–16; 3:10–14). How can Paul have it both ways, thinking that the law should be kept (and is able to be kept by those who have God's Spirit) and thinking that the law must not be kept?

Scholars have a field day with questions such as this, with scholarly opinion ranging all over the map.[8] In my view, the easiest way to solve the problem is to say that Paul somehow imagines that there are two basic kinds of laws given in the Jewish Scriptures. There are some laws that are meant for Jews to show that they are members of God's covenantal community, including the laws mentioned above, of circumcision, kosher diet, Sabbath observance, and so on. These are laws that make Jews Jewish. But salvation in Christ, for Paul, is not for Jews only; it is for Jews and Gentiles. Gentiles are not expected to become Jews in order to be right with God. If they had to do anything of the sort, it would show that the death of Jesus itself was not sufficient for a right standing before God. But it is the death of Jesus alone that makes a person right with God. Gentiles who think they have to become Jews (for example, by being circumcised) have completely misunderstood the gospel.

There is, however, the other kind of law found in Scripture. This is the kind of law that applies to all people—for example, not to murder, not to commit adultery, not to bear false witness, and to love your neighbor as yourself. Everyone, Jew and Gentile, needs to keep these laws. Those who are in Christ are able to keep these laws because the Spirit of God empowers them to do so. So it is not by keeping the law that one is right with God. But one who is right with God will keep the law, at least the law that is designed for all people, though not the law designed to show who is Jewish and who is Gentile. For that reason, even though Paul taught a "law-free gospel"—that is, that a right standing before God does not come from keeping the law—he did not, at least in his opinion, teach a "lawless gospel," that is, a gospel that leads to wild and lawless behavior. Believers in Christ are still expected to live moral upright lives, and the Spirit enables them to do so.

Finally, I should point out one of the most striking aspects of Paul's teaching about the salvation of God that comes apart from the law. Paul claims this teaching is taught by the law itself. In other words, he did not see himself as innovative, coming up with a new religion distinct from Judaism. In his view, his understanding of Jesus as the fulfillment of God's promises to Israel (the promised messiah) was a fulfillment of Judaism. Throughout his writings he appeals to Scripture itself as "proof" for his views. In one famous passage, for example, he points to the father of the Jews, Abraham, who was not, Paul insists, put into a right standing before God by keeping the law (Rom. 4; see also Gal. 3), for Abraham lived centuries before the law was even given. Instead, Abraham was put into a right standing before God because he had faith: "And Abraham believed God, and it was counted to him as righteousness" (Gen. 15:6; quoted by Paul in Rom. 4:3 and Gal. 3:6). For Paul, Abraham pointed the way for all future generations: the Torah itself shows that keeping Torah is not what gives a person a right standing before God, but having faith does. And for Paul, that means faith in what God has now done in fulfillment of the Scriptures, in having Christ die for sins and then being raised from the dead.

Paul's New View of the End of Time

Even as a Pharisee, before his conversion, Paul held to apocalyptic views of the world. Like other apocalypticists, he believed that the present age was dominated by evil forces (such as sin and death, and probably other demonic powers), but that a new age was coming in which God would overthrow evil and bring in a good kingdom where he alone would rule supreme. As with most apocalypticists, Paul probably thought the end of the age was coming very soon.

Once he came to believe that Christ was raised from the dead, Paul did not jettison his apocalyptic expectations. On the contrary, knowing that Jesus had been brought back to life radically confirmed what Paul had already thought, that the end was imminent. But there was one key difference: it would be Jesus himself who brought it.

Like other Pharisees, Paul had thought that the present age would end in a cataclysmic event that would bring this world and all its powers to a crashing halt and usher in the new kingdom. At the end, there would be a resurrection of the dead.

The idea that dead people would be raised from the dead was not shared by all Jews in Paul's day, or before. In fact, you won't find the idea of a future resurrection in most of the Hebrew Bible, only in some of the final books to be written. Most of the writers of the Hebrew Bible thought that when people died, either they would cease to exist or they would go on living in some kind of netherworld called Sheol.

The idea that there would be a future resurrection in which dead bodies were brought back to life came into existence only a couple of centuries before Paul and Jesus. It arose among Jews who were trying to explain how this world could be such a cesspool of suffering, even for the people of God, if God was the one who was ultimately in control of it. Their solution was that God might not *seem* to be in charge of this world, but he ultimately was, and he would demonstrate his control at the end, when all the forces of evil and the people who sided with them would face judgment for their opposition to God and his purposes—even dead people. At the end of this evil age, the dead would be raised, and those who sided with God would be treated to eternal bliss; those who sided with the powers of evil, and thrived as a result, would be subjected to eternal torment. God would have the last word, and there was nothing any-one could do to stop him. We have seen that this was the teaching of Jesus. It was also the belief of other apocalypticists of his day, including Paul.

Now, if the resurrection was an event that was to happen at the end of the age, what would an apocalypticist such as Paul naturally conclude if he came to believe that Jesus had been raised from the dead? He would conclude that the resurrection of the end of days had started—which meant he was living at the end of the age, and the whole thing was about to come to a crashing halt. And it was to be brought by Jesus.

Why Jesus? Because he was the first one God raised from the dead, to be the leader of all those who now would also be raised. That is why Paul speaks of Jesus as "the first fruit of the resurrection" (see 1 Cor. 15:20, 23). This is an agricultural metaphor: just as when the harvest is ready, the farmer goes out to bring in the "first fruit," and then the next day goes for the rest, so too with Jesus: he was the first to be raised from the dead, and everyone else would follow. And when would that be? The metaphor suggested it would be right away. (The farmer doesn't wait years to get the rest of the harvest in, but gathers it in the next day.) For Paul, the resurrection of the dead was about to occur, and people needed to be ready. No wonder he felt such urgency in his proclamation of the gospel. For Paul, the world was soon to come to a screaming climax and the word needed to be proclaimed. Everyone needed a chance to be put in a good standing with God, or else they would face judgment when the end arrived.

The End of Time in 1 Thessalonians

One of the most interesting passages in all of Paul's writings occurs in his first surviving letter, 1 Thessalonians. This is a warm and loving letter (in contrast to Galatians), in which Paul is responding to some of the concerns of his converts in the city of Thessalonica. Among the issues that he addresses is the Thessalonians' expectation that the end of the age is to come soon. These believers apparently accept Paul's teaching that Jesus will bring the Kingdom of God to earth any day now. But it obviously hasn't happened yet, and in the meantime, some of the members of their Christian community have died. This raises serious concerns among those left behind: have those who have already departed lost out on the glorious kingdom that Jesus is bringing?

Paul writes an intriguing response in which he comforts his readers by telling them not to "grieve as the other people do, since they have no hope." For, as it turns out, even the dead will inherit the kingdom when Jesus arrives in glory:

> For since we believe that Jesus died and arose, so also, through Jesus, God will bring with him those who are asleep [i.e., dead]. For we say this to you by a word of the Lord, that we who are living who remain until the coming of the Lord, will in no way precede those who have slept. For the Lord himself will descend from heaven with a shout, with the voice of the archangel, and with the trumpet of God. And the dead in Christ will rise first. Then we who are living, who remain, will be snatched up together with them in the clouds to meet the Lord in the air. And so we will always be with the Lord. (1 Thess. 4:14–17)

In no small measure this passage is interesting because in it Paul does not presuppose that he will be one of the "dead in Christ"; rather, he thinks that he will be one of those "who are living, who remain." Paul anticipates this end of the age to come within his lifetime.

This is the passage that some evangelical Christians point to in support of their view that there will be a future "rapture," in which believers are taken out of this world before all hell breaks out (the "tribulation"). I should point out that this entire notion of the Christians being taken out of the world is completely absent from the favorite book of futuristically minded Christians of the present day, the book of Revelation. It is striking that this passage in 1 Thessalonians speaks not about a coming tribulation on earth, but only of the end of the age when Jesus returns in glory with his faithful ones. The idea that there will be a rapture followed by a tribulation can only be derived by taking what Paul says here along with what John says in the book of Revelation and smashing them together as if each were giving one part of a timeline. In other words, it's a teaching that neither one of them appears to have held.

One of the other interesting features of the passage in 1 Thessalonians is that it presupposes a view of the universe that no educated person holds today, namely, that the universe can be conceived of as a house having three "stories." In the basement is the realm of the dead (below us); where we are now is the realm of the living (on the ground floor); and up above us in the sky (the second floor) is the realm of God and his angels. The idea, then, is that when someone dies, they go down to the place of the dead. Jesus died and went down. Then he was raised up, and he kept going, up to the realm of God. Soon he will come back down, and those who are below us will themselves be raised up, and we who are here on ground level will also be taken up and live forever in the realm of God.

There is nothing to suggest that Paul meant all this symbolically. He, like most Jews of his period, appears to have thought that God really was "up there." The same thought lies behind the story of Jesus' ascension to heaven in Acts 1 and in the intriguing scene in the book of Revelation, where the prophet John sees a "window in the sky" and suddenly finds himself shooting up through it (Rev. 4:1–2). It is hard to know how these authors would have expressed themselves if they knew that in fact there *is* no "up" or "down" in our universe, but that there are billions of galaxies, with billions of stars in each of them, all expanding to incredible distances, as they have been for billions of years. Like it or not, we live in a world very different from the one of the authors of the New Testament.

The other important point to stress about Paul's description about the "return" of Jesus is that he understands—as did all Jewish apocalypticists, so far as we know—that the future resurrection of the dead will be an actual physical resurrection. He does not teach that when you die, your soul goes to heaven, where you lead a bodiless existence for all eternity. No, there will be a future resurrection of the body, in which your physical self is reconstituted, so as to live forever. This view is presupposed in the passage in 1 Thessalonians and is explicitly set forth in another of Paul's letters, 1 Corinthians, where he vehemently objects to those who find the idea of a bodily existence in the afterlife ridiculous (1 Cor. 15:35–41). For Paul, we will all live in bodies: but they will be perfected bodies, like the body of Jesus after his resurrection, made immortal and no longer subject to pain and death, an "imperishable" body (15:50).

> See, I tell you a mystery: we will not all fall asleep [i.e. die] but we will all be changed, in an instant in the twinkling of an eye, at the last trumpet. For the trumpet will blow and the dead will be raised imperishable; and we will be changed. For this perishable self must be clothed in the imperishable and this mortal self must be clothed in the immortal.

This was the fervent hope and the urgent proclamation of Paul. His mission was to convince others so that they too could be transformed into imperishable beings when the end of this age came to a grand climax with the appearance of Jesus from heaven. No wonder he saw his mission as so urgent. The end was upon him, and people needed to be told.

Chapter Nine

Paul the Apostle

It would be easy to argue that after Jesus himself, Paul was the most important figure in the history of Christianity. It was Paul's missionary work that helped transform the followers of Jesus from a small Jewish sectarian movement in Palestine to a worldwide religion comprising both Jews and Gentiles. It was his theological reflections on the significance of the death and resurrection of Jesus that came to form the heart of the Christian message for all time. And it was his writings that were to play such an enormous role in the canon of the new Christian Scriptures, the New Testament, of whose twenty-seven books thirteen are attributed to Paul.

Paul might have been surprised to learn of his own historical significance. After all, he did not expect history to continue for two thousand years after his day. He thought that history was soon to come to a crashing halt, with the return of Jesus on the clouds of heaven in judgment on the earth. Moreover, there are good indications that throughout his ministry, Paul was besieged on every side. It must not have been at all clear to either Paul or outside observers that his voice would be the one to emerge as dominant, to be canonized in Christian theology and Scripture. But that is what happened. Paul has become enormously important for the history of Christianity, because of his mission and his message.

The Mission of Paul

Even if Paul could not have anticipated his ultimate significance, he was not one to minimize what was happening in his work among the Gentiles, as he converted pagans to believe in the one God of the Jews and in Jesus his Son, through whose death God had reconciled the world to himself. Paul's apocalyptic sense that he was living at the end of time dovetailed perfectly with his belief that he had been specially called by God to convert the Gentiles. For Paul, the conversion of the Gentiles was the final major event in the history of the world before the end came. And he was the one chosen by God to make it happen.

Paul's Prophetic Call

We have seen that Paul did not understand his conversion to be a change of religions. In those rare moments when Paul does talk about his coming to believe in Christ, he uses language reminiscent of the Scriptures that he knew so well. He was particularly drawn to the Jewish prophets who claimed that God had called them to proclaim his message. Recall how Paul speaks of his moment of revelation:

> God, the one who set me apart for something special from my mother's womb and called me through his grace, was well pleased to reveal his son to me, so that I might proclaim his good news among the Gentiles. (Gal. 1:15–16)

This sounds remarkably like the prophets of the Hebrew Bible, who spoke about their own call. The prophet Jeremiah, for example, indicates that God said to him, "Before I formed you in the womb I knew you, and before you were born I consecrated you; I appointed you a prophet to the nations" (Jeremiah 1:5). Here is someone who was appointed by God to be his spokesperson, even before he had been born. Paul thought the same thing about himself.

Or consider the writings of the prophet Isaiah:

> And now the Lord says, who formed me in the womb to be his servant, to bring Jacob back to him, and that Israel might be gathered to him . . . "I will give you as a light to the nations, that my salvation may reach to the end of the earth." (Isaiah 49:5–6)

Paul thus saw himself as standing in the line of prophets, chosen before his birth for a special mission. But he was not simply one in a long series of God-inspired spokespeople. In his own estimation, he was far more than that, for Paul took seriously the words of the prophets that at the end of time God's salvation would extend not only to his people, Israel, but to all the nations of the earth. When history was to draw to its divinely appointed close, all those who commit idolatry (i.e., the pagans) would realize the error of their ways and turn to God (Isaiah 42:17). They would realize that "God is with you alone, and there is no other; there is no god besides him" (Isaiah 45:14). Once they came to that realization, all peoples of the earth would worship the one true God: "To me every knee shall bow and every tongue will swear" (Isaiah 45:23), and "all the ends of the earth shall see the salvation of our God" (Isaiah 52:10).

The word of salvation, therefore, was not only for the people of Israel, but for all people. And the news of this salvation was to be delivered by none other than Paul, the one God had chosen to be the "apostle to the Gentiles." No wonder Paul felt a sense of urgency. The hopes and dreams of all the prophets looked forward to his own day—to his own ministry. He was the one God had chosen to bring about the long-awaited fulfillment of the prophets.

Paul's Apostolic Authority

Thus it is easy to see why Paul attached such importance to his work. It is also easy to see why others saw Paul as arrogant and unbending. It all comes down to whether he was actually the one called to take the message to the Gentiles. This became a point of controversy whenever the character of his proclamation came under challenge. And nowhere was the challenge more explicit than among the Christian churches Paul had established in the region of Galatia, in central Asia Minor (modern Turkey).

Our information about how Paul established churches in this region is a bit spotty. Evidently he had been traveling on a mission in the area and was taken seriously ill. While being nursed back to health, he preached his gospel of Christ to those who tended to him. One thing led to another, until there were a number of converts (Gal. 4:12–14). These began to meet together on a regular basis, to learn more about their new faith and to worship the God they had accepted. These converts were former pagans who did not, obviously, keep the Jewish law or Jewish customs. And Paul, as we have seen in the previous chapter, was quite insistent that as Gentiles, they *not* convert to Judaism, for what would be the point? If salvation came on the basis of faith in the death and resurrection of Jesus as God's Son, and not by following the law of the Jews, why would Gentiles decide to follow this law? The only imaginable reason (to Paul) was somehow to improve their standing before God. But how could the complete and perfect salvation provided by Christ be improved upon? Anyone who thought that keeping the law was necessary—or even marginally useful—for salvation obviously misunderstood the true nature of the gospel.

Paul eventually was restored to health and moved on from Galatia to take his message elsewhere. As often happened, other Christians arrived on the scene, proclaiming a different message. It is not completely clear what these other "apostles" told the Galatians, but they evidently insisted that when God gave the law to the Jews it was an eternal provision for his chosen people.[1] It was never meant simply as a temporary or limited set of optional requirements. The Scriptures commanded that males be circumcised as a sign of their belonging to the people of God (Genesis 17:12–14). This commandment is called an eternal provision, not a temporary one. Men who worship God therefore had to be circumcised. These other apostles also pointed out that the disciples of Jesus, who were the original heads of the church and who continued to lead the church in Jerusalem, agreed with them on this issue. They concluded that if Paul taught a different message, he had corrupted the original teaching of Jesus and his followers.

When Paul got word of the conflict in Galatia, he hit the roof and wrote a response. Unlike most of his other letters, this is not a friendly bit of correspondence written out of a warm regard for his good friends. This is a letter dashed off in white-hot anger. It is the only letter of Paul's that does not begin by thanking God for the congregation. Instead, it begins with an accusation:

> I am astounded that you are so quickly deserting the one who called you by the grace of Christ for some other gospel—not that there is any other, but there are some people who have been disturbing you, wanting to corrupt the gospel of Christ. (Gal. 1:6–7)

He goes on to say that if anyone preaches a gospel that is at odds with the one that he himself preached, "that person stands under a curse" (1:8–9). No flexibility here! There is one truth, and Paul has proclaimed it. Anyone who says anything different is completely and utterly wrong.

But on what grounds can Paul claim to be so certain? This is where Paul begins to speak about his past as a righteous Jew and his revelation from God. Christ appeared to him, calling him to take his gospel to the Gentiles. Paul knows that his version of the gospel is the correct one because Christ himself told him. This is why Paul (in contrast to Acts) insists that after his conversion he did not go to Jerusalem to consult with the apostles who were before him. He can't very well be accused of altering their message: he got his message not from them but directly from God. And when one of these Jerusalem apostles seemed to cross him on the matter—Peter, when they were together in Antioch— Paul took him on publicly, accusing him of behaving like a hypocrite, and insisting that no one could be made right with God by keeping the law. And so, he writes to the Galatians, it is an insult to the gospel (and to God) to require, or even suggest, that Gentiles be circumcised or keep other aspects of the law (Gal. 2:11–15).

As I've intimated, Paul's own writings show that not everyone agreed with this view of the law, including Peter. We never hear his side of the argument in Antioch—just Paul's. One can only wonder whether Peter readily yielded and agreed that he'd been bested. It seems rather unlikely. Certainly the other missionaries who came to Galatia in Paul's wake disagreed with him, insisting that it was their message that had been given by God. In fact, as we'll see in a later chapter, virtually everywhere Paul went, he had opponents who taught different understandings of the Christian message, all of whom, naturally, believed they were right and Paul was wrong. What a pity for historians that the other sides of these stories have not been preserved.

We do get hints of what Paul's opponents may have said on occasion. In an earlier chapter I referred to the group of writings that were forged in the name of Clement of Rome, called the Pseudo-Clementines. In these legendary accounts, Peter attacks the "heretic" Simon Magus, who is for this anonymous author a thinly veiled cipher for none other than Paul. Among other things, Peter argues that in the history of God's people, important figures appear in twos, and the first is always inferior to the second. Paul, as the first to appear in the Gentile mission field, is inferior to Peter, who came next.

As to Paul's vision of Jesus that allegedly gave him ultimate divine authority for his views, as we saw previously, Peter is said to have scoffed:

> And if our Jesus appeared to you and became known in a vision and met you as angry and an enemy, yet he has spoken only through visions and dreams or through external revelations. But can anyone be made competent to teach through a vision? And if your opinion is that that is possible, why then did our teacher spend a whole year with us who were awake? How can we believe you even if he has appeared to you? . . . But if you were visited by him for the space of an hour and were instructed by him and thereby have become an apostle, then proclaim his words, expound what he has taught, be a friend to his apostles, and do not contend with me, who am his confidant; for you have in hostility withstood me, who am a firm rock, the foundation stone of the Church. (*Homilies* 17.19)

One can imagine Peter himself saying such a thing to Paul in their controversy in Antioch: "You think you're right because you saw Jesus for a few moments on the road to Damascus? I spent years with him!"

Paul's Modus Operandi

Once Paul converted to faith in Christ and saw himself as the apostle to the Gentiles, he engaged in missionary journeys throughout the urban areas of the northern Mediterranean. In his own words:

> From Jerusalem and as far around as Illyricum I have fully preached the gospel of Christ, and so have aimed to spread the gospel not where Christ is already named, in order that I might not build upon the foundation laid by someone else. (Rom. 15:19–20)

In other words, from the far eastern part of the empire (Judea) to the area just east of its center, Illyricum, across the Adriatic from Italy, Paul always wanted to be there first. He was not interested in evangelizing areas already reached by other Christian missionaries; he wanted to take the word to pagans who had never heard of Christ. The reason he says this to the Christians in Rome is clear from his letter: he now wants to head to the far regions of the west, as far as Spain, so that "all the nations" could hear the truth of salvation.

But how exactly did Paul proceed in his mission? That is to say, thinking purely in terms of logistics, what did he do when visiting a city in order to make converts and start a church?

You might think that he would work like modern evangelists: set up some kind of tent rally, advertise around town, get some interested folks out to hear him preach, make an evangelistic proclamation, extend an altar call, and so get some converts. But modern evangelistic efforts require teamwork and preparation by those already devoted to the cause. When Paul went to a city, he was the first Christian on the scene. It is clear from his other letters that he would typically be accompanied by one or two other Christian companions, and they would work the town on their own, with no backup support, no groundwork already laid, nothing to start with. Paul never speaks of anything like modern evangelistic campaigns.

Is it possible that he simply went into a town, stood on a street corner, and started shouting his message to passersby, hoping to get some interested listeners and go from there? This is certainly possible, but neither the book of Acts nor Paul himself gives any indication that that was how he proceeded.

Paul does occasionally say that the gospel went "to the Jew first, and also to the Greek" (e.g., Rom. 1:16). This has led some to suspect that Paul used local Jewish synagogues as a kind of base of operation. And this in fact is how he is portrayed as proceeding in the book of Acts. Whenever he visits a new town or city he first visits the local synagogue of the Jews and there, as a guest in town, he is given the opportunity to comment on the Scripture text of the day. In the context of his remarks, he moves quickly to proclaim that Jesus is the messiah who was rejected by the leaders of the Jews but vindicated by God, who raised him from the dead. In the stories of Acts, Paul typically makes several converts in this context. Most Jews find his views offensive, and they reject him and his message, driving him to take the message elsewhere, among the Gentiles. So the message literally goes to the Jews first and then the Gentiles (see, for example, Acts 13:14–74; 17:2–6).

This is a missionary strategy that would have made good sense. The problem with it as a historical explanation of how Paul proceeded is that Paul himself says nothing about using local synagogues as a forum for his preaching.[2] In fact, Paul is quite clear that his mission is not at all to the Jews—whom he sees as Peter's bailiwick, not his own—but to the Gentiles exclusively (Gal. 2:7–8). This no doubt was because he saw his mission as a fulfillment of the predictions of the prophet Isaiah, that "all the nations" (which could also be translated as "all the Gentiles") would learn the good news and come to the God of salvation at the end of time. Moreover, there's good evidence to suggest that Paul did not spend his time converting Jews in the synagogue, in that his letters written to the congregations that he established are not addressed, typically, to mixed congregations of Jews and Gentiles, but to churches made up of converts from paganism.

Sometimes this stands at odds with how the book of Acts portrays these very same congregations. For example, in Acts 17, Paul is said to have preached in the Jewish synagogue in Thessalonica for three weeks and to have converted some to faith in Christ before being run out of town. One would think, then, that the Thessalonian church was predominantly, if not exclusively, made up of Jewish converts. But when Paul himself writes a letter to the Thessalonian church, he clearly presupposes that they were not Jews but Gentiles—former pagans who used to worship other gods. He speaks, for example, of how they had "turned to God from idols, to serve a living and true God" (1 Thess. 1:9–10). In Corinth too his congregation was not made up of Jews, for there he reminds them, "You know that you were once outsiders [or Gentiles], led astray by idols who could not speak" (1 Cor. 12:2).

So even though the book of Acts portrays Paul as starting out converting Jews in the synagogue, that is not how he portrays his own work. What, then, was the modus operandi of his mission? He provides us with some hints in his letters, especially the one to the Thessalonians, where he lovingly recalls to them how he spent his time among them:

> For you remember, brothers, our toil and labor among you. For we worked night and day, so as not to be any kind of burden to you, proclaiming to you the gospel of God. (1 Thess. 2:9)

When Paul says he and his companions worked "night and day" among the Thessalonians, he can't mean that they spent all of their time preaching. He indicates that they constantly worked in order to avoid being a financial burden to the community. In other words, they were actually *working*—earning money for themselves. And they were preaching the gospel while at work. Scholars have recently recognized the significance of passages such as this for understanding how Paul established churches in the various cities he visited.[3] According to the book of Acts, Paul was a "tent maker" (Acts 18:3). The word Acts uses there can actually have a range of meanings, but all of them have to do with working with leather. Evidently Paul was a skilled laborer, and he used his skills to allow him to proclaim his gospel.

The way it appears to have happened is this. Paul and his companions would come to a new city, knowing no one in town. They would rent out a space, presumably near the city center, and set up a small business—a kind of Christian leather goods shop. As people would come in to do business with them, they would use the opportunity to proclaim to them the good news of salvation in Christ. What this message entailed we will see momentarily. For now it is enough to know that they preached on the job. This would not have been an altogether unusual undertaking. In the ancient world, a local shop or business was a place for passing along news, reports, rumors, small talk—a place for conversation and discussion and an exchange of views. For Christian missionaries, it was a place where the gospel would be proclaimed.

That's how Paul did it. He preached on the job, working night and day. He converted some people to believe in Jesus' death and resurrection for salvation. These people would start to frequent his shop to learn more and more. They would begin to meet together weekly after working hours for more instruction and worship. They themselves would convert their family members, neighbors, and fellow workers to their new faith. They would sometimes face

A shoemaker and cordmaker at work, from an ancient sarcophagus. These were manual laborers like Paul, who, according to Acts 18:3, was a leather-worker.

opposition, occasionally violent, for their new faith. This would make them band together yet more closely as a new community, made up of the people of God living in the end of time, expecting God soon to intervene in the course of this world and establish a better world removed from pain and suffering.

Once Paul had established a sizable community in one place, he would decide that it was time to move on, to take the gospel to another city where the name of Christ had not yet been heard. And so the mission proceeded, one city at a time.

Paul's Message

Thus Paul converted pagans whom he met in his workplace. They stopped worshiping the many gods of their tradition—the gods of the state, the gods of the city, the gods of their home and family, the gods of various places and functions. They came to believe in only one God, the God of the Jews, whose son, Jesus, had died and been raised from the dead. What did Paul say that was so convincing? What historians would give to know! Unfortunately, all we have are occasional hints found in Paul's own letters and references to his preaching in later sources such as the Acts of the Apostles and the second-century Acts of Paul.

The One Powerful God

In the earliest of Paul's surviving letters, 1 Thessalonians, he does make an allusion to the message that he proclaimed to his pagan audience in Thessalonica, when he reminds them of the

> welcome that we had from you, and how you turned to God from idols, to serve the living and true God and to await his son from heaven, whom he raised from the dead, Jesus—who saves us from the wrath that is coming. (1:9–10)

The first part of his proclamation to pagans (polytheists), obviously, was that there was only one "living and true" God, and that he alone was to be worshiped. By implication, Paul had to convince them that their own gods, by contrast, were "dead and false." We don't know exactly what he said to convince people, but it may be that Paul engaged in the kind of attack on pagan idolatry that we find in other Jewish texts from the period and earlier, in which Jews mock pagan idols as powerless and ineffectual. Some such texts can be found already in the Hebrew Bible, including portions that Paul frequently appealed to. Consider the prophet Isaiah, who humorously maligns the pagan carpenter who makes idols:

> He plants a cedar and the rain nourishes it. Then it can be used as fuel. Part of it he takes and warms himself; he kindles a fire and bakes bread. Then he makes a god and worships it, makes it a carved image and bows down before it. Half of it he burns in the fire; over this half he roasts meat, eats it, and is satisfied. He also warms himself and says, "Ah, I am warm, I can feel the fire!" The rest of it he makes into a god, his idol, bows down to it and worships it; he prays to it and says, "Save me, for you are my god!" (Isaiah 44:14–17)

Isaiah concludes about the pagans who worship such divinities: "They do not know, nor do they comprehend; for their eyes are shut, so that they cannot see, and their minds as well, so that they cannot understand" (Isaiah 44:18).

Possibly Paul himself made some such argument to his pagan listeners: their gods were made by hand from dead materials and have no more power than the tree trunk lying in the backyard; but the true God, who made heaven and earth, is all-powerful and can do what people need in this life, working his marvels for all who worship him.

It is not clear how Paul convinced his hearers that the Jewish God, in contrast to other gods, was all-powerful. It may be that he told stories of how this God had interacted with his people during their history, for example, saving them from their slavery in Egypt through the miracles wrought by Moses, or performing miracles through prophets such as Elijah and Elisha. Or possibly he told his hearers of the miracles done more recently in their own time by Jesus and his followers.

Proof of the Gospel: Paul's "Signs and Wonders"

It is even possible that Paul told of miracles that he himself performed. In his letters Paul is quite reticent to speak about his own miracle-working ability. But he does refer to it on occasion, for example, in his letter to the Romans, where he indicates that it was God's own power that worked through him to convince others of the gospel:

> For I will not dare to say anything except what Christ worked through me to bring the Gentiles to obedience, by my word and deed, performed through the power of signs and wonders through the power of the Spirit of God, so that from Jerusalem and as far around as Illyricum I have fully preached the gospel of Christ. (Rom. 15:18–19)

What were these "signs and wonders" that Paul performed that proved so convincing to people that they came to believe that his God was at work in him? Did he heal the sick? Cast out demons? Raise the dead? Or was the conversion of numerous pagans itself taken to be a wondrous sign of God's power? Would that we knew. Paul, unfortunately, gives only allusions and hints, presumably because his readers knew full well what he was referring to. So in his first letter to the Thessalonians he can speak of how his gospel proclamation came "not in word only but also in power and in the Holy Spirit" (1 Thess. 1:5). And he could remind the Corinthians that his original message to them "was not in persuasive words of wisdom but in a demonstration of the Spirit and of power" (1 Cor. 2:4). Somewhat more explicitly, he says in his second letter to the Corinthians that "the signs of the apostle were performed among you in all patience, both signs and wonders and miracles" (2 Cor. 12:12).

What these signs and wonders and miracles actually were is anyone's guess. Later authors did in fact take a stab at guessing. The book of Acts, written a generation after Paul himself had passed off the scene, goes out of its way to show Paul as the great miracle-working apostle whose deeds rival those of his predecessor, Peter. We have already seen that when on the isle of Cyprus, Paul is confronted with the false magician Barjesus, also called Elymas, whom he strikes blind for interfering with his proclamation of the Gospel: "And now, behold, the hand of the Lord is upon you and you will be blind, unable to see the sun for some time." Immediately a darkness descended on this nefarious opponent of God's salvation. And the miracle leads to an important conversion: the Roman proconsul of Cyprus (Acts 13:7–12).

When Paul and his companion Barnabas move on to the town of Lystra, they find a cripple who has never been able to walk. Paul looks at him intently and says in a loud voice, "Stand upright on your feet." The man springs up and begins to walk. When the pagan crowds see what has happened, they naturally interpret the healing in terms of their own religion: they assume that Paul and Barnabas are two of the (pagan) gods—Zeus and Hermes—come down to visit them in a display of divine power. It is only with difficulty that the apostles manage to keep the multitudes from offering sacrifices to them as immortal beings (Acts 14:8–18).

Later on, in the city of Philippi, Paul and his companions are harassed by a slave girl who is possessed by a demon. Paul casts the demon out, but the girl's owners are not pleased: this spirit had enabled her to predict the future, and they had been turning a nice profit off her supernatural abilities. Now their little soothsaying venture has been shot to pieces. They arrange to have Paul arrested. But the apostle is not one to stay down for long. As he and his companion Silas are singing hymns in jail through the night, God sends an earthquake that destroys the prison. The apostles take the opportunity to preach to the jailor, who immediately converts, along with his whole family, and they all talk until dawn, when Paul baptizes them (Acts 16:16–34).

And the miracles keep on coming. At one point Paul's power is so great that his followers can take handkerchiefs or aprons that he has touched and carry them to the sick and demon-possessed, and they are immediately cured (19:11–12). A boy falls from a window (listening to Paul preach too long) and dies; Paul raises him from the dead (20:7–12). Paul gets bitten by a deadly viper and suffers no harm (28:3–6). Those who see decide that he must be a god, or if not a god, then at least someone who manifests the power of a god. And Paul's proclamation states in no uncertain terms who this god is. It is the only true God, the one who created the heavens and the earth, whose son, Jesus, died for sins and was raised from the dead. In the book of Acts, it is precisely Paul's miracles that authorize and validate his message. With power such as this, it is no wonder that the multitudes convert.

Paul's miracle-working power becomes the stuff of legend. As we have already seen, in the early chapters of the Acts of Peter, Paul is said to have paralyzed a young woman who tried taking communion after having just committed adultery (Acts of Peter 1–2). It is a pity that the second-century narrative that describes Paul's missionary exploits, the so-called Acts of Paul, is so fragmentary, for it clearly included a number of remarkable stories about Paul during his missionary escapades.

The most famous is the incident of the talking lion, which rivals the story of Peter and the talking dog that we saw earlier. In this instance, Paul is in the wilderness on his travels and is confronted with an enormous lion. But the lion somehow knows who this is—the apostle of God—and speaks to Paul in a human voice, asking to be baptized. Not one to refuse a sacrament to anyone (or anything) in need, Paul immediately complies. Going to a river and grabbing the lion by the mane, he baptizes it three times in the name of Jesus. They both then go their respective ways.

It is only later that the two, man and lion, meet up again. Paul has been arrested for his Christian missionary activities and is taken to the Forum to face the wild beasts. But it is his friend the lion who is set loose upon him. Rather than creating a bloody scene, Paul and the lion begin reminiscing together, before God sends an enormous hailstorm that kills all the other beasts and a number of the human spectators besides. Both lion and Paul escape, the former to his natural habitat in the mountains and the latter to resume his missionary exploits.

Readers of this tale may be struck by its similarity to the much better-known story of Androcles and the lion, preserved by the pagan writer Apion in his now-lost work *The Aigyptiaka*. In this account, when Androcles first meets the lion in the wilderness, he does not speak with it, but notices that it is limping because of a large splinter in its paw. Summing up his courage, Androcles takes paw in hand and extracts the splinter. Later, he too is arrested for illegal activity and is thrown to the wild beasts. And behold, he confronts the lion whom he had previously befriended, who, naturally, protects rather than eats him.

The story of man and lion appears to have been a common theme among ancient storytellers. The natural scientist and prolific author of the mid-first century, Pliny the Elder, gives several examples of lions who are grateful to humans for pulling out splinters or bones from their teeth (*Natural History* 8.42, 48, 56, 58).[4] As he indicates, "among beasts only the lion pardons his suppliants." In Paul's case the story of the baptized lion may have been a legend that developed out of a vague reference in his own letters, when in 1 Corinthians he speaks of having "fought the wild beasts in Ephesus" (1 Cor. 15:32). He obviously survived, but how? The legend tells the tale, possibly based as well on the comment found in 2 Timothy, a book that scholars are reasonably certain came not from Paul but from a later follower: "But the Lord stood by me and empowered me, so that through me the proclamation could be fully made and all the Gentiles might hear; and he saved me from the mouth of the lion" (4:17).

All of these stories of Paul's miraculous activities serve to provide incontrovertible "proof" of Paul's proclamation: there was only one God who had the power to intervene in human affairs to provide people with what they need. This is the God that Paul worshiped, the God of his Jewish ancestors. All other gods were dead and false.

Christ Returning in Judgment

But Paul was intent on converting pagans not only to believe in the God of the Jews. For this God had now acted decisively for salvation not just of the Jews but of the whole world, as predicted by the Jewish prophets themselves. This salvation had been brought by his son, Jesus, who died for the sins of the world and was then raised from the dead. Just as important, he was returning soon in judgment. People needed to be ready. Otherwise they would not survive the ensuing onslaught.

That this was the heart of Paul's message is clear in the earliest summary of his preaching, where he reminds his readers

> how you turned to God from the idols, to serve the living and true God and to await his Son from heaven, whom he raised from the dead, Jesus—who saves us from the wrath that is coming. (1 Thess. 1:9–10)

God's wrath is coming against this world, and Jesus alone can save people from it. It is tempting to see Paul's urgent proclamation as a kind of apocalypticized fire and brimstone. But his message is not that people need to believe in Jesus to avoid hell when they die. It is that God is soon to transform this world of evil into a paradise of glory, and all who have sided with the forces of evil—or have refused to side with God (which for Paul was the same thing)—will be destroyed when it happens. People need to repent, and the matter is urgent.

In Thessalonians, it is clear that Jesus' future role as savior from God's impending wrath lies at the core of Paul's message. Throughout the letter, Paul speaks repeatedly of Jesus' (second) coming (2:19; 3:13; 4:14). This will occur suddenly, bringing destruction in its wake (5:2). It will be like a thief in the night, unexpected by most (5:2). The Thessalonian Christians therefore need to be ready for it, to "stay awake" and to "stay sober," lest it catch them, too, unawares (5:1–12). For when Jesus comes, those who have died will be raised from the dead, and the living will arise to meet their Lord in the air, to live with him forever (4:13–18).

Christ Raised from the Dead

But is this all that Paul taught the Thessalonians about Jesus, that he was the one coming from heaven to bring judgment and salvation? There are hints that Paul must have taught them other things as well: for example, he refers to Jesus being killed by his compatriots in Judea (2:14–15). And throughout the letter he speaks of Jesus as the one who died and was raised from the dead (4:14). Moreover, it is clear from his other letters that these were the central points of his preaching: the death and resurrection of Jesus, the messiah. Consider one of the key passages of all his writings:

> For I delivered over to you as of first importance what I also received, that Christ died for our sins in accordance with the Scripture and that he was buried; and that he was raised on the third day in accordance with the Scriptures, and that he appeared to Cephas then to the Twelve. (1 Cor. 15:3–5)

The passage is important because it summarizes what Paul himself thought was of "primary importance" in his message: that Christ died for sins and was raised from the dead. Both events were in fulfillment of what the prophets of Scripture had proclaimed ("in accordance with the Scriptures"). And both events were subject to public verification. They were not secret, hidden events that someone may have made up. Jesus' death is proved by the fact that he was buried, and his resurrection by the fact that he appeared to his followers afterward.

Paul mentions the core of his proclamation, of course, for a reason, just as he had an occasion for everything he wrote. In this instance, it appears that the occasion involved a very big problem that the Corinthians were experiencing. As we have seen, Paul believed that at the resurrection Christians would be raised to enter into the glories of God's kingdom. Some of the Corinthians, however, believed that it had already happened. For these Christians, the resurrection was not a future event that would happen in some kind of crass material way when the bodies of the dead somehow became revivified to live forever. The resurrection was something that had already happened to believers when they were baptized into Christ and received the Holy Spirit. Such people were already leading lives in the Spirit; they were already experiencing the full benefits of salvation.

There have always been Christians like this, who have thought that they are somehow already perfect and are already living a kind of heavenly existence in this transient world. It may be hard for most of us to understand how they could possibly think so. Even people like this get the flu and experience the ravages of age and eventually die like the rest of us. But there it is: from the first century until now, there have always been people who maintain that their lives are being lived on a higher, more spiritual plane than the rest of us.

For Paul, the Jewish apocalypticist turned apostle of Christ, this was an absolutely mistaken notion, and in his letter he refers back to his preaching that originally converted these people in order to prove it. The reason he stresses that Christ "was raised on the third day . . . and appeared to Cephas and the Twelve" is not, as is sometimes said about this passage, because he wanted to prove that Jesus was resurrected. He is referring to Jesus' resurrection precisely because the Corinthians had always agreed about it. Paul wants to point out that when Jesus was raised from the dead, he was actually, physically raised from the dead, in a real body. To be sure, the body wasn't like ours (it wouldn't get the flu or age or die). It was, in fact, an immortal body. But it was a body nonetheless.

Why does this matter? Because the resurrection of Jesus' followers will be like the resurrection of Jesus: a bodily resurrection, not simply a resurrection of the spirit. And since it is to be a bodily resurrection, it is obviously a resurrection that believers have not yet experienced, whatever the more spiritually minded among them might say. Our bodies are still weak, mortal, and subject to the ravages of time and pain. The resurrection is yet to come.

Understanding this mattered for Paul, in large part because it shows that we have not yet enjoyed the full benefits of salvation. There is more to come. This is not as good as it gets. Moreover, the fact that God will be raising the body from the dead shows that, to God, the body matters. God is the creator of this world and of the human body, and he will be the redeemer of this world and the body. Why is this important to know? Because some people—in Corinth, and then later, throughout history—have maintained that the body simply doesn't matter to God, who is concerned instead with the spirit. But if the body doesn't matter, some people have argued (and did argue in Corinth) that it doesn't matter what you do with your body.

The church in Corinth may have been one of the most disturbed bunches of Christians that Paul had to deal with. It is portrayed in 1 Corinthians as having massive divisions in the community, with different groups following different spiritual leaders, all claiming to have superior spiritual power. Some of the divisions have gotten personal: members of the congregation are taking other members to court over their differences. There are cases of rampant immorality: some Christian men are visiting prostitutes and bragging about it in church, and one man is actually shacking up with his stepmother. There are church members who are living in total disregard of how their actions might affect others who are weaker in the faith. There are people coming together for the weekly meal and getting drunk and gorged, while others who must work show up late and find that there is nothing left to eat. The worship services are complete chaos, as those who consider themselves especially spiritual are speaking in tongues (i.e., foreign languages that no one knows) loudly and in competition with one another to demonstrate that they have a particularly strong endowment of the Spirit. And on and on.

But the big problem is the one that Paul deals with at the end of the letter, after addressing all the other issues one by one. This is that the Corinthians don't understand that they are not already leading a spiritual existence in the heavenly places now; they are still here in this world of sin and flesh and pain and suffering. The resurrection is a future physical occurrence, not a past spiritual one. Since it will be a bodily resurrection, God is clearly concerned with the body. And since the body matters, it matters what one does with the body. No more prostitutes, living in sin with stepmothers, getting drunk at the Lord's supper, taking each other to court, and so on. When the end comes, then there will be a glorious, paradisal existence. But until then, followers of Christ need to live in loving, committed relationships with one another, being more concerned for the needs of others than for themselves.

This is the message Paul drew from his proclamation that had originally been received by these former pagans, that Christ had been raised from the dead. A similar message could be learned from the other part of his proclamation, that Christ had died in accordance with the Scriptures.

Christ Crucified

For Paul, the death of Jesus was all-important, not only because it brought salvation in the first place but also because it showed what life is like in this world. This particular aspect of Paul's preaching stands in stark contrast with what you hear in some Christian churches today, where fabulously gifted and flashy preachers proclaim that those who side with God will be successful, happy, and prosperous. For Paul, it was just the opposite. For him, those who follow the one true God cannot expect to live flourishing and glorious lives. They are followers of a crucified man, and if they follow the one who was crucified, they too can expect pain and death for their efforts. This is why Paul insists to his Corinthian readers that he "decided to know nothing among you except Jesus Christ as he was crucified" (1 Cor. 2:2).

Paul, in short, did not stress the glories of Christ available to his followers today. To be sure, Christ's death will eventually lead to the triumph of God over all that is opposed to him. But that is yet to come. In the meantime, we are still living in a world controlled by powers that are alien and antagonistic to God, his purposes, and his people. Those who believe in Jesus are by no means exempt from the ravages of these alien powers. On the contrary, until Jesus returns, believers are living the lives of the crucified.

From Paul's perspective, the hyperspiritual leaders in Corinth, who considered themselves above the menial problems and weaknesses of this world, had gotten the message wrong. They thought that by supernatural power and heightened rhetorical skill they showed that they were especially endowed with God's spirit. But Paul thought the opposite. So he stresses that "I was with you in weakness and in much fear and trembling" (1 Cor. 2:3).

In a truly remarkable passage, in Paul's second letter to the Corinthians, he wants to prove his qualifications to his converts, showing his spiritual superiority to others who are trying to claim their allegiance. What is striking is that he does so by pointing not to all the spectacular feats of power he has performed (contrast some modern preachers) but to his weakness, his pain, and his suffering. In short, he has been beaten up more than anyone else, showing that he is more like Christ:

> Are they servants of Christ? (I speak like a fool!) I am more so. In far more labors, in far more imprisonments, in countless beatings, often to the point of death. Five times I received the forty lashes minus one from the Jews; three times I was beaten with rods; once I was stoned. Three times was I shipwrecked; I have spent night and day awash at sea. On frequent journeys, in danger from rivers, in danger from robbers, in danger from my own people, in danger from the Gentiles, in danger in the city, in danger in the wilderness, in danger in the sea, in danger from false brothers, in labor and toil, often in sleepless nights, in famine and thirst, often hungry, cold and exposed. . . . If I must boast, I will boast of the things that show my weakness. (2 Cor. 11:23–30)

Christ was crucified. Those who are his followers will lead lives of pain and suffering. It may not be the kind of message that converts the hordes in our day, but it was the message Paul proclaimed. It's no wonder that some of the Corinthians started following other spiritual leaders.

Christ's Death for Sinners

For Paul, it was not the mere fact that Jesus had been crucified that mattered. Lots of people were crucified. According to the Gospels, just in Jerusalem on the day Jesus was killed, two others were crucified with him. The next day there may have been two or three more, with the same the day after that. And that's just in one midsized city in a remote part of the empire. God knows how many people the Romans killed this way.

As we have seen, what made Jesus' death different for Paul was his belief that Jesus was the Christ of God. The death mattered because God vindicated Jesus by raising him from the dead, showing that he had suffered his fate not because of something that he himself had done to offend God (or the Romans), but because of the sins of others.

In none of Paul's other letters is the death of Jesus and its effect on the salvation of both Jews and Gentiles discussed in greater length or depth than in his letter to the Romans. Romans has long been seen as the most important of Paul's letters for anyone interested in establishing the content of his understanding of the gospel. This is because Romans is an exception to what we have otherwise seen as the rule for Paul's letters, that they are all written to address situations that had arisen in the churches he had himself established. The church in Rome was not established by Paul, and so he is not writing to one of his own congregations. As we have seen, we don't know exactly who did start the church in Rome. Possibly it was simply anonymous travelers either coming to the city for the first time or returning home there, people who had learned the gospel of Christ in other lands and then brought the message back to the capital.

Still, even though Paul did not write Romans to address the problems of one of his own churches, the letter gives hints that it was written for a specific occasion. Paul was evidently planning to take his worldwide mission from the east, where he had been working, to the western parts of the empire—to Spain, which for him would have been the "ends of the earth." He wrote to the Roman Christians because he wanted to use Rome as a kind of base of operation, and he wanted their support—moral and/or material.

The problem was that the Roman Christians had heard about Paul, and some of the things they'd heard were unsettling. Was it true that he taught a gospel apart from law? That he proclaimed a lawless form of Christianity? Moreover, if he thought that Gentiles were made right with God on the same grounds as the Jews, then did he think that God had abandoned the Jews? Weren't they his holy people? Had God gone back on his promises to the Jewish ancestors? What kind of God would make laws and then nullify them?

These and numerous other questions were being asked about Paul and his gospel message, and he wrote the letter to the Romans in order to answer them. He wanted to describe his proclamation of Christ's death and resurrection and indicate its implications for such things as how Christians should live (*not* lawlessly) and how God can still be faithful to his promises to the Jews if Gentiles are admitted among the people of God without keeping the Jewish law.

Paul is clear in this exposition that all people—Jew and Gentile—stand in need of God's salvation. All people have violated God's will—pagans by willfully ignoring their knowledge that there was only one God who is to be worshiped (1:18–32), Jews for breaking God's law even though they were given it (2:1–29)—and so all people are subject to God's wrath, for all are subject to the power of sin that has enslaved everyone, both those who have the law and those who do not (3:1–20).

But God has now provided a way for people to be put into a restored relationship with himself. In a sense this is a new way, in that it was not available before Christ; but in another sense it is old, in that it was the way predicted by "the law and the prophets." Moreover, it is based on faith, which is how people have always been right with God, not by "doing the works of the law" (3:21–22). This way of justification (being put into a right standing with God) comes through Jesus, whom "God put forward as an atoning sacrifice in his blood," which is to be received by faith (3:24–25).

In other words, just as the animals sacrificed in the Jewish temple could bring a temporary right standing before God for those who had broken his law, the death of Jesus, as a perfect sacrifice, brings a permanent right standing. Jesus' death covers over the sins others have committed, and this is true for both law-observant Jews and lawless pagans. This sacrifice needs simply to be trusted as effective, that is, it needs to be received by faith.

For Paul, this way of understanding how a person obtains a right standing before God is not contrary to what the law of the Jews teaches. Rather, it is taught by the law itself (3:31), as seen in the example of Abraham, the father of the Jews, who was put right with God *before* he received any of God's commandments, simply by trusting that what God said was true. It is by faith, not by keeping the law, that a person is justified (4:1–25).

Paul wants to insist, however, that even though God's act of salvation through Christ is for all people, Jew and Gentile, this does not mean that God has gone back on his promise to Israel that they will be his special people (Rom. 9–11). They are still the chosen ones, called by God to be luminaries to all peoples on earth, given the great gift of his law (which reveals his character and will—something no one else has had direct access to), and promised a special standing with himself. But Jews have by and large rejected the message of salvation in Christ. This too, though, is part of God's ultimate plan: since Jews rejected the message, it has gone out to the Gentiles in fulfillment of the prophecies of Scripture. As a result, the Jewish people will see that others have entered into a special relationship with God, and this will drive them, through a kind of spiritual jealousy, to believe in the salvation God has wrought. And so, according to Paul, "all Israel will be saved" (11:26).

Moreover, the fact that justification comes apart from the law does not mean that the gospel leads to lawless behavior. Quite the contrary, it is those who are in Christ by faith who have the power to overcome the forces of this world that lead to alienation from God. Christians have participated in Christ's death to these worldly powers, such as the power of sin (Rom. 5–7). They no longer need to lead lives in alienation from God, but are empowered now to do what God really wants.

A good bit of the end of Paul's letter to the Romans spells out the ethical obligations of the Christians, who are able to lead lives pleasing to God now that they have a restored relationship with him, obeying his commands, being subject to all ruling authorities, and loving others as themselves (Rom. 12–15).

Here in Romans, then, we have the clearest statement from Paul's own hand concerning the gospel message he preached during his missionary activities in pagan lands. As we will see, this message would be changed by later followers of Paul, who often "remembered" him in ways that he himself may never have recognized.

Chapter Ten

Paul's Proclamation According to Later Sources

A friend of mine once pointed out that there are two kinds of people in the world: those who think there are two kinds of people in the world and those who don't.[1] I'm definitely of the former persuasion. Since the 1980s, teaching graduate students year in and year out, I've found two different kinds of students. Some of my students look at a range of ancient Christian texts and think everything looks the same. All the texts are mashed together into one big megatext, so that at the end of the day, each text is basically saying the same thing. Others of my students look at a range of texts and think everything looks different. Every text is taken as its own discrete entity with its own author, its own message, its own assumptions, so that at the end of the day, every text is basically saying something different.

I must confess that when I was in college and a bit later, when I was a beginning graduate student myself, I belonged to the first set of people. Everything looked pretty much alike. When it came to the New Testament, the Gospel of Mark seemed a lot like Luke, which was very much like John, which had a good deal in common with the writings of Paul, which reflected the things said in the book of Acts, and so on. But the more rigorously I was trained in reading these texts in their original languages, the more I developed a refined sense of just how different they really are from each other. I guess this was a conversion experience of my own, as I moved away from thinking everything is basically the same to seeing that everything is richly unique.

The Message of Paul in Acts

Nowhere is this more clear to me today than in the comparisons and contrasts I see between the book of Acts and the writings of Paul. As I've indicated before, my basic assumption now is that Paul is the best authority for knowing about Paul, and that if an author living thirty years after Paul indicates that Paul said or did something that contradicts what Paul himself says, then it is probably Paul who has gotten the facts right and the other author has given a modified version. I don't mean to say that this modified account is therefore of no value: it is extremely valuable, but principally for what it is, not for what it is not. It is less valuable for knowing what Paul was *actually* like, what he really said and did. But it is more valuable for knowing how Paul was remembered in the generation after his death. That too is a historical matter and of real interest to anyone concerned to know about the development of the Christian religion in its formative years.

It is relatively easy to contrast what Paul says about his proclamation of the gospel with how Acts portrays it: simply take one of Paul's speeches in Acts and see how it stacks up against Paul's own statements. We have already seen some points of contrast, when I noted the differences between what Paul allegedly says about pagan idolatry in the book of Acts in his speech to pagan philosophers on the Athenian Areopogus with what he himself says in the letter to the Romans. The perspectives of these two passages are not simply different; they are at odds. In Acts, "Paul" indicates that God overlooks the error of the pagans in committing idolatry, since, after all, they are ignorant of his existence and don't know any better. In Romans, Paul says just the opposite: God does not forgive the pagans but pours his wrath out on them, because they know full well that he is the only God and they reject this innate knowledge in order to worship idols.

Further contrasts between what Paul says about his proclamation and what Acts says about it can be seen in the first major speech Paul delivers in Acts, on the first of his three missionary journeys in the book, in the town of Antioch, Pisidia (central Asia Minor). Paul and his companion Barnabas arrive in town, and on the Sabbath they go to the synagogue for worship with their fellow Jews. As outside guests, they are asked if they have anything to say to the congregation. Paul stands up and delivers a long sermon (Acts 13:16–42). He addresses his hearers as "Israelites" and gives them a brief summary of the history of the Jewish people, down to the time of King David. He then skips to speak of the descendant of David, Jesus, indicating that he was proclaimed as the long-expected one by John the Baptist but came to be rejected by the Jews of Jerusalem, who handed him over to Pilate to be executed. But God raised him from the dead, as was predicted by none other than David himself in the Jewish Scriptures. It is in Jesus, Paul continues, that everyone can find forgiveness of their sins.

This sermon receives a warm welcome, with many devout Jews following Paul to learn more about what he had been saying. The next week, the synagogue is packed, as people have come out to hear Paul speak again. But the Jewish authorities are jealous (*they* can't get this kind of turnout) and publicly dispute Paul's words. Paul and Barnabas respond by saying that since their message is being rejected by the Jews, they will have to take it to the Gentiles. Eventually, they are run out of town by a Jewish mob.

Now, the reader who sees everything as basically the same can look at this sermon and find in it reflections of Paul's own preaching: Jesus is the Son of God who was executed and raised from the dead for salvation. But the reader who sees everything as unique can discern striking differences between this sermon and anything Paul was likely to have said (and done). To begin with, as we have seen, Paul never gives any indication that he first took his gospel to Jews in the synagogue, and that only when they rejected his message did he, rather reluctantly, turn to try his luck with the Gentiles. Instead, he saw himself as an apostle to the Gentiles.[2] His modus operandi was evidently to use not the synagogue but rather his workshop as the place of his proclamation.

Moreover, in the sermon itself, it is striking that "Paul" stresses the history of Israel, especially Jesus' ties to his ancestor David. This is not at all an emphasis that we find in Paul's letters (where he never recounts the events of Jewish history). More striking still, Paul's sermon gives a summary of the life of Jesus—a kind of précis of the Gospel narratives about Jesus, which begin with John the Baptist and end with Jesus' crucifixion and resurrection. But there is nothing in Paul's own writings to indicate that Jesus' earthly life was of primary (or any) importance to him.

This last point strikes many of my undergraduate students as odd, and so I have them do another little exercise: I tell them to read through all of Paul's letters in the New Testament and to make a list of everything that Paul says about what Jesus said and did during his life. Many students are surprised to learn that they don't need a three-by-five card. We will be exploring the question of why Paul doesn't speak more about the life of Jesus in a later chapter. At this stage it's enough to note that references to such key figures as John the Baptist and Pontius Pilate—in fact, to just about everyone mentioned in the Gospels—are absent from Paul's letters.

Finally, there is an important theological contrast between this sermon in Acts and Paul's own writings. It has to do with one of the most fundamental questions of Christian doctrine: how is it that Christ's death brings salvation? Paul had a definite view of the matter; so did Luke, the author of Acts. What careful readers have realized over the years is that Paul and Luke express their doctrines of salvation quite differently. According to Paul, Christ's death provides an atonement for sins; according to Luke, Christ's death leads to forgiveness of sins. These are not the same thing.

The idea of atonement is that something needs to be done in order to deal with sins. A sacrifice has to be made that can compensate for the fact that someone has transgressed the divine law. The sacrifice satisfies the just demands of God, whose law has been broken and who requires a penalty. In Paul's view, Jesus' death brought about an atonement: it was a sacrifice made for the sake of others so that they would not have to pay for their sins themselves. This atonement purchased a right standing before God.

The idea of forgiveness is that someone lets you off the hook for something that you've done wrong, without any requirement of payment. If you forgive a debt, it means you don't make the other person pay. That's quite different from accepting the payment of your debt from someone else (which would be the basic idea of atonement). In Paul's own way of looking at salvation, Christ had to be sacrificed to pay the debt of others; in Luke's way of looking at it, God forgives the debt without requiring a sacrifice.

Why then, for Luke, did Jesus have to die, if not as a sacrifice for sins? When you read through the speeches in Acts the answer becomes quite clear. It doesn't matter whether you look at Paul's speeches or Peter's, since, if you'll recall, all these speeches sound pretty much alike (they were, after all, written by Luke). Jesus was wrongly put to death. This was a gross miscarriage of justice. When people realize what they (or their compatriots) did to Jesus, they are overcome by guilt, which leads them to repent and ask for forgiveness. And God forgives them.

Thus Jesus' death, for Luke, is not an atonement for sins; it is an occasion for repentance. It is the repentance that leads to the forgiveness of sins, and thus a restored relationship with God (see, for example, Peter's first speech in Acts 2:37–39). This is fundamentally different from a doctrine of atonement such as you find in Paul.

The Message of Paul According to Later Legends

The book of Acts was not the only account of later times to modify the proclamation of Paul. We have several legendary sources that record his preaching, often in ways that make the Paul of later days sound quite remote from the Paul of history. None of these accounts is more interesting than the two we will consider here, the Acts of Paul and Thecla and the Apocalypse of Paul. Both books indicate that Paul proclaimed a gospel of renunciation, arguing that salvation comes from leading an ascetic life that spurns the pleasures of this world in exchange for the bliss of the world to come.

The Acts of Paul and Thecla

One of the most popular legends about the apostle Paul in circulation from the late second century down through the Middle Ages involved his female convert, Thecla, and their interactions in the spreading of the gospel. The tale is usually called the Acts of Paul and Thecla, although some scholars have argued that since Paul is only peripheral to the main account, it should perhaps be called simply the Acts of Thecla.

This was a controversial tale when first penned, for some Christians used it to provide apostolic support for the idea that women could exercise a prominent role in the church and, for example, be allowed to baptize Christian initiates. So incensed over this issue was the church father Tertullian (ca. 200 CE)—one of the great Christian misogynists of antiquity—that he insisted that the book had been forged by a presbyter of a church in Asia Minor, who had been caught red-handed in the act and severely punished for it. For Tertullian, women were to play no leadership role in the church, and Thecla's example was simply an old wives' tale that was to be given no credence.

Others clearly thought otherwise. Thecla became an enormously influential figure of Christian tradition for centuries, adored as a female saint of the highest standing. In some parts of the church, her following came to rival even that of the Blessed Virgin Mary herself.[3]

Her story in its oldest version is easily summarized.[4] Paul on his missionary journeys arrives in the city of Iconium, where he is welcomed into the house of a Christian named Onesiphorus. There he spends his days preaching to all who will come to hear his message. Next door to Onesiphorus lives a young virgin named Thecla, with her mother, Theoclia. They are an upper-class pagan family, and Thecla is engaged to be married to the leading citizen of the city, a man named Thamyris.

As it happens, the window of Thecla's room overlooks the street next to Onesiphorus's house, and she can hear Paul preach from there, although she can't see him. She becomes enraptured by his words and refuses to budge from her window seat for three days. Her mother is in some distress over this odd behavior and calls on Thamyris to come to rescue his future bride from the seductive proclamation of this stranger in town. Thamyris tries to woo her away from the window, but to no effect. Out of frustration he goes out, tracks down Paul, and has him arrested for disturbing the peace.

Thecla's allegiance has now been secured, however. She bribes her way into the prison to be with her beloved (in a Platonic sense) Paul. Thamyris and her family find her there, and they drag the two of them off to the tribunal for judgment. It is Thecla's own mother who, out of frustration at the situation, calls for her execution if she refuses to marry Thamyris.

The governor has Paul flogged, and Paul then disappears from the scene. Thecla, however, is sent off to be burned at the stake. But God works a great miracle, sending an enormous thunderstorm to douse the flames and set Thecla free.

The story gets a bit complicated at this point. Essentially what happens is this: Thecla tracks down Paul and they go together to Antioch, where Thecla is assaulted by another wealthy aristocrat, Alexander. Refusing his advances, she publicly humiliates him by pulling off his crown. This leads him to charge her before the local authorities, who decide to have her thrown to the wild beasts. Amid a number of subplots, the narrative shows Thecla in the arena, under attack by the animals. She, after all this time as a follower of Paul, has never yet received baptism. Seeing a vat of water nearby, she decides to baptize herself by throwing herself in. This creates great consternation among some of the audience—the women of the crowd are on her side in all this—because the vat is full of man-eating seals. But God performs another miracle, sending a lightning bolt down into the vat, killing the seals and allowing Thecla once again to escape.

Portrayal of Paul preaching his gospel, seated by a tower, from which his soon-to-be disciple Thecla listens with rapt attention, from an ivory panel of the fifth century.

Once more she tracks down Paul and informs him that she has now been baptized. She receives his blessing, as he tells her to go forth to "teach the word of God." She does so and lives a long and happy life as a single and celibate proclaimer of the gospel.[5]

Remaining single and celibate is one of the keys to this fascinating narrative. The theology represented here is not one you might expect if all you knew were the seven letters that undisputedly came from Paul's own hand. The reason that Thecla spurns her marriage to Thamyris and rejects the advances of the aristocrat Alexander is not simply that she is now a Christian and wants nothing to do with a husband or lover who is pagan. It is that she has accepted the message of Paul as found in this book: that it is only through sexual renunciation that one will inherit the kingdom of heaven. It is this, rather than the proclamation of the atoning sacrifice of Christ, that lies at the heart of his message.

This message is best seen at the outset of the narrative, where Paul preaches to those gathered in Onesiphorus's house, while Thecla listens from the upstairs window next door:

Blessed are the pure in heart, for they will see God;

Blessed are those who have kept the flesh chaste, for they will become a temple of God;

Blessed are those who are self-controlled, for God will speak to them;

Blessed are those who have renounced this world, for they will be pleasing to God;

Blessed are those who have wives as if they did not have them, for they will be the heirs of God . . .

Blessed are those who have departed from the shell of this world because of the love of God, for they will judge angels and be blessed at the right hand of the Father . . .

Blessed are the bodies of the virgins, for these will be pleasing to God and will not lose the reward for their chastity; for the word of the Father will be an accomplished act of salvation for them on the day of his Son, and they will receive an eternal rest.

From these extracts Paul's message is clear. It is important to renounce this world and all the pleasures it holds. What matters before God is a chaste life of self-control. People are not to engage in acts of sex, even if they are already married. Eternal life is the reward for chastity. This is the gospel that Thecla embraces. No wonder her fiancé is so disturbed.

One might ask where such a message actually came from, since it seems so far removed from the actual proclamation of the historical Paul about the death and resurrection of Jesus. In fact, there is precedent for this stress on sexual chastity in the writings of Paul himself. Paul had to deal with the problem of sexual relations in his lifetime, especially when it came to the church in—you guessed it—Corinth.

As has happened in a lot of Christian congregations, ancient and modern, there was a wide range of opinion about sexual matters in the Corinthian church of Paul's day. I've already mentioned that some members of the church did not think that the body much mattered to God, so for them it didn't matter what one did with the body. But there were other people in Corinth who took the opposite view, thinking that since the human spirit was all that mattered, one should ignore all bodily concerns and live only the spiritual life. Some of these people had written Paul a letter in which they asked whether it wasn't, in fact, better for "a man not to touch a woman"—that is, never to have sexual relations of any kind (see 1 Cor. 7:1). One problem with this approach to sex—not the biggest problem, you might think—is that if there are no avenues for licit sexual activities, things can blow up in one's face, leading to illicit sexual activities. These spiritual Corinthians were, after all, human.

Paul had to address this and a whole range of related issues. As you might expect, he condemns visiting prostitutes and sleeping with stepmothers. But his response to those who think sexual activity of any kind is out of the question is rather interesting, in part because it is so nuanced, to the point that some interpreters think that Paul doesn't actually give a consistent answer to the Corinthians' question (see 1 Cor. 7). His basic reply is that "because of sexual immorality" (i.e., the possibility of illicit sexual activity), every man and woman should be married. Moreover, when married, they should grant one another their conjugal rights (i.e., they should have sex). But Paul then admits that he is giving these guidelines as a concession, because in fact he wishes that everyone could be "as I myself am"—meaning that if he had his way, everyone would be, like him, single and celibate. But he concedes that this requires a special gift from God, and not everyone has it. So it is better to go ahead and marry if you are unable to control your sexual desires otherwise.

But Paul then goes on to say that it is better to remain unmarried if possible (this is where he seems to some interpreters to contradict himself). In fact, he argues, it is always better to remain in whatever state you find yourself when you become a Christian. Those who are married should stay married, those unmarried should stay single, those who are slaves should not seek to be set free, and so on. And why is that? It all comes down to Paul's fundamental conviction that he was living at the very end of the age and that the end was soon to come. Why change your social status when what matters is not your present life—which is soon to be overturned when Jesus comes from heaven—but your future life in the kingdom? And so he says:

The time has grown short. For what is left of it, let those who have wives live as if they do not, and let those who mourn live as if not mourning, and those who rejoice as if not rejoicing . . . and those who deal with the world as if they are not dealing with it; for the form of this world is passing away. (1 Cor. 7:29–31)

Because the world "is passing away" it is better for people to remain unmarried if possible, for those who are married need to be concerned for the welfare of their spouse, but the unmarried can devote themselves completely to the kingdom that is coming (7:32–35). Still, for those who can't control their sexual urges (i.e., for most people), it is better to get married and have a sanctioned outlet for them. In Paul's memorable phrase, "it is better to marry than to burn" (1 Cor. 7:9).

Paul's own emphasis on the value of chastity, then, makes sense only within the context of his apocalyptic vision that the world as he knew it would soon change radically with the return of Jesus. What happened, though, when Jesus didn't return? What happened when the expected apocalypse didn't materialize? What happened when the world continued on, year after year, just as it always had?

As Christianity developed, it shifted away from an apocalyptic expectation that there would be a future utopian life here on earth and toward the sense that there would be a future utopian life in heaven. The doctrine of the afterlife—that souls would go to heaven or hell—developed as a kind of deapocalypticized understanding of an originally apocalyptic gospel. When Christians no longer expected Jesus to be returning sometime next week, the emphasis shifted from the kingdom that would arrive in the future to the kingdom that was above. The apocalyptic dualism that proclaimed a dividing line between the current evil age and the future utopian age mutated into a nonapocalyptic dualism between this evil world and the world of God. In other words, a horizontal dualism that was sketched in time—this age and the age to come—was transformed into a vertical dualism sketched in space: this world and the world above.

What happened, then, to Paul's emphasis on chastity once this transformation had taken place? The reason for chastity could no longer be that the end is near and we need to be able to devote ourselves to its coming. It became, instead, that we need to prepare ourselves for the world above. And how better to prepare ourselves for that world than to deny any allegiance to this one? The proclamation of renunciation insists we must not be tied to this world if we want to experience the joys of eternal life in heaven. All the pleasures of this world must be renounced if we are to enter into the kingdom of God when we die. Salvation will come to those who lead the ascetic life of renunciation. That means no fine food, no high-quality wine, no frivolous entertainments, and especially no sex.

The Apocalypse of Paul

There are very few people in the world who are interested in the past simply because they want to know what happened, who are intrigued with history because (in theory at least) it's just there. There is always a question, of course, if history is actually "there" at all. Where exactly is it? And if it isn't anywhere, then how do we know it was ever there? Historians play with this kind of question all the time, pondering whether we are able actually to reconstruct the past or whether doing history is some kind of elaborate game that we've devised to control what happens in the present, to console ourselves with a fictive knowledge of what has transpired before, or for some other purpose.

Some would argue that no one has purely antiquarian interests, that everyone is interested in the past precisely because they are interested in the present. One of the ways that people who are principally interested in the present "use" history is by making the past itself present, for example, by making it relevant to the present day. People do this all the time, and have always done so. The ancient traditions about Paul did this, as we will see even more in the next chapter: they told stories about Paul not because they wanted to know what Paul was really like but because by remembering Paul in certain ways they could present Paul to their own day and convey the message that they thought needed to be heard by their listeners or readers.

Sometimes these re-present-ations of Paul (making him present for the new situation) have fooled subsequent readers of Paul into thinking that these later traditions reflect what Paul was really like. This happens, for example, when the book of Acts, or even the Acts of Paul and Thecla, is taken as a historically accurate narrative. At other times, hardly anyone is fooled. That's the case with the final text I'll be considering in this chapter, the Apocalypse of Paul, which appears to have been originally written near the end of the third century, two hundred years after Paul had passed from this mortal coil. The author of this particular text, at least, was not driven by purely antiquarian interests. He wanted Paul to speak to his own day, and he penned a fabricated account of Paul's journey to the afterlife in order to make it happen.

Some passages in the Apocalypse of Paul are reminiscent of the guided tour of heaven and hell that we saw Peter take in the Apocalypse of Peter, written possibly a century earlier. Scholars are reasonably sure that these similarities are easily explained—that the author of Paul's journey had access to the account of Peter's and copied part of it for his own narrative. This is a very different narrative in other respects, however, and so deserves to be discussed on its own terms.

The account is based on an enigmatic statement that Paul himself made in his letter of 2 Corinthians. If you'll recall, Paul was confronted in Corinth with a group of leaders who believed they were spiritually superior, as proved by their superior knowledge of God. Paul wants to show that he too has superior knowledge, but since his entire point is that it is his weakness, not his strength, that shows him to be an apostle, he is reluctant to do more than indicate that he too has been given insider knowledge. This came in an ecstatic vision that he had, which he refers to only cryptically, in the third person:

> I must boast; I will gain nothing from it, but I will move on to describe visions and revelations from the Lord. I know someone in Christ who fourteen years ago was snatched up to the third heaven, whether in the body, or outside the body, I don't know: God knows. And I know this certain person—whether in the body or outside the body, I don't know (God knows)—that he was snatched up to paradise and he heard words that cannot be spoken, which no one must tell. On behalf of this person I will boast, but on my own behalf, I will not boast, except in my weaknesses. For if I want to boast, I will not be foolish, for I speak the truth. (2 Cor. 12:1–6)

Well, what did Paul actually see when he was taken up to the "third heaven" (which I assume means the highest heaven of all) and was given a vision of "paradise," hearing those ineffable words?

The Apocalypse of Paul tells us.[6] Paul is described as having a range of visions in the account. He sees and hears the sun, moon, stars, sea, and earth accuse humans for sinning against God. He sees angels who watch over the righteous here on earth, who come before God to praise the upright with words that should strike a chord with anyone familiar with Paul's supposed gospel of renunciation:

> We come [say the angels] from those who have renounced this world for the sake of your holy name, wandering as pilgrims in the caves of the rocks, and weeping every hour in which they inhabit the earth, and hungering and thirsting because of your name . . . restraining and overcoming themselves.

Then other angels come, weeping before God, for they have been set to watch over "those who called upon your name, and the impediments of the world made them wretched." In this text, many of the damned are Christians who have not lived on the straight and narrow. No longer for Paul, as he is remembered here, is the atoning death of Jesus sufficient for salvation. What really matters is how a person lives after joining the church.

Paul goes on to see what happens to that happy soul who dies and is carried by angels before the throne of God to be given an eternal reward. He also sees what happens to that miserable soul who dies and is dragged off by some very angry angels to face eternal damnation. Paul then is shown the actual places of bliss and torment. The bliss is amazing, a glorious utopian place of goodness, where Paul meets with the saints of the Jewish tradition and converses with them in paradise. The torment, on the other hand, is horrific. Here are all sorts of punishments arranged for all kinds of sinners, Christian and non-Christian alike.

The first set of torments, in fact, is reserved for Christians. Paul sees a "river of boiling fire" in which a multitude of people are standing, some of them immersed to their knees, some to their navels, some to their lips, and some up to their hairline. The first group "have gone out of church [to] occupy themselves with idle disputes," the second engage in fornication after taking the eucharist, the third are those who slander other Christians, and the fourth are those who hatch plots against their neighbors.

Church leaders are not spared torment. Paul sees an old man who is tortured by hellish angels who pierce his bowels with "an iron instrument with three hooks." And why? He was a bishop who did not administer his office well and did not take care of the widows and orphans. So too there are punishments for deacons and lesser church officers.

Not to be forgotten are the regular sinners, who are tormented in various awful ways: magicians, adulterers, those who lost their virginity without their parents' knowledge, and even people who "broke their fast before the appointed hour." It's clearly not easy to escape the terrors of hell. Nor are heretics exempt. One of the worst torments is a pit whose stench is more excruciatingly painful than all the other tortures so far described; into this pit are thrown those whom God has chosen never to remember, who in fact are none other than the docetists, those who did not believe that Christ actually had a flesh-and-blood existence.

What we have in this text, then, is a remembered Paul who is far removed from the historical Paul. Paul himself refused to reveal what he had seen in his vision of paradise, and indicates that the words spoken to him there could not be pronounced and must never be told. This author, on the other hand, sees and tells all. He clearly had his reasons for doing so. The heady apocalyptic times of Paul had long passed. No longer was there an urgent mission to the "ends of the earth" to let the Gentiles know that the day of judgment was at hand, that the coming of Christ was imminent, that they needed to change their ways, turn to the one true God, and accept by faith the death of his Son, whom he raised from the dead. The church, by the time of the writing of the Apocalypse of Paul, was a force in the world. And it was filled not just with saints but with sinners. It had leaders who were self-serving and not concerned for the poor and oppressed among them. There were heretics at large. And there were people in the Christian congregations who did not live the true life of faith.

This life of faith was not, as it was in the days of Paul, a life of urgent expectation of the imminent return of Christ in judgment. It was a life that renounced this world and all its pleasures for the sake of the world above, a world that would be entered not when this age came to an end but when a person died and faced God for judgment, to be granted a place either in paradise or in the realms of the damned.

Chapter Eleven

Paul's Impassioned Allies

Paul, as we have seen, was a highly controversial figure, both in his own time and afterward. Charismatic figures always are. Charisma is like a magnet, ineluctably drawing some people in and, when the polarity is reversed, forcefully pushing others away. Just think of the reactions generated by public figures with charisma in our own day, from politicians as different as Ronald Reagan and Bill Clinton to political commentators as diverse as Rush Limbaugh and Michael Moore. Or think of the extreme range of reactions to such religious leaders as Jerry Falwell and Bishop John Spong. As different as all these people are, as avidly as they are adored or despised, they all have had one thing in common: an inordinate measure of personal charisma.

It was no different with Paul. He too—if not in his personal appearance, then at least in his writings—exuded a kind of charisma that drew some people in and drove others away.

Friends of Paul We Have Already Met

We have already seen some of the early Christian authors who revered Paul. About thirty years after Paul wrote his surviving letters in the 50s CE, a member of one of his churches (we don't know which one) wrote an account of the history of early Christianity from the days of Jesus up through Paul's time. This book eventually came to be included in the New Testament as the Acts of the Apostles, and the name of the author is traditionally known as Luke, author as well of our third Gospel.

There is no doubt that Paul was Luke's hero in the faith. The narrative of Acts centers on the movement of Christianity from its inauspicious beginnings among a small group of Jesus' Jewish followers in Jerusalem to its glorious spread throughout the entire Roman world, until it arrives in the capital of the empire, Rome itself. The person principally responsible for this Christian mission is none other than Paul, whose conversion, missionary endeavors, arrest, trials, and journey to Rome are the heart of Luke's account, taking up nearly two-thirds of the narrative. Once Paul arrives on the scene, most of the other apostles disappear, as if they had nothing to do with the Christian mission. For Luke, Paul stands next to Jesus as the driving force of the new faith.

This is not to say that Luke necessarily provides a historically accurate portrayal of Paul's life, message, and mission. As we saw in earlier chapters, there are aspects great and small in Acts that appear to stand at odds with what Paul himself had to say, with respect to both his missionary itinerary and his message. One might wonder how this could be. How could someone who revered Paul so highly and who lived so near his own time get so much of his information about him wrong?

In fact, it is not a big surprise if you give it a moment's thought. Even in our own day, supporters and detractors of George W. Bush or Bill Clinton give very different accounts of these presidents' personal and political lives, putting their own slant on events of the past. In some instances it is very difficult indeed to know what really happened in recent events, even though today we have far more reliable methods of establishing the past than they had in Luke's day: enormous number of eyewitness accounts, written sources, computerized data retrieval systems, and so on. What if we had only one source, from thirty years after the fact, to establish what happened leading up to the war with Iraq? Or, for a closer parallel, what if instead of having contemporary reports in the thousands about Watergate or the presidency of Gerald Ford—about as far removed from us as Luke was removed from the life of Paul—suppose we had only one report, and that by someone who, for some reason or other, was personally fond of the characters involved? Is it really surprising that historians need to look for multiple sources to know what actually happened in the past?

In any event, even though Luke saw Paul as his hero, in many respects he portrayed Paul in ways unlike Paul's portrayal of himself. In Acts, Paul preaches that God overlooks the ignorance of pagans who worship idols; in his own writings, Paul claims that God knows that pagans aren't ignorant at all but commit idolatry in full knowledge of what they are doing, and so sends down his wrathful judgment upon them. In Acts, Paul meets with the Jerusalem apostles right after his conversion in Damascus, to show that they all stand in agreement on every major issue of the faith; according to Paul, he explicitly did not meet with the apostles after his conversion, showing that he did not receive any instruction in the gospel from them. In Acts, Paul is portrayed as being in complete harmony with Peter and the other apostles; according to Paul, he had major disagreements with the Jerusalem apostles, especially Peter, in an ugly confrontation in the city of Antioch over significant implications of his gospel message. In Acts, Paul preaches that God forgives those who have sinned and does not mention that the death of Jesus was an atoning sacrifice for sin; according to Paul, God requires blood to be shed to pay for sin, and his entire gospel is that Jesus' death is, in fact, an atonement. In Acts, Paul is portrayed as never doing anything contrary to the dictates of Jewish law; according to Paul, when he was with Gentiles he "lived as a Gentile." In Acts, Paul has the Gentile Timothy circumcised so as not to offend other Jewish Christians; according to Paul, he refused to have the Gentile Titus circumcised despite Jewish-Christian insistence, because for Paul this would have been a violation of his entire gospel message.

And so on. Sometimes you don't see eye to eye even with the person you revere above all others. Think of all the people today who claim an allegiance to Jesus—many of them with wildly discrepant understandings of what Jesus himself actually taught and stood for. Not all of these latter-day proclaimers of the faith can be right. Not all of them can be portraying Jesus as he really was. Do any of them actually know?

Luke was not alone in both revering Paul and casting him into a new and different mold. About a century later a Christian leader from Asia Minor wrote the Acts of Paul. This account too sees Paul as the great hero of the faith, and yet the message that he is said to proclaim seems nothing at all like what Paul himself preached. Paul's own letters show that he principally proclaimed the death and resurrection of Jesus: "I knew nothing among you except Christ, and him crucified." Not so in the Acts of Paul, where he is shown preaching a gospel of renunciation: here, the way to have eternal life is to abstain from all pleasures, especially those involving sex. The church father Tertullian, writing around the year 200 CE, indicates that the author of this account was a church leader in Asia Minor who was caught red-handed in his act of forgery and deposed from office. In his own defense, the forger claimed that he had written the account "out of love for Paul." Even loving someone is no guarantee of understanding him.

These, then, are "friends" of Paul we have already met. There were many others who also revered the apostle to the Gentiles and who also portrayed his life and message in ways that stand at odds with what we know about the historical Paul. Sometimes these later proponents of Paul presented theological views that stood at odds with the views of Paul himself. With friends like these. . . .

Paul and the Deutero-Pauline Epistles

I mentioned earlier that scholars have long thought that some of the New Testament letters ascribed to Paul are pseudonymous, written by other people in his name. In large measure this is because they represent views that are at odds with those of the undisputed Pauline epistles. In fact, six letters have been called into question, nearly half of the entire Pauline corpus: 2 Thessalonians,

Ephesians, Colossians, 1 and 2 Timothy, and Titus. Like Acts and the later Acts of Paul, these appear to have been written by "friends of Paul" who cherished his memory but altered his message.

Scholars continue to debate these issues well over two hundred years since they were first seriously raised, with competent and skilled researchers taking different sides. Little is cut and dried when it comes to doing history.[1] Take the letter of 2 Thessalonians. This certainly looks like a letter Paul could have written: its beginning sounds like the beginning of one of Paul's undisputed letters, especially the one called 1 Thessalonians. The style of writing and vocabulary are a lot like Paul's. The central issue it addresses—the coming of the end of the age—is one that was near and dear to the apostle's own heart. So why *not* simply assume Paul wrote it?[2]

Remember: this is not a question of whether a Christian would forge a letter in Paul's name. No one doubts that Christians did precisely this: we do, after all, have the letter of 3 Corinthians from the second century and the letters of Paul to Seneca from two centuries later, which everyone agrees were forged. Nor is it a question of whether a forged letter could have made it into the New Testament. The church fathers who decided on the contents and contours of the New Testament were living centuries after the books themselves had been produced, and had no inside knowledge as to who actually wrote them. The only question is whether this particular letter is one Paul wrote or not, and that has to be decided on the grounds of whether it is consistent with the other things Paul is known to have written.

In this particular instance, what is interesting is what the author of 2 Thessalonians actually says about the coming of the end of the age, for it seems to stand at odds with what Paul himself says in 1 Thessalonians. There, as we saw earlier, Paul insisted that Jesus was coming back right away, and people needed to be prepared and ready, or else the second coming would overtake them "as a thief in the night." Not so in 2 Thessalonians. In this letter the readers think the end is coming right away, but the author does not. The author is writing them to argue that the end can't come immediately because other things have to happen first (2:1–12). When these events happen, people will know the end is almost here, because they will be adequately warned in advance. Does this sound like Paul?

Well, to many scholars, it doesn't sound like the same Paul who wrote 1 Thessalonians. Maybe it was someone living later who saw that those who expected the sudden arrival of Jesus had become a problem, for example, by quitting their jobs in anticipation of the imminent end—why work and save money if tomorrow the whole thing will be over (2 Thess. 3:10–12)? Such people were sponging off others in the community. To deal with the situation, the author wrote a letter to the group, using Paul's name to establish his authority, telling people to go back to work and not to expect anything to happen right away. This would make sense in a later context, after Paul's expectation of the imminent end was no longer as viable. After all, it had not come to pass.

Paul, then, is being remembered by this author in a way that helps him deal with the present crisis, rather than the crisis Paul was facing in his own day.

The same can be said of the other so-called Deutero-Pauline epistles of the New Testament, books that are called this because they were probably written not by Paul but by a second (deutero) Paul, or rather, a number of second Pauls. The messages of these letters, the historical contexts they presuppose, and often their writing styles and vocabulary differ in important ways from those of Paul himself.

To take another example: Paul was quite clear and explicit in 1 Corinthians that people should not think that the resurrection had already occurred as a kind of spiritual experience, as we have seen. His opponents in Corinth claimed to be leading a resurrected existence. They maintained that at their baptisms they had been raised with Christ from the dead and were now experiencing a glorified existence. Paul writes 1 and 2 Corinthians to argue that it simply is not so, that life in the present in fact is filled with inglorious pain, because the followers of Jesus are the followers of a crucified man. Like him, they too will suffer. The resurrection will occur only when Christ returns and redeems this world, destroying the forces of evil, raising the dead for judgment, and transforming the bodies of his followers into glorified, immortal beings. As Paul puts it in his letter to the Romans, those who have been baptized have died with Christ, in that they have participated in his death, but they have not yet been raised with him (Rom. 6:1–6). That will happen only at the end, when he returns.

Just the opposite message is proclaimed in the letter to the Ephesians, also attributed to Paul, but probably written by a "second" Paul.[3] Here the author spends a good portion of his letter bolstering his readers by letting them know that they have already experienced the spiritual resurrection, and that they are therefore already "sitting in the heavenly places" (see Eph. 2:5–6). It may seem odd that someone would write this in Paul's name, since this is precisely the view that he opposes in his letters to the Corinthians. But there it is: sometimes even one's followers misconstrue the message. (Ask any university professor who has graded final exams.)

An even more pronounced alteration of Paul's views appears to occur in 1 and 2 Timothy and Titus, called the Pastoral Epistles. These are allegedly written by Paul to two pastors under his charge: Timothy, the pastor of the church in Ephesus, and Titus, the pastor of the church on Crete.[4] These letters give good pastoral advice to Paul's underlings, instructing them how to run their churches, whom to choose as the church leaders to help them serve their congregations, how to ward off false teachers who have infiltrated the communities, and so on. It is clear from reading these letters that the churches addressed are efficiently organized and structured. In addition to the pastor, each church has a board of elders as a group of leading decision makers and, possibly serving beneath them, a board of deacons, who take care of the physical needs of the community. The pastors themselves have the ultimate oversight of the congregations and authority to organize its spiritual affairs, discipline its wayward members, and oversee its various ministries.

This all sounds like a sensible way to have a church organized and structured. The problem is that it doesn't look at all like the churches of Paul's own day. Recall for a moment the situation in one of the churches we have already discussed, the one in Corinth. This was an unusually troubled community. There were divisions in the church, with different leaders claiming to be more spiritual than others and acquiring cliquish followings. Some of the church members were taking others to civil court over their differences. Some people were coming to the weekly communion meal (a kind of potluck affair) and getting gorged and drunk, whereas others had to come late and were going without anything to eat and drink. Some members were disregarding the qualms of others by participating in pagan cultic practices and eating meat that had been offered to pagan idols. The church services themselves were completely chaotic, with those who were more spiritual trying to outdo one another by speaking in tongues more loudly and more frequently, disrupting the services and causing general havoc. And this is not to mention the rampant immorality in the community: some men openly visiting prostitutes and one fellow living in sin with his stepmother.

Now, when Paul wrote his letters to the Corinthians, why didn't he address them to the pastor of the church, to tell him to get his troops in order? Why not rely on the elders and deacons to straighten things out? Why not appeal to the church leaders, the head man in particular, to deal with all these problems that had arisen? It is because there were no designated church leaders.

Paul's churches did not have a pastor in charge who could deal with the problems of disunity, false teaching, and immorality. His churches were instead organized as charismatic communities. The term *charisma* comes from the Greek word for "gift." In Paul's view, as indicated in 1 Corinthians itself, everyone who was baptized as a Christian received a gift from the Spirit of God (1 Cor. 12). There were various gifts: the gift of teaching, of prophesying, of speaking in tongues, of interpreting tongues, of healing, of almsgiving, and so forth. But all the gifts were designed to one end: they were to allow the community to function together as a single unit, the "body" of Christ. Just as the body has numerous parts with various functions, so too in the body of Christ everyone has an important role to play and is provided with a gift from God to do so. There is no one part that runs the entire body. Each part has its own function and must cooperate with the other parts for the body to function efficiently.

Paul understood that the body of Christ was a temporary provision, for very soon Jesus himself would return from heaven and set up his good kingdom on earth, where there would be no more problems of any kind to be solved. The gifts given by the Spirit, then, were an interim provision to enable the church to thrive until the end came.

But what would happen if the end didn't come? Well, what happened in Corinth was a good deal of chaos. Eventually it became clear that the charismatic communities Paul had established were going to be around for the long haul. For any social organization to make it through the long haul, there has to be organization and leadership. In the generation after Paul himself had passed off the scene, his communities developed hierarchical structures in which there were established leaders of the churches. There were elders and deacons, for example. And there was one person with ultimate oversight, the pastor or bishop.

That's the situation presupposed and addressed by the Pastoral Epistles. These letters were produced by someone several decades after Paul's day, written to deal with new problems that had arisen in the communities. An unknown author assumed the guise of Paul to address these issues. His approach to them was not the same as Paul's. He was living in a different age and knew the church in a different form. Consequently, some of his teachings stand at odds with Paul's.

Paul, for example, allowed women to have significant roles in the churches. In his letter to the Romans, he names a number of highly placed women, including Phoebe, a deacon; Prisca, who promoted the Gentile mission and supported a congregation in her home; and Junia, whom Paul calls "foremost among the apostles" (Rom. 16:1, 3–4, 7). In 1 Corinthians he indicates that women played a pivotal role during the church's worship services, for example by their public prayers and prophecies (1 Cor. 11:2–16). Not so the author of the Pastoral Epistles. Living in a different age, when women's voices were being suppressed and their roles in the church curtailed, this author allows only men to serve as pastors, elders, and deacons. In fact, he explicitly forbids women even to speak aloud in church, telling them to talk only at home and indicating that if they want to be "saved," they need to bear children (1 Tim. 2:11–15)— not a particularly enlightened view, and also not one that Paul shared. Here again we have a case where Paul is remembered in ways that stand at odds with the Paul of history.

Paul and the Gnostics

The Pastoral Epistles are particularly concerned with false teachers who have invaded their communities (see 1 Tim. 3:1–11). It is a bit difficult to know what exactly these heretics taught, but it is interesting that at one point the author warns against "the profane chatter and contradictions of what is falsely called knowledge" (1 Tim. 6:20). The Greek word for knowledge is *gnosis*. Is this author warning against Gnostic views?

If you'll recall, Christian Gnostics stressed the importance of gnosis for salvation.[5] They insisted that the world we live in was not created by the one true God but was a cosmic disaster created by a lesser deity. This was the god of the Old Testament. The Jewish god *thought* he was the only God, but in fact he was an inferior being who was simply ignorant of the greater spiritual realm above him. The point of the religion was to escape the evil material world created by this lesser god, to allow the spirit within to return to its heavenly home whence it came. This liberation from the constraints of materiality could come when a person's spirit learned the truth about its origin and imprisonment. This special knowledge was given by Christ himself, who appeared on earth to deliver the secret teachings that could bring eternal life.

These teachings were not for everyone. That's why Christ spoke in parables openly to the crowds but explained everything privately to his inner group of disciples. Only they could receive the real knowledge that he came to proclaim (see Mark 4:11–12), and they passed along these teachings in secret. Thus, according to Christian Gnostics, when the apostles wrote their views, they did so in cryptic language, so that outsiders would understand only the surface meaning, whereas those in the know would understand the deeper, underlying truths they contained. So too, these Gnostics thought that the Old Testament contained secret divine revelations beneath the literal meaning of its words. They therefore gave complex and deeply symbolic interpretations of such books as Genesis, part of the law of Moses.

The author of the Pastoral Epistles may well be attacking a group of Christian Gnostics, for example, when he mocks those who are entranced by "myths and endless genealogies" (1 Tim. 1:4). This may be a reference to the Gnostic mythologies that explained how the divine beings above the God of the Jews came into existence. Such mythologies and genealogies of the gods can be seen, for example, in some of the writings of the Nag Hammadi Library. He also maligns those who claim to be "teachers of the law" (1:7), possibly a reference to Gnostic interpreters of Genesis. And he mocks those who "forbid marriage and demand abstinence from foods" (4:3), practices found among some Gnostics, who insisted that since the material body was evil, its desires and pleasures should be denied.

If the author of the Pastorals, writing in the name of Paul, is in fact attacking some early form of Christian Gnosticism, it is all the more remarkable to learn that Christian Gnostics themselves did not think of Paul as their enemy. Quite the contrary—Paul and his writings were revered by many Gnostic Christians. But how could this be? How could Paul be cited both for and against the same views? One might as well ask how the name of Jesus can be invoked both to support and oppose Western capitalism, or how the name of Muhammad can be invoked both to support and oppose radical Islamic terrorism. All great figures of the past are open to a variety of construals.

In any event, Gnostic Christians revered Paul and used his writings to support their points of view.[6] There are certainly passages in Paul that, even on the surface, could be taken in a Gnostic way. Paul speaks of the "god of this world" who has "blinded the minds of the unbelievers" (2 Cor. 4:4). Is this not a reference to the lower creator god (of the Jews) who wreaks havoc among people here on earth? Paul claims that he could not write to the Corinthians "as spiritual people"; rather, he could only do so as "people of the flesh" (1 Cor. 3:1). Is this not an indication that only some of the Christians have the true knowledge that can set free the spirit, whereas others are only superficially among the saved? Paul refers to the "mystery" of the gospel that was "hidden" from rulers of this age and of the "wisdom, secret and hidden," that was given only to those who were "mature" (1 Cor. 2:6–7). Is this not a reference to secret knowledge given only to a few in the church, who could see below the surface of Paul's words and learn the hidden knowledge that could bring liberation?

Some Gnostic Christians claimed Paul for themselves and offered up interpretations of his writings that revealed their 'true" meaning. These interpretations went far beyond the literal meanings to the secrets hidden within them. Obviously, when such interpreters propounded their views, they claimed to be representing what Paul himself really meant. In fact, some Gnostics could claim direct authorization for their views. Probably the greatest Christian Gnostic of the mid-second century was a man named Valentinus, a brilliant rhetorician and scholar who lived and taught in Rome. Valentinus had been the disciple of a man named Theudas, who was allegedly a close companion of the apostle Paul. The followers of Valentinus claimed that their own views had thus come directly from Paul himself, handed on by word of mouth (rather than committed to writing), from one generation to the next.[7]

Paul and Marcion

An even more influential Christian living in Rome at the time of Valentinus, around 140 CE, was a theologian and evangelist named Marcion. Marcion was not a Gnostic Christian. He did not believe, for example, that it was secret knowledge (gnosis) that brought salvation, and he did not think that the divine realm was inhabited by numerous deities. But he did think there were two deities: the wrathful God of the Old Testament and the loving God of Jesus. And he claimed that his views were taught in the writings of Paul.

We have seen that Paul differentiated between the law of the Jews and the gospel of Christ. In his view, a person is made right with God not by following the law but by believing in the gospel of Jesus' death and resurrection. Marcion took this distinction between law and gospel, the preaching of the old and the proclamation of the new, to what he saw as its logical and intended conclusion. For him, there is an absolute distinction between the religion of the Jews and the religion of Paul, and that is because Paul proclaimed a different God from the Jewish God.

According to Marcion, the Jewish God created the world, made a covenant with the people of Israel, gave them his law through Moses, and then inspired their Scriptures, the Jewish Bible. The problem is that no one, in Marcion's view, can keep the law of God, and since he is a just God, there is a penalty for sin. That's why everyone is condemned before the wrath of God. God is not unfair in demanding a payment for sin: after all, people have broken his law. But he is a God of wrath and vengeance.

This stands in stark contrast with the God proclaimed by Jesus, and after him by Paul. For Marcion it was quite easy to see the difference between these two Gods. When, according to the Old Testament, the children of Israel are told to take over the Promised Land, they are instructed to enter Jericho and massacre every man, woman, and child in the city (Joshua 6:1–21). Is this the same God who says to love your enemy, pray for those who persecute you, and turn the other cheek? In the Old Testament, when the prophet Elisha is mocked by a group of boys, he calls God's wrath down upon them, and two she-bears come out of the woods and maul them to death (2 Kings 2:23–24). Is this the same God who says, "Let the little children come unto me"? The God of the Old Testament is not the God of Jesus. Paul is the one, above all others, who recognized this, who proclaimed a radical disjunction between the law of the Jews and the gospel of Christ.

For Marcion, the God of Jesus, proclaimed by Paul, has never had anything to do with this creation, the material world. He sent Jesus in an act of love to redeem people subject to the wrath of the Creator. But how could Jesus come to earth without himself belonging to this creator God? How could he avoid being part of the material world? Marcion maintained that Jesus only *seemed* to be part of this world, for Jesus was not really born and did not really have a material body. As Marcion's hero Paul phrased it, Christ came "in the likeness of sinful flesh" (Rom. 8:3). Marcion, in other words, was a docetist and maintained that the apostle Paul was as well.[8]

Paul and the Proto-Orthodox

Neither the followers of Marcion nor the Gnostics, of course, survived antiquity.[9] Their various writings—and they appear to have been numerous—were either destroyed or lost. Only a cherished few have turned up in modern times, for example, in such spectacular discoveries as the Nag Hammadi Library. Their opponents, on the other hand, fared much better. Because such writings as the Deutero-Pauline epistles form part of the Christian canon, they have long provided a kind of officially sanctioned lens through which the letters of Paul himself would be read. This is true down to the present day, when it is taken simply as common knowledge that Paul was opposed to the Gnostics, for example, or that he forbade women from speaking in church. If the writings of *other* supporters of Paul had been included in the New Testament—instead of, say, the Pastoral Epistles—there's no telling how different things might be. Maybe we would have a woman pope.

In any event, all of these groups, and others besides, claimed Paul as their own and remembered him as saying what they wanted him to say. But only one of the groups ended up winning the battles over the true nature of Christianity.

This is the group that decided which books should be included in the New Testament and that wrote the creeds that continue to be recited by Christians today. This group, naturally, claimed to represent the true belief, and so they called themselves "orthodox" (meaning, literally, "correct opinion"). They had sealed their victory over Christian Gnostics and the followers of Marcion by the middle of the third century. I have called their spiritual forebears, who shared most of their views before they came to be the dominant majority, the "proto-orthodox."[10]

Proto-orthodox authors did not necessarily see themselves as tied directly to Paul. We know, for example, of another prominent Christian in Rome at the time of Valentinus and Marcion, a teacher named Justin. Justin wrote tractates against the Valentinians and entered into a harsh dialogue with the followers of Marcion. Three of Justin's writings survive: two of them defend Christianity against charges brought by its cultured (pagan) despisers, and the other argues for the superiority of Christianity over Judaism. What is striking is that never in these works does Justin quote or refer to Paul, even though he does quote other, earlier writings, including the Gospels. Was Paul too hot a topic in his day? Was he seen as the apostle of the "heretics," claimed by Gnostics and Marcion, and therefore unusable as a reliable source? It is rather hard to say, since Justin himself is silent on the matter.

Not silent, though, are Justin's intellectual and spiritual descendants, proto-orthodox authors such as the late-second-century Irenaeus, the bishop of Lyons, or the feisty defender of the faith, Tertullian, writing some twenty years later still. These authors, and others like them, know Paul's writings and cite them at length, specifically to combat the likes of Marcion and Valentinus. These proto-orthodox authors, whose views roughly coincide with those of the Pastoral Epistles, are the ones who won the day. Does this mean that their understanding of Paul was right? Not necessarily. It simply means that their Paul became the Paul who was more widely remembered.

But as with all great figures of the past, the Paul who was remembered was as much the Paul of legend as the Paul of history. In some sense, I suppose, every recollection of the apostle to the Gentiles (as well as of Peter, the apostle to the Jews) is a legendary recollection, since we always remember the past not for its own sake but for the sake of our present. Most of us, historians included, revisit the past in our minds in order to make sense of it, and in so doing to make sense of how it might affect us and our world today.

Chapter Twelve

Paul's Embittered Enemies

Not only was Paul a divisive figure for the first three centuries, but he continues to divide people today. I enjoy giving talks to groups of all sorts, and over the years I have given a number of lectures on Paul—both the Paul of history and the Paul of legend. I have spoken to some religious communities for whom Paul is a four-letter word, who see the apostle to the Gentiles as the one who perverted the simple gospel of love and faith proclaimed by Jesus into a complicated, guilt-producing, misogynistic, and anti-Semitic doctrine of wrath and atonement. I have spoken to other religious groups for whom the name Paul rhymes with gospel truth. Over my years of teaching graduate students and attending professional meetings with other scholars of the New Testament I have known highly intelligent and committed scholars who have devoted their entire lives to the passionate exploration of his writings. I have known others who want absolutely nothing to do with him. Jesus himself said that he had come to bring fire, sword, and division to earth, and Paul appears to have done the same.

Paul in His Own Day

We have already seen that during his lifetime Paul was a major source of contention, even within the Christian churches that he himself founded. For me, one of the most curious features of scholarship on the New Testament is that it took so long—many, many centuries—for scholars to realize the significance of Paul's constant polemic against other Christians: there were enormous unresolved disputes in early Christianity over the true nature of the religion. Everywhere we turn in these books, Paul is opposing the views of one group or another, and all these other groups called themselves Christian. None of the writings of Paul's opponents has survived, but if they had, what a tale they would tell. Surely the fact that Paul is on the defensive at every turn—at least where he is not on the offensive—shows us that Christianity was enormously variegated in its earliest years, with a wide range of views purporting to be true, correct, and faithful to the gospel.

In his letter to the Romans Paul has to defend himself against charges leveled by other, trusted Christian authorities that he preached a gospel that leads to lawless behavior and that impugned God on the ground that he reneged on his promises to the Jews. In 1 Corinthians he attacks those who think—based on his own teaching, evidently—that they have already experienced the glories of a spiritual resurrection with Christ. In 2 Corinthians he attacks new apostles who have arrived in town with a similar message, sarcastically calling them "super-apostles." In his letter to the Philippians he attacks Christians who urge his converts to be circumcised, calling them "dogs" who were concerned only for their own pleasure and who "worship the belly." And most notably in Galatians, he fires off a letter of reproach for Jewish Christians of similar ilk, who have argued that the covenant God made with the Jews was eternally binding. For Paul, these so-called Judaizers stand under God's curse, and anyone who accepts their message has "fallen from grace." What scholars would give to hear them defend themselves: surely they could do so simply by quoting well-known passages of Scripture to show that God had not and would not change the rules of the game.

After his death, Paul continued to have opponents, not simply among those who took opposing views and claimed his support for them—for example, Marcion and Marcion's opponents, or Valentinus and Valentinus's opponents, or Tertullian and Tertullian's opponents—but also among Christians with a clearly articulated antipathy to Paul himself. We need always remember, though, that when later Christians declared themselves as Paul's opponents, they were opposing the views of Paul as remembered, not necessarily the views that Paul himself held. As we have already seen, this is a distinction that matters.

Paul and James

According to our early Gospel records, none of Jesus' brothers (including James) was among his followers while he was alive, because they did not see him as anything extraordinary (see Mark 3:20–21; 31–35; John 7:3–5). But according to Paul's account in 1 Corinthians 15, after Jesus' resurrection he appeared to James, and this must have changed everything. James came to believe that his brother was in fact the Christ of God. And given his own unusual status—as the earthly brother of the Lord himself—he was thrust into a leadership role among Jesus' followers. He above all others could correctly interpret what Jesus had said and done during his life. Eventually he became the leader of the church in Jerusalem, the birthplace of Christianity.

James, like Jesus before him, was born and raised Jewish, and he maintained his Jewish identity even after coming to faith in Jesus. He was, in other words, a Jewish Christian. This is particularly evident in the comments that Paul makes in Galatians, when he recalls with some bitterness the public dispute that he had in Antioch with Peter over whether or not it was acceptable to eat meals with Gentiles. Paul, of course, insisted that to do otherwise was to compromise the truth of the gospel, which stated that a person is made right with God not by following Jewish laws such as keeping kosher but by believing in the death and resurrection of Jesus. Anyone who insisted that Gentiles keep kosher misunderstood the faith at its very core.

Peter appears to have accepted this view, at least temporarily. But then "certain men came from James" (Gal. 2:12)—that is, some representatives from the Jerusalem church arrived, sent by James himself—and Peter came to think better of his actions: so as not to cause the newcomers offense, he stopped eating meals with the Gentile believers. Paul evidently went ballistic and publicly called Peter a hypocrite. As I pointed out earlier, we don't know Peter's response. Many interpreters have assumed that he didn't take the accusation lying down, but answered back and possibly even got the better of Paul. It is telling that Paul never indicates the outcome of the dispute.

In any event, James appears to have held a different view of a central issue than did Paul, who insisted that "a person is justified by faith in Christ . . . not by the works of the law" (Gal. 2:16). One of the reasons this dispute between Paul and James is interesting to historians is that we have a letter allegedly written by James that eventually came to be included in the New Testament. This letter attacks the view that faith alone makes a person right with God. According to the epistle of James, just the opposite is true: "a person is justified by works, not by faith alone" (2:24). The perspective set forth in this letter is that faith needs to be manifest in how one lives, for "faith without works is dead" (2:26). And strikingly, just as Paul used the example of Abraham, the father of the Jews, to show that "a person is justified by faith," James appeals to Abraham in order to show that "a person is justified by works" (2:24).

For nearly five hundred years now, since the beginning of the Protestant Reformation with Martin Luther, biblical scholars have asked whether the teachings of James and Paul can be reconciled. Luther argued they could not be, and relegated the letter of James to a secondary status in the canon of Scripture. More recent scholars have come to different conclusions.

For one thing, it is not clear that the person who wrote the epistle of James was actually James, the brother of Jesus. As it turns out, the name James was exceedingly common in Jewish antiquity. There are several just within the Gospels, for example. Even though the person who wrote this book claimed to be someone named James, he never indicates that he is in any way related to Jesus. So this book may not represent an ongoing dispute between James, the brother of Jesus, and Paul, his self-proclaimed apostle to the Gentiles, dating back to the incident with Peter in Antioch.

Moreover, it is not entirely certain that the book of James actually contradicts the views of Paul. For Paul also thought that faith in Christ's death and resurrection had ethical implications. Much of his correspondence, in fact, indicates that anyone who believes in Christ will live a morally upright life in the Spirit. This is what the letter of James means when it claims that faith, to be true faith, must be manifest by works. But doesn't the claim that a person is justified by works, not faith alone, contradict Paul's insistence that a person is justified by faith, not by the works of the law?

Most scholars today recognize that the problem is that both Paul and James use the same words but appear to mean different things by them. When Paul speaks of "works" he is explicitly referring to "works of the law," that is, observance of Jewish rules governing circumcision, the Sabbath, kosher foods, and the like. When James speaks of works, he means something like "good deeds." Paul himself would not argue that a person could have faith without doing good deeds.[1]

So against whom, exactly, is the letter of James arguing, if it is not Paul himself? It appears that James is arguing against Paul as he was being remembered in some circles. The way it might have worked is this. Paul taught that a person is made right with God not by doing the works prescribed by the Jewish law but by faith in Christ. After his death, or possibly even before, some of his converts turned this into the catchy but inaccurate saying that one is "justified by faith, not by works." Moreover, some people construed this to mean that all that mattered was what you believed, not how you lived. For them, you could live any way you pleased, so long as you accepted the death of Jesus for your sins. This led some people to behave abysmally, claiming that it didn't matter. It was in response to this that the letter of James was written, either by someone actually named James or by someone taking the name of Jesus' brother to add some cachet to his argument that "without works, faith is dead."

In other words, the memory of Paul is being attacked in a way that Paul himself may have agreed with.

Paul and the Ebionites

The purported differences between Paul and the historical James, the brother of Jesus, is interesting in yet another way. We know of Christians down into the second and third centuries who claimed allegiance with the teachings of James and insisted that these stood at odds with the view of the false apostle to the Gentiles, Paul. The group best known for making this claim was called the Ebionites.

We don't know exactly why the group was given this name. It may have been a self-designation, as the Hebrew word for "poor" is *ebyon*. These may have been Christians who took upon themselves voluntary poverty for the sake of others, giving all their possessions to the needy, much as the earliest Christian community is said to have done in the book of Acts (Acts 2:44–45). What is clear is that the Ebionites, like the earliest Christians of Jerusalem, were a group of Jewish Christians who maintained that to be a follower of the Jewish messiah Jesus, it was necessary to be Jewish.

In the view of the Ebionites, Jesus himself was thoroughly Jewish. He was, in fact, the most righteous Jew ever to have lived, one who kept God's law perfectly. Since he was so righteous, God chose him to be his son. This happened at his baptism by John the Baptist. According to our early accounts, when Jesus emerged from the water he saw the heavens split open and the Spirit of God descend upon him like a dove (see Mark 1:9–11; Luke 3:21–22), and he heard a voice proclaim, "You are my son, today I have begotten you." It was at this point that Jesus became God's son. The Ebionites did not think that Jesus was supernaturally born of a virgin. Their Scriptures did not include the virgin birth stories of Matthew and Luke. Nor did they think he was the Son of God from eternity past. They did not have the Gospel of John either. Jesus was a full flesh-and-blood human whom God adopted to be his son, based on his scrupulous observance of the law.

As the Son of God, Jesus was given a special commission: he was to be a sacrifice for the sins of the world. And this is the task he fulfilled, in faithfulness to his calling. He thus put an end to the need for sacrifices in the Jewish Temple. These sacrifices, prescribed by the Torah, were merely a temporary measure until the perfect sacrifice should come.

The death of Jesus did not abrogate the other laws of Scripture, however. When God instructed his people how to live—for example, by avoiding certain foods, by keeping certain festivals, by observing the Ten Commandments, and so on—he never planned on changing his mind. These laws were still in force and needed to be observed. Anyone who did not do so could not claim to be among the covenant people of God.

In many respects, the Ebionites can be seen as standing precisely at the opposite end of the theological spectrum from Marcion. Marcion was a ditheist, maintaining there were two Gods; the Ebionites were strict monotheists, insisting there was only one. Marcion believed the world was created by a lesser deity, who was not to be worshiped; the Ebionites believed the world was created by the only true God, who alone was to be worshiped. Marcion rejected the Old Testament as having no validity for Christians; the Ebionites revered the Old Testament as the guide for all Christian faith and practice. Marcion was a docetist, maintaining that Jesus was divine but not human; the Ebionites were "adoptionists," claiming that Jesus was human but not divine (except by adoption as God's mortal son at his baptism). Marcion's hero in the faith was Paul, the one apostle who understood the true teachings of Jesus; the Ebionites rejected Paul as a false apostle who had completely perverted the teachings of Jesus and of Christ's apostles. This included James, who insisted that it is important for all followers of Jesus to follow the law, including the law of circumcision.

This Ebionite view appears to be the one embodied in the Pseudo-Clementine epistles that we have discussed on several occasions already, where the great disciple of Christ, Peter, writes a letter to James, the brother of Jesus, and condemns the apostle to the Gentiles as "the man who is my enemy." According to these later writings, Paul's views are based only on a brief encounter with Christ on the road to Damascus and therefore cannot compare with the teachings that Christ delivered during his entire ministry to his disciples: that the law of God is to be observed.

It practically goes without saying that this was an argument the Ebionites eventually lost. Not that proto-orthodox Christians were quick to rush to the side of Marcion. In fact, the proto-orthodox rejected both views as extreme. They agreed with Marcion that the law was no longer in force, but they disagreed when he said that the author of that law was a lesser deity not to be worshiped. Conversely, they agreed with the Ebionites that the God of the Old Testament was the one true God, but they disagreed when they said that his commandments to the children of Israel were still binding. They agreed with Marcion that Jesus was divine, but disagreed when he said he was not human. And they agreed with the Ebionites that Jesus was human, but disagreed when they said that he was not divine. They agreed with Marcion when he embraced Paul as the great apostle of the faith, but disagreed when he rejected the authority of James. They agreed with the Ebionites when they revered James as the successor of Jesus, but disagreed when they rejected Paul as a false apostle.

In many respects, the proto-orthodox group wanted it, and got it, both ways. God was both lawgiver and law abrogator; Jesus was both human and divine; Paul was an apostle par excellence, and so was James. This insistence that both views—those of Marcion and of the Ebionites—were simultaneously right and wrong is, in part, what led to many of the paradoxes that emerged as the hallmark of proto-orthodox theological claims, for example that Jesus was fully God and fully man at the same time, and that God is made up of three persons—Father, Son, and Holy Spirit—and yet he is One. These views cannot be found in any of the earliest Christian authors, not even the great Paul. But they come to be the traditional Christian perspective in later centuries, as proto-orthodoxy emerges as victorious over the various groups that represented other perspectives of the faith, both those who accepted Paul and those who rejected him.

Paul and the Docetists

It may come as no surprise to learn that not only was Paul accepted by some Christians who were docetists (Marcion) and rejected by others who condemned docetism (the Ebionites), but he was accepted by some who rejected docetism (the proto-orthodox) and rejected by others who accepted it. History gets confusing sometimes, and great historical figures are nothing, in hindsight, if not malleable. It is nonetheless the case that we have evidence to suggest that there were docetists who saw themselves, or at least were seen by others, as standing in opposition to the teachings of Paul. This is at least suggested by the letter included in the second-century Acts of Paul, usually known as 3 Corinthians.

The letter does not call itself 3 Corinthians. This is simply the designation given it by readers who know of two other letters by Paul to the church in Corinth, both of them found in the New Testament. This third letter actually came not from Paul but from someone writing in his name and claiming his authority, much as the authors of the Deutero-Pauline epistles of the New Testament had done a century earlier and the forger of the letters to Seneca did a century and a half later.

The context for 3 Corinthians is provided by the narrative of the Acts of Paul. Some of the Christians in the church of Corinth have become upset because two false teachers have appeared in their midst, proclaiming a version of the gospel at odds with Paul's. These two teachers, named Simon (is this Simon Magus?) and Cleobius, are proclaiming a docetic understanding of the faith:

> There is no need to consider the [Hebrew] prophets; that God is not the Almighty; that there is no resurrection of the flesh; that humans are not God's creation; that the Lord did not come (into the world) in the flesh; that he was not born from Mary; and that the world did not come from God but from angels.

In other words, these are docetists who sound a lot like Marcion but appear not to claim Paul for the authority of their teachings (so far as we can tell). They reject the Creator God and his creation, the authority of the Old Testament, and the fleshly character of Christ.

The historical Paul himself, in his surviving writings, presupposes a different view—at least with respect to God, the creation, and the authority of the Jewish Scriptures. He doesn't need to argue that there is only one God, the one who made the heavens and the earth and inspired the law and the prophets, because in his day there weren't any Christians who denied such things. But in later times, with the appearance of Marcion and others of his ilk, these had become major issues, as had their corollary, that Christ himself could not have belonged to this world of flesh. And so a legendary Paul is summoned up to provide a response in this Third Letter to the Corinthians.

In this letter, "Paul" contradicts the false teachers on every point, claiming that by taking such docetic views they have in fact rejected the Lord.

> For in the beginning I delivered over to you the teachings I received from the apostles who were before me . . . : that our Lord Christ Jesus was born from Mary, from the seed of David, when the Holy Spirit was sent from heaven into her by the Father, that he might come into the world and set free all flesh through his flesh, and might raise us from the dead as fleshly beings . . . For God who is

over all, the Almighty, the one who made heaven and earth, sent prophets to the Jews first of all, that they might be pulled away from their sins. . . . But since God the Almighty was righteous, and did not wish to abandon his own creation, he sent down the Spirit through fire into Mary the Galilean, that the evil one might be defeated through that same perishing flesh that he used in his dealings with others.

Here we have a proto-orthodox Paul who opposes a docetic view of his opponents. The historical Paul could not have said it better himself. In fact, he probably would *not* have said it, as these were issues that had not arisen in his own time. So the anti-docetic claims that "Paul" makes here involve affirmations that the apostle himself never addresses, such as about the incarnation of Christ through the virgin Mary.

Paul's Ultimate Enemies

In the political realm, there is an enormous difference between having opponents with whom you respectfully, or disrespectfully, disagree and having opponents who wield power over you, who can persecute you, capture you, imprison you, torture you, and kill you. So too in the realm of religion. Many religious arguments are kept at the level of personal disagreement. The disagreements may be harsh and lead to serious antagonism, but at the end of the day, they only make you feel irritated, incensed, insulted, despised, and rejected. That is bad enough, to be sure. But at other times religious disagreements lead to bodily harm, and that's when things get really ugly.

Paul's Christian opponents had no real physical power that they could wield over him. They may have despised him, rejected him, and mocked him, but there really wasn't a whole lot they could do about him, nor he about them. This was a war of words, ideas, and views, not of daggers, swords, and crosses. But Paul also had non-Christian opponents, and they were not at all remiss in taking their opposition to corporeal lengths. Paul speaks, for example, of being flogged in Jewish synagogues, of being beaten with rods by order of Roman magistrates, and of being imprisoned (2 Cor. 11:23–27). Later traditions claim that he was eventually martyred, beheaded on the order of the Roman emperor Nero.

It is hard to know exactly what led to such violent opposition to Paul by Jewish and Roman authorities. According to the book of Acts, the opposition came entirely from non-Christian Jews who were either jealous of Paul's following or put off by his message. These opponents roused the mobs to violence against him, riding him out of town on a rail or stoning him to the verge of death, and eventually turning him over to the Roman authorities as a troublemaker. This may be a historical recollection in its broad outline: Paul himself refers to the Jews of Judea as those "who killed both the Lord Jesus and the prophets [Christian prophets?] and persecuted us and are not pleasing to God and to all people, preventing us from speaking to the Gentiles that they might be saved" (1 Thess. 2: 15–16). I have never understood how Jews in Judea, or anywhere else, could actually prevent Paul from talking to Gentiles, but he clearly thinks they hindered his work. More than that, he claims they were responsible for violent opposition to him and his mission.

If Roman authorities repeatedly intervened to punish Paul, surely *someone* must have reported him as a troublemaker. Romans were not in the business of punishing people simply because they didn't like their religious views. So it is possible his Jewish opponents took offense at his message of Christ, just as he took offense at the Christian message prior to his conversion. Perhaps they leveled criminal accusations against him to the authorities, who punished him for disturbing the peace. Or possibly the situation was more like the one we observed from the letter of 1 Peter, that the Christian communities he established were seen as antisocial and contrary to the commonweal, and that authorities decided to go after the one ultimately responsible for this blot on the public record. Once more, we are stymied by our sparse source materials.

What is clear is that rather than bemoan his violent opposition, Paul reveled in it. Nowhere is that seen more clearly than in his Second Letter to the Corinthians, where he repeatedly boasts about how badly he has suffered over years, arguing that this shows him to be the true apostle of Christ. And so he says:

> We are afflicted in every way but not crushed, troubled but not despairing, persecuted but not forsaken; cast down but not destroyed, always carrying the death of Christ in our bodies. (4:8–10)

Later he speaks of "afflictions, hardships, calamities, beatings, imprisonments, tumults, labors, sleepless nights, hunger" (6:4). And in his most prolonged discussion he indicates that he far excels his Christian opponents in his sufferings for the sake of Christ:

> Are they servants of Christ? . . . I am more so. In far more labors, in far more imprisonments, in countless beatings, often to the point of death. Five times I received the forty lashes minus one from the Jews; three times I was beaten with rods; once I was stoned. Three times was I shipwrecked; I have spent night and day awash at sea. On frequent journeys, in danger from rivers, in danger from robbers, in danger from my own people, in danger from the Gentiles, in danger in the city, in danger in the wilderness, in danger on the sea, in danger from false brothers, in labor and toil, often in sleepless nights, in famine and thirst, often hungry, cold and exposed. (11:23–27)

This is what it means to be an apostle of Christ. It was not a particularly glorious calling. But it is one that Paul embraced, in part because he knew that followers of a crucified man could not expect to have it easy.

The Martyrdom of Paul

We do not have any contemporary accounts of Paul's death, although traditions from several decades afterward indicate that he was martyred. The earliest reference comes in the letter from the church of Rome to the church of Corinth known as 1 Clement, written around 95 CE, some thirty years after Paul's death. This anonymous author refers to the "pillars" of the Christian faith who were persecuted for their faith, "even to death." He refers especially to the apostles Peter and Paul. About Paul, he states:

> Because of jealousy and strife Paul pointed the way to the prize for endurance. Seven times he bore chains; he was sent into exile and stoned; he served as a herald in both the East and the West; and he received the noble reputation for his faith. He taught righteousness to the whole world, and came to the limits of the West, bearing his witness before the rulers. And so he was set free from this world and transported up to the holy place, having become the greatest example of endurance.

It appears that this author knows of a tradition in which Paul accomplished the plan he himself mentions in his letter to the Romans: to go on to Spain, "the ends of the earth," to proclaim the gospel there. But eventually he was put on trial and, evidently, executed for his faith.

About a century after the writing of 1 Clement we get a narrative of what happened leading up to Paul's martyrdom. This comes in the Acts of Paul, and like most of the book's narrative, it is based on legendary accounts rather than historical events. Paul is said to have arrived in Rome and to have rented out a barn to meet with the Christians there. Among those listening to Paul is a young man named Patroclus, who happens to be the cupbearer of Nero himself, one of his favorite servants. Patroclus is sitting in the window on an upper floor. After a while he begins to doze off; he falls from the window and dies. Word is rushed off to Nero. The emperor is not pleased.

In the meantime, Paul performs one of his patented miracles, going down to the corpse and restoring it to life. When Patroclus later shows up for work at Nero's palace, the emperor is terrified and astounded: "Patroclus, is this you? I thought you were dead!" Patroclus replies that he was dead, but that the "master of the universe, the Lord Jesus Christ," has raised him from the dead. Nero, rather than expressing his gratitude for the miracle, becomes immediately envious of the miracle-working ability of this Jesus, and suspicious of him as a potential usurper of his own power. He interrogates Patroclus and learns that he considers Christ to be the king of all. In his rage—isn't the emperor supposed to be the king of all?—Nero sends Patroclus and two other self-proclaimed Christians in the court to prison to be tortured.

This is what leads to the persecution of Christians at the hands of Nero. He orders the followers of Christ to be rounded up and punished. Only after wiser heads prevail does he agree that no one should be punished without a court trial.

Paul himself is arrested and brought before Nero, who threatens to execute him for his faith. Paul, however, shows no trace of fear but rather a haughty self-assurance in the face of death. He tells Nero that if the emperor kills him, he will rise from the dead and appear to him alive afterward. Nothing can keep a good man down.

Nero orders his execution. The executioners spend some time talking to Paul before they do the deed. As might be expected in a story of this kind, he actually converts them before they perform their duty. But at his death a miracle occurs: once Paul is beheaded, it is not blood that spurts from the wound but milk. It is difficult to say what the milk is meant to signify. It is, of course, a symbol of life, in that it is the food that sustains a newborn after birth. So maybe it means that Paul is being born again into his new life with Christ in the other world. Moreover, in his own letters, Paul himself speaks of nourishing his converts with the "milk" of his teaching (1 Cor. 3:2). So perhaps the milk spurting from his neck signifies the edifying message that his death will bring to others, that death is not the last word, for it can be followed by eternal life with the Lord.

In any event, Paul fulfills his vow to Nero. To the emperor's shock and dismay, the apostle appears to him after his execution, as full of life as can be. The emperor does not repent in the story, but one could scarcely expect him to do so. There is a limit, after all, to how far pious legend can distort the historical facts, and most people in the early church thought of Nero as an unrepentant despot till the time of his own death.

The Afterlife of Paul

Whether or not Paul himself came back to life after his death, it is clear that his writings and teachings lived on. As we have seen so many times, this does not mean that his actual teachings were cherished and remembered. Far more often, his teachings were remembered in ways that bore little resemblance to what he really taught. Maybe that's true of every great religious teacher. In any event, it is surely the explanation for how Paul could appear in so many guises after his life. Some of his followers remembered him as supporting the teachings of the Jewish Scriptures (for example, those who preserved his letter to the Romans). Others saw him as an outspoken opponent of the Scriptures (the Ebionites and the Marcionites). Some remembered him as thinking that the resurrection was to be a future, physical transformation of the bodies of believers (those who preserved 1 Thessalonians and 1 Corinthians). Others saw him as an advocate of a spiritual resurrection that had already happened in Christ (the pseudonymous author of Ephesians). Some remembered him as a supporter of women and their important role in the Christian church (the author of the Acts of Paul and Thecla). Others saw him as an outspoken opponent of women's participation in church, requiring women to remain silent and urging them to be saved by having babies (the author of 1 Timothy). Some remembered him as a supporter of a docetic understanding of the world and Christ (Marcion). Others saw him as a forceful opponent of the docetic view (Tertullian and the author of 3 Corinthians). Some remembered him as the original source for the Gnostic understanding of Scripture and salvation (Valentinus). Others saw him as the apostolic opponent of all things Gnostic (Irenaeus and Tertullian).

Paul, in short, seems to be, if not all things to all people, at least starkly different things to different people—much as Simon Peter was, and much as Jesus was before him. Maybe this is a mark of Christian greatness.

Part Three

MARY MAGDALENE

Chapter Thirteen

Mary Magdalene in Popular Culture and History

Between Peter, Paul, and Mary, there is no question about who is the media star. Peter may be a sentimental favorite among faithful readers of the New Testament, who can identify with his rash behavior but basically good heart. Paul has intrigued and occupied serious theologians for centuries and is still widely revered by laypeople, who perhaps read him more often than they understand him. But neither Peter nor Paul is big news on Broadway, in Hollywood, or at Barnes and Noble. With Mary Magdalene it is a different story. Here is an early follower of Jesus about whom we know very, very little but who has drawn the spotlight for many, many years as a star performer in plays, movies, and novels. Maybe public intrigue and veneration come easier to those whose real lives are vague and shadowy. Screenplay writers rarely like to be constrained by the facts of history.

The Thoroughly Modern Mary

Mary Magdalene was big news when I was in high school and was first starting to read the Bible seriously. Tim Rice and Andrew Lloyd Webber's musical *Jesus Christ Superstar* premiered on Broadway in October 1971. Its key figures were, in addition to Jesus himself, Judas Iscariot and Mary Magdalene, an interesting duo, given the Gospels themselves, where other figures—Peter, James, and John especially—are far more prominent. But if one wants intrigue, it is better to weigh public interest, and who exactly is interested in James, the son of Zebedee? Judas the betrayer, on the other hand, and Mary, an "intimate" of Jesus—these are another story.

Mary in fact is intimate with Jesus in this early Andrew Lloyd Webber–Tim Rice collaboration. Played by Yvonne Elliman, the only actor from the Broadway cast who also starred in the movie version of 1973, Mary is the one follower who stands by Jesus through thick and thin, and who tries to soothe his agony in the face of his coming torment and death:

Try not to get worried
Try not to turn on to
Problems that upset you
(oh) Don't you know everything's alright
Yes everything's fine
And we want you to sleep well tonight
Let the world turn without you tonight . . .

Cooling his forehead with a wet cloth and anointing his head with sweet perfume, she raises the ire of the ever-present and callused Judas: how can Jesus associate with such a woman of low standing and ill repute? Jesus turns the attack on Judas for his hypocrisy, defends Mary, and returns to let her stroke his hair.

There's more than a little sexual tension going on, and not far below the surface. This becomes especially clear in the most popular song from the Broadway soundtrack, a top-40 hit by Elliman, whose character seems genuinely mystified by her hidden passion for Jesus:

I don't know how to love him, what to do, how to move him.
I've been changed, yes, really changed.
In these past few days when I've seen myself, I seem like someone else.

I don't know how to take this, I don't see why he moves me.
He's a man, he's just a man.
And I've had so many men before, in very many ways: he's just one more.

Should I bring him down? Should I scream and shout?
Should I speak of love—let my feelings out?
I never thought I'd come to this—what's it all about? . . .

Yet, if he said he loved me, I'd be lost, I'd be frightened.
I couldn't cope, just couldn't cope. . . .
He scares me so. I want him so. I love him so.

It was never clear to me whether the people who played and listened to the song in the early 1970s knew (like Mary) "what it's all about." This was not your normal outpouring about the pangs of unrequited love. It was about, well, Jesus! But there were some people who knew. My spiritual guru (we didn't call him a guru at the time; we were, after all, budding fundamentalists) was completely incensed at the idea that Mary would ever talk about having sex with Jesus ("Should I bring him down?").

But the idea that Jesus and Mary were sexually attracted was not born with *Jesus Christ Superstar,* nor did it die there. When I started teaching at the University of North Carolina many years later, the Martin Scorsese film *The Last Temptation of Christ* had just come out. This too was a box-office hit, and it also raised a huge public outcry. As it turns out, that first semester in my new position I was teaching an undergraduate course called "Jesus in Myth, Tradition, and History." The course dealt with portrayals of Jesus in the ancient world, especially in the Gospels of the New Testament and in the noncanonical, apocryphal Gospels, including some of the ones I've mentioned here in earlier chapters, such as the Gospel of Peter. I thought it would be an interesting exercise for my students to see the new film, based on the novel by Nikos Kazantzakis, and critique it in light of what they had come to know about the historical Jesus and the apocryphal tales told about him in antiquity. So I announced that one of the course assignments was a five-page movie critique.

This is when I first realized that I had moved to the Bible belt. Where I had taught before, at Rutgers University in New Jersey, this kind of assignment would have caused no tremors at all. But in Chapel Hill, among students from North Carolina, many of them from very conservative religious backgrounds, it provoked a virtual uprising. Several students defiantly announced that they would never go to see such a "blasphemous" film. They would rather fail the class.

This made little sense to me, as it seemed narrow-minded to condemn a movie you haven't seen. But I guess this is how censorship works: an authority tells you that something is bad for your soul, and so you avoid it like the plague, knowing nothing about it. In this case, even the "authorities" (principally fundamentalist leaders) hadn't seen the film either. But they knew about its premise, and that was enough for them. (I ended up rescinding the assignment and went to the film myself with anyone from the class who wanted to go just for fun; as it turns out, the vocal minority notwithstanding, most of the class went.)

The premise of the film is that while being crucified, Jesus, played by Willem Dafoe, has a vision of what it would be like to come down off the cross and to lead a normal life. He gets married to his former girlfriend, Mary Magdalene, and then, after she dies, to another Mary, Mary of Bethany; they have kids, and he grows old surrounded by a loving wife and family. What many viewers didn't (and still don't) realize is that this is all a vision. That is, even though a large portion of the movie deals with Jesus' life after the crucifixion, it is not something that actually happens. It is something that Jesus, in the few moments before his death on the cross, *imagines* as happening. But at the end of his fantasy he realizes that in fact it would be a huge mistake, and so he dies as God originally planned, bringing about the salvation of the world.

If the dream sequence—which to be fair, is not shown to be a dream sequence until the very end of the film—proved offensive to conservative Christians (and to lots of other people as well), what proved more offensive was the relationship of Jesus and Mary Magdalene before his public ministry began. In the film Mary is played by Barbara Hershey—for my money, the best Mary

Magdalene of all time. For one thing, she has this funky tattoo thing going all over her body. I'm not sure what the tattoos mean, but they do make her stand out from the crowd.

Mary in this portrayal is a prostitute, and Scorsese bars no holds in showing her as such. In one of the most intriguing (and offensive to some people) scenes in the film, a caravan has arrived in town and the camel drivers are waiting inside Mary's bordello for their ten minutes with her—much of it shown to viewers with inquiring minds. Jesus himself is in line but waits till the end, not to have sex with Mary but to ask her forgiveness for previously jilting her. As it turns out, his earlier rejection is what drove her to prostitution, and she, frankly, is not in a forgiving mood, especially as he goes on, somewhat pathetically, bemoaning to Mary—who has been having sex all day with a series of strangers—about just how sinful he is. She kicks him out of the house, and it looks like that's where their relationship will end.

But in a later sequence they meet up again, in even less happy circumstances. Mary is being dragged by her hair by a group of angry Jewish men who have had enough of her flagrantly immoral behavior and have decided to stone her. Jesus intervenes, and by pointing out the hypocrisy of the self-righteous antagonists— some of whom are also known for their sexual exploits—he manages to save Mary from being beaten to a bloody pulp. She, as you might imagine, is grateful, and becomes his first follower. So begins Jesus' ministry, which culminates, after a number of twists and turns in the plot, in his crucifixion by the Romans.

And so we have Mary Magdalene in Hollywood. She plays a central role in both these films, *Jesus Christ Superstar* and *The Last Temptation of Christ.* And both actresses played the role well: Yvonne Elliman in 1973 and Barbara Hershey in 1989 were each nominated as Best Supporting Actress for the Golden Globe Awards. In many respects the characterizations of Mary were similar: she is a reformed woman of ill repute who is attached to Jesus and sexually drawn to him. In the latter movie, she is imagined as marrying him.

In the most recent blitz of media attention to Mary Magdalene, she actually is married to him. This is the premise behind the best-selling novel of the twenty-first century: *The Da Vinci Code* by Dan Brown.

The Da Vinci Code is a murder mystery set in modern times, but its intrigue for many people has been its historical claims about Jesus and Mary Magdalene. I won't summarize the entire plot here, as it is familiar to nearly everyone— there are only six people in the English-speaking world who have not read the book—and in any event there are numerous books written about it. What I'm interested in here is the portrayal specifically of Mary Magdalene, which for many readers is the book's most captivating feature. According to the leading characters of *The Da Vinci Code,* who are historical sleuths who appear to know everything there is to be known about the Holy Grail and its origins in the life of Mary Magdalene, Jesus and Mary were married lovers whose union was covered over by the later ecclesiastical authorities. Not only did they have (licit) sex, they produced an offspring: after Jesus was crucified, Mary fled

Palestine for France, where her daughter, Sarah, was born. Sarah was eventually to become the founder of the Merovingian dynasty, so French royalty (and— big surprise—one of the leading characters in the novel) could claim a divine bloodline. This is obviously a significant datum: if your direct ancestor was none other than the Son of God, wouldn't you want people to know?

These historical claims about Mary in *The Da Vinci Code* have intrigued modern readers, a surprising number of whom have simply assumed that it is gospel truth. Over the past year or so, since I published my own book on *The Da Vinci Code* (I didn't want to be left out), I have given lots of talks to lots of audiences about the historical problems in Dan Brown's narrative.[1] There are in fact mistakes all over the place, some of them howlers and some of them simply rooted in a misunderstanding of, or more likely an ignorance of, what our ancient sources actually say about Jesus (and Mary Magdalene). What I have found is that people in my audiences are all too eager to know where Dan Brown got it wrong. But when it comes to Mary Magdalene, there are always two or three people who want to insist that he must have gotten it right. These are never people who are historians, who know the ancient sources and read them in their ancient languages (Greek and Latin, for example). They are just regular folk who think that it *must* be right: Jesus and Mary must have been married with kids, just because it makes sense.

Unfortunately, history cannot be written simply on the basis of what makes sense. It makes best sense to me, for example, to think there should never have been influenza epidemics, tsunamis, hurricanes, earthquakes, mudslides, world wars, killing fields, and black deaths that have wiped millions of otherwise innocent and well-meaning people off the face of the earth. But like it or not, disasters happen, whatever my preferences and best sense. History has to be written on the basis of evidence. And that applies to the history of the 2004 tsunami, the 1970s Khmer Rouge, the 1918 influenza outbreak, the 1860s Civil War, and everything else in history, including such less personally tragic matters such as the life of Mary Magdalene.

Still, we are left with widespread perceptions of Mary Magdalene fueled by Broadway, Hollywood, and Barnes and Noble. But what do historians say about her both as a historical figure and as one who was "remembered," not just since the 1970s, but during the early centuries of the church? Is it true that she was a close companion of Jesus? That they were sexually intimate? That they might have been married? That they had a child? Is it true that she was a prostitute, reformed by the message of Christ? That she was nearly stoned for her illicit sexual activities?

The Medieval Mary

I should point out that these modern portrayals of Mary are not simply the products of modern imaginations (we will see in the chapters that follow that they are not the results of historical scholarship either). Mary has long been an intriguing figure to Christian storytellers down through the ages. In the Middle Ages, for example, she was a highly influential and intriguing figure, and the stories told about her were widespread and well known, even if many of these accounts have not made it onto our modern radar screens. The most famous collection of medieval stories about the Christian saints was produced in 1260 by an Italian author known as Jacobus de Voragine in a book now known as *The Golden Legend*. Rather than portraying Mary in the modern guise as Jesus' spouse, *The Golden Legend* shows her as a chaste, reformed sex offender whose turn to the sacred life made her one of the most holy and powerful of Christ's followers after his death.

Although she is portrayed in her early adulthood as having it all—she is fabulously rich, insanely beautiful, and outrageously sensual—she converts to become a follower of Jesus. Fourteen years after Jesus' ascension to heaven, Mary, her brother Lazarus, and several other followers of Jesus are rounded up by unbelievers and set afloat on the Mediterranean in a rudderless boat, left to die of exposure. But a great miracle happens, and the boat arrives in Marseilles, in southern France (hence the idea that Mary went to France after the crucifixion, as found in *The Da Vinci Code*). They take shelter near a pagan shrine.

The local governor and his wife come to make an offering to their pagan god in the shrine, and Mary preaches the gospel to them, dissuading them from performing the sacrifice. Later the governor confronts Mary and says that he will believe in her God if God can provide a son to him and his wife. Mary prays, and the woman becomes pregnant. The governor decides he needs to learn more about this God who can work miracles, and so plans to set off for Rome to meet the apostle Peter himself. The governor's pregnant wife insists on coming along as well, and this is where the trouble begins.

A violent storm arises on the sea, causing the woman to go into labor. She gives birth to a premature son, and she dies in childbirth. The sailors want to dispose of both mother and son overboard, as being bad luck for the rest of their journey. But the governor convinces them to drop them all off on a nearby island. When he arrives onshore, he covers his deceased wife with his cloak and lays the child, who is still alive, on her breast. He then returns to the boat and goes on to meet Peter in Rome.

Peter greets him and tells him not to be upset over what has happened: "Do not take it amiss. . . . It is in the Lord's power to give gifts to whom he will, to take away what was given, to restore what was taken away, and to turn your grief into joy" (*Golden Legend,* 96). Peter then takes the governor to Jerusalem to show him all the places that Christ had taught and performed his miraculous deeds, where he died and from where he ascended to heaven. The two of them stay together for two years.

Eventually the governor becomes eager to return home. He catches a ship, which happens to pass by the island where he had left his dead wife and exposed son. He begs and bribes the crew to let him see their place of final rest.

But when he arrives, he sees the child, now a two-year-old, traipsing down the hill to his still-dead mother and sucking on her breast for his daily nourishment. We are told that this was a miracle worked long distance by none other than Mary Magdalene. As the governor praises her greatness, a yet greater miracle occurs: his wife rises from the dead to tell him that while he was in Jerusalem with Peter, she was beside him with Mary Magdalene—invisible companions, much as Scrooge and the Ghost of Christmas Past in *A Christmas Carol.*

They return to their home city and greet the flesh-and-blood Mary, reformed sinner and worker of stupendous miracles in the name of her Lord. Other miracles continue to happen throughout this lavish medieval text.

Whatever else we can say about the real, historical Mary Magdalene, her memory lived on for centuries—for millennia—among devotees committed to the wonderful power that she could exude as the (nonsexual) intimate of Christ.

But what can we say about the historical Mary Magdalene?

Mary in Our Earliest Sources

We found that it was difficult to separate historical fact from legendary accretion in the cases of Peter and Paul. We have the same problems when it comes to Mary Magdalene, but the problems manifest themselves in slightly different ways. Modern readers probably don't realize just how little is said about Mary in our surviving sources. This was not a problem with the other two. Peter shows up in scores of places in the Gospels and even more in Acts; two books are (pseudonymously) attributed to him in the New Testament, and several others from outside the New Testament. Paul, on the other hand, is the main character of the book of Acts and is the alleged author of nearly half the books of the New Testament and of other books that did not come to be included in the canon. The problem with writing about these two is knowing what *not* to say, as there is so much information available. With Mary we are in an entirely different situation. Her name occurs only thirteen times in the entire New Testament—and that includes parallel passages (that is, if her name shows up twice in a story in Matthew, and the same story is in Mark and Luke, that would be six of the thirteen occurrences). She is never mentioned in the book of Acts, in the letters of Paul, in any of the other writings of the New Testament, by the ten authors known as the Apostolic Fathers just after the New Testament, or by many of our earliest church fathers.

Moreover, when she does happen to be mentioned in our early sources, not much is said about her. Many people assume that she must have been a particularly close and intimate companion of Jesus. This is often based on their sense of what she must have been like, or on the legendary accounts that have come down to us, whether in the *Golden Legend* or in *The Da Vinci Code.* Some scholars have done nothing to disabuse people of this idea, championing her as Jesus' closest disciple, or as the only one who was faithful to him to the end, or as the one who must have received his special teachings privately in their shared moments together. How much evidence is there for any of this in our most ancient sources, the Gospels of the New Testament? In fact, virtually none. During Jesus' entire public ministry, prior to his crucifixion, Mary is mentioned *once,* and that is in only one Gospel (i.e., the other three don't mention her at all before the crucifixion). Even in that one instance it is not a reference just to her—let alone a reference that suggests she was particularly close to Jesus. The reference comes in Luke 8:2, where we are told that three women traveled with Jesus and his disciples, providing them with financial support from their own private means: Joanna, Susanna, and Mary Magdalene. Two of these women are identified further: Joanna is the wife of an important figure in the administration of King Herod, and Mary is one from whom seven demons had been exorcised (whether by Jesus the text doesn't say).

That's the only reference to Mary's relationship to Jesus during his ministry in the entire New Testament. Obviously it doesn't give us much to go on. In this case we are not dealing with a situation like that of Peter and Paul, where there was so much information that it was difficult to weed out what was historical from what was legendary. Here there is so little information that it is difficult to know even what to talk about.

But that hasn't stopped Christian storytellers (and scholars) from trying. That's because of what happens *after* Jesus' ministry, when he is crucified and then raised from the dead. According to our early accounts, Mary was one of the women who observed the crucifixion, watched his burial, and came on the third day to anoint his body, only to find the tomb empty. In a couple of our sources, the resurrected Jesus appeared to her first, before he appeared to anyone else, even Peter.

This is why Mary was destined to become a figure of paramount importance to Christian storytellers past and present. She is portrayed as the first witness to proclaim Jesus' resurrection. If this is true historically, it is hard to deny or underplay her importance. In some sense, you could argue that Mary started Christianity.

The fact that she is historically important, however, does not mean that we know much about her. Of the thirteen explicit references to her in our sources, all but the one I just mentioned, from Luke 8, deal with her involvement (from a distance, mostly; she wasn't a main player) in observing Jesus' death and burial and then her experience at the empty tomb afterward. As we will see in greater depth later, even these twelve references to Mary are problematic for knowing what really happened to her. I show this to my students by having them do the exercise I mentioned earlier. I ask them to take the four New Testament accounts of Jesus' resurrection and compare them in detail. It is a great eye-opener for many of them, and something I'd suggest for everyone, for if you compare the four New Testament accounts in detail, you'll see that they differ on just about every point. Who went to Jesus' tomb on the third day after his crucifixion? Was it Mary alone or Mary in the company of other women? If there were other women, how many others were there and who were they? Was the stone in front of the tomb when they arrived, or had it been rolled away? Whom did the women see there? Was it a young man? Two men? An angel? What were the women told to do? Were they instructed to tell the disciples to go to Galilee to meet Jesus, or to stay in Jerusalem to meet him? How did the women react? Did they do as they were told, or did they keep silent and not tell, out of fear? And what then did the disciples do in response? Did they believe the women or disbelieve them? Did they check it out for themselves or not? Did they head up to Galilee or stay in Jerusalem? And did the women themselves (or Mary herself) have a vision of the resurrected Jesus? If so, was Mary the first to see him, or was someone else? And when she saw him, did she grab hold of him or not? And on and on. The answers to all these questions, and more, depend entirely on which account you happen to read.

I stress this point because when it comes to Mary in particular, we are dealing not only with sparse and scattered evidence but also with diverging accounts. Little is said about her, and the few episodes that do mention her are so full of discrepancies that it is scarcely possible to know what, if anything, actually happened.

This is not to say that there is nothing to know about Mary Magdalene—at least I hope not, since I still have about five more chapters to write about her. But it is to say that our sources are remarkably problematic, even more so than in the cases of Peter and Paul, where the evidence is quite abundant. There are later sources, of course, that deal with Mary, from well before the *Golden Legend* of the Middle Ages. Most remarkably, there are some of the Gnostic Gospels discovered at Nag Hammadi and elsewhere, including, most significant of all, the Gospel of Mary itself, a firsthand account of a secret revelation that she allegedly received directly from Christ and delivered over to the other disciples, who express considerable doubt of the accuracy of her vision since it was, after all, "given to a woman." These later sources may not be of much use in knowing what the historical Mary was like, but they can provide us with solid information concerning how she was remembered.

Who's Who? The Confusion over Marys in the New Testament

One other feature of our sources makes Mary's case different from those of Peter and Paul, and in some respects far more interesting. Probably in part because there are such sparse references to her involvement with Jesus, readers of the Gospels have always inserted her into stories where her name does not occur. That is how the various traditional interpretations of Mary have come about—for example, that she was a prostitute, that she was nearly stoned for committing adultery, that she had a sister, Martha, and a brother, Lazarus, and so on.

None of these things is actually said about Mary Magdalene. One problem is that there are other people named Mary in the New Testament, and sometimes these other Marys are confused with Mary Magdalene. Another problem is that there are several stories in the Gospels about unnamed women, and readers have sometimes plugged Mary into these stories, assuming that she was the woman in question, when it actually appears otherwise.

First I should say something about the name Mary, which was one of the most popular names among Jewish women in the first century. Just within the New Testament, we know of six women who bore the name, including, for example, Jesus' own mother—and this is out of a total of just sixteen women named in the Gospels. In the first century, nearly one out of four Jewish women from Palestine whose names are known was called Mary. That is why ancient sources sometimes differentiate among these people by identifying them in other ways: thus one woman is called Mary Magdalene (literally, Mary of Magdala), another one is called Mary of (the town of) Bethany, another is called Mary the mother of Jesus, and so on. A problem naturally arises when readers assume that an author is talking about one Mary when in fact he is talking about another. Combined with the problem that some unnamed women are also found in the early stories about Jesus, it's easy to see how identities could get confused.

Let me show how the confusion has led to some of the well-known but nonhistorical traditions about Mary Magdalene. In the Gospel of Mark, an unnamed woman pours ointment over Jesus' head prior to his arrest and trial. He praises her for anointing him for his burial (Mark 14:3–9). There is nothing to tie this woman to Mary Magdalene, who is never mentioned in Mark's Gospel prior to the Passion. But the Gospel of John, written about thirty years later, also speaks about a woman anointing Jesus, and this time it is someone named Mary. It is not Mary Magdalene, however, but Mary of Bethany (John 12:1–8). Moreover, this cannot be the same event mentioned in Mark, because in Mark it takes place in the home of Simon the Pharisee in the land of Galilee and in John it takes place in the house of Mary (of Bethany), Martha, and Lazarus in the land of Judea. But readers have confused the two stories, making both women "Mary." Now, when Luke tells the story it is much like Mark's, but in this case we are told that the woman is a "sinner," and Simon the Pharisee is surprised that Jesus allows her to touch him (Luke 7:37–39). When this third story is taken to refer to the same event as Mark's and John's, then what results is a garbled account, not found in Mark, John, or Luke, in which Jesus is anointed by a sinful woman named Mary. The category "sinner" then somehow gets translated to mean "prostitute" (which it didn't mean—it simply meant a woman who did not keep the law rigorously), with the result that Jesus is thought to have been anointed by a prostitute named Mary.

Elsewhere in Luke's Gospel we have a reference to Mary Magdalene, "from whom had gone out seven demons" (8:2). We aren't told what these demons were—but suppose you imagine that this Mary is the same as the sinful woman who anointed Jesus (which she couldn't be, for reasons I'll point out later). Then possibly it was her demon possession that drove her to prostitution (even though demons are never said to do that in the New Testament). So by smashing all these different stories together, you have the following identification: Mary Magdalene is also Mary of Bethany, who was a prostitute but had reformed because Jesus cast seven demons out of her. This picture is not at all historical—it has come about simply by combining different stories that mention different Marys and yet other stories that mention other women, none of whom were named Mary, leading to one big conglomerate story about Mary Magdalene, the reformed prostitute.

Other stories then get attached to her—for example, the near-fatal attempt on the life of a woman caught in the act of adultery, who is taken out to be stoned before Jesus intervenes. This is thought to be Mary, as, for example, in Scorsese's *Last Temptation of Christ* and as reprised in one of the rare flashbacks found in Mel Gibson's controversial *The Passion of the Christ,* where again Mary Magdalene is the only faithful follower of Jesus (apart from his mother, Mary), whom he had earlier saved when she was about to be stoned.

None of these New Testament stories, however, deals with Mary Magdalene except in popular imagination, which has kept blissfully removed from a careful reading of the texts themselves. In fact, the New Testament texts actually tell a different tale. Mary Magdalene is not the person she is sometimes said to be.

1. Mary Magdalene cannot be the sinful woman who anoints Jesus in Luke 7. This woman, I should repeat, is not called a prostitute. Anyone who assumes that a "sinful woman" must have been someone who was paid for sex is simply misogynist. In fact, for particularly strict Jews of the first century, a sinful woman could be someone who ground her grain on the Sabbath or who ate a bit of shrimp cocktail, for this would be someone who did not assiduously observe the law of Moses. But in any event, this sinful woman who anoints Jesus in Luke 7 is not Mary Magdalene, because Mary Magdalene is actually introduced by Luke in his very next story (Luke 8:1–3), where he gives her name (Mary), her identification (of the town of Magdala), and describes something about her ("from whom seven demons had gone out"). As New Testament scholars today all agree, if the earlier story of Luke 7 were about Mary, he would have introduced her for the first time *there,* not later.

2. Mary Magdalene is not the same person as Mary of Bethany. The name Magdalene indicates the town she comes from: the Galilean town, on the shore of the Sea of Galilee, known as Magdala. The other Mary, however, came from and lived in Bethany, a town near Jerusalem in Judea. They can't be the same person because the one identifying mark for both of them is given precisely to differentiate them.

3. Mary Magdalene was not attacked by a group of angry men who wanted to stone her for committing adultery (a story found in John 8). The woman

in this intriguing story is left unnamed. I should point out that even though this has long been a favorite story for readers of the New Testament—and the one episode from Jesus' ministry that seems to make it into every Hollywood version of his life—it is a story that did not originally occur in any of our Gospels. Today you will find it in your English Bible at the beginning of John chapter 8. But almost all modern translations will place the story in brackets. That's because it does not occur in our oldest and best manuscripts of the Gospel of John. It was evidently added to John's Gospel—as were other verses, just as yet other verses were deleted—by scribes who had heard the story and wanted to include it in their gospel accounts, even though it was not originally there.[2] In any event, there is nothing in the story about Mary Magdalene: the woman caught committing adultery is unnamed. (By the way, if she was caught, where's the man she was caught with? Jewish law condemns them both, not just the woman, to death.)

An Earlier State of Confusion

As I have already indicated, it is not only modern readers who have confused the various women mentioned in the stories of Jesus, resulting in a kind of conglomerate figure, the reformed prostitute and exorcised demoniac Mary Magdalene, who anointed Jesus for burial prior to his Passion. The same view of Mary is found in the thirteenth-century *Golden Legend,* and in fact for centuries before that. Since the view is not set forth in the Gospels themselves, how far back does it go?

As it turns out, we are remarkably fortunate to be able to pinpoint a moment when the sundry New Testament stories were amalgamated into one composite picture. So far as we know, it happened first in the year 591 CE, in a sermon delivered by none other than Pope Gregory the Great (540–604 CE). In his Thirty-third Homily, delivered on the story of Jesus' anointing in Luke 7, the pope stated the following:

> She whom Luke calls the sinful woman, whom John calls Mary, we believe to be the Mary from whom seven devils were ejected according to Mark. And what did these seven devils signify, if not all the vices? . . . It is clear, brothers, that the woman previously used the unguent to perfume her flesh in forbidden acts. What she therefore displayed more scandalously, she was now offering to God in a more praiseworthy manner. She had coveted with earthly eyes, but now through penitence these are consumed with tears. She displayed her hair to set off her face, but now her hair dries her tears. She had spoken proud things with her mouth, but in kissing the Lord's feet, she now planted her mouth on the Redeemer's feet. For every delight, therefore, she had had in herself, she now immolated herself. She turned the mass of her crimes to virtues, in order to serve God entirely in penance, for as much as she had wrongly held God in contempt.[3]

Even though many of Jesus' male contemporaries believed that women should not be involved with business outside the home, many women had to work in order to survive in the ancient Roman world, as seen in this funerary monument portraying two women working in a poultry/butcher shop.

Here is not merely a conflated Mary—the individual parts are taken from discrete Gospel accounts, most of which are not actually about her—but also an imagined Mary, one whose heartfelt and tearstained penance upon her conversion to be a follower of Christ corresponds in inverse proportion to the sins of perfume, eyes, hair, and mouth she had committed as a lost and unrepentant prostitute.

Even if we are also interested in knowing what the actual, historical Mary was like, based on the flimsy evidence that survives about her, it is important to realize that she came to be remembered in this way. Gregory's homily, of course, was written by a man—as were the Golden Legend, all the other recollections of Mary that survive from antiquity down through the Middle Ages, the novel and the screenplay for *The Last Temptation of Christ* and *The Passion of the Christ,* and the music and screenplay for *Jesus Christ Superstar.* Maybe this should tell us something. With Mary we are dealing not only with how an important woman was remembered in the years and centuries after her death but also with how she was remembered by *men.*

I don't know if Gregory's account can be taken as completely representative of this collective act of memory, but it is striking that Mary's body is seen as a threat, something that can be used to seduce men and lead them away. The only redeeming feature of her body is when it turns from its dangerous acts (dangerous, that is, to the men concerned) and falls to the feet of the man Jesus in repentance and sorrow. It is the sorrowful penitent who is acceptable; that is the kind of woman these texts seek. One can't help but think that the men who relish this recollection of Mary the penitent sinner are those who are trying to inform their own world with their own vision of what sexual and gendered relationships ought to be, with women not enticing men with the dangers of sex but falling at their feet in humble submission and penitence.

In any event, our study of the traditions of Mary Magdalene will not focus on her modern-day portrayals in novel and film, or on the medieval legends about her, or even on the sixth-century reflections of powerful Christian figures such as the pope. We will be primarily interested in seeing what we can know about her as a historical figure, and to see how she came to be remembered and portrayed in the earliest surviving sources of Christianity, the Gospels and other writings of the first three hundred years of the church.

Chapter Fourteen

Mary During the Ministry of Jesus

It is extremely difficult to know about people who lived in the past. That's why we need historians. Most of the billions of people who have ever lived on this planet are completely unknown and unknowable: they lived and died, leaving no trace. Of course that's less true today than in earlier centuries. For most people in the American context, at least, there are obituaries. And as the computer age continues to advance, with e-mail and blogs joining the frenzy at breakneck speed, the record of our individual existences grows apace. Presumably some of these electronic traces of our lives are stored *somewhere,* for the amusement of future researchers (and the chagrin of some people who thought for some reason that e-mail was private).

But for people in the past, we are less advantaged. In fact, we don't have a scrap of evidence for the vast majority of people living, say, in the nineteenth century. What about the first century? In most instances, we are extremely lucky to know a name.

What happens, though, when we have more than a name, when we have a written account? That's when historians can get to work. The problem involves figuring out if the written record (if we are fortunate beyond measure, there will be more than one) is accurate. Suppose a private letter is discovered that discusses a previously unknown James MacDougall of Boston, who lived in the 1880s and who is described as the premier American philosopher of his day. No historian could take the description seriously: this MacDougall never published any books or articles, is never mentioned by any other philosopher of his day, cannot be found on the faculty lists of any college or university, and so on. What if it turns out that the letter was written by his widow soon after he died? Then we would have a clear motive for her saying what she did: the letter is historical evidence not of MacDougall's philosophical influence but of her attachment to and admiration of him.

The same kind of investigative procedure applies to people from the distant past. We are always best served when we have multiple references to a figure. It is quite useful when these multiple references come from independent sources, so that they cannot be thought to have collaborated with one another to "get their facts straight." It is always best if these sources are contemporary with the people they discuss, or at least if they are based on contemporary sources. It is particularly useful when these sources happen to agree on what they say, so there is corroboration without collaboration. And it is best of all when the sources don't show any particular bias that would have pushed them to slant their statements one way or another, unlike the widow of James MacDougall.

Now, with Peter and Paul we are in comparatively excellent shape. They are discussed in multiple and independent sources from near their own day— Peter, for example, is spoken of in various Gospels and Acts, and in Paul's case we have some of his own writings. But what about Mary Magdalene?

References to Mary in Our Early Gospels

As we saw in the previous chapter, Mary is mentioned in the four Gospels of the New Testament, though not frequently (thirteen times). These sources are relatively close to the time she was living: within fifty or sixty years, at least. They are based on traditions that had been in circulation in the meantime, many of which must go back to her own lifetime. We also have later sources, such as the Gospel of Peter and Gnostic writings such as the Gospel of Philip and even the Gospel of Mary. These are useful for showing how Mary came to be remembered by Christians of the second and third centuries. But the first issue is to determine what our oldest sources tell us about the historical Mary.

Bits of useful information are found in the terse references of Mark and Luke. The fact that Mary is never mentioned during Jesus' ministry in Mark's Gospel must show that, at least for this author, she was not a major player in Jesus' life, let alone his closest follower, lifelong companion, and lover. The first time Mary is named is near the end, at the scene of Jesus' crucifixion:

> There were also women watching from a distance, among whom were Mary Magdalene, and Mary the mother of James the younger and of Joses, and Salome; these women had followed him when he was in Galilee and had served him; and there were many other women who had come up with him to Jerusalem. (Mark 15:40)

In Luke's Gospel, on the other hand, written some fifteen years after Mark, we do have a brief reference to Mary during Jesus' public ministry. This reference corroborates some of the things Mark had to say:

And [Jesus] was passing through the cities and villages, preaching the kingdom of God; and the Twelve were with him, as were some women who had been healed from evil spirits and illnesses: Mary, who is called Magdalene, from whom seven demons had gone out, and Joanna, the wife of Chuza, Herod's steward, and Susanna and many others, who were serving them out of their own resources. (Luke 8:1–3)

Each of these passages has a different emphasis, but they agree on several important points: Mary was a Galilean Jewish woman of means, nicknamed Magdalene, who followed Jesus and financially supported him during his itinerant ministry of preaching and healing.

On the surface this may not seem like much information, but in fact it is a lot to go on if you play the historian and dig a bit.

A Jewish Woman from Magdala

To begin with, what do we know about what it meant to be a Jewish woman in first-century Palestine? This is one of the many topics that scholars have long been interested in and have devoted entire books to.[1] One of the interesting features of the study of first-century Jewish women is that it has largely been carried out by twentieth-century Christian men. And why would such people be interested in knowing about women in first-century Judaism? For many of these modern scholars, as authority Ross Kraemer has noted, there is a personal agenda involved: they have wanted to show the vast superiority of Christianity over Judaism in the treatment of women.[2]

According to the standard stereotype, Jewish women were especially oppressed during the first century, forced to be silent and stay in the home, unable to enter into the public sphere, expected to devote themselves to cooking, cleaning, making and mending clothes, and raising children. Jesus, however, came to liberate women and so accepted them as his followers and set them free from the constraints of the overbearing Jewish law.

This portrayal, as Kraemer and others have noted, is not a disinterested description of life in the first century. It is a theologically motivated reconstruction meant to celebrate the salvation that Jesus brings, not just for the afterlife but also for life in the present among all people, men and women.

As with most stereotypes, there are some things that are probably right about this portrayal. But the picture is seriously skewed in some ways. For one thing, it is a big mistake to separate Jewish women in the ancient world from non-Jewish women, as if only the former faced strictures on their public (and private) behavior. For most androcentric cultures—that is, for most cultures—women have had to play second fiddle to men, especially to the men closest to them: their fathers, brothers, and husbands. That was true of pagans as well as Jews in the first century. And all cultures, even the most open and liberated, place restrictions, either official or practical, on genders. When was the last time you saw a female pope in Rome or a woman president in the United States?

It is true that Jewish *men* in the first century often did not place a high premium on the independent thought and judgment of their female counterparts.[3] Consider the sayings connected with a Jewish rabbi of first-century Jerusalem, a man named Yose ben Yochanan, who indicated that men should not talk extensively with women (the following account also indicates how his words were sometimes interpreted, by yet other male leaders among Jews):

> Yose ben Yochanan of Jerusalem says . . . "don't talk too much with women." He spoke of a man's wife; all the more so is the rule to be applied to the wife of one's fellow. In this regard did the sages say, "So long as a man talks too much with a woman, he (1) brings trouble on himself, (2) wastes time better spent on studying Torah, and (3) ends up an heir of Gehenna."

Comparable is another passage from ancient Jewish writings, which indicates the conditions under which a woman would not be allowed to receive the payment due to her from her marriage contract, should she be divorced. These include if she (1) goes out with her hair flowing loose, (2) spins in the marketplace, or (3) talks with just anybody. Scholars of this literature have concluded that this ruling indicates that there was to be a difference between a woman's behavior in private (where she can let down her hair, spin, and talk) and in public. But it is not at all clear that these passages indicate the actual social experience of women in first-century Jewish Palestine. They may instead represent what certain men *wanted* women's behavior to be like. Certainly it is the case that women of the upper classes could, and often did, have greater freedom of movement and speech than women among the masses. And wealthy women were in a different camp from the poor.

One of the most surprising archaeological finds of modern times is a set of inscriptions on a Jewish synagogue in the city of Aphrodisias, in Asia Minor. The inscriptions list the names of the major donors to the synagogue and the names of the synagogue leaders. What is striking is that a number of the names are women.[4] The idea that women could not be actively involved in Jewish life and worship in antiquity has been blown apart by this find. Women in some sections of society were oppressed, just as they are now. But in others they could be leaders. Presumably women who wanted to have more freedom of expression and movement would have gravitated, if it was within their means to do so, to those aspects of their culture and to those leaders of their society that could make such freedom possible.

Jesus was not the only one to bring liberation to women of the first century. But it is clear that his particular preaching would have been attractive to some kinds of women. Mary Magdalene was one of the women who followed him. I should stress that she is presented as following Jesus in the company of other women—*many* other women, according to both Mark and Luke. Several of these other women are named, for example, Joanna, Susanna, Salome, and someone else named Mary. This suggests that Mary Magdalene was not Jesus' special companion and trusted friend, at least not according to the records we have. These records are, after all, the only things historians have to go on, unless they want to invent historical claims out of thin air to support their points of view (for example, that Mary and Jesus made love and had babies).

Both Mark and Luke indicate that Mary Magdalene was from Galilee. That is the northern part of what is today the land of Israel. It is also the region Jesus himself was from, as he was raised in the small hamlet of Nazareth. Nazareth was so small and insignificant that it is not found on any map from the ancient world and is never mentioned in the Hebrew Bible. It is also not mentioned in the writings of the first-century historian Josephus, who spent a lot of time in Galilee and discusses a lot of its places. Archaeologists who have dug in Nazareth have concluded that it was remote, isolated, and small.[5] Possibly two hundred to three hundred people lived there in the days of Jesus. If he had four brothers, several sisters, a mother, and a father, as the Gospels indicate, then just his immediate nuclear family would have made up a sizable portion of the population.[6]

Some scholars have claimed that the region of Galilee was somehow less Jewish than the southern part of Israel, the region of Judea. In part this is because there were a couple of large Gentile cities in Galilee: Tiberias and Sepphoris, not too far from Nazareth. And in part it is because the region is sometimes referred to as "Galilee of the Gentiles." Recent studies have demonstrated, however, that outside the two big cities, Jewish customs, culture, and religion dominated the lives of Galilee's inhabitants.[7] Jesus himself was thoroughly Jewish in every respect. So were his followers, including Jewish women such as Mary Magdalene. They worshiped the Jewish God, kept Jewish customs, observed Jewish law. Everything about them was Jewish.

We don't know where or how Mary met Jesus, but it is probably safe to assume that she heard him preaching throughout rural Galilee, as he avoided the cities: Sepphoris, for example, is never even mentioned in the New Testament. She herself did not come from tiny Nazareth. Her name, in fact, indicates her home. She is called Magdalene because she came from Magdala.

Magdala was a much larger place than Nazareth. We know about it from the writings of Josephus, who with some exaggeration (Josephus does this a lot) indicates that it was a good-sized city surrounded by a large wall, with two grain markets, a major aqueduct for the water needs of the population, a Greek-style theater, and a hippodrome for public races, large enough to seat ten thousand people.[8] In the archaeological digs undertaken there, none of these structures has been discovered.

The town was located on the western shore of the Sea of Galilee and was best-known for two things: being a major center for the fishing industry—it was especially known for its pickled sardines—and a very large tower. The word for tower in Aramaic (the language of Jesus, Peter, Mary, and other Jews in the region) is in fact *magdala,* hence the name of the place itself. In some ancient sources it is called Migdal Nunya (Tower of Fish).

Eventually, after the days of Mary and Jesus, Magdala came to be known as a kind of luxury resort. As with most places of that kind, whether Las Vegas today or Corinth in antiquity, this carried with it some connotations of profligate lifestyles and licentious activities. It is hard to know how much Mary's own later but unfounded reputation as a prostitute relates to the fact that her name, Magdalene, came to have those associations.

I have already indicated that Mary must have been a woman of means. According to both Mark and Luke, she and the other named women "served" Jesus. The Greek term used there can be translated as "ministered" to him (and his disciples), but it often has the connotation of "providing financial support for." Jesus, of course, abandoned his livelihood as a carpenter/woodworker to engage in his public ministry.[9] His twelve disciples did likewise. As Peter says at one point: "See, we have left everything to follow you." Jesus replies:

> Truly I tell you, there is no one who has left house or brothers or sisters or mother or father or children or fields for my sake, and for the sake of the good news, who will not receive a hundredfold houses and brothers and sisters and mothers and children and fields . . . and in the age that is coming eternal life. (Mark 10:28–30)

But how were Jesus' followers to receive so much when they had no source of income? Obviously someone had to supply them with what they needed. The new siblings, parents, and children that the disciples acquired would have come from the larger group of people following Jesus. They would be spiritual family members, united around faithful adherence to Jesus' teachings. But the other newly acquired possessions—houses, fields, and so on—would have to be provided by others. We don't know if Jesus and his followers actually begged in order to survive. But since they had no source of income, *someone* had to give them what they needed, if not to pay the bills (they would have had none), then at least to eat a couple of times a day.

Mary and her female companions were the ones, or were among the ones, who did so. We don't have any indication where they themselves received an income. Possibly these women just happened to be wealthy, that is, that they came from wealthy families and/or married into money. That appears to be the case with one of the other women named by Luke: Joanna, who was married to Chuza, King Herod's personal steward (Luke 8:3). What Chuza thought about his wife giving his money away to an itinerant Jewish prophet and his unemployed followers is anyone's guess.

This raises a final question about Mary's background. Was she, like Joanna, married? As we will see more fully in a later chapter, there is absolutely nothing to suggest that she was married to Jesus. In only one passage in our canonical Gospels does she even speak with Jesus, and then she calls him "teacher"—

rather than "darling," for example. But it's not at all implausible that she was married to someone. Most people were—although not everyone, as we will see later. About all we can say is that if she was married, nothing indicates that her husband traveled with her as she accompanied Jesus, with other men and women, throughout Galilee and on to Jerusalem.

Jesus' Appeal to Women

It appears, then, from our early sources that Jesus had a number of female followers during his public ministry, and Mary may have been one of the leaders, if not *the* leader, among these women. That would explain why she is almost always named first when the women are mentioned.

But why were women such as Mary following Jesus while he preached his message and, reportedly, performed his miracles in the Galilean countryside? It's not good enough to think that of course they would have followed him, since he was the Son of God. The brute facts of history are that most people did not follow Jesus. The vast majority of Jews from his day did not accept him as the messiah, did not become his personal followers, did not think he was the one chosen by God to bring about the salvation of the world.

Is there something about his message that was particularly attractive to some people? Especially to some Jewish women of first-century Galilee? I think it would be a mistake to take the view advanced by some historians, otherwise superb scholars, who have claimed that Jesus promoted an agenda of absolute equality between the sexes and was principally concerned with establishing some kind of egalitarian society to replace the hierarchical structures that he found governing gender relations in his day.[10] Jesus had other things on his mind than reforming society for the long haul. Jesus didn't think there was going to *be* a long haul. Society and all its structures were soon to come to a screeching halt when the Son of Man arrived from heaven in judgment on the earth, destroying all that was opposed to God and setting up God's paradisal kingdom here on earth. Jesus was an apocalyptic prophet, not a social reformer.[11]

But could it not be that in his vision of that coming kingdom, there would be greater equality between the sexes, and it is this that attracted women to his message and his movement? This is probably closer to the truth, but even here one needs to be cautious. Like it or not—some people like it, and others do not—Jesus was completely a man of his time. He was not a liberated male of the twenty-first century. He was a man of first-century Palestine. He too had cultural assumptions and unquestioned beliefs about the world and the people in it. These included certain assumptions about men and women. And it appears that one of these assumptions was that men, not women, were to be leaders.

If Jesus thought otherwise—frankly, given when and where he lived, I don't see very well how he *could* have thought otherwise—it is virtually impossible to explain the rather troubling circumstance that he chose twelve male disciples to be his closest followers. Let me be perfectly clear about this point, before anyone goes on the attack: I am decidedly not saying that since Jesus' disciples were men, Christian leaders should always be men, that only men should be pastors and priests and bishops and popes and whatever. That is just the opposite of my view. Times have changed, thank God, and the idea that women in *our* day should be in any way restricted or hindered or held back is absolutely anathema. Saying that only men can be leaders of the churches, or leaders of any organizations, including families, because of what the New Testament says, or because of what happened in the days of Jesus, is like saying that we should still stone children to death when they disobey their parents, and execute bankers who lend money out at interest or textile workers who mix different kinds of fabric. The Bible was written in a particular time and place, and to rip it out of its context and pretend that somehow its words automatically apply to our own time and place, without remainder, is—not to put too fine a point on it—sheer lunacy.

But historians still want to know what the biblical authors themselves actually thought, even if it is not what we think. They want to know what people like Jesus (and Peter, and Paul, and Mary, etc.) actually believed, even if it is not what we believe. And Jesus, so far as we can tell, believed that his chief followers, the Twelve, were to be men, not women. More than that, he believed that in the coming Kingdom of God, there would not be an egalitarian society where everyone had an equal say and everyone was on an equal level. How could he, as a first-century man, even have conceptualized such a thing? Instead, he assumed there would be rulers in the future kingdom, just as there had always been for the people of God. As in the days of old, these rulers would administer the twelve tribes of God's people, the new Israel that entered into that kingdom. And who would these rulers be? The twelve men he had chosen to be his disciples. In one of his best-attested sayings of the Gospels, Jesus informs the Twelve:

> Truly I say to you that in the new world [i.e., the Kingdom of God], when the Son of Man sits on the throne of his glory [as ruler of all], you who follow me [the disciples] will also sit on twelve thrones judging the twelve tribes of Israel. (Matt. 19:28; cf. Luke 22:28–30)

Jesus, in short, did not envisage a future kingdom of God that would be organized and run in a revolutionarily egalitarian way. It would be administered by twelve men.

At the same time, Jesus' message was obviously attractive to women, to such an extent that someone like Mary Magdalene could leave home and traipse around the countryside with him, supporting him out of her own means. What, then, was the attraction?

We should probably consider the question in a broader context. Women were not the only ones drawn to the message of Jesus. His followers were generally those who were outside the realms of influence and power. This was so much the case that Jesus established a solid, though for some people dubious, reputation for attracting the dregs of society: prostitutes, tax collectors, and sinners. The religious leaders did not much like him. In fact, most of them appear to have despised him. None of his followers was a leading rabbi of the day. They were lower-class peasants such as the illiterate fishermen Peter and Andrew, James and John, people of no moment, of no standing in society, with no claims to education, wealth, or prestige. *These* were the people that Jesus thought would be the world leaders in the age to come? Could he have been serious? If such lowlifes were to be the future kings, well, then just about anyone could make it to the top. And maybe that was why Jesus' message was so attractive to the poor, the dispossessed, the outcast, the oppressed— because it was an apocalyptic promise of hope to those who were suffering in the present age.

Like other Jews in his day, Jesus believed that the present age is evil, controlled by cosmic powers that are opposed to God and his people. That's why there is such rampant misery and suffering here. One can hardly blame God for this wretched mortal existence, with its enormous rates of infant mortality, its famines, its plagues, its wars, its injustices, its anguish. It isn't God who is at fault. It is the forces that have aligned themselves against God. They are the ones who, for the time being, are in charge of this cesspool of suffering.

What can one say, then, about those people who have done well in this world, who are wealthy and prestigious and powerful? How have they acquired their wealth, prestige, and power? Obviously by aligning themselves with the forces that are in control of this world. It is the high and mighty who are God's enemies; including those in the reigning religious establishment. No wonder Jesus didn't have many friends in high society. He thought high society was an odious pit, and anyone in it was bound to face a day of reckoning, in which all that is wrong with this world would finally be set to rights.

As a Jewish apocalypticist, Jesus believed that the true followers of God would be vindicated when God brought salvation to the world that he had created. The world had become corrupt, but the corruption was to be rooted out and destroyed. All who suffer now will be vindicated then, just as all those who prosper now will be judged then. "The last shall be first and the first last" (Luke 13:30). This was not simply a clever one-liner that Jesus came up with. It was the core of his apocalyptic proclamation. God was soon to send a deliverer from heaven—one whom Jesus called the "Son of Man"—who would take down the high and mighty and exalt the lowly. "For all who exalt themselves will be humbled, and all those who humble themselves will be exalted" (Luke 14:11).

This radical reversal of fortunes was to take place soon, with the imminent arrival of God's Kingdom: "Truly I tell you, some of those standing here will not taste death before they see that the Kingdom of God has come in power" (Mark 9:1). He spoke these words to his own disciples, some of whom would still be living when they saw it happen: "Truly I tell you, this generation will not pass away before all these things take place" (Mark 13:30). It's no wonder that Peter, Andrew, and the others left their jobs to follow Jesus. The end was coming soon, and they would in the very near future be exalted to places of prominence in God's kingdom, where all those who were downtrodden and oppressed would enjoy the pleasures of God's presence in a world in which there would no longer be any poverty, injustice, or social ostracism.

I began this short excursus into the message of Jesus because I wanted to explain just why his message may have been appealing to women in his day, such as Mary Magdalene. It is precisely because it was an apocalyptic message of a radical reversal when the lowly and oppressed would be exalted and liberated. I don't want to make the mistake of saying that all Jewish women were horribly oppressed and that Jesus was the only one enlightened enough to liberate them—the claim of many Christian theologians taking the guise of historians. But women generally in the ancient world, Jewish women among them, were widely restricted in their movements and interactions, in the roles they could play in their families, their religious societies, their political worlds. There were exceptions. But for the most part, a woman with ambition, especially from the lower classes, had nowhere to go.

Jesus' message may well have seemed inordinately attractive to such women. In the near future there would be a complete and radical change. This world and the society that inhabits it would be overthrown. A new kingdom would come. The lowly will be exalted, the oppressed will be vindicated. Surely the lowly and oppressed, women among them, took this to be extremely good news. This, in fact, was the gospel.

There is more to it than that. One of the key aspects of Jesus' teaching was that those expecting the imminent arrival of God's Kingdom need to prepare by living in ways that are appropriate to it. Life in the future Kingdom will reflect God's own values, such as love, justice, and freedom. These values should be reflected in how the followers of Jesus' message live in the present. In the future kingdom there will be no hatred, and so Jesus' followers should love one another now. In the future kingdom there will be no loneliness, and so Jesus' followers should visit the widows and orphans now. In the future kingdom there will be no poverty, and so Jesus' followers should sell their possessions and give to the poor now. In the future kingdom there will be no hunger, and so Jesus' followers should feed the hungry now. In the future kingdom there will be no sickness, and so Jesus' followers should heal the sick now. In the future kingdom there will be no demons, and so Jesus' followers should cast out demons now. In the future kingdom there will be no war, and so Jesus' followers should work for peace now. In the future kingdom there will be no injustice, and so Jesus' followers should fight injustice now.[12]

The future Kingdom could begin to be realized in the here and now, as Jesus' followers begin to implement its values and standards in the present. That's why, for Jesus, the Kingdom of God is "like a mustard seed" (Mark

4:31). It is a tiny little seed when first planted, but then it grows into an enormous bush. The Kingdom is like that because it has a small, inauspicious beginning in the lives of Jesus' followers in the here and now. But when the Son of Man arrives in judgment on the earth, the plant that emerges will be enormous. It will, in fact, take over the world.

If women will no longer be silenced and oppressed in the future kingdom, what about now? It is no surprise that Jesus had many women followers, according to early sources such as Mark and Luke. Who more suited to hear his message! So both while Jesus was alive and soon after his death, women played a significant role in his communities of followers. Just as they would be liberated in the future kingdom, so they could already begin to feel the fruits of their liberation in the present. No wonder that in the earliest Christian communities that we know about, those of Paul, there are women patrons of the churches, women deacons, women missionaries, and even women apostles. Women found the apocalyptic proclamation of Jesus, and of Paul after him, liberating.[13]

There is another aspect of Jesus' apocalyptic message that may have provided a source of comfort and hope for some of his women followers. One of the things he taught his disciples was that earthly families are of no moment. This is one of those teachings that tends to be watered down in our current craze for what have come to be known as "family values." The assumption of most (American) Christians, and the explicit claim of many Christian preachers, is that Jesus himself was a proponent of our own view of such values: family, home, obedience to parents, one husband/one wife, or whatever. But the earliest traditions about Jesus ring a troubling note for such claims. We've already seen that Jesus does not upbraid his followers for leaving their parents, spouses, and children to follow him; he praises them for doing so. In fact, at one point—this comes as a shock to my students, who can't believe Jesus would say such a thing—Jesus indicates that no one can be his follower unless he "hates his father and mother" (Luke 14:26).

Jesus appears to have taught that his own followers were to constitute a new family for those who had left everything to accompany him on his path. As found in our earliest Gospel:

> And a crowd was sitting around him, and they told him: "Look, your mother and your brothers and sisters are looking for you outside." And he replied to them, "Who is my mother and brothers?" Looking at those who were sitting in a circle around him he said: "See, here is my mother and my brothers. For whoever does the will of God, this is my brother, sister, and mother." (Mark 3:31–34)

This may not be a comforting thought to those who cherish the nuclear family over, say, friends and acquaintances on the outside. But for some this new teaching could be good news—especially for some women. Women throughout the Greco-Roman world—both within Judaism and outside of it—were normally under the authority of the male figures of their own families:

their fathers at first, and then, after marriage, their husbands. But what if the family unit is declared of no binding force? Women are no longer under male authority.

In fact, Jesus' teaching goes even farther than this. Not only did he deny the authority of the nuclear family, he also preached that the institution of marriage is itself merely a temporary measure, to be dissolved when the kingdom of God arrived.

In one of the most intriguing stories of our early Gospels, Jesus is confronted by his opponents, the Jewish Sadducees, over the matter of whether there will be a future resurrection of the dead (Mark 12:12–27). Jewish apocalypticists such as Jesus thought that at the end of the age, God would raise all people from the dead, some to face judgment and others to receive an eternal reward. But the Sadducees were not apocalypticists and did not subscribe to the idea that there would be a future resurrection. They thought—as did a lot of other nonapocalyptic Jews, and as did most pagans—that once you died, that was the end of the story: you simply ceased to exist.

We have a story in Mark's Gospel in which a group of Sadducees try to convince Jesus that a resurrection makes no sense. They present him with a hypothetical situation: there was a man who died before his wife conceived a child. According to the law of Moses, in a situation like this the man's brother is to marry the widow and give her children, to preserve the family line. As it turns out, the man was one of seven brothers. The woman married each one of them in turn, as they all died and left her childless. Then she herself died. So, ask the Sadducees, when the resurrection of the dead occurs, whose wife will she be? For she was married to all seven, but she can have only one husband at a time, even in the supposed afterlife.

It's a good question and a nice trap. But, as is his wont, Jesus easily gets out of it. In this case he does so by arguing that marriage happens only in this age. It is a temporary measure. In the kingdom of God "they neither marry nor are given in marriage, but are like the angels in heaven" (Mark 12:25). Angels don't marry, and in the future kingdom, neither will people.

Why would that be good news for women? Remember: in the first century, when a woman was married, she was under the authority of her husband. But if there was no marriage (and if her father was no longer living), then she would be free to be her own person. More than that, Jesus indicated that his followers should begin implementing the values of the kingdom in the present. It is not surprising to find that some of Jesus' followers—including the apostle Paul, as one salient example—maintained that it was in fact better to remain single and celibate (1 Cor. 7:7, 25–26). We know of female Christians of later times who followed precisely this teaching. The social payoff for them was significant: they were free from the restrictions otherwise imposed on women in a patriarchal society, where fathers and husbands could dictate what women could do and how they should act.

Once again, it should be clear why some women found this message so compelling. We have no hard-and-fast information on the matter with regard to Mary Magdalene herself. None of our texts says exactly why she followed Jesus. But it is not at all implausible that she found his message not only persuasive but also personally liberating.

Chapter Fifteen

Jesus and Mary in Conversation

People attach themselves to religious leaders for all sorts of reasons. Sometimes it is because of the message, a teaching so powerful and life-transforming that it is worth giving up everything to follow. Sometimes it is because of personal charm or charisma that naturally and irresistibly draws people in. Sometimes it is because of a personal interaction—special attention paid to one in need, repaid by a complete devotion to the cause. And sometimes it is all of these things.

That may have been the case with Mary when she committed herself as one of Jesus' followers. She may well have been drawn to Jesus' charisma and found his message of the coming Kingdom of God liberating. Possibly she had been searching for some such message as a way to escape from the humdrum of the everyday or, perhaps, from the oppressive structures of a patriarchal society. But it may not have been only Jesus' message that Mary found liberating. He may have personally liberated her—freed her from a terrible affliction she was suffering.

Jesus and Mary: A Possible First Encounter

In the one reference to Mary during Jesus' public ministry (Luke 8:2–3), we are told that she belonged to a group of his women followers who "had been healed from evil spirits and illnesses." More specifically, we're told that "seven demons had gone out" of her. The number seven in this context may not be meant to be taken literally. It is often used to refer to a "complete" number. In this case, it may simply mean that she was completely overwhelmed by a demonic disorder before she joined Jesus' followers. Luke doesn't actually say that it was Jesus who healed her of her ailment, but it can probably be inferred. Just a few verses earlier he indicates that "Jesus cured many people of sicknesses and plagues and evil spirits" (Luke 7:21). And it is explicitly stated in the ending to the Gospel of Mark that was added by a later scribe (Mark himself ended his story at 16:8).[1] In this addition we learn that after his resurrection, Jesus first appeared "to Mary Magdalene, from whom he had cast out seven demons" (Mark 16:9). Whether or not we are dealing with a historical datum, it is clear that Mary was remembered as a demon-possessed woman who had been exorcised by Jesus. This would help explain, obviously, her profound attachment to him.

What else can our earliest Gospels tell us about Mary and her interaction with Jesus during his public ministry? Unfortunately, as I've already emphasized, the Gospels of the New Testament (and Paul, and the other authors of the New Testament, and the Apostolic Fathers) tell us nothing else.

Jesus and Mary in Ongoing Discussion

What is interesting, however, is that Mary does play a significant role in the ministry of Jesus as it was remembered in the writings of early Gnostic Christians. Mary, in fact, is a key figure in some of these books—including several of the Nag Hammadi writings and one book found about fifty years before this library was discovered, the Gospel of Mary.

I will devote a good deal of attention to the Gospel of Mary in a later chapter, where I discuss the stories of Jesus' encounter with Mary after his resurrection. Other conversations that are reported in our sources may also be situated in that context, but in some instances they may represent conversations that reportedly took place during his public ministry. In any event, as you might imagine, these Gnostic texts probably do not preserve historically reliable accounts of things that Jesus and Mary actually said. These are conversations as they are being imagined by later Christians, who are in fact putting words on Jesus' and Mary's lips to promote their own, Gnostic understandings of things. But for someone who wants to know about how the traditions of Mary came to be perpetuated after her death, they are a source of endless fascination.

The Dialogue of the Savior

Probably the earliest account of a discussion—or, rather, of a series of questions and answers—between Mary and Jesus is in one of the treatises of the Nag Hammadi Library, usually known as the Dialogue of the Savior. This dialogue is found in one of those manuscripts that is full of holes, having been eroded away over the centuries, making parts of it very difficult (impossible, actually) to read. But the basic thrust of the work is clear. Jesus here speaks to his disciples and delivers to them the true knowledge that leads to salvation.

The disciples are not originally from this miserable world. They have come down into it from the great world above, becoming somehow entrapped in this deficient sphere of matter. But once they know the truth that Jesus brings, they will escape and return to their heavenly home. At one point Jesus says to the disciples, including Mary, "You are from the fullness and you dwell in the place where the deficiency is. And lo! His light has poured down upon me!" (saying 55).[2]

What is striking is that a good deal of this document consists of questions asked by three of the disciples, Judas Thomas (not the betrayer Judas Iscariot), Matthew, and Mary. Thus it appears that for this writer, Mary was more important than others of the twelve. In fact, Mary is portrayed as a superior Gnostic. At one point she utters three aphorisms found in the New Testament on Jesus' own lips: "The wickedness of each day [is sufficient]. Workers deserve their food. Disciples resemble their teachers." The narrator concludes that "she spoke this utterance as a woman who understood everything" (saying 53). What better commendation for a Gnostic seeking true knowledge?

Or consider this later conversation: "Mary said, 'I want to understand all things [just as] they are.' The master said, 'Whoever seeks life, this is their wealth. For the world's [rest] is false, and its gold and silver are deceptive'" (sayings 69–70). In other words, the true wealth that brings eternal life is complete understanding. The material things of this world simply deceive people into imagining that they matter.

Or finally, consider this back-and-forth:

> Mary asked, "Tell me, master, why have I come to this place, to gain or to lose?"
> The master replied, "You show the greatness of the revealer."
> Mary asked him, "Master, then is there a place that is abandoned or without truth?"
> The master replied, "The place where I am not."
> Mary said, "Master, you are awesome and marvelous. . . ."
> The master said, "When you leave behind what cannot accompany you, then you will rest." (sayings 60–64, 68)

Only in the presence of Jesus, the revealer, is there truth; only when we leave behind the material things of this world will we find eternal rest. This is the lesson taught to Mary, who understood "everything." Mary is a completed Gnostic.

The *Pistis Sophia*

If the attention Mary receives in the Dialogue of the Savior is surprising, her role in the Gnostic work called the *Pistis Sophia* (which means "faith-wisdom") is astounding. This work was not a part of the Nag Hammadi Library but was discovered in the eighteenth century as part of a large book containing several

Gnostic treatises. Like other Christian Gnostic books that we are considering, this one consists of a series of revelations that Jesus gives to his disciples in which he explains the truth about this material world and the need to escape it through acquiring proper understanding. It is a long, drawn-out book. At one point, the discussion shifts to a question-and-answer session, and here again Mary figures prominently. In fact, the conversation is dominated by Mary and "the virgin John"—and far more by her than him. She asks four out of every five questions that Jesus addresses.

Her dominance in the back-and-forth is not meant to indicate that she knows less than the other disciples. Just the contrary—Mary is portrayed as the one who is beyond the others in her spiritual perception and progress. At one point, Jesus says to her:

> Blessed Mary, you whom I shall complete with all the mysteries on high [i.e., he will perfect her with knowledge], speak openly, for you are one whose heart is set on heaven's kingdom more than all your brothers.

Mary does as she is bidden and recounts her understanding of how Jesus has overcome the evil powers that control this material world and has freed those with true understanding from the power of fate. Jesus' response shows that she has understood:

> When Mary finished saying these things, Jesus said, "Well done, Mary. You are more blessed than all women on earth, because you will be the fullness of fullnesses and the completion of completions."

The other disciples, however, especially Peter, are not pleased with how this particular conversation is going. Peter thinks, in fact, that Mary is hogging all of Jesus' time. And so we are told:

> Peter stepped forward and said to Jesus, "My master, we cannot endure this woman who gets in our way and does not let any of us speak, though she talks all the time." (*Pistis Sophia*, 36)

Mary finds this bit of male testosterone threatening: "My master, I understand in my mind that I can come forward at any time to interpret what Pistis Sophia [the divine being who gives wisdom] has said, but I am afraid of Peter, because he threatens me and hates our gender" (*Pistis Sophia*, 72).

The divine realm, however, is not a place where gender matters. Gender involves material, outward appearance, whereas true knowledge involves inward understanding. Thus Mary is told: "Any of those filled with the spirit of light will come forward to interpret what I say: no one will be able to oppose them."

We have seen that the apocalyptic message of the real, historical Jesus may have seemed liberating for women, since they could expect that in the future kingdom they would no longer experience the oppression of a patriarchal state.

How much more liberating is the message of the Gnostic Jesus? For now women with full understanding are completely on a par with men. They are superior, in fact, to most men, who fail to recognize the truth and continue, like Peter himself, to make judgments based on external forms such as gender.

In the *Pistis Sophia* we find Jesus' final commendation to Mary for coming to a full realization of the truth that brings salvation:

> When Mary finished saying these things, the savior marveled greatly at the answers she gave, for she had become entirely pure spirit. Jesus answered and said, "Well done, Mary, pure spiritual woman."

Thus even a woman can transcend her physical nature and find salvation as a pure spirit.

This is not the first time we have seen a controversy in Christian circles over whether women were allowed to engage in religious conversation in the presence of men. As we saw earlier, even though the apostle Paul allowed women to be active participants in the worship services in his church, a later scribe modified his letter of 1 Corinthians by telling the women that they must "keep silence." So too a later author, forging a letter in Paul's name, demanded that women are "to keep silent" (1 Tim. 2:12). How different that is from the Paul remembered in the Acts of Paul and Thecla, who commissions his female apostle to go forth and "proclaim the Word." And how different from the Gnostic Jesus of the *Pistis Sophia,* who praises Mary for her complete knowledge of the truth that liberates.

Nor will this be the last contretemps between Peter and Mary over her standing in the community of the saved.

The Gospel of Thomas

By all accounts Peter's harshest attack on Mary comes in the most famous tractate of the Nag Hammadi Library, the Coptic Gospel of Thomas. Scholars continue to be intrigued by this text and to write large tomes about it sixty years after its discovery. To some extent, that is because of its potential historical value: in the opinion of some scholars, the Gospel of Thomas includes authentic sayings of Jesus that did not make it into the New Testament. Needless to say, any additional information discovered about Jesus is bound to make a stir. No discovery of modern times is more likely to provide such information than the Gospel of Thomas.

The Gospel consists of 114 sayings of Jesus and nothing else. The Gospel says nothing about what he did, contains no miracle stories, does not describe his last week, last hours, death, or resurrection. It is a list of sayings, one after the other, sometimes in response to questions or comments made by one or another of his disciples. Many of these sayings are quite similar to what we find in the books of the New Testament, including the parable of the mustard seed and the comment about the blind leading the blind. But many others are

completely unlike those of the New Testament, and it is these in particular that
have sparked interest among scholars of early Christianity.

Mary Magdalene shows up twice in the text. She asks an innocent question
in saying 21: "Mary said to Jesus, 'Whom are your disciples like?'" Jesus
gives a lengthy response. But then she appears again in the final passage of the
collection, the infamous saying 114, where she is discussed by Jesus and Peter
in a way that has made many modern readers cringe.

> Simon Peter said to them, "Let Mary leave us, for women are not worthy of
> life."
> Jesus said, "I myself shall lead her in order to make her male, so that she too
> may become a living spirit resembling you males. For every woman who will
> make herself male will enter the kingdom of heaven."

As you might imagine, no other saying of the Gospel has generated as much
heat as this one. Some parts of it are not that difficult to understand: Peter
clearly has a low opinion of women in general and Mary in particular, and is
perturbed that Mary is present with the other (male) disciples. We have encountered Peter's resistance to Mary before, for example, in the *Pistis Sophia*.
Even in canonical texts there appears to be some controversy between the two.
In Luke's Gospel, when Mary and the other women find Jesus' tomb empty
and learn that he has been raised from the dead, they go off to tell Peter and the
others, who do not believe them, because it seems to be "an idle tale" (Luke
24:11). Mary, throughout our traditions, seems to have trouble getting Peter's
respect. The theme is repeated even more forcefully in the Gospel of Mary, as
we will see in the next chapter.

In any event, Peter in the Gospel of Thomas maligns not only Mary but all
women as being "unworthy of [eternal] life." You might think that Peter would
find heaven a boring place with just men around, but there it is. Misogynists
don't always look ahead.

What is more puzzling, in some respects, is Jesus' response, that he will
make Mary (and other women, one would assume) male, so that she too can be
a living spirit like other males, and thereby enter into the kingdom. What's
wrong with women the way they are? Why should they have to become males
in order to enter the kingdom of heaven?

What is most surprising about the discussions of this verse is how often
readers have failed to realize that it needs to be interpreted in light of ancient
understandings of gender.[3] Whoever wrote this account was living in the ancient Roman world.[4] To understand what he meant by his comments, we need
to understand what people living in the Roman world normally understood
about the relationship between the male and female.

Fortunately, we know a good deal about such things. A number of ancient
authors talk about the matter, including philosophers, scholars of religion, natural scientists, medical doctors—in fact, even ancient gynecologists. When you

read what these writers said about gender, it becomes quite clear that they did not think what *we* think about it.[5]

People today usually think about male and female as two kinds of the same thing. There's one thing, the human being, and it comes in two types: male and female. There are problems with this understanding, as we ourselves sometimes admit. There are hermaphrodites, for example. But basically this is how we see it. It is not, however, how people in antiquity saw it. For them, male and female were not two kinds of human being, they were two degrees of human being. Women, in fact, were imperfect men.

The way to make sense of the ancient understanding is to imagine all living creatures on a kind of continuum. At the far left of the spectrum are plants, to the right of them are animals, and to the right of (other) animals are humans. There are different degrees of intelligence and perfection among animals: slugs might be on the left of the continuum and chimpanzees might be further along. So it is among humans as well. Children and slaves are not perfect as humans, so they would be to the left of the scale. Women too are not perfect, as they have not reached the level of the men. The male body is the perfect human ideal. Moving along the continuum, beyond humans altogether, are other living beings: the gods, who are in fact superhuman, the very pinnacle of living existence.

The goal of humans is to become like the gods, and that requires movement along the continuum. Men have to transcend their mortal limitations. For women to transcend theirs, they first have to move along the continuum through the place occupied by men. For a woman to have life, she must first become a male.

Women, then, were imperfect humans, or as some authors would have it, imperfect men. Many ancients held this view in quite literal terms: women were men who had never developed. Their penises hadn't grown (the vagina was an inverted penis that never emerged); their muscles hadn't fully developed; their lungs hadn't matured; their voices hadn't deepened; their facial hair hadn't appeared. Women were men who hadn't yet reached perfection.

To go off on a bit of a digression for a moment, that is the reason that some ancient texts are opposed to certain same-sex relationships. The problem with such relationships in Greek and Roman antiquity was not that it was unnatural for two people of the same gender to have physical intimacy, as some people today feel. The problem had to do with the ancient ideology of dominance as it related to the understanding of the genders.

In the Greco-Roman world, dominance was a firmly held and seldom questioned ideal. It was simply common sense that human relationships were organized around power. Those who were more powerful were supposed to dominate those who were less powerful. Thus one empire could destroy another with impunity. They had no particular qualms about it. The stronger could and should dominate the weaker. Masters had complete control over slaves. Parents had total dominance over children. Men could, and should, assert their power over women, who were literally the weaker sex.

This ideology of power affected not only military and political ideology but also personal and sexual relations. Free men were made to be dominant. Modern people have trouble understanding how the ancient Greeks could accept the practice of pederasty, where an adult man took a preadolescent boy as a lover. In this system, the man would inculcate moral and cultural values into the boy, teaching him the ways of society and politics, in exchange for sexual favors. But wasn't that "unnatural"? Not at all. In fact, Greeks talk about it as the most natural thing in the world. The reason is not hard to find once you understand the ideology of dominance. Boys were imperfect men. The more perfect was to dominate the less perfect. It was natural for a free man to have sex with a young boy. And that's why pederasty applied only to preadolescent youths. Once a boy reached puberty, he started attaining his manhood, and from that point on it was a shameful thing to be dominated by someone else, since men were to be dominators, not dominated.

That is also why in the ancient world it was widely acceptable for a free man to have sex with his slaves, whether male or female. He was dominant over them. What about when two free men had sex, though: wasn't that unnatural? As it turns out, most ancient people thought that same-sex relations between men was unnatural for only *one* of the two involved, the one who was on the receiving end of the sex act. Since the "unnaturalness" of sex involved being dominated by someone when you were to be the dominator, then only the dominated partner acted unnaturally. So when Julius Caesar was known to have been involved in a sexual relationship with the king of Galatia and was suspected of having himself been the submissive partner in the relationship, his troops composed humorous little ditties making fun of him for it. The king of Galatia hadn't done anything immoral or unnatural, though. He had acted like a man.

When ancient texts, therefore, condemn same-sex relations, it is important to understand what it is they're condemning. They are condemning a man for acting like a member of the weaker sex, or a woman for acting like a member of the stronger sex.

Now, what does all this have to do with Peter, Mary, Jesus, and the Gospel of Thomas? In this text, Peter, in typical ancient male fashion, looks down on Mary as a member of the weaker sex. But Jesus sees her as one who will, like Peter and other males, find salvation. How will that be? The only way to find life—to live the life of the gods, or in the case of Christian teaching, to live life with God—is to progress beyond the human realm to the divine. For a woman, that would require her first to become more perfect. Women will have help in this task, for Jesus will make them male, so that they can then transcend the male and move on to the divine, becoming, as Jesus puts it, "living spirits."

For the Gnostic system—which, in my opinion, the Gospel of Thomas subscribes to[6]—this involves learning the secret teachings that Jesus delivers, the gnosis about how the spirit came into this world in the first place and how it can return to its heavenly home. This secret knowledge is available to all people, both men and women, Peter *and* Mary.

The Gospel of Philip

More than any other book from Christian antiquity, the Gospel of Philip, discovered at Nag Hammadi, has become known as a source of information for the relationship between Mary and Jesus. And that is because it plays such a prominent role in Dan Brown's blockbuster hit *The Da Vinci Code*. The historical backdrop to the novel involves Jesus' alleged marriage and sexual relationship with Mary Magdalene. After his death, Mary flees to France, pregnant with his child, who was to become the ancestor to the Merovingian dynasty and whose bloodline is preserved down to the present day.

All this is presented not as part of the fiction of *The Da Vinci Code* but as the historical facts underlying the fiction. And where did these facts come from? Well, in actual fact they come from a book written in the 1980s that Dan Brown relied heavily upon. He relied so heavily on it that its authors have reportedly threatened to take him to court. This is a book called *Holy Blood, Holy Grail*. It is a conspiracy theorist's dream, written by three so-called independent researchers (when someone calls himself an independent researcher, it usually means that he is not a scholar trained in the field). But the characters of *The Da Vinci Code* itself do not claim to have gotten their information from *Holy Blood, Holy Grail*. They claim to have gotten them from the noncanonical Gospels that have been discovered in modern times, especially the Gospel of Philip.

Some of the historical claims about the noncanonical Gospels in *The Da Vinci Code* have struck scholars as outrageous, or at least outrageously funny. The book claims, for example, that some of these Gospels were discovered among the Dead Sea Scrolls. That is completely wrong: the Dead Sea Scrolls do not contain any Gospels, or any Christian writings of any sort. They are Jewish texts, which never mention Jesus or any of his followers. And the novel claims that Jesus' marriage to Mary Magdalene is frequently reported in the Gospels that did not make it into the New Testament. On the contrary, not only is their marriage not reported frequently, it is never reported at all, in any surviving Gospel, canonical or noncanonical. I'll have more to say about this in a later chapter. For now I want to consider the Gospel of Philip, which is *The Da Vinci Code*'s star witness for the case that Jesus and Mary were husband and wife.

The Gospel of Philip is one of the most puzzling and convoluted of the writings discovered at Nag Hammadi. It consists of a number of sayings and reflections about the nature of reality and humans' relationship to it, all within the context of a Gnostic understanding of the world. The book is filled with hard-to-interpret parables, metaphorical statements, theological claims, analogies, exhortations and so on, in what appears to be a random sequence. This is not an easy text to interpret. Many readers simply throw up their hands in despair. Just to give you a taste, consider one of its early statements:

> A Gentile does not die, for he has never lived in order that he may die. He who
> has believed in the truth has found life, and this one is in danger of dying, for he

is alive. Since Christ came the world has been created, the cities adorned, the dead carried out. When we were Hebrews we were orphans and had only our mother, but when we became Christians we had both father and mother. Those who sow in winter reap in summer. The winter is the world, the summer the other eternal realm.

And so it goes.

Despite its generally opaque quality there are some fascinating statements made in the Gospel of Philip, and two of them involve Mary Magdalene. These are the two that come to be quoted in *The Da Vinci Code*. Unfortunately, both of them are problematic in ways that Brown, or at least his fictional characters, evidently don't realize. The first involves one of the real historical howlers of the novel. This involves the passage of the Gospel of Philip where we are told:

> There were three who always walked with the lord: Mary his mother and her sister and Magdalene, the one who was called his companion. His sister and his mother and his companion were each a Mary.

One of the main characters in *The Da Vinci Code*, the historical sleuth and Holy Grail expert Leigh Teabing, quotes this saying and then points out that it shows that Jesus and Mary Magdalene were married, because, as he indicates, "as any Aramaic scholar will tell you, the word *companion*, in those days, literally meant *spouse*" (*Da Vinci Code*, p. 246).

The problem (perhaps unbeknownst to Brown) is that the Gospel of Philip was not written in Aramaic. It was written in the ancient Egyptian language Coptic. Moreover, when you look up the passage in the Coptic, the word used there is actually a loan word from Greek, *koinônos*. This is not the Greek word for "spouse." It normally means "associate" or "companion." Thus this passage from the Gospel of Philip tells us only that Mary was an associate of Jesus—the same information that we can glean from the canonical Gospels.

The other passage of relevance in the Gospel of Philip may appear more promising for showing an intimate relationship between Jesus and Mary. According to *The Da Vinci Code* (and in the view of many interpreters), the passage indicates that Jesus and Mary used to kiss each other frequently on the mouth. The problem with this particular passage, however, is the same one that we saw earlier with respect to the Dialogue of the Savior: the manuscript has worn out in places, so there are holes where some of the words used to be, making it hard to know exactly what the author wrote. The text reads as follows:

> And the companion of the [gap in the manuscript] Mary Magdalene. [Gap in the manuscript] her more than [gap] the disciples [gap] kiss her [gap] on her [gap].

It *looks* as if the passage must have indicated that Jesus loved Mary more than the others and used to kiss her—on her mouth, or on some other body part? We'll probably never know.

But if nothing else, this passage appears to show that this author remembered Mary as being particularly close and intimate with Jesus. It would be going too far, however, to think that he is portraying them as *sexually* intimate. That might be our own natural response: they are, after all, kissing. But here again it is important to put the text in its own context. As it turns out, the Gospel of Philip and other Christian Gnostic texts mention kissing on other occasions. It is clear from these other passages that whatever is going on, it is not some kind of divine foreplay.[7]

At an earlier point, for example, the Gospel of Philip says the following:

> It is from being promised to the heavenly place that man receives nourishment. [Gap in the manuscript] him from the mouth. And had the word gone out from that place it would be nourished from the mouth and it would become perfect. For it is by a kiss that the perfect conceive and give birth. For this reason we also kiss one another. We receive conception from the grace that is in one another.

As with other passages in the Gospel of Philip, it is difficult to understand what all of this means. What is reasonably clear is that a person reaches perfection through what issues forth from the mouth—that is, the words of knowledge that are delivered by an inspired teacher. It is this perfect issuance that leads people to experience the new birth, as they come to know the truth that brings liberation from their entrapment here as material beings. This notion was symbolically portrayed in the Christian ritual of the kiss of peace, which was practiced throughout the early church, just as many churches today have a moment during their worship services when people in the pews greet one another with a chaste kiss or handshake. By kissing another, you show that it is through the mouth, and the truths it delivers, that one can find life. One thereby "conceives" and "gives birth."

When Jesus kisses Mary, then, it is not a prelude to sex. It is a symbolic statement that she received the revelation of truth that he conveyed to his disciples. According to the Gospel of Philip, she understood this truth even better than the others. If this notion was widespread throughout Christian Gnostic circles, it is no wonder that Peter and the others felt more than a twinge of jealousy toward her. She had usurped their place as the one most intimate with Jesus, not sexually but spiritually.

Chapter Sixteen

Mary at the Passion

Nothing sears our memory like a tragic death. No one in my generation can forget where they were when they learned that John F. Kennedy had been assassinated. And who can erase the memory of his widow, Jacqueline, still spattered with his blood, standing beside Lyndon Johnson as he took the oath of office to ensure a smooth transition of government at the moment of its greatest peril?

Even scenes we have not observed can imprint themselves on our brains—the body of Marilyn Monroe sprawled on her bed, naked and alone, an empty bottle of sleeping pills beside her. Yet more vivid are the scenes that have replayed themselves time and again before our eyes: the tragic accident that took Princess Diana from us as her car was mindlessly chased by paparazzi through the early morning streets of Paris.

With respect to Jesus of Nazareth, it is no surprise that many people think of him, first and foremost, as a figure on the cross, bloodied and wearing a crown of thorns. This recollection of Christ as crucifix is not only a modern phenomenon. Our very earliest Christian author, the apostle Paul, reminds his readers in Galatia that "before your eyes Christ was publicly portrayed as crucified" (Gal. 3:1). And he tells his church in Corinth that "I decided to know nothing among you except Jesus Christ as he was crucified" (1 Cor. 2:2).

What about Mary Magdalene? I suppose today most people think of her principally as a prostitute who followed Jesus. But for centuries her memory was indelibly etched on the Christian collective memory as the one who stood by to observe Jesus suffer on the cross, and who then visited his tomb on the third day, only to find it empty. She too was principally associated with death.

The Passion Narratives in Early Christianity

To make sense of this recollection of Mary, we need to know more about the narratives of Jesus' death as they were circulated orally in the early church and then written down in our surviving Gospels. As I pointed out earlier, the Passion narratives take up a disproportionate amount of space in the Gospels. John's Gospel is the most striking, for here Jesus' three-year ministry is recounted in the first eleven chapters but his final week in the last ten. The other Gospels are comparable: in Mark the ministry lasts ten chapters and the final week six.

For those interested in seeing how the early Christians told stories about Jesus and in learning about the theological significance they attached to the last days and hours of his life, these narratives are absolutely fundamental. They are also important for historians interested in knowing what really happened to Jesus, the founder of the largest religion in the history of Western civilization. These Gospel narratives are our main source of information not just about Jesus but about his followers, both men and women, including his best-known female follower, Mary Magdalene.

One of the problems involved in using these accounts to establish what actually happened during Jesus' last hours is that they are filled with internal discrepancies, both large and small. According to Mark's account, for example, Jesus was arrested after he had eaten the Passover meal with his disciples, and was crucified at nine o'clock the next morning (see Mark 14:12; 15:25); but according to John's account Jesus was arrested the night before the Passover meal was to be eaten and was crucified just after noon on the day devoted to the meal's preparation (John 19:14). Well, which is right? According to Matthew, when Jesus was put on trial the Jewish leaders and all the people were present before Pilate, as they cried out what they wanted him to do (Matt. 27:15–26). According to John, Jesus was sent inside the governor's residence, and no one else was there with him; Pilate had to go back and forth between Jesus on the inside and the Jewish leaders and people on the outside, talking first to Jesus, then to the leaders (John 18:28–19:14). Is one of these accounts more reliable than the other? According to Mark's account, it was Simon of Cyrene, not Jesus, who carried the cross to the place of crucifixion (15:21); according to John, Jesus carried the cross the whole way by himself (19:17). According to Mark, the curtain in the Temple was destroyed after Jesus breathed his last (Mark 15:38). According to Luke, it was destroyed before he died (Luke 23:45). John says nothing about it being destroyed at all. And so on. Read the stories carefully for yourself, comparing them to one another, and you'll find differences all over the map.

The Passion Narratives as Theological Retellings

Scholars of the New Testament have long recognized the reason for these differences. Our surviving accounts have all been modified in the process of retelling. The modifications sometimes contribute to an author's or storyteller's overall portrayal of Jesus in his last hours. That is to say, when someone changed the story, it usually was not because he had new information and simply wanted to set the record straight. More commonly it was because he wanted to make a point about Jesus and did so by altering the details of the story.

Let me give an illustration of how the process worked. To understand this illustration it is important to recall that the Gospel of Mark was the first of our surviving accounts to be written, and that, as scholars have long recognized, Matthew and Luke used his stories as a basis for their own. Sometimes they borrowed Mark's account wholesale without changing it much or at all. At other times they modified it to suit their own purposes.

In Mark's account of the Passion, Jesus is silent during the whole proceeding. He says nothing on the way to be crucified, while being nailed to the cross, or when being abused by everyone on the scene, including the two other criminals being crucified with him. It is only at the end that he speaks, as he cries out the words of Psalm 22: "Eloi, eloi, lama sabachthani," which means "My God, my God, why have you forsaken me?" (Mark 15:34). He then gives a final shout and dies. Here Jesus is portrayed as a man in despair, silent as if in shock, betrayed by one of his followers, deserted by his friends, mocked by his own religious leaders, castigated even by the two robbers crucified by his side, and at the end sensing that he has been abandoned even by God himself. It is a deeply wrenching moment filled with pathos.

It is important to remember here that I am reading only Mark. I am not bringing in other Gospel texts to soften this portrayal of the rejected Jesus in deep anguish. Mark's original readers would not have access, say, to Matthew, Luke, or John to give them a differently nuanced perspective. If you want to know what Mark thought of the crucifixion, you have to read just Mark.

At the same time, it is clear that for Mark, even though Jesus himself may not understand what is happening, the reader knows. Immediately after Jesus breathes his last, two crucial events occur: the curtain in the Temple is ripped in half, and the centurion standing beside the cross confesses, "Truly this man was the Son of God" (Mark 15:38–39). Both events are key to understanding Mark's portrayal of Jesus' death. In Jewish tradition, the curtain in the Temple was what separated the holiest room in the place—the so-called Holy of Holies—from the rest of the Temple. It was inside the Holy of Holies that God's very presence was manifest; it was here that God dwelt on earth. But no one could go into the Holy of Holies, into God's presence, except once a year. This was on the Day of Atonement, when the Jewish high priest would go behind the curtain and offer two sacrifices. One was for his own sins; then, after he was purified, he would offer a sacrifice for the sins of the people, that they too might again be right with God.

In Mark's Gospel, when Jesus dies this curtain is ripped in half (Mark 15:38). The meaning? God is no longer removed from his people. In the death of Jesus, God is now available to all people—not through the Jewish sacrificial system, but through the death of Jesus, his messiah. The sacrificial system is now done away with. People can stand before God on their own, through the work accomplished by Jesus.

This work of salvation is finally recognized—not by the followers of Jesus who have fled the scene, not by the Jewish leaders who remain opposed to Jesus and all he stood for, not even by faithful Jews who had followed Jesus during his lifetime. The salvation brought by the death of Jesus is recognized by a complete outsider: the pagan soldier who crucified him, who now sees that Jesus really is "the Son of God" (Mark 15:39). This recognition is highly significant for Mark's Gospel, because no one else in the story ever seems to understand who Jesus really is. Early on in the Gospel we learn that Jesus' own family thinks he has gone out of his mind (Mark 3:21), the leaders of his people think that he is inspired by the devil (3:22), the people from his hometown reject him as an upstart (6:1–6), and even his own disciples never understand who he is (6:51–52; 8:21). Throughout the Gospel Jesus repeatedly tells his followers that he must go to Jerusalem in order to be rejected and executed, and every time he tells them, they show that they don't know what he's talking about (8:32–33; 9:32; 10:35–40). When the moment finally comes, they are not there to see it happen. They have all fled.

But the centurion who observes Jesus' death knows what it is all about, and makes the confession that Peter and the other disciples never could make. It is precisely in his death on the cross—not in his powerful manifestations of miracles, for example—that Jesus is the Son of God.

My point is that Mark has shaped his narrative of Jesus' crucifixion in order to make a theological claim: it was this death that brought salvation to the world. There are, no doubt, historically accurate reminiscences embodied in this account. But Mark was not interested in providing a dispassionate history lesson about what happened one April morning in Roman Palestine. He wanted to teach a theological lesson about the death of the messiah for the sins of the world. Historians who want to know what *really* happened have to take the theological character of the story into account. Otherwise they'll end up simply using Mark as if it were a videotape of an event, rather than a theologically motivated retelling of the story.

That the Gospel writers were principally interested in theological retellings is evident when you compare Mark's version with the other accounts we have. Here I'll not make an exhaustive comparison, but simply consider Luke's narration of the same events.

Mark's emphasis on Jesus' silence prior to his crucifixion and on his seeming despair in the face of death are completely changed by Luke. Here Jesus is not silent during the proceeding. On the way to crucifixion (only in Luke, not Mark) Jesus sees some women weeping by the side of the road and turns to them to say, "Daughters of Jerusalem, don't weep for me but for yourselves and your children" (Luke 23:27–31). When being nailed to the cross, he does not writhe in silent agony, but prays (only in Luke), "Father, forgive them, for they don't know what they're doing" (23:34). And while on the cross, far from remaining silent, he actually has an intelligent conversation with one of the robbers crucified next to him. Unlike in Mark's Gospel, where both criminals mock Jesus, in Luke only one of them does so. The other tells him to be silent and then asks Jesus, "Remember me when you come into your Kingdom." And Jesus gives him the comforting reply, "Truly I tell you, today you will be with me in Paradise" (23:39–43).

The Jesus of Luke's Gospel—unlike the one portrayed in Mark's—is not silent as if in shock, unsure of why this is happening to him. He does not feel forsaken and abandoned by God. He knows exactly what is happening to him and why. He has compassion for others (the daughters of Jerusalem). He speaks of God as his "Father." He prays for forgiveness for others. Most important, he knows that he is to die but that he will wake up in paradise, in the presence of God himself, with this robber next to him. This is seen most clearly at the very end. In Luke's Gospel, Jesus does not utter a final cry of despair—known traditionally as the cry of dereliction ("My God, my God, why have you forsaken me"). Instead he humbly prays to God, showing that he knows that his good Father is on his side till the very end: "Father, into your hands I commit my spirit" (Luke 23:46). And then he dies.

The difference from Mark is striking and should not be smoothed over as if both are historically right. This is what happens when readers take what Mark says, combine it with what Luke says, and then for good measure throw in Matthew and John—thereby coming up with a view of Jesus found in *none* of the Gospels. There's certainly no one who can stop you from doing this. But you need to realize that if this is how you treat the Gospels—smashing the four discrete accounts into one large account, where Jesus says and does everything narrated in each version—what you have done in effect is to create your *own* Gospel, rather than pay careful attention to the Gospels as they were themselves written. The reality is that Luke's portrayal of Jesus is different from Mark's (and from Matthew's, and from John's, etc.). Rather than silent and despairing, Luke's Jesus is calm and in control, knowing full well his fate, trusting God that all will be well in the end, and knowing how, in fact, it will turn out ("Today you will be with me in Paradise").

Luke no doubt had reasons for changing Mark's account in the ways that he did. Some scholars have thought that Luke was writing for a persecuted Christian community and was trying to show them how they themselves should face death, should it come to that. They, like Jesus, could be calm and in control, knowing that ultimately God was in charge. If they could put up with the torments of the moment in full confidence that God was their Father, they too would be rewarded with the blessings of Paradise. This narrative, in other words, is not a historical account written to show what really happened in the life of Jesus. It is an exemplary account written to show what can happen in the lives of his followers.

I have a reason for stressing this point in a discussion of Mary Magdalene. If she is shown observing the death of Jesus on the cross in some of the accounts, this is not necessarily an innocent historical recollection of something that actually happened. It may be that, but it also may be part of a larger theological point that the authors of the Gospels were trying to make.

These narratives of Jesus' life and death were written many decades after the events they narrate by people who were not there to see these things happen. They based their accounts on stories that had been in circulation by word of mouth for year after year. It would have been very hard indeed even for Christians in the first century to have done historical research to find out the details of what really took place. Remember that even according to the accounts themselves, Jesus' followers had fled the scene. So where did the Gospel writers acquire their information about what Jesus said on the cross? There was no one there taking notes. Looking at the matter with the critical eye of an experienced historian, it seems highly unlikely that Roman soldiers who were trying to do their job of executing criminals and then disposing of their bodies would have been sympathetic to anyone asking to stand beneath the cross to record last words of the dying Jesus.

It is striking to note, in this connection, that many of the events narrated in the Gospel stories of Jesus' death have clear parallels to prophecies of Scripture that later Christians claimed that Jesus fulfilled. That Jesus was killed with two robbers, that his garments were divided up between the soldiers, that he was silent during the entire proceeding, that he called out the words of the Psalms at the end, that his legs were not broken—all these, and many other events besides, were seen by Christians as rooted in biblical passages such as Isaiah 53 and Psalm 22. Some scholars have stressed that this relationship between the events narrated and the biblical passages to which Christians turned to make sense of the events is not accidental—that in fact when Christians came to attach salvific significance to the death of Jesus they searched their Scriptures to help them understand why it had happened. They landed on passages that talked about the suffering and death of God's righteous one. These passages affected the ways they told the stories of Jesus' suffering and death. The Psalms and the book of Isaiah, then, colored the ways Jesus' crucifixion was remembered. Later authors wrote down the stories as they had heard them. Only later readers would be able to look at the stories and say, "See—Jesus fulfilled Scripture by the way he died." Of course it would look that way. Scripture itself was the basis for many of the stories in the first place. The stories are not dispassionate accounts of what happened by eyewitnesses who took careful records. They are orally transmitted accounts that have been shaped by the Christians' knowledge of Scripture in the first place.

Having said all that, I should point out that there are aspects of the crucifixion narratives that stand up to historical scrutiny, as embodying historical fact rather than Christian theology. As one salient example: all of our accounts agree that Jesus was crucified on the order of the Roman governor Pontius

Pilate, and that the death sentence was imposed because Jesus claimed to be the "king of the Jews," a political charge of treason against the state (thus, independently, write Mark and John; see also the Gospel of Peter). Moreover, this charge was inscribed on a placard over Jesus' head on the cross. This information is attested in a range of independent sources and accords perfectly well with what we know about the Roman administration of justice in first-century Palestine.

But now finally on to the key question of this chapter. What about Mary Magdalene and the other women with her at the scene of Jesus' crucifixion? Were they really there to see these things happen, and if so, what role did they play in the events?

The Women at the Crucifixion

All four of our Gospels agree that Mary Magdalene, along with some other women, observed the crucifixion. Our earliest account is Mark's:

> And there were women watching from a distance, among whom were Mary Magdalene and Mary the mother of James the less and Joses, and Salome, who had followed him when he was in Galilee and had ministered to him, and many other women who went up with him to Jerusalem. (Mark 15:40–41)

Matthew says something very similar but indicates that the women were Mary Magdalene; Mary, the mother of James and Joseph; and the mother of the sons of Zebedee (this may be Mark's Salome) (Matt. 27:55–56). Luke doesn't actually name the women but says that everyone whom Jesus knew looked on, including the women who had followed him from Galilee (Luke 23:49). This may be a reference back to the three women we considered before in connection with Luke 8: Mary Magdalene, Joanna, and Susanna. John's Gospel indicates that the women did not look on from a distance but were right at the foot of the cross (19:25), and he too names either three or four women: Jesus' own mother, her sister, Mary the mother of Cleopas (is this Jesus' mother's sister or someone else?), and Mary Magdalene.

Moreover, in all four of the New Testament Gospels and the Gospel of Peter we are told that Jesus was buried by a previously unnamed follower of Jesus, Joseph of Arimathea. The three earliest accounts, Matthew, Mark, and Luke, indicate that the burial was observed, again by the women. In Mark the observant women are Mary Magdalene and Mary the mother of Joses (but not Salome, evidently) (Mark 15:47); Matthew indicates that it was Mary Magdalene and "another Mary" (which one, we're not told) (Matt. 27:61); and Luke indicates that it was "the women who had followed him from Galilee" (Luke 23:55). John says nothing about the women observing the burial, possibly because there is a different witness here to the event: Nicodemus, with whom Jesus had a conversation near the beginning of John's Gospel (chapter 3).

As we will see at greater length later, all the Gospels also agree that it was women, headed by Mary Magdalene, not the men disciples or anyone else, who went to the tomb on the third day and learned that Jesus had been raised from the dead.

What is one to make of these curious references to women as the ones who observed that Jesus was crucified, buried, and raised? Why do these stories recur in our sources? Did Christian storytellers make them up? Or do they represent historical recollections of things that really happened?

Historians would have no trouble coming up with reasons for thinking that someone may have wanted to make up the stories. The very heart of the Christian faith, as it developed in a variety of circles in the years after Jesus' life here on earth, was rooted in the confession that "Christ died for our sins according to the Scriptures, that he was buried, and that he was raised from the dead on the third day according to the Scriptures" (see 1 Cor. 15:3–4). But anyone inclined to doubt this confession could well ask: how do you know that Jesus actually died? Maybe he simply passed out on the cross. Others were known to have done so. How do you know he was actually buried? Even if he was killed by the Romans, he would more likely have been left to rot on the cross, as was sometimes done, or thrown into a common burial pit with all the other corpses of criminal lowlifes. And even if he was actually buried in a tomb, how do you know that on the third day the tomb was empty? Surely this defies belief. Possibly someone went to the wrong tomb, or maybe someone stole the body from the tomb, or maybe the body was taken by scavenging dogs. How do you *know* that Jesus died, was buried, and was then raised? After all, everyone knows that the disciples of Jesus themselves saw none of these things happen, since they had fled and gone into hiding.

The stories of the women, one could argue, were made up precisely to counter the charges that the stories were invented. Christian storytellers could not reply that the disciples provided firsthand knowledge of these events. The disciples weren't there. But maybe other people were there—a group of women who observed these things from afar. The women, in other words, could have served an apologetic purpose. That is, they may have functioned to defend (the root meaning of the Greek term *apologia*) the claims that were central to the Christian profession of faith.

One of the great things about being a historian is that for every historical argument, there is almost always a historical counterargument. That is certainly true in this case, for someone who wants to argue that Christians made up the story about Mary Magdalene and other women observing Jesus' death, burial, and empty tomb faces a problem. If Christian storytellers wanted to prove that what they said was historically, actually true, why would they invent *women* to be the witnesses? Wouldn't that in fact be counterproductive, in that the accounts then could be all too readily written off as old wives' tales, silly stories told by foolish women who simply didn't know better? If you, an ancient storyteller, wanted to verify the central claims of the faith by inventing witnesses, wouldn't you invent male witnesses?

This seems like an effective counterargument and may dispose one to think that the stories of Mary observing Jesus' death and burial (and seeing him after the resurrection) must go back to historical events, for otherwise it is difficult to account for their having been made up. But one other great thing about being a historian, engaging in historical work, is that most counterarguments can themselves be countered by a counterargument. My students love this (the ones still awake at this point). In fact, one could imagine reasons for storytellers—someone such as the author of the Gospel of Mark, for instance—coming up with the idea that it was precisely women on the periphery of Jesus' followers who observed the critical events of his death, burial, and resurrection.

The reality is that Mark's Gospel is almost entirely about men and their reactions to Jesus, and none of the men, frankly, comes off that well. Working our way backward through the account, there are the (male) Roman soldiers who mock, torment, and kill Jesus. There are the two robbers who malign him on the cross. There is Pontius Pilate, who condemns him to death even though he can't find that Jesus has done anything wrong. There are the Jewish high priest Caiaphas and his ruling council, the Sanhedrin—all men—who find Jesus guilty of blasphemy even though he hasn't committed any. There are the Sadducees with whom Jesus is in angry confrontation, and the Pharisees before them, who claim that Jesus' work is inspired by the Devil.

And then there are his own male followers, one who betrays him, another who denies him three times, and all who abandon him and run for their lives. These are the twelve men who have spent the entire time of Jesus' ministry with him, who repeatedly show that they don't realize that Jesus' mission is to die on a cross, whom Jesus has to rebuke for not understanding him or his message. Throughout this Gospel Jesus tells these men that he must go to Jerusalem and suffer and die, and that if they want to be his disciples they must take up their crosses and follow him. And how do they respond? They discuss, repeatedly, who among themselves is the greatest and who will have the superior roles in the future kingdom. In other words, despite his repeated assertions, they think following Jesus will lead not to a cross but to a throne.

Who does understand that Jesus is to die in this Gospel? Not the insiders, but an unnamed woman who anoints his body for burial (Mark 14:3–9). Who actually takes up the cross for Jesus? Not Peter, James, or John, but a complete outsider, Simon of Cyrene, who is commissioned for the purpose (Mark 15:21). Who confesses his faith in Jesus as the Son of God precisely in his death? Not any of the disciples, but a pagan Roman soldier at the foot of the cross (Mark 15:39). Who cares for Jesus' dead body after his death? Not any of those closest to him, but a previously unknown and obscure figure named Joseph of Arimathea (Mark 15:43). And who is there to see all these things take place? None of the male disciples, but some of the women followers, who are faithful to the end and observe from afar the events that bring about the salvation of the world (Mark 15:40–41; 47).

The salvation that Jesus brings is not recognized by the high and the mighty, by the Pilates and Caiaphases and Sanhedrins of this world. It is a salvation that involves a complete reversal of the values and priorities of this world. It is a glory that comes in the form of suffering, a salvation that comes through pain. It is a salvation in which slaves will exult over masters, the oppressed over the powerful, the dispossessed over the mighty, a salvation where the last shall be first and the first last. And who observes this salvation? Not witnesses who are thought to be credible to this world, not the future bishops of the powerful churches of Christendom, but a group of lowly women. This is a salvation that appears to the world as "foolishness" but in fact, as the apostle Paul would have it, is "the wisdom of God" (1 Cor. 1:24).

My point is that the observation of Jesus' death, burial, and resurrection precisely by women could indeed be taken to be a theologically motivated "memory" of what happened, rather than an actual historical occurrence. It could have been invented by Christian storytellers who, like Mark after them, wanted their hearers to know that God "uses the weak things of this world to confound the powerful," that the salvation brought by Jesus was meant not for the high and mighty but for the lowly and the oppressed. It is a salvation first known not to the great leaders of this world, and not even to the not-so-great male leaders of Jesus' apostolic band, but to a group of women otherwise virtually unknown except by name.

In short, based on this argument, it is not clear if the women actually did observe the events of Jesus' death and burial. It is *possible* that this is a historical recollection. But it is also possible that it is an invented story designed to show how Mary Magdalene and the others were being remembered—as the first to know the salvation brought by Christ.

There is a problem, however, with this counter to the counterargument (i.e., there is a counter to it). As a historian, I am struck by a certain consistency among otherwise independent witnesses in placing Mary Magdalene both at the cross and at the tomb on the third day. If this is not a historical datum but something that a Christian storyteller just made up and then passed along to others, how is it that this specific bit of information has found its way into accounts that otherwise did not make use of one another? Mary's presence at the cross is found in Mark (and in Luke and Matthew, which used Mark) and also in John, which is independent of Mark. More significant still, all of our early Gospels—not just John and Mark (with Matthew and Luke as well) but also the Gospel of Peter, which appears to be independent of all of them—indicate that it was Mary Magdalene who discovered Jesus' empty tomb. How did all of these independent accounts happen to name exactly the same person in this role? It seems hard to believe that this just happened by a way of a fluke of storytelling. It seems much more likely that, at least with the traditions involving the empty tomb, we are dealing with something actually rooted in history.

The Women at the Tomb

The stories about the discovery of Jesus' empty tomb, even more than other stories in the Gospels, are almost impossible to reconcile with one another in all their details. Some of the undergraduate students who take my course on the New Testament, who believe that there cannot be any discrepancies in the Bible, have a tough time with this one. I have them list everything each Gospel has to say, in detail, and then compare their lists. It's hard not to be struck by the differences. To be sure, some of the differences can be chalked up to different emphases between one of the Gospels and another, or reconciled if you are bound and determined to do so. Mary is said to go to the tomb on the third day, but sometimes she is alone, and other times she is said to be with other women. But the names of the women differ from one account to the next (it is "the other Mary" in Matthew; "Mary the mother of James and Salome" in Mark; a group of unnamed women in Luke; Mary goes by herself in John). If you are intent on reconciling these accounts, you can argue that an entire group of women went: John's Gospel mentioned only Mary, while the other Gospels mentioned Mary and other women, one naming one of the women, another naming two others, and another naming none of them. Fair enough, I suppose. And if Mark says the women saw a young man at the tomb and Matthew says they saw an angel and Luke says they saw two men, then maybe what they really saw was two angels, whom they mistook as men in Luke's Gospel, and of whom Mark mentions only one, again mistaken as a man. (If that's the solution one adopts, by the way, it means that what really happened is something that none of the Gospels says—for none of them indicates that the women saw two angels.)

There are other differences that are even more difficult to reconcile, which I think we might as well admit are simply discrepancies. In John's Gospel, for example, when Mary Magdalene arrives at the tomb she finds that the stone has already been rolled away, and she runs off to tell two of the disciples (John 20:1). In Matthew's version, however, Mary and another woman named Mary arrive at the tomb and watch as an angel descends from heaven and rolls the stone away and sits on it. They are terrified, but the angel reassures them, urging them to see that Jesus' body is not there and to go tell the disciples (Matt. 28:1–2). In Mark's account they don't see an angel roll away the stone: they come to the tomb, find it open, and enter to see a young man sitting inside the tomb (not an angel on top of the stone that he has just rolled away, as in Matthew), who tells them that Jesus has been raised and that they are to tell the others (Mark 16:4–5). Well, which is it?

What the women are told differs in the different accounts as well. In Mark's version, they are told to have the disciples return to Galilee to meet with the raised Jesus, just as he had previously told them. In Luke they are not told to leave Jerusalem at all, but are reminded what Jesus had told them while he was still in Galilee, that he must be raised. Rather than going to Galilee to see

Jesus, they stay in Jerusalem and see him there. They are instructed, in fact, not to leave (see Acts 1:4—written by the same author as Luke). Well, did they leave or not?[1]

Or did they even see Jesus raised from the dead? In Matthew, Luke, and John we have accounts of Mary Magdalene (sometimes with other women) going off to tell the disciples what they had seen at the empty tomb (it's actually not empty in Matthew and Luke, as there is someone in there: it just isn't Jesus). But Mark's Gospel ends in a far more elusive and mysterious way. There the women are instructed to tell the disciples that Jesus would meet them in Galilee (not in Jerusalem, as in Luke), but they fail to do so. They flee from the tomb and say nothing to anyone, for they were afraid (Mark 16:8). And that's where Mark's Gospel ends. So did the women tell what they found or not? One Gospel says one thing and the others say something else. In fact, the others say several different things, depending on which one you read.

Does Mary herself have a vision of Jesus raised from the dead? In Mark, neither she nor anyone else sees Jesus. In Luke the male disciples see Jesus, but there is no account of Mary and the women seeing him. In Matthew Mary is the very first to see Jesus raised from the dead, in the company of other women, and clings to his feet in adoration. In John she is the first to see him, but in the company of no one, and Jesus does not allow her to touch him: this is the famous *noli me tangere* scene: "Don't touch me, for I have not yet ascended to my father" (20:17). Somewhat curiously, a week later Jesus reappears to the disciples and changes his instructions, telling the doubting Thomas to touch his hands and side (John 20:24–28). Had he ascended to heaven in the meantime and dropped back down for a brief visit afterward?

Nowhere else in the Gospels do you find such a confusion of reporting. Some readers have argued that this is precisely what you might expect. If something as mind-boggling as a resurrection had occurred and these women were the first to learn, they may well have been completely discombobulated and the stories may have gotten jumbled up in no time. But even if that is true, the historian is still left with the problem of knowing what most likely happened, given the fact that our various sources don't appear to agree in the

Painting of a Christian woman in prayer, from the Catacomb of Priscilla.

numerous details they narrate. And if all the details are at odds, what does that do to the overall story?

Still, there are several points on which the sources do agree, for example, that Jesus was buried and that on the third day his body was no longer in the tomb, and that Mary Magdalene was the first to find out. This is found independently in Mark, in John, and in the Gospel of Peter. Moreover, Matthew, Luke, and John, all of which are independent of one another, indicate that Mary (by herself or with other women) went and informed some, or all, of the male disciples.

At the very least, I think we have secure historical data to suggest that Mary Magdalene was the first to discover and proclaim the resurrection of Jesus. I have argued earlier that we do not know a lot about this woman historically. Most of our information about her is either legendary accretion as she was remembered in later ages or needs to be inferred from the very few references to her that do happen to survive in our early sources. But that is not to minimize her importance. The Christian religion is founded on the belief that Jesus was raised from the dead. And it appears virtually certain that it was Mary Magdalene of all people, an otherwise unknown Galilean Jewish woman of means, who first propounded this belief. It is not at all farfetched to claim that Mary was the founder of Christianity.

This is a matter we will want to pursue in a later chapter. Mary may not have been Jesus' lifetime partner, spouse, and lover; she may not have had children with him; she may not have been the reformed prostitute of later legend who became a model of chastity for women to imitate and follow. But it could be argued that she was the most important person in the early history of Christianity, that without her declaration of Jesus' empty tomb, the male disciples themselves may never have been inspired to proclaim the new religion.

Chapter Seventeen

Mary and Her Revelations

It may be difficult to justify some of the exaggerated claims that one hears these days about Mary Magdalene, from both scholars and popularizers. She was Jesus' closest disciple! She was his most intimate lifelong companion! She was his wife! She bore his children! In fact, none of these claims holds up to historical scrutiny. What makes Mary special is not her relationship to Jesus while he was living but what happened to her after he died. She was the one who found him missing from the tomb.

Sometimes the course of one's entire life is determined by a solitary incident—some kind of defining moment that changes everything. Mary's decision to anoint Jesus' body for burial on the third day after his death was just such a moment. When she arrived, she found that his body was not there. She went and told the others. They came to believe that he had been raised from the dead. And so Christianity started.

Christianity became the most powerful and influential religious, political, social, and cultural institution in the history of Western civilization. It began one Sunday morning with an act of piety and devotion that turned into a moment of confusion, consternation, and excitement. Despite her relative unimportance during Jesus' life, Mary Magdalene was the most important figure immediately after his death. She was more important than Peter, James, or John. She was the first to believe Jesus had been raised.

What if she hadn't gone there that morning? Would someone else have gone? It is impossible to say. There's no evidence that any of the men disciples or any of the women not connected with Mary thought about going to the tomb. If no one else had gone, would anyone have come to know that the tomb was empty? Would we have Christianity? Mary changed the course of human history, arguably more so than anyone else in the history of the West—not because she had Jesus' babies but because she found his empty crypt.

Some early Christians recognized the significance of Mary and invented stories about her. Not surprisingly, many of these stories are not about her connections to Jesus while he was alive, since it was widely known that she didn't have many connections to him then. They are about what happened when she saw him after his death. The idea that he had appeared to her led to the assumption that he must have talked with her and revealed to her secret knowledge that could be given only to the chosen few, those in the inner circle among his followers. And who would be closer to him than the one to whom he first appeared after rising from the dead? It was to Mary, therefore, that Jesus was thought (by some storytellers) to have made his ultimate revelations about the meaning of life, the nature of this world, and the way of salvation.

These revelations—which principally occur in Gospels outside the New Testament—embody the concerns, beliefs, and perspectives of the storytellers who originally dreamt them up. As a result, different stories about the revelations to Mary stand at odds with one another, as these are not what Jesus actually told her but what storytellers would have wanted him to have told her. What is striking is that most of these revelations in one way or another deal directly with the issue that must have been on everyone's mind once they realized that Mary Magdalene was of central importance to the beginning of Christian religion: how is it that a *woman* could play a pivotal role? Recall that women throughout the Roman world, including Judaism, were generally not seen as public leaders, teachers, or philosophers. Yet a woman was the one who began the proclamation that stands at the foundation of the newfound faith in Christ's death and resurrection. How could this be?

Many of the revelations allegedly delivered to Mary by Jesus deal with this issue. In most instances these revelations come not to Mary alone but to Mary among others in the inner circle. And it is often difficult to know whether the revelations are meant to be understood as being given before Jesus' death or after his resurrection (although in other instances it is clear).

Destroying the Works of the Female

One of the most ancient accounts is the Dialogue of the Savior, which includes a conversation in addition to the one we have already discussed (see chapter 15). This other conversation allegedly took place between Jesus and his three followers Judas (i.e., Judas Thomas—Jesus' brother), Matthew, and Mary. As with many discussions recorded in this Gnostic work, it is a bit difficult to make sense of the back-and-forth. It needs to be "unpacked" a bit. The conversation begins with a comment to Jesus from Judas (the bracketed portions are words that have to be restored because there are holes in the manuscript):

Judas said, "You have told us this from the mind of truth. When we pray, how should we pray?"

The master said, "Pray in the place where there is no woman."

Matthew says, "He tells us, 'Pray in the place where there is no woman,' which means destroy the works of the female, not because there is another form of birth, but because they should stop [giving birth]."

Mary said, "Will they never be destroyed?"

The master said, "[You] know they will perish [once again], and [the works] of [the female here] will be [destroyed as well]."

Judas begins with a question about prayer, that is, about how one can enjoy communion with God. Jesus' reply, that communion with God comes "in the place where there is no woman," is then interpreted by Matthew: it means that communion with God will happen when "the works of the female" are done away with. This doesn't sound very liberated or gender-affirming, but what does it mean? As Matthew's words show, the "works of the female" involve those activities that are uniquely connected with women, namely, the conception of a child and childbirth.

We should remember here that Gnostic Christians maintained that this material world and all that belongs to it are the result of a cosmic disaster: this is not a good place created by the one true God. It was created by a lesser deity, and the point of the Gnostic religions was not to affirm this material existence or to hope for its ultimate redemption. The point was to *escape* the material world. What happens, though, when a child is conceived and born into the world, that is, when a female accomplishes "her works"? The material world continues to perpetuate itself. But if the point of the religion is to escape material existence, then procreation is to be avoided at all costs. That is what it means, then, to destroy the works of the female. It is to refuse to participate in sexual activities that lead to childbirth.

Someday this destruction will be complete. Someday those who are true Gnostics will escape this world of entrapment and return to their heavenly home, a nonmaterial realm of the spirit. So in response to Mary's query, Jesus indicates that the works of the female will be destroyed. Procreation will no longer happen, babies will no longer be born, and salvation will ultimately come. I suppose this could be seen as an ancient counterattack on what we might think of as "family values," with Jesus himself leading the charge. Rather than affirming the family, he condemns it.

I might point out that a similar lesson was taught in another early Christian Gospel in which Jesus' principal interlocutor was a woman, this time not Mary Magdalene but her companion at the empty tomb, Salome. This other text is called the Gospel of the Egyptians. Unfortunately, we do not have the entire document, only a few quotations from it in the writings of the late-second-century author Clement of Alexandria. These quotations are enough, however, to give us a general sense of some of the main emphases of the Gospel. Interestingly enough, they involve the role of women in attaining salvation from this material world.

At one point in the Gospel of the Egyptians Salome asks Jesus, "How long will death prevail?" That is to say, how long will this miserable material world and all its finitudes last? Jesus gives a terse response: "For as long as you women bear children." Once there are no more bodies being produced, there will be no more prisons for the divine sparks to inhabit, and death will, obviously, be no more. Salome then responds, "Then I have done well not to bear children." Jesus affirms her choice, saying, "Eat every herb, but not the one that is bitter." In other words, it is best to avoid the painful life experience of giving birth.

That is why in another back-and-forth with Salome Jesus strikes a note that will sound familiar to those who have read the Dialogue of the Savior. Here in the Gospel of the Egyptians Jesus says, "I have come to destroy the works of the female." Clement explains that by "the female" Jesus means physical desire and by "works" he means birth and decay. In other words, Jesus has come to destroy the passions that lead to offspring. What matters is not existence in this evil material world—with all its pleasures and pains—but life in the spiritual world, where there is no pain, suffering, or death.

Salome wants to know when this will happen. Jesus replies in words similar to those found in the Coptic Gospel of Thomas: "When you trample on the shameful garment and when the two become one and the male with the female is neither male nor female." In the Gospel of Thomas it is clear that trampling on the garment refers to escaping this material body that clothes or, rather, entraps us (Gospel of Thomas 37). Moreover, the "two" will "become one" when the genders are reunited as they were before the human being became male and female (Adam and Eve in Genesis 2). For books such as Thomas, and presumably the Gospel of the Egyptians, the first step toward this superhuman existence is for women to become male, whence both male and female, who are no longer differentiated, can progress to a higher plane, to live the life of the divine.

Eating the Seed

As strange as the revelation to Mary in the Dialogue of the Savior might seem, it pales in comparison with another episode allegedly involving her after Jesus' resurrection, in a now-lost work called the Greater Questions of Mary. This is one of those many, many books from the ancient Christian world that we know about but which did not survive. It may well be that a book such as this was destroyed by offended readers. From what we can tell, there certainly was a lot to give offense.

We know of the book only from a reference to it in the work of a feisty and not always reliable heresy hunter of the fourth century named Epiphanius.

Epiphanius was intent on eliminating every trace of Christian heresy from the face of the world, and he wrote an extensive critique of all the heresies he knew about, eighty of them altogether. His attacks on these unacceptable forms of religion are mean-spirited and vitriolic. Epiphanius was a master of name-calling and mud-slinging. There are places where he attacks heresies that we have reason to suspect never even existed. These provide him with a chance to vent his wrath on an imaginary target. There are other places where what he says about alternative forms of Christianity is known, in fact, to be wrong.

Epiphanius's book is called the *Panarion,* which literally means something like "medicine chest." He called it this because in the book he tries to provide the antidote for the bites of the serpents of heresy, indicating the nature of the heretical poison (false teaching) and showing how it can be countered by an appeal to the orthodox truth. On some occasions in the Panarion Epiphanius actually quotes from written texts that he has managed to collect. Even if his interpretations of these texts are questionable, it is useful to have the words of the authors that he cites, as in most instances these books don't survive otherwise. This is the case with the Greater Questions of Mary, allegedly used by a group of Gnostic Christians that Epiphanius claims to know firsthand, a group that he calls by a variety of names, one of which is the Phibionites.

No other group was more notorious to Epiphanius, more insidious in its beliefs and practices, more dangerous to otherwise unwary Christians, more open to a barrage of slur, slander, and outrageous castigation from Epiphanius's pen. In part the Phibionites may have earned a special dose of Epiphanius's vitriol for personal reasons: Epiphanius indicates that when he was a young man he was nearly seduced into joining the group, before learning about its nefarious practices. These practices were allegedly justified by the literature they read and accepted as authoritative, including the revelation allegedly given to Mary Magdalene by Jesus after his resurrection.[1]

And just what were those practices? According to Epiphanius, they involved an altogether bizarre celebration of the Lord's Supper. If you'll recall, the early Christians did not celebrate the Lord's Supper by taking a wafer and a sip of wine or grape juice, as happens commonly today. In the early church, it was a kind of potluck supper. People would bring food and drink together and, in the course of the meal, have a special time in which they celebrated the bread as the body of Christ that had been broken for salvation, and the wine as the blood of Christ that had been shed for the sins of the world. Epiphanius maintains that the Phibionites put a completely different spin on the celebration, based on their Gnostic understanding of the material world and the need to escape it. Somewhat like in the Dialogue of the Savior, this understanding denigrated the "works of the female," that is, conception and childbirth.

According to Epiphanius, the Phibionites celebrated the Lord's Supper by engaging in a nonprocreative sex ritual involving sacred coitus interruptus. After the evening meal, members of the community would pair off (with someone other than their own spouse, Epiphanius is quick to point out) and have sex. But when the man reached climax he would pull out of the woman and together they would collect his semen and consume it, saying, "This is the Body of Christ." If the woman happened to be menstruating at the time, they would also take some of her menstrual blood and consume it, saying "This is the Blood of Christ."

It is difficult to know if Epiphanius is just making all this up. But it is striking that this ritual appears to enact an opposition to the "works of the female" (conception and birth). Sexual activity here is intentionally nonprocreative. Did Epiphanius know that the Phibionites were opposed to procreation and, based on that knowledge, *invent* a set of rituals that could embody their views? Did he then attack the group for holding such rituals, when in fact they came from his own fertile mind? Or did he really know what was going on at the Phibionite Wednesday night prayer meetings?

What is clear is that he claims that the Phibionite Christians justified their extraordinary eucharistic practices by appealing to their sacred writings, which were not the books that came to be included in our New Testament, but other books allegedly written by apostles. In particular he mentions the Greater Questions of Mary (he indicates that they had a Lesser Questions of Mary as well, but he doesn't tell us anything about it). This book allegedly contained one of the more stunning encounters between Jesus and Mary Magdalene on record. In the episode in question, Epiphanius claims, Jesus was said to have taken Mary up to a mountaintop and to have miraculously drawn a woman from his side—somewhat like the birth of Eve from the rib of Adam. He then proceeded to have sexual intercourse with her. But when he reached his climax Jesus took his semen and ate it, telling Mary, "Thus must we do, that we may live." Mary, understandably, was quite alarmed and fell to the ground in a faint. But Jesus raised her up and said to her, "O you of little faith, why did you doubt?" If Martin Scorsese's movie *The Last Temptation of Christ* caused an uproar when it was released, imagine the public reaction to the Greater Questions of Mary.

In any event, as I've indicated, it is not at all clear to me that Epiphanius actually knew what he was talking about. It seems unlikely that the Phibionites themselves would have been spreading reports about their illegal and outrageous nocturnal orgies. And the details of Epiphanius's description sound very much like what you can find in the ancient rumor mill about many secret societies in the ancient world.[2] It is possible, however, as I've suggested, that he had read some of the Phibionites' books and allowed his mind to wander a bit until it hit upon a (nonexistent) ritualistic expression for their belief that we are to escape this material world and not bring any more people into it, since salvation will not be complete until all souls have returned to their heavenly home in the spiritual realm. According to this view, having offspring means prolonging the experience of pain and suffering.

So even if Epiphanius's description of the Phibionites' eucharistic practices is made up, it may be that the group did in fact practice nonprocreative sex, in order to "destroy the works of the female." Without procreation, there is no more conception and childbearing. And it is just possible that this practice was rooted in the Gnostic belief that women must become men in order to enter into the Kingdom of Heaven. That is to say, nonprocreative sex may have represented a symbolic statement by women that they had already advanced toward becoming men, on the road to becoming "living spirits like you males" (Gospel of Thomas, 114).

The Subordination of Women

From a modern point of view, I scarcely need to say, the perspectives on women embodied in these texts—the Dialogue of the Savior, the Gospel of the Egyptians, and the Greater Questions of Mary—are rather disturbing. I suppose someone *could* argue that these are progressive views of women, in that they acknowledge that women have an active role in the religion and can enjoy nonprocreative sex. Here Jesus is directly revealing his truths not to a man but to a woman, Mary Magdalene or Salome. And he is showing that women can be partners in the salvation he brings, along with the men. But the way for women to inherit salvation in these texts is to forgo precisely those aspects of existence that make women women (for these authors): procreative sex, conception, and childbearing. In other words, as long as you stop being a woman, you can be saved. This is hardly a liberating message. But I suppose, on the other hand, that it could also be seen as a step up from some of the options facing women in other, non-Gnostic Christian groups.

In some circles connected with the apostle Paul, for example, women were expected not to stop being women but to remain women. And as women, they were assigned a subordinate role to the men, with no hope of ever seeing a change or improvement. This point of view wasn't embraced by all the circles connected with Paul, but it was certainly the view that came to be dominant in Pauline churches, so much so that it came to be canonized in Scripture and is largely responsible for the sense among some scholars today that Paul himself was one of the great misogynists of Christian antiquity.

In particular, this view can be found in the Pastoral Epistles, written in Paul's name by a later follower sometime near the end of the first century:

> Let a woman learn in silence in all submission. I do not permit a woman to teach or to exercise authority over a man,; but she is to be silent. For Adam was created first and then Eve. And Adam was not deceived, but the woman was deceived and so committed a transgression. But she will be saved through bearing children, if they remain in faith and love and holiness with modesty. (1 Tim. 2:11–15)

It is interesting that, just as with the Greater Questions of Mary, so too here Adam and Eve are invoked in order to support an author's view of women in relationship to men and to salvation. But now the opposite lesson is drawn. In this case, women are *not* to cease performing the "works of the female" in order to be saved. Just the contrary: Eve was made as a woman for the purpose of man (not vice versa) and so is meant to serve men (not to become a man). For this author, the story of Adam and Eve shows what happens when women try to usurp the position of men: women are easily duped. Never forget, he reminds his readers, what happened to Eve when she was tempted by the serpent to eat the fruit of the tree of the knowledge of good and evil. She led the man astray. That is what happens every time a woman exercises authority, and that is why women must be silent and completely submissive. The only way they can be saved is by bearing children—that is, by bearing the curse that God called down upon woman ("pain in childbearing") as a result of the sin in the Garden (see Genesis 3:16).

So we have two radically different views of women from early Christianity. Both are patronizing, telling women what they have to do in order to be saved. Both are promoted by the men who wrote these texts. Both accept an essential difference between men and women. Both presume that the difference puts women in the inferior position to men. Both use the myth of Adam and Eve to promote their agenda. And both only begrudgingly allow for the possibility of salvation to the inferior human being.

The difference between the two views is striking, but maybe at the end of the day it is immaterial. Which is better, to be told that you can attain salvation as a woman by no longer being a woman, or to be told that you can attain it by subjecting yourself to the whims of your man? Pick your poison.

It is striking that the position associated with Paul in the Pastoral Epistles is opposed by a different position, also associated with Paul, in yet other texts of early Christianity. We saw this already in our discussion of the Acts of Paul and Thecla, where a woman "becomes a man" and thereby earns her salvation. In the case of Thecla, she becomes a man by accepting Paul's proclamation of a gospel of renunciation. Women should not engage in sex at all if they want to be saved (and neither should men). This ascetic gospel obviously stands at odds with what we find in the pseudonymous letter of 1 Timothy, where it is precisely through having sex and bearing children that a woman can be saved.

Thecla in fact does become like a man. At one point of the story, she cuts off her hair and modifies her outer cloak to make it look like a man's. Christian cross-dressing never really caught on, but in Thecla's case it proved highly effective. Not only does she appear like a man, she acts like one: baptizing herself (rather than having a man baptize her) and being commissioned by Paul to go forth and "proclaim the word."

The view of women embodied by Paul in the Acts of Paul and Thecla stands at odds with what he allegedly embraces in 1 Timothy. In one text women are to become men; in the other they are doomed to remain subordinate as women. Something similar can be said about views of women associated with Mary Magdalene. In some ancient traditions she is seen as urging women to stop being women so as to become men and thus enter into the kingdom. But in others she insists that women can have their salvation precisely as women.

Nowhere is this latter view taught more clearly than in the most important work connected with Mary in all of Christian antiquity, the Gnostic Gospel of Mary.

The Gospel of Mary

The Gospel of Mary was one of the most significant discoveries of the late nineteenth century. Unfortunately, it was unavailable to the reading public for nearly sixty years after it was found. The story of its discovery and the Candide-like circumstances that prevented its publication is engagingly told by Harvard professor Karen King in one of the best studies of the book to date.[3] The manuscript that contains the Gospel, along with three other Coptic texts (including the Act of Peter, which we considered in an earlier chapter) was purchased in Cairo in 1896 and taken back to Berlin. There, in Berlin, a German scholar of Egyptian antiquity named Carl Schmidt transcribed the manuscript and prepared an edition of it. His edition was ready for publication by 1912. But the press that was publishing it experienced a disaster: a water main burst, destroying the edition (and lots of other things as well). So Schmidt had to start all over. Then World War I intervened, and German scholars suddenly had other things on their minds and in their lives. It wasn't until after the war that Schmidt could resume his work. Unfortunately, he had numerous other obligations as well. He died in 1938, before completing the task. The project was then taken on by another German scholar, named Walter Till. Till finished his work by 1943, but this, obviously, was also a bad time in Germany, at the height of World War II.

It was soon after the war that the remarkable discovery of Gnostic documents at Nag Hammadi was made. Till reasonably thought that there might be another copy of the Gospel of Mary among the Nag Hammadi treatises, and so he delayed publication of his work until he could know for sure. Eventually it became clear that his manuscript was the only copy of the book in existence. He published his edition in 1955—nearly a full lifetime after the document was first uncovered in Egypt.

The book Till produced was worth the wait. The Gospel of Mary is a significant and previously unknown Gospel text from early Christianity. Most scholars think it was written sometime in the second century, possibly in the early part of the century. That would make it one of the earliest Gospels outside the New Testament. And it is the only Gospel from antiquity named after a woman. It is no surprise, I suppose, that the woman is Mary Magdalene.

Since Till's edition appeared, several small fragments of the Gospel have turned up in Egypt. These fragments are written in Greek, which is usually thought to have been the original language of the document (so the Coptic edition published by Till is a translation of the Greek original). But even with these additional fragments, nearly half the original Gospel of Mary is lost. The more complete Coptic manuscript of 1896 is missing its first six pages and an additional four pages right in the middle. Thus we have only a fragmentary knowledge of what was originally in the document. But what survives is spectacular enough, for the text records an appearance of Jesus to his disciples after his resurrection, and a description of a revelation he had previously given to Mary.

The text divides itself neatly into three parts. The first part begins in medias res, with Jesus talking to his disciples and answering their questions. They are principally concerned about the nature of this world and of sin. Jesus tells them what they need to know, and delivers a short set of warnings to them to avoid false leaders and not to impose legalistic requirements on others. He then leaves.

The second part is where Mary appears. The disciples are disconsolate that Jesus is gone, and are concerned that they might suffer his fate of execution. Mary comforts them, and Peter suggests that they would all benefit if she would tell them what Jesus revealed to her privately. Mary begins to describe a vision she had. Unfortunately, this is where the text breaks off for four pages. It resumes in the middle of Mary's description of the human soul as it ascends through the heavenly spheres controlled by forces opposed to it, on its way to its heavenly home.

In the third part, the disciples discuss Mary's vision and question its validity. It was, after all, given to a woman. Can it be trusted? Andrew and Peter express their doubts, but Levi comes to Mary's aid. The Gospel ends with the disciples going forth to preach the good news.

Even from this brief summary it should be obvious that this is an important text for understanding aspects of early Gnostic Christianity, including its understanding of the world, sin, and salvation, as the soul learns to escape this material world to return to the world of the spirit. It is equally important for its distinctive portrayal of Mary and its understanding of women, especially in relationship to men, to the savior, and to the events of salvation themselves. We will do well to consider each of the parts of the book at greater length. As we will see, the perspectives embodied in the book stand very much at odds with views that eventually triumphed in orthodox Christianity. Indeed, they represent a Gnostic understanding of the faith that came to be suppressed by Christian leaders of later centuries.

Part One: Jesus' Parting Words to His Disciples

The text begins with a question, presumably from one of the disciples: "Will matter be destroyed or not?" This is a fundamental question that early Christians had to deal with, a question that lay at the heart of the conflict between Gnostic and proto-orthodox Christians in the second and third centuries. The proto-orthodox view was that this material world and everything in it were created by the one true God, as described in the opening chapters of the book of Genesis. This does not mean that the proto-orthodox believed there was nothing wrong with this world. They too could look around and see that material existence is anything but pleasant for the majority of people living here. There are tsunamis, hurricanes, tornados, earthquakes, mudslides; there are poverty, famine, drought; there are epidemics, life-threatening diseases of all kinds, and the ravages of aging. No one can look at the world we live in and make an unqualified pronouncement that it is good.

But for the proto-orthodox, the world was originally *created* good. The evil that now afflicts it is not the world's natural state. Instead, the good creation has become corrupted. Among humans, this corruption manifests itself in acts of sin, as humans murder, rape, pillage, oppress, and malign one another. Evil is manifest in nature as well, for example, in the natural disasters that have always occurred (since the Fall, for theologians) and seemingly always will occur.

It is interesting to contrast the understanding of the world in the Gospel of Mary with that found in early Christian apocalyptic thinkers, such as Paul. In the apocalyptic view, the evil that has so corrupted nature will one day be destroyed. God will intervene in history and overthrow the forces of evil and everyone (sinners) siding with them. He will then reestablish this material world as he had originally designed it in its pristine state. There will be a glorious, paradisal kingdom here on earth, where all people will enjoy the lush benefits of the earth and experience none of the hardship, pain, and suffering that are the lot of humans in the present. According to this apocalyptic view, then, matter will be not destroyed but redeemed when God reasserts his will over the good creation that he made.

Not so for many Gnostic Christians, including the one responsible for penning the Gospel of Mary. Jesus here replies to the question of whether matter will be destroyed by affirming that "all natures, all formed things, all creatures . . . will dissolve into their own root."[4] In other words, everything will melt away, even matter itself: "The nature of matter is dissolved into the root of its nature." In the Gnostic view, the material world is not a good creation that is to be redeemed. It is the source of pain and suffering, and it will be done away with. Eternal life is not a material existence but a nonmaterial existence. That which is spirit will return to the spiritual realm, whereas that which is matter will face ultimate dissolution.

This leads to another question, asked now by Peter: "What is the sin of the world?" For an apocalyptic thinker such as Paul, there were several answers to what sin is. On one hand, sin is an act of disobedience to God. But the act of disobedience, for Paul and others like him, is rooted in something deep within human nature, because people are enslaved to the cosmic forces that are in control of this world, including the power of sin. As an apocalypticist, Paul maintained that sin is a very real presence in the world, standing in opposition to God and enslaving people to do its will. Alienation from God occurs when sin succeeds (as it always does) in driving people to disobey God's injunctions for human life.

This is not the view of the Gospel of Mary, however, for Jesus replies to Peter that "there is no such thing as sin, but you create sin when you mingle in adultery, and this is called sin." Sin does not exist, then, as an independent entity. When Jesus refers to mingling "in adultery" he evidently means the illicit combination of things, specifically the combination of what is spiritual with what is material. When spirit comes to be entrapped in matter (illicit mixing, i.e., adultery), that is where alienation occurs. And that is the human dilemma that needs to be resolved. What is needed is not an atonement for (or forgiveness of) sins against God, or the destruction of the cosmic power of sin. Instead, everything needs to be restored "to its root." This happens when the material world dissolves and the spirit returns to its heavenly abode. For the Gospel of Mary, that was the mission of Jesus: "For this reason the good came among you, to those of every nature, in order to restore nature to its root."

Jesus goes on to talk about the problem created by human desires. Since the spirit is in its true state when it is no longer entrapped in the body, it should not yield to the desires of the flesh. These desires in fact came into being when the spirit "committed adultery," that is, when it came to be united with a material body. Jesus says, "Matter gave birth to passion that is without form, because it comes from what is contrary to nature." God did not unite spirit and matter: this unification is unnatural, leading to passion and the internal suffering that passion creates. All this is contrary to nature. The way to escape this untenable situation of being controlled by desires, of course, is to escape the body.

At this point, the disciples' questions have ended, and Jesus gives them several parting exhortations. He first bestows his peace upon them, and says:

> Be careful that no one leads you astray by saying "Look here" or "Look there."
> The child of humanity [literally "the son of man"] is within you. Follow that.
> Those who seek it will find it.

These exhortations are reminiscent of some sayings from the Coptic Gospel of Thomas, which also insists that the Kingdom of God is not a physical presence here in this material world but a kingdom within, in one's spirit, which is itself divine. One cannot, therefore, go searching for a future kingdom on earth, for it will not be found here. In Thomas's words:

> Jesus said, "If those who lead you say to you, 'See, the kingdom is in the sky,' then the birds of the sky will precede you. If they say to you, 'It is in the sea,' then the fish will precede you. Rather the kingdom is inside of you, and it is outside of you. When you come to know yourselves, then you will become known, and you will realize that it is you who are the sons of the living father. But if you will not know yourselves you dwell in poverty and it is you who are that poverty." (Saying 3)

The Kingdom is not something that can be pointed to outside a person; it is within one. And it is within others as well (that's why it is also "outside of you"). It is by knowing yourself, who you really are, that you come to realize the kingdom within. Those who have this gnosis are the children of God. Those who do not have the gnosis are impoverished. This is true for the Gospel of Mary as well. One is to follow the hidden spark (the child of humanity) that is within in order to attain to salvation, and "those who seek it will find it."

This teaching also stands at odds with apocalyptic views represented by someone such as Paul. Christian apocalypticists believed that God created this material world; they maintained that he will also redeem it and that his Kingdom will come here, to the world in which we live. It is not some kind of mystical kingdom inside each of us. It is a kingdom yet to come, in which God will stand supreme.

The first part of the Gospel of Mary ends with Jesus urging his followers not to "lay down any rules other than what I have given you, and do not establish law, as the lawgiver did, or you will be bound by it." Throughout history, of course, Christian leaders have been quite intent on legislating moral behavior, dictating what can and cannot be done with one's own body and in interaction with the bodies of others. And so there are rules of sexual conduct (no extramarital sex), community conduct (don't steal your neighbor's property), political conduct (pay your taxes), and so on—all taken to be the "Christian" way of life. But according to the Gospel of Mary, external regulations are not what it means to follow the way of Christ. It is the internal recognition of the truth that matters.

Part Two: The Revelation to Mary

After making these exhortations, Jesus leaves the disciples, presumably returning to his heavenly home. But rather than taking his exhortations to heart and moving on to "preach the good news," they wallow in doubt and self-pity, showing that they have not understood Jesus' teaching about the glorious kingdom within. Just when Jesus has told them that the material body is of no importance, they worry about saving their own skins:

> The disciples were grieved. They wept profoundly and said, "How can we go to the Gentiles and preach the good news of the kingdom of the child of humanity [literally "son of man"]? If they did not spare him, how will we be spared?"

And that is when Mary appears on the scene. She alone understands her master's teaching. She, the female follower of Jesus, is the true disciple, who has gnosis. We read her opening words of comfort to the disciples:

> Mary stood up, greeted them all, and said to her brothers, "Do not weep or grieve or be in doubt, for his grace will be with you all and will protect you. Rather, let us praise his greatness, for he has prepared us and made us truly human."

This is a key passage in the book. Mary does not have to cease being a woman in order to be perfect. Which of us are truly human? Not those concerned with their material bodies, but those who accept Christ's teachings. Mary alone realizes this, and so she calls the men away from their anxieties and fears over their material well-being. Humans are more than bodies, and that means they are more than gendered bodies. For this Gospel, the gender of a person does not count. What counts is the self-knowledge precipitated by the revelation of Christ. Mary is the one and only disciple to see it. And her words had their effect: "When Mary said this, she turned their hearts to the good."

Peter, almost as if by way of concession, asks Mary to describe what the savior had told her privately:

> Peter said to Mary, "Sister, we know the savior loved you more than any other woman. Tell us the words of the savior that you remember, which you know but we do not, because we have not heard them."

There are several striking features of Peter's request. First, he acknowledges that Mary is the most beloved woman to Christ. This should not be taken in a sexual way: it is not that Christ loved Mary *differently* from other women (or other men). He loved her *more*. She is the one specially favored with a revelation from Christ. Peter also acknowledges that this revelation was given to Mary alone. This statement will be significant later in the text, where Peter flat-out denies what he admits here. Possibly the most significant point is precisely that it is to Mary—a woman—that Christ has given this secret revelation. Once more we see that for this text, external, material features such as sexual differences are literally immaterial. What matters is the knowledge that Christ bestows.

Mary's description of her vision begins with her query to Christ concerning how one actually receives a vision—whether it is through the soul or the spirit. Christ indicates that visions come neither through soul nor spirit but through the mind. It is there that the text breaks off, leaving us to wonder how he would have explained the differences among soul, spirit, and mind. It appears that he is about to explain the superiority of the mind as the receptor of the vision, as he indicates: "The mind, which is between the [other] two, sees the vision." But when the text resumes after four missing pages, it is the soul, not the mind, that is all-important. Mary describes her vision in which the soul is ascending to its heavenly home, passing through realms controlled by hostile forces intent on keeping it entrapped here in the world of matter.

In her vision the soul is holding a conversation with the second heavenly power, named Desire. The soul needs to pass through the realm controlled by this power in order to reach its heavenly goal. The first power—already bypassed in the missing portion of the text—was evidently called Darkness. This of course is linked to spiritual blindness, the inability to perceive the truth. By passing darkness by, the soul shows that it has become enlightened; it has now moved to the second sphere, that of Desire.

Desire does not want to allow the soul to ascend through its realm and claims that the soul is an earthbound creature that did not have a heavenly origin. For this reason, it has no right to travel to the spiritual realm above. And so Desire says: "I did not see you descending, but now I see you ascending. Why are you lying, since you belong to me?"

There are, of course, some people who are completely overwhelmed by Desire, who are slaves of Desire, who belong to it. But not this soul. This is a true soul from the upper world, who was entrapped within the garment of the body. Contrary to what Desire thought, the soul was not identical with the body. And so the soul can say to Desire: "I saw you, but you did not see me or know me. To you I was only a garment and you did not recognize me." Desire has no power over the nonmaterial entity, the soul. And so the soul can continue on its journey.

It next encounters the third power, called Ignorance. Ignorance too wants to keep the soul tied to its material moorings, and claims that the soul has been "bound by wickedness" and so has no right to ascend to the spiritual realm. But the soul responds that Ignorance is wrongly passing judgment. Being bound to the material realm was a temporary, not permanent, state of affairs. The soul has now realized that the material realm is soon to pass away. It informs Ignorance: "I was bound, but I have not bound. I was not recognized, but I have recognized that all is to be dissolved, both what is earthly and what is heavenly."

Ignorance cannot recognize truth, but the truth (within the soul) knows that the material world—all things on earth and in heaven—are to be dissolved. This truth is what sets the soul free. It ascends above the realm of Ignorance, to encounter the fourth and final power.

This power is called Wrath and is said to take seven forms (the first three of which conform to the powers already confronted by the soul): darkness, desire, ignorance, death wish, fleshly kingdom, foolish fleshly wisdom, and angry person's wisdom. This sevenfold power of Wrath asks the soul: "Where are you coming from, slayer of humans, and where are you going, destroyer of realms?" How well does this power know the soul! The soul slays the human, in that it overcomes the human body. And it destroys realms in that it overcomes the material world that has tried to keep it hostage.

The soul makes an apt response to this fourth power:

> What binds me is slain, what surrounds me is destroyed, my desire is gone, ignorance is dead. In a world I was freed through another world, and in an image I was freed through a heavenly image. The fetter of forgetfulness is temporary. From now on I shall rest, through the course of the time of the age, in silence.

What better expression can there be of the Gnostic belief in salvation? What binds the immortal soul—the body—is to be slain, and with its destruction comes liberation. No longer is the soul constrained by desire or plagued by ignorance. It is a true spiritual being, freed from bodily passions and fully knowing who it is.

This knowledge did not come from the present material world, but from the heavenly world above, as the soul saw its true spiritual image. Once it comes to the knowledge of itself, it is freed from the temporary forgetfulness that has plagued it. And it can return to a place of rest, for all time.

As anyone familiar with traditional Christianity will recognize, this understanding of salvation stands very much at odds with what came to be called "orthodoxy." In orthodox Christianity, the body and its desires are not evils to be escaped. The body will be redeemed, and all desires will be directed to their rightful object: God himself. Desire, for orthodox Christianity, is not in itself the problem; the problem is misplaced desire. Salvation is not a matter of setting the spirit free from its material trappings; it is a matter of redeeming the material world that God himself created, so that it can return to its pristine state and humans—composed of both body and soul—can worship their creator for all time. This salvation does not come through self-knowledge brought by Christ. It comes through the sacrifice that Christ paid for sins. It is the death and resurrection of Jesus—not the secret revelation that he delivered—that bring about a restored relationship with God. This restored relationship does not mean that individual personalities are dissolved into the oneness of the godhead. It means that humans will be redeemed from their alienation from God, reconciled into a passionately loving and faithful relationship with their Creator.

To say the least, the revelation to Mary in this Gospel presents an alternative vision of what it means to be a follower of Jesus.

Part Three: The Male Response to Mary's Revelation

It should be clear already from this text that Mary—the one woman mentioned—is the only one who has understood the teaching that Christ himself revealed. She is the true Gnostic, the one with full self-understanding who will be set free from the constraints of this material body. As it turns out, the male disciples don't like it.

Andrew is the first to speak out, saying to his "brothers": "Say what you think about what she said, but I do not believe the savior said this. These teachings certainly are strange ideas." In other words, this must be another old wives' tale. Andrew's comments themselves, of course, are revealing: here is a man who doesn't understand, who hasn't attained self-knowledge, who is still constricted by his own ignorance of the truth, which prevents him from attaining to his salvation. For this text, men do not have a leg up on salvation. Quite the contrary, it is the men who don't "get it."

Peter then responds, showing that he too is outside the divine revelation that can bring salvation: "He [Peter] asked the others about the savior: 'Did he really speak with a woman in private, without our knowledge? Should we all turn and listen to her? Did he prefer her to us?'"

Peter, of course, means this as a rhetorical question. Unfortunately, he has gotten the answer wrong. Christ *has* preferred Mary to them, the male disciples, as seen in the circumstance that he really did speak with her privately without their knowledge, revealing to her the truth that can bring salvation. Peter's comments betray both belligerence and hypocrisy, since, as you'll remember, he first asked Mary to describe what Christ had revealed to her alone. Now that she has done so, he refuses to believe that it is possible. Could a woman receive the revelation when the men had not? Evidently so.

We will have more to say about the personal struggles between Peter and Mary—an early Christian battle of the sexes—in the next chapter. For now it is enough to notice Mary's reaction: she begins to weep and asks him, "My brother Peter, what do you think? Do you think that I made this up by myself or that I am lying about the savior?" Whichever way Peter answers he will be wrong: Mary is neither self-deceived nor deceptive.

The apostle Levi stands up for Mary and brings the discussion to a close: "Levi answered and said to Peter, 'Peter, you always are angry. Now I see you arguing against this woman like an adversary. If the savior made her worthy, who are you to reject her? Surely the savior knows her well. That is why he has loved her more than us.'"

As the closing argument, Levi's words carry special weight. Peter is portrayed as a hothead (recall our earlier discussions of Peter's reputation). And he is treating Mary as the enemy, when in fact she has just described the real enemies: desire, ignorance, and wrath, all of which Peter seems to have in full measure.

It is striking that Levi affirms Mary's standing before Christ. He has "made her worthy." Christ has done that by taking her as she already is, not by making her like one of the male disciples, who apart from Levi continue to seem a bit dense. It is because the savior knew her so well, knew what she was really like, that "he loved her more than us."

This last statement marks a significant progression in the thought of the book. If you'll recall, Peter asked Mary to recount her vision because Christ loved her "more than any other woman." Now, as it turns out, Christ loved her even more than the male disciples. Mary here is exalted to the highest level possible. She is the one whom Christ fully knew, to whom he revealed the truth necessary for salvation, who has come to be exalted in his presence even more than Andrew, Peter, Levi, and the other men disciples. Mary is the true Gnostic, the free spirit who is bound to return to her heavenly home.

Levi concludes his words by urging Peter and the others to be humble and human—truly and perfectly (i.e., spiritually) human. They are to proclaim the good news of salvation, and not to impose any rules or laws on their converts other than what the savior commanded. In response, the disciples go forth to teach and preach, presumably the message that Mary, the most beloved of them all, had delivered to them.[5]

Chapter Eighteen

Mary: The Residual Questions

Like many of my friends who are scholars of the New Testament and early Christianity, I get asked to do a lot of lectures around the country. Over the past few years I've been struck by what seems to pique the interest of a crowd— whether they are church people committed to their beliefs in Christ or secular audiences interested in Christianity as a cultural and historical phenomenon. If I'm giving a lecture on Peter or Paul, there will always be a few interested souls. But if I'm talking about Mary, the throngs will flock in. Mary is the hot topic of the day; Peter and Paul seem old and tired by comparison.

That may be a pity, given the far-reaching importance and real intrigue of Peter and Paul in their own right. But it is not a surprise. Since Mary is less known, there is so much more room to speculate. It is always more interesting to come up with wild and outlandish theories than to describe what is reasonably well-documented. For most folk, fiction is more compelling than fact any day.

The fact is, we know very little about Mary. Unlike Paul, she left us no writings. Indeed, she probably was illiterate. Unlike Peter, there are no lengthy accounts written about her from within a few years of her life. And unlike both Paul and Peter, there are no writings forged in her name by later followers. Even the Gospel of Mary, written probably a century after her death, is about her, not allegedly by her.

Since she was the best-known woman follower of Jesus, the doors of speculation have been thrown wide open, both in the modern world and in antiquity. Was she *especially* close to Jesus? Did they have a sexual relationship? Were they married, with children? Was she his closest follower? Was she the first leader of the apostolic band? Did her real story come to be squelched by the patriarchal forces of the young religion, when the men took over the church and rewrote the history of its early years, leaving Mary, and all other women, out of the story? These are a few of the intriguing questions surrounding the least-known but, for many, most interesting of the trio I've been considering in this book. In this concluding chapter, I would like to address some of these residual questions.

Question One:
Were Mary and Jesus Married, with Children?

This is the one question that seems to be on everyone's mind, the one I get asked more than any other. The question has long been in the air, I suppose. But it has been stoked into a raging fire by the best-selling novel of modern times, *The Da Vinci Code*. What evidence is there? Well, as I've asked before, if the theory is intriguing enough, why do you need evidence?

As we've seen, a lot of the historical claims of *The Da Vinci Code* are simply wrong. It is not true, for example, that the Dead Sea Scrolls contained Gospels that discussed Mary and Jesus. Serious historians have found such claims outrageous. Those of us with a better sense of humor have just seen them as outrageously funny.

Nor is it true that the marriage of Mary and Jesus is repeatedly discussed in the Gospels that didn't make it into the New Testament. In fact, it is never discussed at all—never even mentioned, not even once. It is not true that the Gospel of Philip calls Mary Jesus' spouse. In fact, few of the historical claims about Mary and Jesus in *The Da Vinci Code* are right. But it's still a terrific book if you like a fast-paced murder mystery built on a conspiracy theory that involves a cover-up by the Vatican. Thirty-six million readers can't all be wrong. (And that's before the book has come out in paperback and the movie has been released!)

So what does the historical evidence tell us about Mary and Jesus? As we have seen, it tells us almost nothing—certainly nothing to indicate that Jesus and Mary had a sexual relationship of any kind. When I tell this to an audience, I inevitably have one or two people raise their hands to ask, "Isn't it *possible,* though, that they were married?" And I reply that of *course* it's possible—just as it's possible that Jesus was married to Susanna, or Salome, or to Mary of Bethany (who also gets mentioned several times in the Gospels—far more frequently, in more than one Gospel, during Jesus' ministry), or to her sister Martha, or to one of the other women mentioned in the New Testament. Or that he was married to someone who isn't named at all. Or that he was gay. Why not? It's *possible*. But historians have to deal not only with what's possible but also with what's probable. Was Jesus probably intimate with Mary? Or Susanna? Or Peter? Well, how would we know? We need evidence.

From the historian's point of view, it is interesting to note that it is in our later sources, not our early ones, that Mary becomes more prominent in Jesus' life. These also are the sources that hint at their possible intimacy. Just consider the sources we've discussed already, in reverse chronological order. The latest source that I've mentioned is the Greater Questions of Mary, allegedly used by the Gnostic Phibionites in the fourth century. In this account, Jesus takes Mary privately up to a mountain and forces her to watch as he has sex with a woman he draws out from his side. In this case Mary is not herself intimate with Jesus but is a rather unwilling voyeur into his sex life otherwise. An earlier source is the Gospel of Philip, where we are told that Jesus loved Mary more than others, and frequently used to kiss her. This kissing is not sexual foreplay, as I showed in my discussion in chapter 15, but it does indicate a particular closeness. In this Gospel we are also told that she was his companion.

Somewhat earlier is the Gospel of Mary, where there is nothing at all sexual between Jesus and Mary, but where Jesus is said to have loved her more than the men disciples. It's not that he loves her differently (for example, as a lover); it is that he understands her fully and has granted her a special revelation unknown to the others. Somewhat earlier still is the Gospel of John. Here Mary is never mentioned during Jesus' lifetime, but she is the one who discovers his empty tomb and to whom he first appears after rising from the dead. She is surprised and ecstatic at seeing him alive, and is told not to cling to him but to go tell the disciples that he has been raised.

Earlier still is the Gospel of Luke, where Mary is not alone when she sees Jesus raised from the dead, but is in the company of other women. She is not even named in the account, but one can assume she is one of the women at the tomb, since she is earlier named as one of the women who had followed Jesus from Galilee to Jerusalem before his arrest. Here, in this Gospel, we have the one reference to her accompanying Jesus during his ministry, along with Joanna, Susanna, and lots of other women. Our earliest Gospel is Mark, and here Mary is not named at all until the end; she and other women find Jesus' tomb empty and flee out of fear, telling no one what they have seen.

My point is that the later sources begin to suggest an intimacy between Jesus and Mary that is not found in the earlier sources. In fact, in the earliest sources, there is not a hint, not a glimmer of hope, that there was anything special between them.

But is there any evidence that they were *not* married or at least intimate? Sometimes it is argued—for example, in *The Da Vinci Code*—that Jesus must have been married, because Jewish men in the first century were *always* married. If Jesus himself was not married, then one of our sources would have said something about his "unnatural state of bachelorhood." (And if he was married, who more likely as a spouse than Mary, the woman more commonly named than any other?) Once again, this claim, as plausible as it sounds, is in fact wrong. We do know of Jewish men in the first century who were single and celibate. Strikingly, they are men who shared a religious perspective similar to that of the historical Jesus.

One of the most significant aspects of the Dead Sea Scrolls—not that they contained Gospels—is that they were written by a group of Jews known to historians as the Essenes.[1] We know about the Essenes from a number of sources outside the Dead Sea Scrolls. They are mentioned, for example, in the writings of a Jewish historian of the first century, Josephus. What these other sources tell us is that the Essenes were a group of single, celibate men. They lived at the same time, and in approximately the same place, as Jesus. And as we now know from the Dead Sea Scrolls, they, like Jesus, were Jewish apocalypticists. They too believed that they were living at the end of time, that God was soon to intervene in the course of history to overthrow the forces of evil and bring in his kingdom. In preparation for this imminent cataclysmic event, the Essenes stayed in the wilderness, maintaining their ritual purity, removed from the presence and influence of women.

Jesus differed from the Essenes in a number of significant ways. For example, he did not believe in living an isolated life in order to preserve his ritual purity. In contrast, he spent his time with prostitutes, tax collectors, and sundry other sinners. But he did share with the Essenes an apocalyptic worldview, sensing that the Kingdom of God was soon to arrive in power and insisting that people prepare for it. It simply isn't true that someone like Jesus—a Jewish man of the first century—would necessarily have been married. Other apocalypticists weren't.

We know of one other Jewish bachelor from the first century. Strikingly, it was one of Jesus' most important followers: none other than the apostle Paul. As we have seen, Paul told his Christian converts in Corinth that since the "time is short" they should remain in whatever social state they were already in. If they were slaves, they should not seek to be free; if they were married, they should not seek to be separated; if they were single, they should not seek to be married. More than that, he argued that it was better, in view of the "approaching crisis" to remain single, just as he himself was (1 Cor. 7:7, 25–26).

The like-minded Essenes before Jesus and the like-minded Paul after him—all of them apocalyptic Jewish men—lived life as single and celibate. It is not at all implausible that Jesus did as well.

But there is more evidence than just that. We earlier saw that Jesus taught that in the coming Kingdom of God, there would be no "marriage or giving in marriage" (Mark 12:25). People would live in that coming age "like the angels"—that is, a marriageless and sexless existence. It may not be paradise the way *we* might imagine it, but for some people it was pretty attractive. In any event, it is what Jesus believed. Moreover, he instructed his followers that they should begin to implement the ideals of the kingdom in the present. In the kingdom there would be no hatred, war, disease, demonic powers, loneliness, or suffering of any kind; so people should live lives appropriate to the kingdom here and now, loving one another, making peace, healing the sick, casting out the demons, visiting the lonely, relieving suffering. If the ideals of the Kingdom are to be replicated in the here and now, and if there is no sex and no marriage in the Kingdom, what does that say about life in the present? It would seem that Jesus thought that sex and marriage should be forgone in the present, in light of the coming of the End (unless, of course, you were already married). On these grounds, my best guess as a historian is that Jesus was single and celibate.

But in particular there is evidence to suggest that he was not married to Mary Magdalene. For one thing, if he was, and if it was at all known, why do the Gospel writers never mention it? Moreover, why is it that most of them never mention her during Jesus' public ministry? And why is it that the one who does so, Luke, mentions her only in the company of two other women (one of them married) and a large group of others? These writers mention Jesus' mother, his father, his brothers (four of them by name), and his sisters. Why would they never mention his wife? And if his wife was Mary Magdalene, why would they never say so, given the fact they do mention her?

Moreover, it is significant just how they do mention her. They call her Mary of Magdala. As I've pointed out, they indicate the town she came from in order to differentiate her from the other Marys named in the New Testament—for example, Mary the mother of Jesus and Mary of Bethany. Each Mary is identified by the striking feature that differentiates her from the others. Now, if this particular Mary was the one to whom Jesus was actually married, wouldn't *that* be the thing that would differentiate her most clearly from any of the others, rather than, say, the town that she happened to come from?

At the end of the day, as titillating as it might be to think of Jesus having a clandestine sexual relationship with Mary, or as "sensible" as it might be to think that they had a normal married relationship with children, the evidence seems to speak against it. As a professional historian I hate to admit it, but sometimes history just is not as interesting as fiction.

Question Two:
Was Mary the First Apostle?

The term *apostle* comes from a Greek word that means something like "one who has been sent." It can refer to anyone who is sent on a mission. In Christian parlance, it is used to refer to those who were specially commissioned and sent by Christ to spread his gospel. The word is sometimes distinguished from the term *disciple,* which means "follower." In a technical sense, there were twelve disciples. These were the closest followers of Jesus during his public ministry, the ones (all of them men) he chose to be his inner circle. But in a broader sense, all of the followers of Jesus, men and women, could be called his disciples.

Who, then, were the apostles? Normally they are understood to be the closest followers of Jesus *after* his death, who took his message abroad to convert others to the belief that in his life, death, and resurrection Jesus had performed

the act of salvation, making it possible for people now to have a right relationship with God. In other words, the apostles were the first witnesses to Christ,
commissioned by him, after his resurrection, to proclaim his gospel.

We usually think of the apostles as men: the eleven remaining disciples
(Judas having committed suicide), the one who replaced Judas according to
the book of Acts (a man named Matthias), and one or two others, including
James, Jesus' earthly brother, and Paul. Early traditions indicate that Jesus
appeared to these others after his resurrection, to commission them as missionaries and leaders of the church. What most people don't realize is that in
the early days of the church, there were also women apostles.

There really shouldn't be any dispute about this matter, since the apostle
Paul himself mentions a woman apostle by name in the letter he wrote to the
Christians of Rome. At the end of his letter Paul sends greetings to various
members of the congregation whom he happens to know (even though he has
never visited Rome; he must have met these people elsewhere). Included in his
greetings is the following: "Greet Andronicus and Junia, my compatriots and
fellow prisoners, who are preeminent among the apostles" (Rom. 16:7).
Andronicus is a man's name, and Junia a woman's. We know nothing else
about these two: were they husband and wife? Brother and sister? Unmarried
missionary partners? Here again historians can't help feeling desperately frus-
trated by the scarcity of our sources. Who *were* these people? How did they
convert to faith in Christ? What did they do with their lives? What was their
mission? How did they achieve it? What made them so special in the eyes of
Paul? Why were they preeminent? Did Paul see them as even more important
than, say, Peter, whom he does not mention here? Unfortunately, we will probably never know.

But we do know that one of them was a woman, and that she was an apostle,
and a preeminent one at that. I should point out that not everyone has known
this. As it turns out, English Bible translators have sometimes allowed their
own biases to affect how they have translated this passage (Rom. 16:7). In
such venerable editions as the Revised Standard Version, Junia has undergone
a sex change. In these translations she is called not Junia (a woman's name)
but Junias (a man's name).[2]

Why would translators make this change? It is not because of what Paul
actually wrote. What he wrote was Junia, the name of a woman. In fact, while
Junia (feminine) was a common name in the ancient world, Junias (masculine)
was not a name at all: it doesn't occur in any ancient Greek text. So what is
going on with translations such as the Revised Standard Version? It is purely a
matter of patriarchal bias. The translators couldn't believe that a woman could
be an apostle, so they made the woman Junia into a nonexistent man, Junias.

Were there other women apostles? Other women who understood themselves, and were understood by others, to be commissioned by Christ in order
to spread the word of his death and resurrection? We know of at least one
other, one who could be thought of, in fact, as the original apostle: Mary

Magdalene. Mary is called an apostle by some early Christian writers. This would include an anonymous writer sometimes thought to have been Hippolytus, a Christian leader in Rome around 200 CE. In a commentary written on the Old Testament book, the Song of Songs, this writer points out that Jesus first appeared to the women at the tomb and instructed them to tell the disciples that he had been raised. He then appeared to the male disciples, upbraiding them for not believing the women's report. As the author indicates: "Christ showed himself to the (male) apostles and said to them, 'It is I who appeared to these women and I who wanted to send them to you as apostles.'" Mary and the others, therefore, could be thought of as "apostles sent to the apostles," a title that Mary herself came to bear in the Middle Ages (Latin: *apostola apostolorum*).

As I've intimated, this view that Mary was the original apostle—the one commissioned to tell the good news of Christ's resurrection—is found already in the books of the New Testament. In the Gospel of Mark, it is Mary Magdalene along with Mary the mother of James and Salome who come to the tomb on the third day, learn from a young man there that Jesus has been raised, and are told then to go tell the disciples. In this account, it is true, they say nothing to anyone "for they were afraid" (Mark 16:8). And there is no word here of Christ himself appearing to these women (or to the other disciples, for that matter). But in the later account of Matthew, Mary and "the other Mary" not only learn of Jesus' resurrection from an angel at the tomb but are also instructed to tell the others. Jesus himself appears to the women and commissions them to "tell my brothers (i.e., the men disciples) to go to Galilee; and they will see me there" (Matt. 28:11). We are not explicitly told that the women did what they were told, but we do learn that the disciples made a trip to Galilee and that Jesus appeared to them there—so one can assume that the women fulfilled their commission.

It is in the last New Testament Gospel to be written, John, that Mary herself is singled out as the first to see Jesus raised from the dead. According to this account, Mary comes alone to the tomb, finds it empty, and goes to tell Peter and the "beloved disciple." They race each other to the tomb to see that Jesus' body is not there. When they return to their homes, Mary is left outside the tomb, and Jesus suddenly appears to her. She mistakes him for the gardener and asks where he has taken the body. But then he calls her by her name, and she recognizes him, calling him *rabbouni* (which means "teacher"). (Note: she does not call him "hubby.") Jesus commissions her to tell the disciples that he is about to ascend to heaven, and she does as she is told.

Here Mary is the first to be commissioned to proclaim the resurrection. In this account, at least, Mary is the first apostle. It is striking that in other traditions that we have, it is not Mary but Peter who is the first to see Jesus alive after his crucifixion. This is the case, for example, in the Gospel of Luke, where there is no mention of Jesus appearing to the women at the tomb, but several stories of his appearing to his men followers. The first appearance is to

Peter, as the disciples proclaim: "He has appeared to Simon" (Luke 24:36). But even here, before Jesus appears to anyone, it is the women—Mary Magdalene along with Joanna, Mary the mother of James, and several other women—who discover the empty tomb and inform the disciples. Somewhat typically, one might think, the men dismiss the women's account as an "idle story." It is not until Jesus himself shows up that they believe.

Even more striking is the earliest account of Jesus' resurrection that we have, found not in the writings of the Gospels but in a letter of Paul, some fifteen or twenty years before the Gospels were composed. In his first letter to the Corinthians, Paul reminds his converts of the message that he had originally delivered to them when trying to persuade them to join him in his faith in Christ:

> For I delivered over to you as of first importance what I in turn received, that Christ died in accordance with the Scriptures, and that he was buried; and that he was raised on the third day in accordance with the Scriptures, and that he appeared to Cephas, then to the Twelve. Then he appeared to more than five hundred brothers at one time. . . . Then he appeared to James, and then to all the apostles. Last of all, as to a miscarriage, he appeared to me. (1 Cor 15:3–7)

It is interesting that Paul never mentions the women discovering the empty tomb. In fact, he never mentions the empty tomb, or the women at all—any women. He instead refers to the appearances of Jesus after his death, all of which are to men (unless one wants to argue that the "five hundred brothers" included "brothers and sisters," but if that's what Paul meant, at least it is not what he said).

Some scholars have thought that Paul recounted only the stories of Christ's appearances he knew about. This would mean that the stories about the women at the tomb were not in broad circulation. Others have pointed out that Paul is giving evidence for the Christian claims about Christ. The evidence that he died is that he was buried, and the evidence that he was raised is that he appeared alive afterward. But since the point is evidence, it is sometimes argued, Paul has restricted himself to naming the *men* that Christ appeared to, since the testimony of women would not be admissible in a Jewish court.[3]

This may be right, but it's hard to know. What is clear is that there were two competing traditions in early Christianity. In one set of traditions, Christ first appeared to Mary Magdalene (and possibly other women); in the other he first appeared to Peter (and possibly other men). One of the reasons this is interesting is that we have repeatedly seen through our discussion of Mary that there is a steady stream of stories that show her in competition with Peter, or at least show Peter constantly becoming upset by the high status Christ gives her. In the *Pistis Sophia,* Peter complains that Mary gets to do all the talking. In the Gospel of Thomas Peter asks that Mary leave Jesus and the disciples, "for women are not worthy of life." And in the Gospel of Mary, Peter argues, in typically hotheaded fashion, that Mary's revelation cannot have come from Christ, who would not have revealed his secrets privately to a woman rather than publicly to the men. This contest between Peter and Mary seems to go back to our earliest traditions, some of which claim that he was the first to see Jesus raised from the dead, and others that give the nod to her.

Question Three:
Did Mary Start Christianity?

There is no doubt that Peter became dominant as the leader of the church early in the Christian movement, and Mary receded into the background. We have scores of passages that talk about Peter, his involvement with Jesus during his life, and his leadership of the church after his death. There are scarcely any references to Mary.

Somewhat ironically, this is what makes a number of scholars conclude that the religion actually started with Mary, rather than Peter. The logic is this: later storytellers were fully aware of Peter's vast importance to the burgeoning Christian movement. How could they not be? He was the main figure during Jesus' ministry, one of the inner circle, the leader of the Twelve. After Jesus' death he became the head of the church in Jerusalem and eventually the main missionary to the Jewish people. He along with the apostle Paul was responsible for the spread of the religion from its tiny, inauspicious beginnings to its relative triumph throughout the empire. Peter was huge.

And what about Mary? She was scarcely known and little talked about. So if storytellers were to make up, or at least to modify, the stories of Christianity's beginnings, would they invent the story that it was a woman who started it? Wouldn't they be more likely to celebrate the greatness of the illustrious apostle Peter? Wouldn't they show that although he had denied Christ at the moment of crisis, he had redeemed himself in the aftermath by being the first to realize that Christ had been vindicated by God, raised from the dead, and exalted to heaven? Why would someone make up a story about a virtually unknown woman discovering the empty tomb and proclaiming the resurrection?[4] Especially if the point of the stories is to give evidence that Jesus' death was not the last word, that God himself had the last word by reversing the illicit judgment of the Jewish leaders and the Roman authorities by raising his son from the dead, would the "idle tale" of a woman be invented as evidence for the resurrection?

It seems unlikely. But then where did the stories of Mary Magdalene, either by herself or in the company of other women, originally come from? If it is hard to imagine them being made up by a number of early Christian storytellers, then maybe the stories have a real historical basis. Maybe it actually was Mary who found the tomb empty on the third day and who proclaimed that Jesus had been raised from the dead. I should emphasize that even though Christianity is based ultimately on the life and ministry of Jesus, it is much more than that. Traditional Christianity is the belief that he died for the sins of the world and was raised from the dead. Technically speaking, Christianity could not begin until someone proclaimed Jesus raised from the dead. It appears that the first to do so was Mary Magdalene. If so, as I argued in the previous chapter, Mary really is the one who started Christianity. There could scarcely be a more significant woman for the history of Western civilization—or man, for that matter—who is at the same time less known than Mary Magdalene.

Her role in the story came to be minimized in some places, especially as men became increasingly in charge of the church and the women leaders—some of them apostles—came to be silenced. In other places her role and reputation lived on, as evidenced in the scattered references to her in various sources from the early Christian movement, especially among the Gnostics. But for orthodox Christianity, Peter and Paul eventually triumphed.

In what ways were Peter's and Paul's understandings of the Christian faith different from Mary's? Unfortunately, we will never know for sure, since Mary left us no writings and is scarcely referred to in our early sources. We do learn from the early-third-century author Origen that Mary had followers devoted to her understanding of the religion. But unfortunately, we know nothing about what that might have been—what she herself actually believed about Christ—except what can be inferred from certain facts of history.

These include the fact that she was a Jewish woman from Galilee who was a devoted disciple of Jesus. She must have been drawn to his message, otherwise she would not have followed him and supported his mission from her own means. That means that she too must have been a Jewish apocalypticist, anticipating that this evil age of pain, suffering, and oppression was soon to be overthrown and God's kingdom was soon to arrive here on earth. In that kingdom there would be no more war, hatred, injustice, poverty, disease, demonic forces, oppression. It would be a paradisal age in which God and all he stood for ruled supreme. And it would be an age in which there would be no more oppression based on class, wealth, prestige, or gender. There would be no destitution, no underclass, no slavery, no sexual differentiation. Women would no longer be subject to the control of the men in their lives. They, along with the men, would be like the angels of heaven. In Jesus' message of the future liberation of the earth, Mary herself must have seen a message of her own liberation, in a future age filled only with what is good, when God would reign supreme.

And once she came to believe that Jesus had been raised from the dead, she, like other apocalyptic Jews such as Paul, probably drew the logical conclusion: The end is upon us. The Kingdom of God is almost here. The expectations of Jesus are soon to be realized, and the promises of God are about to be fulfilled. Mary may well have expected to see the liberation of the earth within her own lifetime.

Conclusion: Peter, Paul, and Mary in Perspective

Throughout this study I have argued that Peter, Paul, and Mary, like Jesus before them, were Jewish apocalypticists. Apocalyptic thinkers thought that the end of all things would be like the beginning: the earth would return to its original paradisal state—a new Garden of Eden, in which there would be no more sin, evil, pain, or suffering. In this spirit—that the end is to be like the beginning—I would like to conclude this book on the same note that I began it on, with reference to the Peter, Paul, and Mary of modern times.

This folk-singing trio of the 1960s were storytellers for their age. As with most storytellers, many of their most popular songs were in fact reproductions of songs written by others. These reproductions were themselves subject to a number of interpretations, applicable to a wide range of situations.

Some of Peter, Paul, and Mary's best-known songs involved personal loss and separation. The popular tune "500 Miles," for example, speaks of one's lover missing the train she is on, only to hear the whistle blow from a hundred miles away.

Even better known is a song (written by John Denver, no less) that tugged at our heartstrings in ninth grade, even if it does seem a bit hokey now:

All my bags are packed, I'm ready to go
I'm standin' here outside your door
I hate to wake you up to say goodbye

But the dawn is breakin', it's early morn
The taxi's waitin', he's blowin' his horn
Already I'm so lonesome I could die . . .

'Cause I'm leavin' on a jet plane
Don't know when I'll be back again
Oh, babe, I hate to go . . .

Are these songs merely about the heart-rending pain of going on a trip? Are they about losing a loved one forever? Or could they be about moving into the modern world of the 1960s, away from the comforts of the postwar '50s, into an age of armament, protest, racial tension? Could they be about a sense of loss as we move into a new world, leaving the old, comfortable one behind?

The early Christians would have related to some such sense of estrangement from the world. In fact, it was one of their own major refrains. This was certainly true of Gnostic Christians, including the author of the Gospel of Mary. In their view, there was deep within themselves, at their inner core, a spark of the divine that had become estranged from its heavenly home. This spark was entrapped here in this evil world of matter, separated from the spiritual realm from which it came and to which it was eager to return. Other Christians felt a sense of alienation as well, including the apostle Paul and the author of 1 Peter, who believed that their real home was in heaven. For them, when it came to this world of pain and misery, they were just passing through.

Many early followers of Christ told tales about the glories of this other world, whose power was sometimes manifest here on earth and whose blessings awaited those who remained faithful to the death. How are these stories to be interpreted? Are the glories of God's coming Kingdom meant to be taken literally as an expression of what would happen here on earth? Would God overthrow the forces of evil to establish his sovereignty once and for all, as Jesus himself seems to have taught and his followers Peter, Paul, and Mary evidently believed? Or do the stories refer to life in heaven that will come to souls once they have passed from this mortal coil, as seems to be the message of the apocryphal Apocalypse of Peter? Or could they refer to the blessings of life in the here and now for those who have experienced the full benefits of salvation at the point of their baptism and who, therefore, are already "ruling in the heavenly places," as taught by the opponents of Paul in Corinth and by some of Paul's own later followers, including the author of the book of Ephesians?

The thing about stories is that no one, not even their authors, can control their interpretation. Stories continue to live once they are produced. And as they live, they change. This was especially true in the ancient world, when there were none of the possibilities and limitations given to us by modern mass media. When I buy a CD with Peter, Paul, and Mary singing "Lemon tree very pretty and the lemon flower is sweet / But the fruit of the poor lemon is impossible to eat," I can go to another town in another state and buy another of the same song, and it will be exactly the same song. And I can do it time after time.

In the ancient world it was never that way, because there were no means for mechanical or electronic reproduction that could guarantee the accuracy of the product. As a result, people living in the ancient world did not understand or see the need to preserve traditions unchanged from one retelling to another. This is true of people who live in oral cultures generally, as opposed to written or electronic cultures. In antiquity such people changed their songs and stories depending on their own feelings and emotions and on the situation within which they sang or recited them. Changes could be made based on the audience, the time of day, the historical, cultural, or political context, and so on. Sometimes the stories simply changed because it seemed that they ought to change. The words of "Lemon Tree" might be changed simply because some of them make no sense. Truth be told, the fruit of the lemon is not "impossible" to eat. And so someone might change it to say "The fruit of the poor lemon is not very pleasant to eat." But then the rhythm would be thrown off, so it would need to be changed again, in some other way. Someone else might decide that the song makes better sense if it refers not to lemons but, say, to kumquats. Then the rhyming scheme wouldn't work, and the whole thing would need to be reworked. And so it would go.

If this is true for songs about lemons, how much more for matters that really and truly mattered to those who passed along their cherished traditions? In our written cultures, we might think that the really important historical events of antiquity—the life of Socrates, the conquests of Rome, the death of Jesus—would have been remembered with pinpoint accuracy precisely because they *were* so important. Not so for ancient people. Stories were changed with what would strike us today as reckless abandon, precisely because they did matter so much to those telling them. They were modified, amplified, and embellished. And sometimes they were made up.

For historians who study the ancient world, it is important to know what actually did happened, insofar as this is possible. It is important, for example, to know what Jesus really said and did, to know why he faced such opposition, to know why he was crucified, to know why his followers continued to believe in him after his death. But it is also important to know how the tales about him were retold: sometimes modified, amplified, and embellished. And sometimes made up.

So too with his followers, including the three we have focused on here, the ancient trio of Simon Peter, the Apostle Paul, and Mary Magdalene. They too lived real historical lives, and it is important—or at least intriguing—to know what these lives were like, to know what they said and did and experienced, insofar as we can. But it is also important to know how their stories lived on in the decades and centuries after their deaths, as Christian storytellers told and retold their tales.

Some of these tales will not get us back to the historical Peter, Paul, and Mary. Peter probably did not make a tuna fish come back to life; Paul probably did not baptize a talking lion; Mary probably did not restore a woman to life after she lay dead for two years on a deserted island. But many Christians *believed* these things happened. When they told these stories and others like them—even stories that happened to be historically accurate—they did so for reasons. These stories meant something to the storytellers—the stories spoke to them, expressed their understanding of the world, embodied their beliefs, values, and concerns—just as the folk songs of the 1960s do for some of us.

At the end of the day, probably not too many of us are all that concerned about the proper interpretation of "If I Had a Hammer" or "Lemon Tree." More of us may be concerned about the meaning of the life of Jesus, and possibly even the lives of his followers. But it is always important to remember that in pursuing these concerns we are not only trying to reconstruct something like the brute facts of history. We are also involved in seeing how history was interpreted by those who have handed it down to us.

The reality is that history does not come to us in unmediated guise. It comes to us in stories from the past, told by real flesh-and-blood humans who were interpreting their stories—even their historically accurate ones—in light of their own situations, concerns, beliefs, practices, needs, and values. This is true even of us today, living in a written culture and an electronic age. We too speak about the past because it means something to us in the present; we too re-present what we know and think and believe in ways that matter to us; we too seek to understand the past while trying to make sense of the world we live in today.

Notes

Introduction

1. Like many of the songs popularized by Peter, Paul, and Mary, they did not compose this one. It was written by Lee Hays and Pete Seeger in 1958.

Chapter One
The Quarry: Our Sources for Peter the Rock

1. For apocryphal texts throughout this book I have used the translations found in J. K. Elliott, *The Apocryphal New Testament: A Collection of Apocryphal Christian Literature in an English Translation* (Oxford: Clarendon Press, 1993).
2. The first Christian on record who indicated that the twenty-seven books we now have as the New Testament were to be *the* canon of Scripture was the bishop of Alexandria, Athanasius, in the year 367 CE—that is, some three hundred years after most of the books had been written. For the debates over which books to include and which to exclude, and a discussion of the grounds for making such decisions, see Bart D. Ehrman, *Lost Christianities: The Battles for Scripture and the Faiths We Never Knew* (New York: Oxford University Press, 2003).
3. See Bart D. Ehrman, *The New Testament: A Historical Introduction to the Early Christian Writings,* 3rd ed. (New York: Oxford University Press, 2003), chap. 5.
4. All the quotations from Papias are my own translation. This one comes from Eusebius's *Church History,* 3, 39. See Bart D. Ehrman, *The Apostolic Fathers,*

Loeb Classical Library (Cambridge, MA: Harvard University Press, 2004), 2:93–95.

5. Thus, for example, Carsten P. Thiede, *Simon Peter: From Galilee to Rome* (Grand Rapids: Academie Books, 1988).

6. A moment's reflection shows that he wouldn't have called it that: authors may sign their book and they may give them titles, but they do not give them titles that indicate whom they are written by. The author of this account might have called it "the Gospel" or "the Gospel of Jesus Christ," but whoever called it "the Gospel according to Mark" is telling you which anonymous author actually wrote it.

7. The author of Matthew copied a number of his stories from Mark, which was also originally written in Greek. This means that he too must have been writing in Greek. For a further discussion, see my *The New Testament,* chap. 6.

8. I might point out that some readers have thought that Papias's claim that Peter was Mark's source is confirmed by the way Peter is portrayed in Mark's Gospel, as rather brash, dense, and ultimately unfaithful. The argument is that Mark must have learned the truth about Peter's personality and actions from Peter himself. It's a clever argument, but it doesn't really work. Whether Peter decided not to whitewash his own character or whether Mark decided not to whitewash it, either way it's not evidence of who wrote the book; there are lots of negative portrayals of lots of people in lots of books, and no one thinks that the person in question was always the source of information. Was Judas the source for the Gospel of Matthew, since he comes off badly? Or was Herod? Or James and John? And so on.

9. Johnson M. Cheney, ed., *The Life of Christ in Stereo* (Portland: Western Conservative Baptist Seminary, 1969).

Chapter Two
Peter: Solid Rock or Shifting Sand?

1. See the fuller discussion on pp. 35–36.

2. See p. 33.

3. At one point in my scholarly career I wondered if Paul's controversy was with Peter or with someone else also named Cephas. The reason for my question was that in Galatians 2:8–9, Paul mentions both Peter and Cephas, and if you didn't know any better, you would think he was talking about two different people. Could there have been two with the same nickname, Cephas the leader of the church in Jerusalem and Peter the missionary to the Jews outside of Jerusalem? Well, probably not. It wasn't a common nickname. In fact, so far as we know, only one person had it. Still, there was an ancient church tradition that these were two separate

people. See my article "Cephas and Peter," *Journal of Biblical Literature* 109 (1990): 463–74.

Chapter Three
The Rocky Beginning

1. See Jonathan Reed, *Archaeology and the Galilean Jesus: A Re-examination of the Evidence* (Harrisburg, PA: Trinity Press International, 2000).
2. The best study, in my opinion, remains William V. Harris, *Ancient Literacy* (Cambridge, MA: Harvard University Press, 1989); for Jewish literacy in Palestine in the period, see Catherine Heszer, *Jewish Literacy in Roman Palestine* (Tübingen: Mohr-Siebeck, 2001).
3. This was not simply a matter of social class, in that slaves, who were very low on the class scale, were sometimes trained in literacy to assist in their masters' household duties. But fishermen such as Peter needed no such training. This raises the interesting question of how Peter communicated later in life when he met with Jews to try to convert them, and then associated with them, and Gentiles, outside of Palestine. Did he have an interpreter with him?
4. See the discussion in John Dominic Crossan and Jonathan Reed, *Excavating Jesus: Beneath the Stones, Behind the Texts* (San Francisco: HarperSanFrancisco, 2001), 92–93.
5. I give a bibliography of the works I consider to be the most important (or at least the most interesting), in my study *Jesus: Apocalyptic Prophet of the New Millennium* (New York: Oxford University Press, 1999).
6. For a fuller account, see my book *Jesus: Apocalyptic Prophet of the New Millennium.*
7. For a fuller explanation of Jesus' apocalyptic message, see my book *Jesus: Apocalyptic Prophet of the New Millennium.*
8. For a fuller discussion of what first-century Jews meant by the term *messiah,* see John Collins, *The Scepter and the Star: The Messiahs of the Dead Sea Scrolls and Other Ancient Literature* (New York: Doubleday, 1995).
9. These are my own translations. See Bart D. Ehrman, *The Apostolic Fathers,* Loeb Classical Library (Cambridge, MA: Harvard University Press, 2004), 1:171–73.

Chapter Four
Peter at the Passion

1. The term *synoptic* literally means "seen together." It is used to refer to Matthew, Mark, and Luke because these three Gospels are so similar in

the stories that they tell that they can be placed next to each other in parallel columns and be read together.

2. According to John 19:14, Jesus was crucified on the afternoon when preparations were under way to eat the Passover meal that evening. In other words, Jesus is crucified the morning after the meal was eaten in Mark (at 9:00 a.m.; Mark 15:25), but the afternoon before the meal in John.

3. For a fuller discussion of the Gospel of Peter, see Bart Ehrman, *Lost Christianities: The Battles for Scripture and the Faiths We Never Knew* (New York: Oxford University Press, 2003), 13–28.

4. A person who was crucified died by asphyxiation, as the weight of the body would cause the lungs to distend, making it impossible to breathe. If a person was nailed through the ankles, he could push up with his legs to relieve the pressure on the lungs. If the legs were broken, this was no longer possible, and death would come more quickly.

5. For a more detailed account, see the Introduction in James A. Robinson, ed., *The Nag Hammadi Library in English,* 4th ed. (Leiden: E. J. Brill, 1996).

6. We know this because whoever manufactured the books used scrap paper to strengthen the spines of the leather covers, and included among the scrap paper were dated receipts.

7. Translation by James Brasher and Robert Bullard, in Robinson, ed., *Nag Hammadi Library.*

8. Translation of Frederik Wisse in Robinson, ed., *Nag Hammadi Library in English.*

9. For a fuller discussion of these matters, see my book *Misquoting Jesus: The Story Behind Who Changed the Bible and Why* (San Francisco: HarperSanFrancisco, 2005).

10. For a detailed discussion of why this verse should not be thought of as original to Luke, and of the reasons why it was added later by scribes, see Bart D. Ehrman, *The Orthodox Corruption of Scripture: The Effects of Early Christological Controversies on the Text of the New Testament* (New York: Oxford University Press, 1993), 212–17.

11. The Gospel itself is actually anonymous, and John, the son of Zebedee, interestingly enough, is never mentioned in it by name.

12. For a discussion of this verse and of the various endings that scribes tacked on to the Gospel of Mark, including the last twelve verses familiar to the readers of the King James Version (and other English translations), see Ehrman, *Misquoting Jesus,* 65–68.

13. Some readers of this passage in Greek have thought that there is a nuance being conveyed that is hard to translate into English, for on the first two occasions Jesus asks Peter, "Do you love me?"—using the word *agapaw,* which may refer to a deeply committed love, and Peter replies, "Yes, Lord, you know I love you," using a different word for love, *philew,* which may connote something more like "fondness." The third time Jesus asks his question he uses the word *philew,* and then is satisfied with the

answer. This may be an attractive interpretation; the problem with it is that the two words did not have hard-and-fast meanings or nuances in Greek, but were sometimes used interchangeably with no difference in meaning.

14. It seems odd that the Gospel of Peter speaks about the "twelve" being grief-stricken after the crucifixion: hasn't Judas gone off to kill himself, leaving only eleven? It should also be noted that when Paul talks about Christ's resurrection appearances in 1 Corinthians, he indicates that Christ "appeared first to Cephas and then to the twelve." What's going on here? It is interesting that neither the Gospel of Peter nor the apostle Paul ever refers explicitly to Judas Iscariot, one of the twelve, as the one who betrayed Jesus. Did they not know about it?

Chapter Five
On This Rock I Will Build My Church

1. See the brief discussion in Bart D. Ehrman, *The New Testament: A Historical Introduction to the Early Christian Writings,* 3rd ed. (New York: Oxford University Press, 2003), 133–34.
2. That these various sermons represent Luke's views, rather than the views of the apostles who are said to deliver the sermons, is particularly clear with respect to Paul. As we will see later, what Luke says Paul preached and what Paul says he preached are often very different—sometimes at odds.

Chapter Six
Peter: Christian Author and Martyr

1. This is in the famous Abgar Legend recounted by Eusebius, *Church History* 1, 13.
2. Some have suggested that the Greek in the letter—with its stylistic quality and its familiarity with the Greek Bible—is due to the circumstance that Peter used Silvanus as an amanuensis (see 5:12). On this theory, Silvanus is the one who then composed the letter, as instructed by Peter in Aramaic. The problem with this theory is that it would mean that Silvanus, not Peter, was the letter's actual author. Moreover, the letter mentions Silvanus as the carrier of the letter, not its writer.
3. This clever ploy—to condemn forgery in a book that is itself forged—can be found, for example in the book called the *Apostolic Constitutions,* written in the fourth century. The book claims to have been written by the apostles of Jesus soon after his death. And it warns its readers not to read books that *claim* to be written by apostles when in fact they are

not. Presumably this ploy was used in order to throw readers off the scent of one's own deceit.

4. See my discussion in *The New Testament: A Historical Introduction to the Early Christian Writings,* 3rd ed. (New York: Oxford University Press, 2003), 456–58.

5. See the Introduction to the Shepherd of Hermas in vol. 2 of Bart D. Ehrman, *The Apostolic Fathers,* Loeb Classical Library (Cambridge, MA: Harvard University Press, 2003).

Chapter Seven
The Apostle Paul: Polling Our Sources

1. See the discussion in my book *Lost Christianities: The Battles for Scripture and the Faiths We Never Knew* (New York: Oxford University Press, 2003). The most authoritative study is Bruce M. Metzger, *The Canon of the New Testament: Its Origin, Development, and Significance* (New York: Oxford University Press, 1987).

2. For a place to start, see my textbook on the New Testament, *The New Testament: A Historical Introduction to the Early Christian Writings,* 3rd ed. (New York: Oxford University Press, 2003), and the bibliographies that I cite at the end of each discussion of one of the Pauline letters.

3. For a fuller discussion of this issue, see Gordon Fee's commentary on these verses in his book *The First Epistle to the Corinthians* (Grand Rapids: Eerdmans, 1987).

Chapter Eight
Paul the Convert

1. The Diaspora started six hundred years before Paul, when the Babylonian empire headed by the general Nebuchadnezzar overthrew Judea (586 BCE), causing numerous Judeans (whence we get the word *Jew*) to relocate in other parts of the world.

2. It is called this because of the tradition that it had been rendered into Greek from Hebrew by seventy (Latin root: *sept-*) Jewish translators.

3. There is nothing to suggest that in Paul's day there was anything like a closed canon of Scripture. That would come later. But there were numerous books in addition to the Torah that many Jews accepted also as authoritative.

4. There are lots of books written about the Pharisees and other Jews at the time when Christianity arose. Two excellent resources are Shaye Cohen, *From the Maccabees to the Mishnah* (Philadelphia: Westminster, 1987) and E. P. Sanders, *Judaism: Practice and Belief 63 BCE–66 CE* (Philadelphia: Trinity Press International, 1992).

5.   See the articles by Jan Bremmer and by János Bollók in Jan Bremmer, ed., *The Apocryphal Acts of Paul and Thecla* (Kampen: Kok Pharos, 1996).
6.   Sanders's most influential book is *Paul and Palestinian Judaism* (Philadelphia: Fortress Press, 1977).
7.   Scholars who have studied Paul's view of the law have come to quite different understandings. This is an inordinately complicated subject. To get a sense of some of the options, held by some very bright scholars, see Stephen Westerholm, *Israel's Law and the Church's Faith: Paul and His Recent Interpreters* (Grand Rapids: Eerdmans, 1988).
8.   See note 7.

Chapter Nine
Paul the Apostle

1.   The term *apostle* comes from the Greek and literally means "one who is sent." It is used to refer not only to the twelve apostles of Jesus but to anyone who considered him- or herself to be commissioned by Christ to take his message abroad.
2.   In 2 Cor. 11:24 he does indicate that on five occasions he was subjected to "the forty lashes minus one," which most interpreters have taken as a reference to corporal punishment meted out by synagogue authorities. If that's right, then he must have regularly caused a stir in the synagogues he visited on his journeys, as Acts itself indicates.
3.   See Ronald Hock, *The Social Context of Paul's Ministry: Tent-making and Apostleship* (Philadelphia: Fortress, 1980).
4.   See Tamás Adamik, "The Baptized Lion in the Acts of Paul," in Jan Bremmer, ed., *The Apocryphal Acts of Paul and Thecla* (Kampen: Kok Pharos, 1996), 60–74.

Chapter Ten
Paul's Proclamation According to Later Sources

1.   Dale Martin, who scribbled comments all over a first draft of this book in a vain attempt to make me improve it, has asked me to tell you, the reader, that he is the one who came up with this life-transforming insight.
2.   Even if he did occasionally preach in the synagogues, which might be suspected on the basis of 2 Cor. 11:24 (see note 2 in the preceding chapter), he never indicates that he had any Jewish converts, and his letters seem to be addressed to converted pagans.

3. See especially Stephen Davis, *The Cult of Saint Thecla: A Tradition of Women's Piety in Late Antiquity* (New York: Oxford University Press, 2001).

4. For a recent translation, see "The Acts of Thecla," in Bart D. Ehrman, ed., *Lost Scriptures: Books That Did Not Make It into the New Testament* (New York: Oxford University Press, 2003), 113–21.

5. Readers have often noticed that Paul does not come off with flying colors in some of these stories connected with Thecla. In one of the oddest moments of the book, when the aristocrat Alexander sees Thecla and wants her for himself, he asks Paul to give her to him. Paul claims he doesn't know who she is!

6. For a translation, see J. K. Elliott, *The Apocryphal New Testament: A Collection of Apocryphal Christian Literature in an English Translation* (Oxford: Clarendon Press, 1993), 620ff.

Chapter Eleven
Paul's Impassioned Allies

1. On the issue of who actually wrote these letters, see the discussions of each of them (and the accompanying bibliographies) in Bart Ehrman, *The New Testament: A Historical Introduction to the Early Christian Writings,* 3rd ed. (New York: Oxford University Press, 2003).

2. See the discussion in Ehrman, *The New Testament: A Historical Introduction,* 376–78.

3. See the discussion in Ehrman, *The New Testament: A Historical Introduction,* 381–85.

4. See the discussion in Ehrman, *The New Testament: A Historical Introduction,* pp. 385–93.

5. For more on the Gnostics and their views, see Bart D. Ehrman, *Lost Christianities: The Battles for Scripture and the Faiths We Never Knew* (New York: Oxford University Press, 2003), chap. 7.

6. This is the thesis of Elaine Pagels, *The Gnostic Paul: Gnostic Exegesis of the Pauline Letters* (Philadelphia: Fortress, 1975).

7. This tradition can be found in Clement of Alexandria, *Stromateis,* 7, 17, 106.

8. For more on Marcion and his teachings, see Ehrman, *Lost Christianities,* chap. 6.

9. There are Gnostic churches still today—check out the Yellow Pages in a California phone book—but these do not have a historical lineage back to the second century. They are modern developments, arising out of the "rediscovery" of Gnostics and their long-lost writings.

10. On the victory of the proto-orthodox party, see Ehrman, *Lost Christianities,* chaps. 9–13.

Chapter Twelve
Paul's Embittered Enemies

1. James and Paul also seem to mean something different by the term *faith*. For Paul, faith means a trusting acceptance of Christ's death; for James, it means something like intellectual acceptance of a proposition. See, for example, James 2:19—even the demons "believe." That is, even they "know" there is only one God. That simply isn't what Paul means by faith, for example, in Romans 3. For a further discussion see Bart D. Ehrman, *The New Testament: A Historical Introduction to the Early Christian Writings,* 3rd ed. (New York: Oxford University Press, 2003), 366–68.

Chapter Thirteen
Mary Magdalene in Popular Culture and History

1. My book is *Truth and Fiction in the Da Vinci Code* (New York: Oxford University Press, 2004).
2. For a fuller discussion of how scribes sometimes altered the texts of Scripture that they copied, see my book *Misquoting Jesus: The Story of Who Changed the New Testament and Why* (San Francisco: HarperSanFrancisco, 2005). I include there, on 63–65, a more extended discussion of this passage.
3. Gregory the Great, Homily 33; quoted from Susan Haskins, *Mary Magdalene: Myth and Metaphor* (New York: Harcourt Brace and Co., 1993), 96. For scholars interested in such things, the Latin text itself can be found in J. P. Migne, *Patrologia Latina,* XXXVI, col. 1239.

Chapter Fourteen
Mary During the Ministry of Jesus

1. See the bibliography in one of the more even-handed and learned, though accessible, treatments, Ross Kraemer, *Her Share of the Blessings: Women's Religions Among Pagans, Jews, and Christians in the Graeco-Roman World* (New York: Oxford University Press, 1992).
2. Ross Kraemer, "Jewish Woman and Christian Origins: Some Caveats," in Ross Shepard Kraemer and Mary Rose D'Angelo, eds., *Women and Christian Origins* (New York: Oxford University Press, 1999).
3. These examples and reflections are from Kraemer and D'Angelo, eds., *Women and Christian Origins,* 38–39.
4. The groundbreaking study was by Bernadette Brooten, *Women Leaders in the Ancient Synagogue: Inscriptional Evidence and Background Issues* (Chico, CA: Scholars Press, 1982).

5. See the study by Jonathan Reed, *Archaeology and the Galilean Jesus: A Re-examination of the Evidence* (Harrisburg, PA: Trinity Press International, 2000).

6. See John Dominic Crossan and Jonathan Reed, *Excavating Jesus: Beneath the Stones, Behind the Texts* (San Francisco: HarperSanFrancisco, 2001), 31–36.

7. See the important study by Mark Chancey, *The Myth of a Gentile Galilee* (Cambridge: Cambridge University Press, 2002).

8. Josephus, *The Jewish Wars,* Book 2, 598–99. One of the best, full discussions of the town of Magdala can be found in Jane Schaberg, *The Resurrection of Mary Magdalene* (New York: Continuum, 2002), chap. 2.

9. In fact, there is only one reference in the entire New Testament to Jesus as a carpenter, and that is in Mark 6:3. As it turns out, the word *carpenter* there—the Greek is τεκτον—has a range of meanings, all involving someone who works with his hands to fashion things. So it could also mean "stonemason" or "blacksmith," for example. If it does mean that Jesus worked with wood, it would probably indicate that he made things like gates and yokes. It is unlikely, given his historical context in a small hamlet in rural Galilee, that he did fine cabinetry.

10. One of the now classics in the field of feminist interpretations of Jesus and early Christianity is by the influential New Testament scholar Elisabeth Schüssler Fiorenza, *In Memory of Her: A Feminist Theological Reconstruction of Early Christianity* (New York: Crossroads, 1983).

11. At the same time, even though this was not his intent, his teachings could be socially revolutionary. See note 12.

12. I earlier said that Jesus was not a social reformer, in that he was not interested in improving society for the long haul. His teachings did lead to a kind of social reform, however, to the extent that his followers were to implement new values and priorities in expectation of the coming kingdom.

13. See my discussion, and the bibliography I cite, in Bart D. Ehrman, *The New Testament: A Historical Introduction to the Early Christian Writings,* 3rd ed. (New York: Oxford University Press, 2003), chapter 24.

Chapter Fifteen
Jesus and Mary in Conversation

1. See the discussion on pp. 53–54.

2. I am using the translation of Stephen Emmel in James A. Robinson, ed., *The Nag Hammadi Library in English,* 4th ed. (Leiden: E. J. Brill, 1996).

3. There are exceptions, of course. One of the most penetrating analyses is by Elizabeth Castelli, "'I Will Make Mary Male': Pieties of the Body and Gender Transformation of Christian Women in Late Antiquity," in

J. Epstein and K. Straub, eds., *Body Guards: The Cultural Politics of Gender Ambiguity* (New York: Routledge, 1991). For a range of interpretations, see Jane Schaberg, *The Resurrection of Mary Magdalene: Legends, Apocrypha, and the Christian Testament* (New York: Continuum, 2002), 156–60.

4. The author claims to be Judas Thomas, who in other early Christian traditions is portrayed as the brother of Jesus (for example, in the apocryphal Acts of Thomas). But everyone realizes that the real author is writing pseudonymously.

5. The literature on this subject is immense. For a good place to start, see Thomas Lequeur, *Body and Gender from the Greeks to Freud* (Cambridge, MA: Harvard University Press, 1990).

6. See the fuller discussion in Bart D. Ehrman, *Lost Christianities: The Battles for Scripture and the Faiths We Never Knew* (New York: Oxford University Press, 2003), 55–65.

7. For an intriguing history of kissing in early Christianity, see Michael Penn, *Kissing Christians: Ritual and Community in the Late Ancient Church* (Philadelphia: University of Pennsylvania Press, 2005).

Chapter Sixteen
Mary at the Passion

1. This difference may result from a different geographical emphasis of the different Gospels. Mark sees Galilee as the place of salvation but Jerusalem as a city of demons. Luke sees Jerusalem as the city of God from which salvation must go forth.

Chapter Seventeen
Mary and Her Revelations

1. For an English translation of Epiphanius's work, see Frank Williams, *The Panarion of Epiphanius of Salamis* (Leiden: E. J. Brill, 1997).

2. See the discussion and bibliography in Bart D. Ehrman, *Lost Christianities: The Battles for Scripture and the Faiths We Never Knew* (New York: Oxford University Press, 2003), 198–201.

3. I find Karen King's exposition of the text to be very enlightening; see her *The Gospel of Mary of Magdala: Jesus and the First Woman Apostle* (Santa Rosa, CA: Polebridge Press, 2003). But I strongly disagree with one of her major premises, that the Gospel is best understood something other than "Gnostic." Her ground for thinking so is related to her claim that scholars have regularly, and wrongly, labeled some texts as Gnostic— applying the term to any early Christian writings that are not Jewish. I

have to say that this view (that she is attacking) is not one that I see represented very often among other scholars.

4. I have used the translation of Marvin Meyer, *The Gospels of Mary: The Secret Tradition of Mary Magdalene, the Companion of Jesus* (San Francisco: HarperSanFrancisco, 2004).

5. The surviving Greek fragment indicates that it is only Levi who goes forth to preach the gospel. Maybe Peter never did get it.

Chapter Eighteen

Mary: The Residual Questions

1. There are numerous treatments of the Dead Sea Scrolls and their relationship to the Essenes. For a quick overview, see Joseph Fitzmyer, *Responses to 101 Questions About the Dead Sea Scrolls* (Mahwah, NJ: Paulist Press, 1992); for an overview by another highly competent scholar, see James Vanderkam, *The Dead Sea Scrolls Today* (Grand Rapids: Eerdmans, 1994).

2. For a full discussion of this and related issues, see Eldon Jay Epp, *Junia: The First Woman Apostle* (Philadelphia: Augsburg Fortress, 2005).

3. This is the view first set forth by the German scholar Martin Hengel.

4. We have seen that the author of Mark may have had a reason to come up with a story like this. But recall my earlier point: since the accounts of Mary at the empty tomb are found throughout our sources, it must be a very early tradition (well before Mark got hold of it). It is hard to imagine so many Christian storytellers coming up with the *same* story about Mary, independently of one another, if it were not historical.

Credits and Permissions

Index

Note: Page numbers in *italics* refer to illustrations. Numbered books of the Bible can be found under "first" and "second."